WHITE HOUSE
HISTORY

A journal published by the

White House Historical Association

Washington

White House History (ISSN 0748-8114) features articles on the
historic White House, especially those related to the building itself and
life as lived there through the years. The views presented by the authors
are theirs and do not necessarily reflect the position or policy
of the White House Historical Association.

The White House Historical Association is a nonprofit organization,
chartered on November 3, 1961, to enhance understanding, appreciation,
and enjoyment of the historic White House. Income from the sale of
White House History and all the Association's books and guides
is returned to the publications program and is used as well to
acquire historical furnishings and memorabilia for the White House.
Address inquiries to: White House Historical Association,
740 Jackson Place, N.W., Washington, D.C. 20006
www.whitehousehistory.org

*Opposite: Plasterwork (detail) at Belcamp House in Dublin, Ireland. Its owner,
Sir Edward Newenham, was inspired by the American Revolution, and built the first monument to
George Washington on the Belcamp House grounds in 1778. Sir Edward corresponded with both
President Washington and Benjamin Franklin.*

ISBN 978-1-931917-09-4
Library of Congress Number 2009939895
Printed in China

Printed in China.

Foreword

The fourth volume in the collections of articles from White House History, the journal of the White House Historical Association includes thirty-nine articles from seven issues. They vary from biographical articles to various focus pieces on aspects of life in and the operations of the White House.

Our celebration of President Lincoln's 200th year is in our two issues on his life and presidency. Both are included here. Notable in these issues are heretofore unpublished—and only recently found—photographs of the White House in Lincoln's time. They are very rare, giving us glimpses as through windows heretofore unknown, on the presidential enclave during the Civil War. Not always easy to pin down as to their precise dates, they fascinate us because of the details they show of a particular time while in the midst the White House is so unchanged.

The biographical articles also surround the White House years of President Eisenhower, who maintained a White House painting studio and pursued his oils devotedly. We also visit his childhood home, which was restored and made central to his presidential library in Abilene, Kansas, with his approval. The original architect of the White House, James Hoban, was given an entire issue, which is reprinted here. His role in the creation of the White House for George Washington was celebrated in Ireland and America, on the 250th anniversary of his birth. Articles from both countries explore his architecture and the architecture of Ireland that may have influenced him.

We visit the White House stables, which flourished during the first century of the White House. The kitchens are not overlooked in seven articles on the kitchens and presidential appetites. And we offer a series of articles on flowers, flower gardens, and floral decorations for state dinners and White House weddings, a special subject in White House life that began in about 1859, when the then-customary artificial wax flowers were removed and fresh flowers first introduced to White House vases. Old worries about flowers thinning the oxygen in the air and causing sickness seem at that time to have been discarded. The White House has been filled with flowers ever since.

William Seale
Editor, *White House History*

*Opposite:
The Monroe Plateau (detail) in the State Dining Room is surrounded by a balustrade featuring classical figures balanced on spheres atop plinths, with reclining Bacchantes on either side. Denière et Matelin, Paris, c. 1817.*

WHITE HOUSE HISTORY

COLLECTION 4, NUMBERS 19 THROUGH 25

PRESIDENTIAL HORSES • NUMBER 19

WHITE HOUSE KITCHENS AND COOKING • NUMBER 20

PRESIDENT EISENHOWER'S WHITE HOUSE • NUMBER 21

JAMES HOBAN: ARCHITECT OF THE WHITE HOUSE • NUMBER 22

WHITE HOUSE FLOWERS: EMBELLISHING THE PRESIDENT'S TABLE • NUMBER 23

LIFE IN THE LINCOLN WHITE HOUSE: PART ONE • NUMBER 24

LIFE IN THE LINCOLN WHITE HOUSE: PART TW0 • NUMBER 25

WHITE HOUSE
HISTORY

White House Historical Association
Washington

PRESIDENTIAL HORSES • NUMBER 19
PUBLISHED FALL 2006

Foreword

The horse and the White House parted company rather abruptly in 1909 when President William Howard Taft introduced the automobile to presidential transportation. His predecessor, Theodore Roosevelt, had stayed the gasoline tide, but Taft, although something of a horseman, like most people of the time, was also one who welcomed innovation. Except for a brief time during World War I and pleasure riding at times since, the horse faded from White House life.

But the horse had its day. From the earliest time horses and carriages were associated with the ceremonies and honor of being head of state. Even early in the Revolution, before there was a presidency, the Pennsylvania legislature ordered for Martha Washington a very finely appointed carriage and horses, that she might journey in a style appropriate to the public rank of her husband. George Washington's own taste in horses and equipages is well known. Uniformed mounted militia accompanied his coach, itself an elaborate vehicle of white and gold with cherubs painted on the doors. In approving Pennsylvania Avenue in Pierre Charles L'Enfant's design, the first president endorsed a ceremonial way along which members of the House and Senate would parade, horse-drawn, from the Capitol to attend the White House, where they would bring their legislation to the "Audience chamber" (East Room) for presidential approval.

John Adams brought his horses to the White House when he moved there and tried to sell them to his successor, Thomas Jefferson, who declined rather rudely. Making a point about republican simplicity, Jefferson insisted upon riding his own horse, which he did to his inauguration in the most theatrically humble way, acquiring a road coach later on for trips home to Monticello. Any horse tradition at the White House was eclipsed in 1829 by Andrew Jackson, who brought from Tennessee not only fine mounts but racehorses. However, Jackson went to Washington by horse and left by railroad train, foreshadowing the end of presidential horse transportation yet seventy years in the future.

Through the nineteenth century horses were always a major feature of White House life. The stables were extensively populated and always managed by expert horsemen, the coachman being also manager of the operation. Horse celebrities included Old Whitey, President Zachary Taylor's mount from the Mexican War; tourists pulled hairs from the tail of this gentle, "comfortable" horse for souvenirs, until the

Equestrian statue in bronze of Andrew Jackson by Clark Mills, placed in Lafayette Park before the White House in 1853. It is shown here in a Daguerreotype made at about the time the process was invented.

tail was bald. President Ulysses S. Grant's favorite relaxations included horses, when he raced his sulky down Pennsylvania Avenue, whip in his teeth, stopping for no one. Without fail he spent some time in the afternoons around the woodstove at the White House stable, talking horses with the grooms.

This issue of White House History *is about horses at the White House. Sources for our authors are many, in part the public record, in which a clear accounting survives of White House stables and those horse-related amenities taxpayers provided, and the private papers of the presidents, for the bulk of the cost of presidential horses was carried from the president's own salary for the more than a century that the horse was both necessity and friend to the presidency.*

William Seale
Editor, *White House History*

Presidents as Horsemen

W I L L I A M   B .   B U S H O N G

*T*he nineteenth century might be called the golden age of the horse. Horsepower pulled plow, canal boat, and wagon to market; horse-drawn stages linked towns; and omnibuses and carriages conveyed people to work within cities, to shop, or to the train station, which, a decade after the Civil War, emerged as the hub of a transcontinental transportation system. Before automobiles, the residents of the White House, like most of humankind, depended essentially on horses for transportation and the movement of goods and services. The president's stables, long demolished and largely forgotten today, were once integral to the operation of White House.

The Sequence of Stables

The primacy of the horse at the White House ended in 1909 when President William Howard Taft converted the carriage room into a garage for his giant steam-powered cars. The Taft family cow, Pauline Wayne, remained the sole inhabitant of the stable until the structure was razed in 1911. Horses remained available to the White House at nearby army stables for recreational riding into the late twentieth century. It was not until 1951

Major General Andrew Jackson, President of the United States, *engraved by James B. Longacre after painting by Thomas Sully c. 1820. Jackson's favorite horses were not warhorses but racehorses. He was the only president to maintain a racing stable at the White House.*

that Congress struck an expenditure from the White House budget for horses and stables.[1]

The various executive stables that were built on the White House grounds over a period of a century were never intended to be great architecture. Public interest was keen simply because they were the president's stables. The first executive stable was a distance away from the White House, a Georgian-style brick structure erected by builder William Lovell on the southeast corner of 14th and G Streets, NW, in 1800. Six years later President Thomas Jefferson designed a stable and carriage house in new wing dependencies flanking the White House on the east and west. The west wing housed the coach house and tack room, and the stable with a cowshed were in the east wing.[2]

After the British burned the White House in 1814, a temporary frame stable was appended to the end of the rebuilt east wing. President James Monroe moved the stable to the west wing in 1819 for greater convenience to the coach house. James Hoban, who had built and rebuilt the White House, prepared plans and directed the construction of the new stable, turning it toward the south where it made an ell to the existing wing. The colonnades of the stable and wing created a stately enclosure for a brick-paved courtyard, but the location below the windows of the State Dining Room was not ideal.[3]

President Andrew Jackson, a passionate horseman, stabled not only workhorses at the White House but also thoroughbreds that raced at courses in Washington and Baltimore. His horses so overflowed the Monroe stable

STABLES

The first White House stable was built in 1800 on the corner of 14th and G Streets, in Northwest Washington. It was remodeled as a school in 1821 and demolished about 1886.

Above: Stable employees were photographed in front of the carriage entrance to the president's stable with saddle horses, Algonquin—the Roosevelt children's pony—and Theodore Roosevelt's landau. The image appeared in Town and Country, January 10, 1903.

Left: President Ulysses S. Grant's prized warhorses, Cincinnati and Egypt, are shown centered in this engraving of the executive stables, which appeared in Harper's Weekly, April 17, 1869. The White House is in the background.

The White House stables in 1890. The gateway of the executive stables faced 17th Street, NW. At the center of the U-shaped building was an open courtyard, which was enclosed by frame and glass in 1890. The stable, carriage, tack, and harness rooms, and a cozy sitting room for the coachmen and stable hands, were located on the first floor. An apartment for the coachman and his family was in the second story.

The official White House fleet with drivers and motorcycle police in 1909 at the time the White House stable became a garage.

that wooden shanties had to be built for further housing along the west fence of the grounds. Eventually Jackson persuaded Congress to fund the construction of a free-standing neoclassical brick stable trimmed with Aquia sandstone about 100 yards east of the east wing of the White House. Washington builder William P. Elliot erected the structure at a cost of about $3,600.[4] In 1834, the *National Intelligencer* reported that "a fine stable, having a handsome picturesque appearance, calculated to accommodate about ten horses" had been completed.[5] Tall and wide, the stuccoed brick stable had a porch on the south side with six round columns of plastered brick with stone bases. A brick wall with a flagstone court-yard enclosed it. The flagstone continued into the sta-ble's center hall, which was bordered by two ranges of stalls. Grooms fed the horses from the passage without entering the stalls. A feed and tack room and a space for coaches and other smaller vehicles also flanked the hall and extended into an ell to the side. On the second level were a hayloft and living quarters for grooms and a coachman.[6] According to the public gardener James Maher, Jackson told him: "Plant me a tree of rapid growth to protect my stable from a northwester." Maher planted silver maples calculated to create a shade canopy of 425 square yards.[7]

Andrew Jackson's stable was razed in 1857 to make way for the present south wing of the Treasury Department. Workers salvaged the stone and bricks and used them to erect a new structure on the east grounds, south of the Treasury. The project was planned and directed by Edward Clark, superintendent of construc-tion work then under way at the Patent Office extension and an assistant to Thomas U. Walter, architect of the Capitol. Costing approximately $8,000, the new stable was slightly larger and wider than Jackson's stable. The areas along its central passage accommodated twelve horses, the White House carriages, and feed and tack, and upstairs were bedchambers for the grooms. The brick building was stuccoed and whitewashed and had a painted tin roof.[8] Fire consumed this building in 1864, destroying the Lincoln children's ponies, Mary Todd Lincoln's black carriage horses, and John Nicolay's sad-dle horse. Abraham Lincoln witnessed the tragedy and in his determination to save the pony of his son Willie, who had died, had to be restrained by guards from rush-ing into the blazing stable.[9]

Once again workmen salvaged bricks and stone and, with additional new materials, erected the replacement stable on the west grounds. Designed by Walter, this utilitarian structure cost $12,000. Illustrated in *Harper's Weekly* in 1869, the two-story stable appears to have had a side-gable roof with a wide porch supported by thin Tuscan columns sheltering the carriage entrance. Functionally, it mirrored its predecessor in providing spaces for the care and feeding of the horses, a carriage room, and second floor living quarters. In 1871, this structure made way for the excavation of the foundation for the imposing State, War and Navy Building (today's Eisenhower Executive Office Building).[10]

The last White House stable, a High Victorian mansard-roofed structure, was completed during the Ulysses S. Grant administration in 1872. Funds for con-struction were drawn from the appropriation allotted for the new Executive Office Building amounting to $27,025.15.[11] Alfred B. Mullett, supervising architect of the Treasury Department, the chief architect for the fed-eral government, had charge of the design. He became renowned for his massive granite Second Empire–style post offices and federal courthouses built in major cities across the United States.[12] In 1890, the Army Corps of Engineers expanded Grant's stable substantially by adding new stalls and rooms for the grooms to the rear of the building. The project also covered the area within the two wings with glass.[13]

Mullett gave the executive stables a formal gateway entrance that faced 17th Street. At the center of the U-shaped building was an open asphalt courtyard enclosed by a wrought-iron fence. The stable, carriage, feed, tack, and harness rooms, and a cozy sitting room for the coachmen and stable hands, were located on the first floor. An apartment for the coachman and his family was in the second story. A reporter for *The Evening Star* described the White House stables in 1889:

> A few rods south of the southern entrance
> to the great State, War, and Navy buildings
> is a grove of young trees, from above the
> verdant tops of which peep out an odd-looking

*Thomas "Tad" Lincoln,
the president's son, posed
on his pony, c. 1865.*

*Carriages of ambassadors and dignitaries park on the North
Drive during a New Year's Day reception at the White House
in the late 1890s. Guests arrived at the White House in a
wide variety of conveyances, from the elegant coaches of
ambassadors and ministers plenipotentiary to the hired cab,
shown on the right. A great many came on foot.*

continuation of mansard roof. . . . The uniformed stranger wonders what manner of mansion it is which is thus secluded and finds that it is the White House stables. The stables are extensive enough to contain twenty-five horses and twelve vehicles. Nothing but a pass from the President's private secretary will secure admission to the sacred precincts where Albert Hawkins is king.[14]

The Coachmen

Albert Hawkins was a coachman who began his service under Ulysses S. Grant. By the 1880s, he was among the most celebrated of Washington's African American community. Tall and well made, the smartly uniformed Hawkins was considered the "beau ideal" of a coachman. He served the White House until 1889, when his eyesight began to fail.[15] Occasional anecdotes about the White House stables appeared in newspapers and magazines, providing a profile of the reserved coachman. One of the best stories highlighted his sense of humor. First Lady Frances Folsom Cleveland, the bright and beautiful young wife of President Grover Cleveland, was in high demand on the social scene. Mrs. Cleveland devised a novel way to set aside several hours a week for French lessons. Her teacher joined her for a carriage ride, driven by Hawkins, one morning a week. In the privacy of the carriage, the first lady could take her lessons undisturbed. Mrs. Cleveland became so absorbed that she

LIBRARY OF CONGRESS

Left: Coachman Charlie Lee supervised the groomsmen and stablemen and had charge of the care and feeding of fifteen horses, eight of which were owned by Theodore Roosevelt. The photograph appeared in the Washington Post, *January 7, 1906.*

Opposite: Portrait of First Lady Frances Cleveland by Frances B. Johnston, 1886.

THE HUB, NEW YORK, NEW YORK

Left: This custom-made landau was built for President Grover Cleveland at a cost of $2,000 in 1885. The top threw back in opposing directions, making an open carriage.

Opposite: Neatness and order—an interior view of the stalls in the White House stable in 1903.

LIBRARY OF CONGRESS

would often direct Hawkins in French. With a grin and a nod, Hawkins smartly replied, "Oui, Oui Madame."[16]

What is known about the grooms, coachmen, outriders, and other horsemen is episodic, like much of what is known about Hawkins, and comes from surviving documents in the public building commissioner's records, newspapers, and periodicals of that time. The coachman, conspicuous in formal livery on the box of the president's carriage, was always the most recognized member of the domestic staff. William Willis, an expert horseman, succeeded Hawkins in 1889. He was of mixed African American descent and described by reporters as "mulatto." Prominent in African American society, Willis was a Freemason and Odd Fellow and was invited to work at the White House by Colonel William H. Crook, disbursing agent of the office staff, who appointed him the driver of the carriage for the president's private secretaries.[17] A widower, Willis lived in the stables with his daughter and mother until he suffered a sudden stroke and died in 1895. Another well-known White House coachman was Charlie Lee, the driver for Theodore Roosevelt. His livery consisted of a blue coat, white doeskin trousers, high boots, and a top hat with a red white and blue cockade. Lee, the last White House coachman, was among the employees who moved with the Roosevelts to the White House from their home in Oyster Bay, New York.[18]

During the nineteenth century, it was customary to employ a coachman and a few grooms to care for the

VEHICLE DEALER

horses and manage the White House stables. In 1889, *The Evening Star* reported that the president's stables had four employees, including coachman Hawkins, who managed the operations. By 1901, the stable staff included a foreman or manager of the stables, three coachmen, four grooms, and a general laborer. The president paid for his coachman from his personal funds. Two drivers for the executive and domestic staff and three grooms were paid out of the executive budget. The remaining workers with the White House horses were employees of the U.S. Army Quartermaster Corps assigned to presidential stable duty.[19]

The Horses and Carriages

The U.S. government maintained the stable and paid the salaries of most of the staff, but it did not furnish horses or carriages for the president's personal use. This policy began during the Jefferson administration. President John Adams had purchased a carriage and horses with government funds allocated for the White House household and offered them to his successor. Jefferson elected not to keep them, believing that the president should avoid any regal trappings of office by providing his own carriage and horses.[20]

By the late 19th century a traditional division of the president's and the government's horses was well established. "A great many people think," said Colonel Crook, "that the expense of keeping the president's horses [is] borne by the government. Such is not the case. The government keeps up the office stable, of course, but all those horses on the north side [of the stable] are the president's own property, and their keeping is paid for by him. There are practically two distinct stables. When Albert [Hawkins] needs feed he buys it from a private firm, while the feed for the government horses comes from the quartermaster's department."[21]

Presidential horses received the most attention and occupied larger box stalls, while the government horses had smaller open stalls. However, all the White House horses earned their oats and were on call twenty-four hours a day. Years of pounding the asphalt streets of Washington would take a toll on the hoofs and legs of these horses, so they required and were given the best of care. Messengers, secretaries, clerks, and the housekeeper used the government horses for daily business and for hauling produce and goods. The White House stables became a hub of activity as messengers on horseback and horse-drawn carriages conveying executive and domestic staff came and went.[22]

Before the twentieth century the president's vehicles were neither armored-plated nor specially built. Their carriages were similar to those of citizens of wealth. Often they were gifts from admirers. George Washington had the most elaborate turnout of the presidents for state occasions—a cream-colored carriage drawn by six matched horses "all brilliantly caparisoned." Coachmen and footmen wore livery trimmed with white and brilliant red-orange that Washington had selected long before for his racing silks. President Franklin Pierce preferred an informal coach and often rode through Washington in an "unpretentious one-horse shay." Chester A. Arthur was far more conspicuous in his stylish dark green landau, drawn by two perfectly matched mahogany bays with flowing manes and tails. The harness was mounted with silver, and the horse blankets were dark green kersey ornamented with the president's monogram.[23]

Grover Cleveland and Mrs. Cleveland kept fine matched brown horses in the White House stable for their carriages. Their favorite was the open landau that was taken out for drives in the Rock Creek valley and the surrounding hills of Washington. Andrew Johnson, James A. Garfield, and William McKinley also greatly enjoyed such relaxing excursions with their wives and families. Ulysses S. Grant and Rutherford B. Hayes were the most avid enthusiasts of driving. No matter what the purpose, presidential style always was on display in carriages, equipage, and livery.[24]

The horses, carriage, and livery of the president added beauty and spectacle to state events, inaugural parades, and official ceremonies. Horse-drawn vehicles ceremoniously conveyed the president to and from the White House to the Capitol until Warren G. Harding's inaugural parade in 1921, when automobiles took over. Nineteenth-century presidential funerals were pageants, with elaborate horse-drawn funeral cars and long processions. In the twentieth century, the president's flag-draped casket has been carried on an artillery caisson drawn by six matched horses followed by a riderless horse.[25]

Military heroes who risked their lives in devotion to the nation have long been attractive presidential candidates. The image of a uniformed officer on a warhorse was once a powerful symbol of leadership and executive ability. Military heroes, such as George Washington, Andrew Jackson, William Henry Harrison, Zachary Taylor, Franklin Pierce, Ulysses S. Grant, Rutherford B. Hayes, James A. Garfield, and Benjamin Harrison, were fine riders. However, Washington, Jackson, and Grant stand out as the most ardent of presidential horsemen. It is no surprise that Jackson and Grant have monumental equestrian statues in the nation's capital and that some of Washington's finest portraits are equestrian. These men formed a recognized bond with the horse that became a part of their presidential image and defined them as men.[26]

George Washington and Thomas Jefferson took immense pride in their horses and bred them to improve the bloodlines of saddle, work, carriage, and racehorses. Early presidents loved horse racing, the most popular sport in America at that time. Considered essential to the improvement of the speed and stamina of the American horse, racing created more excitement, enthusiasm, and interest in the colonial period and the early republic than any other sport. Considered by his peers the best horseman of his era, Washington helped organize races in Alexandria, Virginia, and frequently attended race meetings throughout the region. Jefferson rarely missed the meets at the National Race Course in Washington, which opened just outside the city boundary two miles north of the White House in 1802. The best horses in the country competed at the National Race Course into the 1840s, and the Jockey Club dinner and ball, a highlight of the

Above: "Come on Boys!" General Benjamin Harrison on his mount at the battle of Resaca, Georgia, 1864.

Woodcut scene of a race meeting in 1834. The "carriage folk" paid a toll to look on from covered stands for spectators, especially for the ladies. Standees watched the races for free outside the rails.

Always comfortable in the saddle, President Theodore Roosevelt poses for the Clinedinst Photographic Company, c. 1908.

President Warren Harding, accompanied by a secret service agent, rides Harbel in Potomac Park, Washington, D.C., c. 1921.

President Lyndon B. Johnson and Vice President Hubert Humphrey pose on horseback at the Johnson ranch on election day, November 2, 1964. Photograph by Cecil Stoughton, Lyndon B. Johnson Library.

President Ronald Reagan and Vice President George H. W. Bush on a pleasure ride at Quantico, Virginia, July 22, 1981.

Jacqueline Kennedy takes Sardar over a jump in Middleburg, Virginia, in 1962.

RONALD REAGAN LIBRARY

ROBERT T. KNUDSEN, JOHN F. KENNEDY LIBRARY

Washington social season, concluded the meeting.[27]

Andrew Jackson's renowned passion for horseracing was accompanied by an inclination to gamble. A wager sparked one of his duels. Jackson was a fierce competitor and wagered large sums on his horses. Once he lost a hefty bet at the Washington races and to his chagrin had to pay off wagers of almost $1,000 when his favored horse was beaten in an upset.[28]

Jackson bred racehorses at The Hermitage, his home in Tennessee, and operated a racing stable from the White House during his presidency. It was an open secret that he entered runners in the name of his nephew and private secretary, Andrew Jackson Donelson. Jackson stabled his filly Bolivia and the colt Busiris, owned by his friend General Callender Irvine of Philadelphia, at the White House.[29] One day at the National Race Course, President Jackson took Vice President Martin Van Buren to watch Busiris train. When the horse on the track became unruly, Jackson shouted, "Get behind me, Mr. Van Buren. He will run you over!" Although Van Buren was an accomplished rider, for a long time afterward newspapers and cartoonists used this incident to ridicule Van Buren's reliance on Jackson's fatherly political support.[30]

Ulysses S. Grant was the last president actively interested in horse racing. While a presidential candidate, Grant held the ribbons of the great champion trotter Dexter owned by Robert Bonner. Quite an event was made of it, commemorated by Currier and Ives in a popular print. As president, Grant bred trotters and, in the late 1870s, Arabians. He loved mounting a sulky and driving at high speed down Pennsylvania Avenue, often in a race with his friend and neighbor, General Edward Beale of Decatur House on Lafayette Square. Once Grant engaged in a friendly race on the streets of Washington with a butcher's wagon and was amazed when the horse pulling the wagon outpaced his horse. Subsequently, he sent a representative around to the butcher's shop and eventually bought the horse. Butcher's Boy became his favorite trotter.[31]

The last true horseman to use the White House stables was Theodore Roosevelt. His love of fine horses was legendary and played a part in shaping his vigorous personal image and advocacy of the "strenuous life." Roosevelt had been a rancher in the Dakota Territory, and his volunteer, mounted Rough Riders emerged as national heroes after the famous charge at San Juan Hill during the Spanish-American War. After the assassination of President William McKinley in 1901, Roosevelt brought his image as a rugged outdoorsman and war hero very successfully to the presidency.

The Roosevelt family loved horseback riding and driving and did both often in the public eye. Late in his tenure, Roosevelt's presidential schedule included daily rides to Potomac and Rock Creek parks with his military aide, Archie Butt, a superb horseman. Roosevelt, with three companions, once rode more than ninety miles in one day through sleet and snow between the White House and Warrenton, Virginia, to prove that the test ride for army and naval officers was not too difficult. The Roosevelts were the last family to fully utilize the White House stables. When offered an automobile, the president refused, saying that the Roosevelts were horse people.[32]

With the invention of photography and the popularity of illustrated magazines and newspapers by the late nineteenth century, images of the chief executives and their families on horseback became familiar subjects for news photographs. Presidents William Howard Taft, Warren G. Harding, and Calvin Coolidge and Eleanor Roosevelt as first lady regularly rode horses for exercise and relaxation in public both in the city parks of Washington and on vacation. Many modern presidents and first ladies have had a casual interest in horseback riding, particularly as a vacation sport. Most notable were Jacqueline Kennedy and Ronald Reagan. Mrs. Kennedy was a skilled rider with a passion for jumping and hunt riding. She stabled ponies, Macaroni and Tex, at the White House for her children to learn to ride. Ronald Reagan was the last president who might be considered an accomplished rider and horseman. His career in films had demanded that he ride well. As president, he was comfortable in the saddle or simply working with his horses.

American presidents throughout history have admired the grandeur and appreciated the utility of the horse. George Washington regarded horses as a source of pardonable pride, and his warhorses were of great importance to him as loyal companions and symbols of his leadership. Many presidents since his time have enjoyed the beauty and skill of these uncomplaining public servants for work, sport, and leisure. Everyday use of horses at the White House has long passed, but at special ceremonies and state occasions the horse regains the stage.

I would like to thank Gwen White, Sally Stokes, Pamela Scott, and Loni Hovey for their research contributions to this article.

1. For the construction history of the White House stables, see Herbert R. Collins, "The White House Stables and Garages," *Records of the Columbia Historical Society*, vol. 63–65 (1963–65), 366–85; for Pauline Wayne's fate, see "White House Stables Will Be Torn Down," *Washington Evening Star*, July 10, 1911; and for background on the end of an appropriation for horses and stables, see "To Change the Subject: Presidential Stables Just a Memory," *Christian Science Monitor*, January 3, 1952.

2. William Seale, *The President's House: A History* (Washington, D.C.: White House Historical Association with the cooperation of the National Geographic Society, 1986), 1:114. See also Julius Trousdale Sadler Jr. and Jacquelin D. J. Sadler, *American Stables: An Architectural Tour* (Boston: New York Graphic Society, 1981), 59–60.

3. Seale, *President's House*, 1:151–52, 172.

4. Collins, "White House Stables and Garages," 374.

5. "The City of Washington," *Washington National Intelligencer*, November 18, 1834.

6. Seale, *President's House*, 1:197–98.

7. "Ornamental Trees for Sale," *Washington Evening Star*, November 21, 1855.

8. Seale, *President's House*, 1:343–45.

9. "From Washington," *New York Times*, February 11, 1864; Smith Stimmel, *Personal Reminiscences of Abraham Lincoln* (Minneapolis: William H. M. Adams, 1928), 37–40.

10. Collins, "White House Stables and Garages," 382.

11. Alfred B. Mullett's progress report to Secretary of State Hamilton Fish, January 9, 1872, quoted in *Executive Office Building, General Services Administration Historical Study* vol. 3, Washington, D.C., December 1964, 43–44.

12. For a study of Mullett's tenure as supervising architect, see Antoinette J. Lee, *Architects to the Nation* (New York: Oxford University Press, 2000), 73–110.

13. *Annual Report of the Chief of Engineers, United States Army to the Secretary of War for the Year 1890* (Washington, D.C.: Government Printing Office, 1890), 3535–36.

14. "Harrison's Horses," *The Evening Star*, April 13, 1889.

15. For contemporaneous descriptions of Albert Hawkins and William Willis, described below, see "President's Coachman May Live" *Washington Post*, July 28, 1895.

16. "The Tattler," *The Stable* 3, no. 5 (June 1888): 120.

17. "President's Coachman May Live."

18. Seale, *President's House*, 2:728; "The White House Stable and Its Occupants," *Washington Post*, January 7, 1906.

19. "Harrison's Horses," *Washington Post*, April 13, 1889; "Employees at Stable of the Executive Mansion," 1901–1903 Stable Employees, Record Group 42, entry 91, box 24, letter 1234, National Archives, Washington, D.C.

20. Betty Monkman, *The White House: Its Historic Furnishings and First Families* (New York: Abbeville Press, 2000), 32.

21. Colonel William H. Crook, "The President's Horses," *Washington Evening Star*, April 5, 1884.

22. Gilson Willetts, *Inside History of the White House* (New York: Christian Herald, 1908), 429.

23. Ibid., 430–31. See also Frank G. Carpenter, "Our Presidents as Horsemen," *Magazine of American History* 17 (June 1887): 483–93; "All Fond of Horses," *Washington Post*, March 5, 1905. See also Herbert R. Collins, *Presidents on Wheels* (New York: Bonanza Books, 1991). Collins covers the history of carriages and automobiles of the presidents by administration.

24. John Durant, *The Sports of Our Presidents* (New York: Hastings House Publications, 1964), 130–31.

25. See "Presidents' and Ex-Presidents' Funerals," in *Horse-Drawn Funeral Vehicles*, ed. Michael P. D'Amato (Bird-in-Hand, Pa.: Carriage Museum of America, 2004), 337–402.

26. Carpenter, "Our Presidents as Horsemen," 483.

27. For background on the presidents and horseracing, see Lyman Horace Weeks, *The American Turf: An Historical Account in the United States.* (New York: Historical Company, 1898): 32–33, 452; John Hervey, *Horse Racing in America* (New York: privately printed, 1944), 2:5–6, 57–70; John Hervey, *The American Trotter* (New York: Coward-McCann, 1947), 457–58; Roger Longrigg, *The History of Horse Racing* (New York: Macmillan, 1972), 205–8; Jennie Holliman, *American Sports, 1785–1895* (Philadelphia: Porcupine Press, 1975), 108–23.

28. Benjamin Perley Poore, *Perley's Reminiscences of Sixty Years in the National Metropolis* (Philadelphia: Hubbard Brothers, 1886), 1:190–91.

29. President Jackson brought several of his horses, slave jockeys, and a trainer from Tennessee and installed them in the White House stable. Busiris was noted as being at the White House stable in Hervey, *Horse Racing in America*, 2:70. Jackson brought his gray filly Bolivia to Washington in the spring of 1834 along with Ratler and Lady Nashville, owned by Andrew Jackson Donelson. Equestrian artist Edward Troye painted both Busiris and Bolivia in 1834. See Alexander Mackay-Smith, *The Races Horses of America, 1832–1872: Portraits and Other Paintings by Edward Troye* (Saratoga Springs, N.Y.: National Museum of Racing, 1981), 46–47. See also "Washington Jockey Club Races," *Washington National Intelligencer*, October 16, 1834. The race results noted that Bolivia, entered by Donelson, had won an important sweepstakes for three-year-old colts and fillies contested over two two-mile heats. Bolivia, by Jackson's Bolivar, won both heats. By the time of the race, she had been purchased by Colonel John Crowell of Alabama. See also Edward Hotaling, *The Great Black Jockeys* (Rocklin, Calif.: Forum, 1999), 97–102.

30. For the importance of horse racing to Jackson and the complex circumstances of the duel with Charles Dickinson, see Robert V. Remini, *Andrew Jackson and the Course of American Empire, 1767–1821* (New York: History Book Club reprint, 1998), 1:136–42, and *Andrew Jackson and the Course of American Democracy, 1833–1845* (New York: History Book Club reprint, 1998), 3:434.

31. Carpenter, "Our Presidents as Horsemen," 492.

32. Seale, *President's House*, 2:728. For a description of the president's ride to Warrenton, Virginia, see Archibald Butt to Clara (Mrs. Lewis F. Butt), January 14, 1909, *The Letters of Archie Butt*, ed. Lawrence F. Abbott (Garden City and New York: Doubleday, Page and Company, 1924), 285–96.

Arlington's Ceremonial Horses and Funerals at the White House

CLAIRE A. FAULKNER

*T*hough presidential personalities and policies can generate deep chasms during their term of service, the death of a president evokes a genuine sadness that transcends partisan politics. Rarely are Americans as united in emotion and sensibility as at such a time. In a eulogy following President James A. Garfield's death in 1881, Henry Watterson, journalist, editor, and later Pulitzer Prize winner, stated, "Today, the people of the United States are one with one another, and stand hand in hand and heart to heart."[1] There is an immediate synthesis of feeling surrounding news of the loss of a national leader, especially one who resided in the White House. American presidents have led their country through economic hardship, world wars, and national crises, and the simple fact that they have held the highest office in the land affords them a unique place in American hearts.

Private funerals allow mourners to stand together to remember a loved one with ritual and ceremony that allay many of the tensions associated with the loss. State funerals "lend a degree of order during the threatening, chaotic experience" of losing a president or other high-ranking official.[2] The strict timing, ritual, and protocol inherent in state funerals reassure and comfort a grieving nation through tradition. Presidential funerals are exceptional in their pageantry, pomp, and precision, and burial

View of President John F. Kennedy's funeral procession to Arlington National Cemetery.

with full military honors includes color-bearers, body-bearers (the official U.S. government name for pall bearers), a caisson, an escort, a band, a firing party (the official name for rifle honor corps), and a bugler. Gene Gurney, author of a book on Arlington National Cemetery, explains that "other elements of the funeral—the slow, measured pace of the cortege, the somber music and the muffled drums—exemplify the reversal of the normal order of things" and serve to underscore the nation's loss.[3]

The primary responsibility for state funeral arrangements is borne by the commanding general of the Military District of Washington. However, specific decisions regarding each presidential funeral are made with family members, often well in advance of the actual death. President Gerald Ford made specific mention of this fact when eulogizing journalist and presidential historian Hugh Sidey in November 2005. In his opening remarks Ford said to mourners, "Like most men my age, I have given a thought or two to my funeral. As a former president, I'm almost required to, since the military periodically updates its own plans, and each presidential family is solicited for personal touches."[4]

The Third United States Infantry, better known as the Old Guard, is the military unit charged with overseeing diplomatic arrivals and departures and maintaining the perpetual guard at the Tomb of the Unknowns; however, it may be more widely recognized for performing burials in Arlington Cemetery with all the ceremonial accoutrements and for providing the caisson platoon and pall bearers for state funerals. Members of the Old Guard also serve as escort to the president for ceremonial

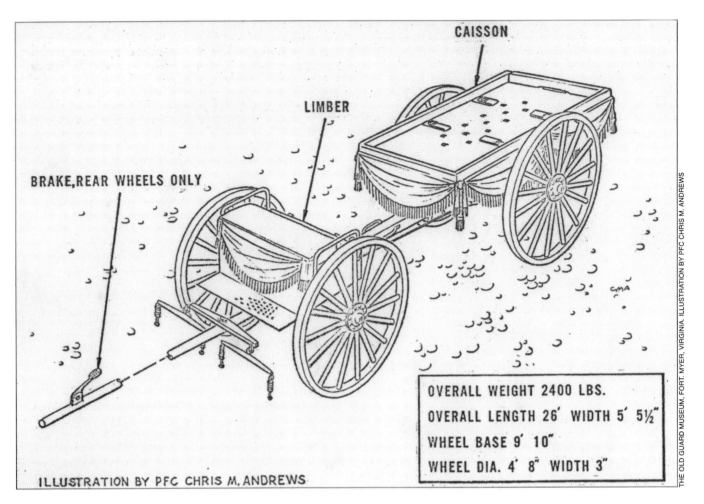

CAISSON

LIMBER

BRAKE, REAR WHEELS ONLY

OVERALL WEIGHT 2400 LBS.
OVERALL LENGTH 26' WIDTH 5' 5½"
WHEEL BASE 9' 10"
WHEEL DIA. 4' 8" WIDTH 3"

ILLUSTRATION BY PFC CHRIS M. ANDREWS

Illustration of limber and caisson currently used by the Caisson Platoon, Third Infantry.

purposes. As the Old Guard is the oldest active infantry regiment in the United States Army, it is fitting that this unit should bear the responsibility for the supervision, direction, and performance of ceremonial functions and funerals; however, it is also appropriately tasked with safeguarding the nation's capital through the coordination and maintenance of situational awareness, the employment of forces for homeland defense, and military assistance to civil authorities.

Following the Revolutionary War, the Old Guard was created on June 3, 1784, after the victorious Continental Army had been disbanded. According to the provisions of the 1783 Peace of Paris, Congress was required to create an army. Only a small artillery detachment, posted to West Point, had been retained, and this became the Old Guard.[5] Although the Third Infantry Regiment has been stationed at numerous military facilities since its inception, its home has been at Fort Myer, Virginia, just across the Potomac from the nation's capital since 1948.

For some, it is perhaps a stark reality that the famous Third Infantry Regiment, most especially the Caisson Platoon, spends five days a week practicing and performing burials (averaging six per day) at Arlington

National Cemetery. In 2005, the Caisson Platoon participated in 1,780 funerals. These troops are selected for their soldierly appearance and superior discipline; similarly, the horses for the unit are chosen for their color, height, and temperament. The solemn dignity that the men and horses lend to each funeral service is "not simply accidental or instinctive," explains the regiment's public information office. "Both men and horses train constantly for this duty. Most of the soldiers come to Fort Myer not as expert horsemen, but as trained infantrymen. Many come from rural areas of the South and West and bring with them a knowledge and love of animals. In addition to caring for the horses, he or she must learn to ride at the position of somber attention with a military forward seat in a flat saddle."[6]

The saddle used by the Caisson Platoon dates from the Civil War and was designed by then Army Captain George B. McClellan. Although it underwent multiple alterations during the latter half of the nineteenth century, the same basic split-seat design remains. The field artillery harness design dates to the 1890s. Old manuals from the U.S. Army Quartermaster Corps, have allowed soldiers to act as farriers and also to handcraft all the saddles, bridles, and tack needed for their missions. Specifically, Eugene Burks has served as saddlemaker for the Caisson Platoon since 1981. He currently produces and maintains the tack for over forty head of horses, including a large assortment of military saddles, postillion harnesses for several teams of six horses, strap goods, bridles, halters, saddlebags, and girths.

As in the leather shop, all facets of the unit are highly specialized, and the horses and riders train, drill, and live together until they are deemed qualified to conduct the ceremonial missions. Most horses undergo extensive training to prepare them for the sights and sounds in Arlington National Cemetery. They must be able to maintain their composure around gunfire, cannon fire, vehicular traffic, bands, flags, and low-flying aircraft. Six horses pull each caisson through its specified route, and the horses are matched and sent out in either light- or dark-colored teams. The website of the Military District of Washington describes the arrangement: "Each team is grouped into three pairs: the lead pair is in front, the swing team follows and the nearest the caisson is the wheel pair. Although all six animals are saddled, only those on the left have mounted riders. This is a tradition which began in the early horse-drawn artillery days

when one horse of each pair was mounted, while the other carried provisions and feed." Horses for the Caisson Platoon come from ranch owners across the United States. Currently there are about forty-seven horses, most of which are stabled at Fort Myer; the rest are at a training facility at Fort Belvoir, Virginia.[7]

The use of limbers and caissons (from the French for "artillery wagon") for the burial of military personnel appears to have originated in the beginning of the era of light mobile field artillery in the eighteenth century. When a caisson was unloaded on the battlefield, presumably it would reload with wounded, dead, or dying soldiers of the battery it had just resupplied. This matter of conveyance was later carried over and formalized into the use of a caisson for the burial of a singular fallen soldier in his coffin.

Tradition is highly valued by members of the Third Infantry Regiment. Old customs and habits are studied, practiced, and employed in the execution of their duties. The practice of having the charger of a deceased military officer led in the funeral procession, for example, is a survival of the ancient custom of sacrificing a horse at the burial of a warrior. The Mongols and Tatars in the days of Genghis Khan and Tamerlane believed that the spirit of a sacrificed horse went through the "gate of the sky" to serve its master in the afterworld. According to European folk belief, the spirit of a dead horse would find its dead master if permitted to follow him into the hereafter. Otherwise the dead master's spirit would have to walk. Some of the Plains Indians in America also adopted the custom of sacrificing the horse at the burial of a warrior after they came into possession of horses following the Spanish discovery. In 1804, Meriwether Lewis and William Clark visited the grave of Blackbird, a great Omaha chief who had been buried sitting on his favorite horse. Although horses are no longer sacrificed, riderless horses are still led in funeral processions to symbolize the custom.[8]

The riderless, or caparisoned (ornamentally covered), horse is considered a symbolic representation that the deceased was mounted in this life and will continue to be mounted in the hereafter. In American state ceremonies, for a caparisoned horse to be included, the person honored must have, at one time, achieved the rank of army or marine corps colonel or above. Because the president of the United States is the commander in chief of the armed forces, he is automatically entitled to the

Above: President James Garfield's funeral procession, Cleveland, Ohio, 1881.

Right: Abraham Lincoln's caparisoned horse, Old Bob, waits in front of the president's mourning draped residence in Springfield, Illinois, 1865.

Opposite: The Old Guard escorted the coffin of Former President William Howard Taft from the Taft residence to the Capitol and from the cemetery gate to his gravesite, 1930.

use of the horse. Some historical records indicate that Abraham Lincoln was the first president to have been honored by the inclusion of the caparisoned horse in his funeral cortege. When his coffin was being carried to his grave in Springfield, Illinois, it was followed by his personal horse, Old Bob, with its master's boots backward in the stirrups to signify that the deceased would never ride again. However, Tobias Lear, George Washington's personal secretary, recorded that Washington's horse was a part of Washington's funeral: "The General's horse, with his saddle, holsters, and pistols, [was] led by two grooms, Cyrus and Wilson, in black."[9] In addition, Zachary Taylor's personal horse, Old Whitey, was in his funeral procession. The use of reversed boots in the stirrups during a funeral is comparable to the infantry's custom of "slope arms," a position in which the rifle is reversed so that the muzzle is pointed to the ground during burial ceremonies.

The equipment a caparisoned horse bears differs according to its color: if black, the horse carries saddle blanket, saddle, and bridle; if any other color, the horse carries a folded hood and cape, along with a blanket, saddle and bridle. All of the caparison is black. The hood,

saddle blanket, and cape are made of wool or serge—a strong, twilled fabric with diagonal rib—and all brass and leather is highly polished. Also, in the case of a presidential death, the Presidential Seal is placed on the rear corners of the blanket, four inches from the bottom.

Perhaps the most famous caparisoned horse was Black Jack, named after General John J. "Black Jack" Pershing. Black Jack was foaled January 19, 1947, and came to Fort Myer from Fort Reno, Oklahoma, on November 22, 1952. He was the last of horses issued by the U.S. Army Quartermaster Corps and the last to be branded with the army's "US" on the left shoulder, with his army serial number, "2V56," on the left side of his neck. Black Jack weighed 1,050 pounds and stood fifteen hands high. On Black Jack's twenty-ninth birthday, President Richard Nixon wrote, "Black Jack has been a poignant symbol of our nation's grief on many occasions over the years. Citizens in mourning felt dignity and purpose conveyed, a simpler yet deeper tribute to the memory of those heroic 'riders' who have given so much for our nation. Our people are grateful to Black Jack for helping us bear the burden of sorrow during difficult times."[10] Nixon's penned words highlight the way in

BLACK JACK

Right: A birthday celebration for Black Jack at Fort Myer, in 1970. Nancy Shado, Black Jack's biggest fan, feeds him butter pecan cake.

Opposite: Pfc. Arthur Carlson and Black Jack wait for President Kennedy's coffin to descend the Capitol steps, November 25, 1963.

Below: Black Jack's tombstone. His gravesite is on the parade grounds at Fort Myer surrounded by a manicured hedge in the shape of a horseshoe.

THE OLD GUARD MUSEUM, FORT MYER, VIRGINIA

ROBERT LAUTMAN FOR THE WHITE HOUSE HISTORICAL ASSOCIATION

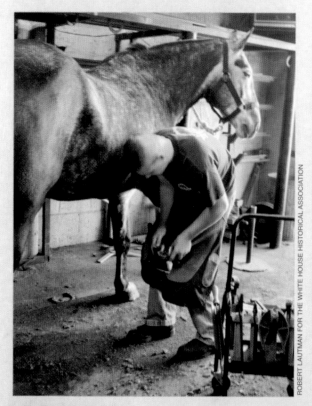

ROBERT LAUTMAN FOR THE WHITE HOUSE HISTORICAL ASSOCIATION

ROBERT LAUTMAN FOR THE WHITE HOUSE HISTORICAL ASSOCIATION

ROBERT LAUTMAN FOR THE WHITE HOUSE HISTORICAL ASSOCIATION

Above and left: Scenes in and around the stables at Fort Myer.

Opposite, top: Eugene Burks displays items made in the leather shop at Fort Myer. He has been the saddlemaker for the Caisson Platoon since 1981. Specialist Troy Call displays cowhide tanned for use in the leather shop.

Right: Each leather item used by the ceremonial horses is made to specifications in the leather shop's historical manu-al, including a large assortment of military saddles, harnesses, strap goods, bridles, halters, saddlebags, and girths.

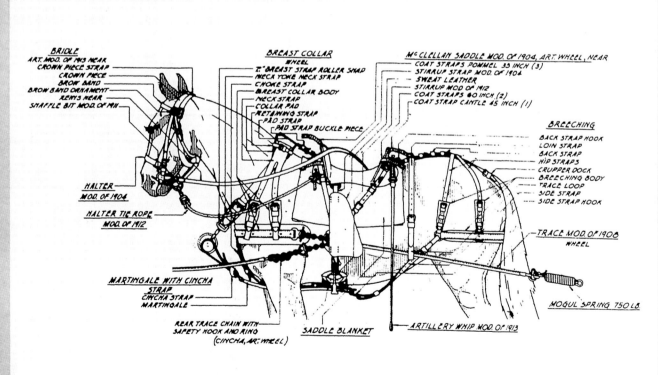

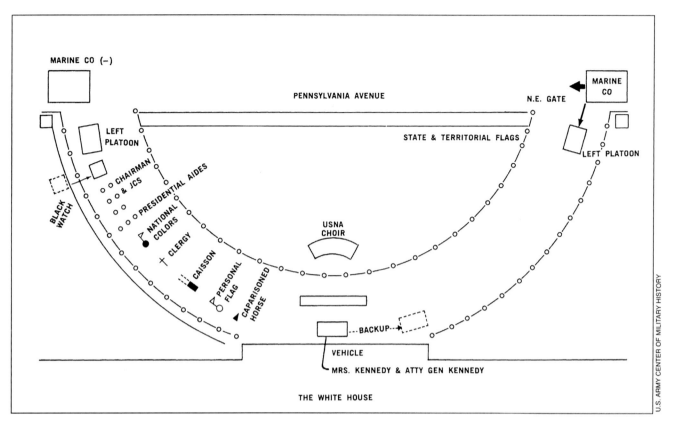

MARINE CO (−)

PENNSYLVANIA AVENUE

N.E. GATE

MARINE CO

STATE & TERRITORIAL FLAGS

LEFT PLATOON

LEFT PLATOON

BLACK WATCH

CHAIRMAN & JCS

PRESIDENTIAL AIDES

NATIONAL COLORS

CLERGY

CAISSON

PERSONAL FLAG

CAPARISONED HORSE

USNA CHOIR

BACKUP

VEHICLE

MRS. KENNEDY & ATTY GEN KENNEDY

THE WHITE HOUSE

U.S. ARMY CENTER OF MILITARY HISTORY

which the use of a caparisoned horse was becoming synonymous with laying a national hero to rest.

Although Black Jack garnered fame during the funeral of President John F. Kennedy, he also took part in the funerals of Herbert Hoover, Douglas MacArthur, Lyndon Johnson, and literally thousands of others in Arlington Cemetery during his many years of service with the Old Guard. Black Jack was retired to the Fort Myer stables on June 1, 1973, and lived for three more years in a stall decorated with red, white, and blue. Until his death on February 6, 1976, Black Jack received an average of fifty visitors a day. He also received fan mail, Christmas cards from all over the world, and "numerous requests for clippings from his tail and horseshoes."[11] Clearly, he captured many hearts. He is buried on the post parade ground at Fort Myer, Summerall Field, near the post headquarters flagpole. At the time of Black Jack's retirement, a horse named Raven assumed his duties. Currently, the most well recognized horse in the Fort Myer stables is Sergeant York, the caparisoned horse that participated in President Ronald Reagan's funeral in 2004.

The incorporation of specialized music, gunfire, and flags are other facets of a ceremonial state funeral. For example, "Taps" is widely recognized as the music that

Above: Diagram of the Kennedy processional from the North Portico of the White House to Saint Matthew's Cathedral, November 25, 1963.

Opposite: Kennedy's coffin taken from the White House in procession. Black Jack follows in the background.

concludes a ceremonial funeral honoring the deceased's service to country. The music and words to "Taps" were composed by General Dan Butterfield at Harrison's Landing in July 1862, to replace the earlier "Tattoo," or "Lights Out," which he thought too formal. The call became known as "Taps" because it was often tapped out on a drum in the absence of a bugler. It was officially adopted by the U.S. Army in 1874 and later was used as a figurative call to the sleep of death for soldiers. Graveside military honors also include the firing of three volleys each by seven service members. This practice also recalls old battlefield customs of ceasing hostilities while both sides cleared their dead from the battlefield. Once the dead had been properly cared for, each side would fire three volleys to indicate they were ready to resume the battle.

The death of a U.S. president involves other ceremonial gun salutes and military traditions. On the day after the death of the president, former president, or president-elect (unless this day falls on a Sunday or holiday, in which case the honor will be rendered the following day), the commanders of army installations with the necessary personnel order that one gun be fired every half hour, beginning at reveille and ending at retreat. On the day of burial, these same installations fire a twenty-one-gun salute starting at noon and a fifty-gun salute (one round for each state) at five second intervals immediately following the lowering of the flag.

Yet perhaps the most recognizable trapping of a military or state funeral is the flag-draped coffin. The blue of the flag is placed at the head of the coffin, over the left shoulder of the deceased. In 1918 the U.S. Army, at the suggestion of Major General George W. Cocheu, officially began the practice of placing a flag over the coffin and presenting it to the next of kin at the conclusion of the funeral service, though the custom dates to the Napoleonic Wars of the late eighteenth and early nineteenth centuries, when a flag was used to cover the dead

as they were taken from the battlefield on a caisson. Today the flag-covered coffin is a symbol that a soldier's country assumes the solemn and sacred obligation of burying its fallen.

Although not every president has received a state funeral with all of these trappings, each is entitled to the honor. Over time, presidents and their families have increasingly chosen to use one of the most poignant aspects of a state funeral ceremony—horses in the funeral cortege. Following a service for Abraham Lincoln in the East Room of the White House, the late president's coffin was drawn to the Capitol by six horses pulling a "fourteen-foot long hearse that very much resembled a draped and decorated wagon."[12] Less than two decades had passed since President Lincoln's death when President Garfield was also struck down by an assassin's bullet. Although Garfield was buried in his home state of Ohio, his funeral procession from the Capitol to the train station included a horse-drawn caisson. According to eyewitness reports, the hearse "was drawn by six iron-gray horses, each led by a colored groom."[13] There is no

TIME LIFE PICTURES / GETTY IMAGES

Right: At the Capitol, Black Jack waits for President Kennedy's coffin to be removed from the caisson. Mrs. Kennedy, the president's children, and President and Mrs. Lyndon B. Johnson can be seen in the distance.

Below: Black Jack marching in President Lyndon B. Johnson's funeral, January 1973.

JOHN F. KENNEDY LIBRARY

LYNDON B. JOHNSON LIBRARY AUSTIN

Left: Black Jack and the caisson unit bearing President Herbert Hoover's coffin arriving at the Capitol, October 1964.

Below: Former President Dwight D. Eisenhower's caisson arrives at the Capitol, March 30, 1969. Notice the similarity between this and other presidential funerals.

evidence of a caparisoned horse being used. Similarly, upon the death of former President William Howard Taft in 1930, the Old Guard supplied the caisson and caisson detachment for the escort from the Taft residence to the Capitol and from the cemetery gate to the grave. Taft was the first of two presidents to be buried at Arlington National Cemetery. Again, there is no reference to a caparisoned horse being employed.

When President John F. Kennedy was assassinated in 1963, Mrs. Kennedy was desirous that her husband's funeral rites be memorable and historic, and his ceremo-

Above: Stereopticon slide showing the body of President Warren G. Harding leaving the White House, August 8, 1923.

Right: President Harry Truman presenting the Presidential Baton to Colonel William W. Jenna, commanding officer of the Third Infantry, in the Rose Garden, April 10, 1952.

nial processions be given dramatic impact for the world to see. The first cortege bore his body on a flag-draped caisson from the White House to the Capitol on November 24, 1963. Three pairs of matched gray horses pulled the caisson. Behind the caisson, a member of the Coast Guard carried the presidential flag, and behind the flag walked Black Jack. The biographer of this horse observed, "Black Jack's vitality was impressive. Every step of the way his head bobbed up and down as he energetically tugged on his walker's line."[14] Black Jack was later a part of the processional that carried Kennedy's coffin from the Capitol to a brief stop at the White House and on to the church service at Saint Matthew's Cathedral. Following the service, the caisson and caparisoned horse took the final walk with the president's remains to Arlington National Cemetery. Just as the Old Guard followed decades-old protocol in carrying out a funeral, Mrs. Kennedy, together with the designer of the Kennedy gravesite, architect John Carl Warnecke, worked to make the gravesite "combine the ideas and feelings of the present with the traditions of the past,"[14] and the idea for the eternal flame was born.

The death of President Kennedy introduced military tradition and state ceremonies to a new generation of Americans, and Robert Hazel, novelist and poet, composed a poem entitled "Riderless Horse" that crystallized the haunting images surrounding the funeral for the late president:

Riderless Horse

From Andrews Field you ride into the Capital.
A guard of honor escorts your sudden corpse
    down an aluminum ladder.
Your widow stalks your body through an avenue
of bare sycamores, and one answering bell,
leading heads of state to altar and precipice.
On the birthday of your son, your widow
walks bars of a dirge on the pavement
    towards fountain and abyss.
Among swords of sunlight drawn by the spokes
    of the caisson
and the white manes of horses, she walks
    into noon and midnight.
Above the muffled drums,
the high voice of a young soldier
tells the white horses how slow to go
before your widow and children, walking
behind the flag-anchored coffin—
and one riderless black horse dancing![16]

Although the death of President Kennedy brought the Old Guard and its military traditions into the national spotlight, the activities surrounding the funeral also brought tragedy to the members of the Third Infantry Regiment. Captain Michael D. Groves, the officer responsible for the military arrangements at the funeral of the president, died of a heart attack the next month, on December 3, 1963, at home while dining with his family, at the age of twenty seven. He was responsible for the training and supervision of the body-bearers, deathwatch, rifle firing party, and caisson escort for the services at the White House, the Capitol, and Arlington Cemetery. According to a speech on the floor of the House of Representatives by Congressman James G. Fulton of Pennsylvania, "Captain Groves worked day and night to handle the arrangements . . . and overtaxed himself."[17]

Above: The Caisson Platoon at the funeral of former President Ronald Reagan, 2004.

President Herbert Hoover's death the following year once more triggered the Old Guard into action, and the Caisson Platoon and caparisoned horse were again deployed. Early funeral plans had indicated that President Hoover would be buried in West Branch, Iowa, and, at the time of his death, the caisson unit and horses should be transported by air to Iowa for the services. On a veterinarian's recommendation the Old Guard had "rehearsed the logistics of the transfer by trucking the horses to Andrews Air Force Base, loading them onto a transport plane, and flying over the Chesapeake Bay for about twenty minutes" to make sure the process would be smooth and seamless when the inevitable time came.[18] However, when Hoover died, his original funeral plans were changed, and a caisson unit was not required to travel to Iowa. Black Jack and a caisson team simply participated in the escort of the coffin from Union Station to the Capitol.

It is especially fitting that a caisson unit and caparisoned horse functioned in President Dwight D. Eisenhower's funeral, because he had a direct impact on the continuation of the program at Fort Myer. During his presidency, controversy rose over the considerable cost of horse-drawn funerals when it was found that the government could save funds by substituting motorized hearses in place of the caissons. The

army vice chief of staff issued an order to abolish all future horse-drawn units. President Eisenhower immediately interceded and ordered horse-drawn funerals to continue.

Upon President Ronald Reagan's death in California in 2004, his body was transported to Washington for the state funeral. At 16th Street and Constitution Avenue, NW, on June 9, 2004, President Reagan's coffin was transferred to an Old Guard horse-drawn caisson from a hearse for the journey to the Capitol. This was the same location in which President Lyndon Johnson's coffin had been transferred to a caisson in 1973. Reagan had been an avid horseman, and the boots that were reversed in Sergeant York's stirrups were the president's own brown riding boots provided by Mrs. Reagan, who asked that they not be altered in any way. This arrangement was unusual; under most circumstances, the boots used with the caparisoned horse are ceremonial pairs maintained and stored by the Old Guard.

Members of the Old Guard have furnished their services to their commanders in chief on numerous mournful occasions, and presidents have elected to highlight their singular service in various ways. On the bicentennial of the Third Infantry Regiment in 1984, President Ronald Reagan sent a letter to the unit espousing its "unparalleled reputation for discipline, precision, and dedication"[19] to each distinctive mission. President Harry Truman, on the other hand, chose to present a trophy baton to representatives of the Third Infantry Regiment in commemoration of its long and embattled service in the army as well as the years spent in the Washington area as the escort to the president at official and ceremonial functions. Named the "Presidential Baton" by members of the regiment, it was presented on April 10, 1952, by President Truman to Colonel William W. Jenna, commanding officer of the regiment. The baton was fashioned from 136-year-old white pine used in the reconstruction of the White House after the British burned the residence in 1814. It is just over 3½ feet long, weighing about 1½ pounds, with silver ferrules. The wood was turned by a member of the U.S. Army Band, and the silver was donated by jewelers in the Washington, D.C., area. The baton is decorated with red, white, and blue braided cords and tassels. It is marked by a gold band just below the head with twelve stars, the Presidential Seal, and the inscription, "Original White House Material / Removed in 1950."[20] Oddly enough, during the historic Truman renovation of the White House between 1948 and 1952, much of the wood, paneling, and bricks were stored in warehouses and buried on the grounds of Fort Myer, the home of the famed regiment.

With the dedication and assistance of members of the Old Guard stationed at Fort Myer, national farewells inexorably intertwine their horses and our presidents who speak to us, metaphorically, one last time through the rhythmic cadence of the horses' hooves on the Washington pavement, slowly drawing them toward their final resting place. In a distinctive way, horses help us say our last good-byes. Whether a president is taken from his nation through old age, disease, or an assassin's bullet, the nation sustains a sharp and biting wound. Following the assassination of President Garfield, the Reverend Henry Ward Beecher said, "We are all under a cloud. . . . We are gathered together to-night as a household would be gathered where the father had been stricken down."[21] The loss of a president temporarily cloaks the nation in darkness, and Reverend Beecher aptly speaks for all Americans.

NOTES

1. Quoted in *Gen. Garfield from the Log Cabin to the White House: Including His Early History, War Record, Public Speeches, Nomination, Inauguration, Assassination, Death and Burial,* ed. J. B. McClure (Chicago: Rhodes & McClure, 1881), 8.

2. In *Children and the Death of a President: Multi-Disciplinary Studies,* ed. Martha Wofenstein and Gilbert Kliman (Gloucester, Mass.: P. Smith, 1969), 197.

3. Gene Gurney, *Arlington National Cemetery: A Picture Story of America's Most Famous Burial Grounds from the Civil War to President John F. Kennedy's Burial* (New York: Crown Publishers, 1965), 19.

4. Former President Gerald R. Ford, eulogy for Hugh Sidey, *Washington Post,* November 30, 2005.

5. *A Short History of the Old Guard* (Fort Myer, Va.: Old Guard Museum, April 2005), 2.

6. "The Army's Last Horses," press release from the Public Information Office, Third United States Infantry, The Old Guard, November 11, 1977.

7. See the home page of the Military District of Washington, www.mdw.army.mil.

8. The historical information is taken from George Stimpson, *A Book About a Thousand Things* (New York: Harper & Brothers, 1946), 76.

9. Tobias Lear, quoted in *The Writings of George Washington,* ed. Worthington Chauncey Ford (New York: G. P. Putnam's Sons, 1893), 14:254–55.

10. President Richard Nixon on Black Jack's 29th birthday.

11. *Pentagram News,* January 29, 1976, 15.

12. Robert Knuckle, *Black Jack: America's Famous Riderless Horse* (Burnstown, Ont.: General Store Publishing House, 2002), 3.

13. Russell Conwell, *The Life, Speeches and Public Services of James A. Garfield,* (Portland, Maine; George Stenson and Co.,. 366.)

14. Knuckle, *Black Jack,* 9.

15. Gurney, *Arlington National Cemetery,* 135.

16. Robert Hazel, "Riderless Horse," in *Of Poetry and Power: Poems Occasioned by the Presidency and by the Death of John F. Kennedy* ed. Erwin A. Glikes and Paul Schwaber, (New York: Basic Books, 1964) 65.

17. *Congressional Record—House,* December 4, 1963, 23272.

18. Knuckle, *Black Jack,* 116.

19. President Ronald Reagan to the Third Infantry Regiment, May 30, 1984, Old Guard Museum, Fort Myer, Virginia.

20. Information regarding the Presidential Baton is from the Old Guard Museum Historical Property Catalog, no. OG1952.001.

21. Quoted in *Gen. Garfield from the Log Cabin to the White House,* ed. McClure, 69.

Addendum

A Presidential Funeral

Flags lowered. A flag-draped coffin. A stoic first lady on the arm of a military aide. The fly over of twenty one fighter aircraft. Gunfire salutes at military installations across the country. These are the familiar sights and sounds of a state funeral for a modern day American president. With the ceremonies attendant to the passing of President Ford fresh in mind, it is timely to reexamine the funeral proceedings that sear the final images of a president into the consciousness of the American public.

The nation has witnessed the deaths of just four presidents over the past three decades, and only three of those chose to have state funerals—Lyndon B. Johnson (1973), Ronald Reagan (2004), and Gerald R. Ford (2007). Although Richard Nixon's family had the option of a state funeral, they decided instead to hold a simple service at the Nixon Library in California, where in 1974 President Nixon, the first president to resign from office, was buried beside his wife, Patricia Nixon, who predeceased him. Traditionally five days in length, presidential state funerals are meticulously choreographed. Coordination for the events is conducted by the army's Military District of Washington and begins early in each presidential term, when a new president is asked to attend to the strange task of imagining his own funeral service. It is a cold realization that greets a new president at the White House door.

By helping plan their own funeral, presidents are able to incorporate personal touches that can elucidate their character and legacy on a national stage for the last time. In many ways, funeral services are final conversation with the nation, and illustrate something about the man and the way in which he wishes to be remembered. We recently observed this following the death in the funeral of President Ford. Tailored to fit his particular persona, the services and events surrounding the five

days of remembrance departed from tradition and provided Americans a glimpse at the complexion of the man who served the nation in multiple capacities, including the presidency, over his lengthy career.

In both what he elected to include in his services and what he chose to leave out, President Ford painted in symbols the portrait of his public life. For example, he determined to lie in state in front of both the House and Senate chambers in the Capitol to honor and highlight his service in each. "I know personally how much those two tributes themselves meant to President Ford," remarked Gregory D. Willard, a Ford family representative during a news conference at the time. In contrast, President Ford did not want his body to be borne along Pennsylvania Avenue to the Capitol by the horse-drawn caisson, traditional in so many presidential funerals. Instead he requested a motorcade that passed through

Above: President Gerald. R. Ford's portrait was draped in black at the White House while the country mourned his death.

Alexandria, Virginia, hometown while he was in public service and went by the World War II Memorial on the National Mall, to pay tribute to his military service and an entire generation of fellow Americans who brought victory in that conflict.

An unassuming President Ford had to be persuaded to include many of the ceremonial formalities attached to state funerals. "The folks that handle protocol for the country worked with him to help him understand that the service was for the nation as well as for his family, and he agreed reluctantly to certain elements," said the Reverend Robert Certain of St. Margaret's Episcopal Church in Palm Desert, California, where President and Mrs. Ford worshipped. During his last symbolic journey to Washington, Ford's body lay in state in the Capitol rotunda and this may remain as one of the most memorable and poignant images. In a proclamation announcing his death, President Bush characterized Ford as "a true gentleman who reflected the best in America's character." In an unprecedented and extraordinary act, Ford's children greeted mourners and well-wishers personally as thousands streamed through the Capitol, paying their respects to the late president.

Upon arrival at the rotunda, President Ford's flag-draped coffin was placed on the same bier originally constructed for Abraham Lincoln 142 years ago by government carpenters and used in the funerals of ten subsequent presidents. This connection to the past underscores the importance of tradition in honoring a president as one in a distinguished line. In the nineteenth century, while news of a presidential death carried the same significance it does today, information traveled by telegraph, not twenty-four hour cable news, and there was no pre-set form for official mourning.

Traditions for presidential funerals found models in royal funerals and Washington merchants Alexander Hunter and Darius Clagett staged the first, that of William Henry Harrison, in 1841. This funeral was held in the East Room at the White House, the mirrors and chandeliers elaborately draped in black crape. Following the service the lead-lined mahogany coffin was mounted on a splendid "funeral car" or float, and drawn by black draped horses to the Congressional Cemetery for temporary burial until winter ice melted and it would be taken to Ohio for burial. Great numbers of pallbearers and dignitaries marched in the procession to dirges played

by the Marine Band, punctuated by artillery salutes. Nineteenth century presidential funerals followed this pattern somewhat, Lincoln's being even more elaborate and including a funeral train and "viewings" in city halls and state capitols from the East Coast to the final resting place in Springfield, Illinois.

Sorrowful grandeur of this sort faded with the twentieth century, still the flavor of presidential mourning remained highly ceremonial. The first president to die in the twentieth century was William McKinley, assassinated in September 1901. Decorations of mourning for him were greatly simplified from what had taken place for President Garfield twenty years before. His body lay in state in the Capitol. Likewise Warren G. Harding's funeral ornaments were even simpler. First he lay in state in the East Room, but his official funeral service took place in the Capitol rotunda, where the public was admitted to view the coffin adorned with a flag and eagle made of flowers in red, white and blue, designed by his widow Florence Harding, hence a personal touch.

Funerals of Presidents Franklin D. Roosevelt and John F. Kennedy continued the trend for subtle, yet distinct mourning decorations. Both, like Harding, having died in office, they first lay in state in the East Room, where trim black drapery dimmed the festive sparkle of the chandeliers. The coffins stood on the Lincoln bier, flag-draped with a limited surrounding of flowers. After a day, usually, the procession began to the Capitol for the public lying in state prior to the religious service. The general pattern of the presidential funerals have thus been established for the better part of a century.

Upon President Ford's passing, his official portrait hanging in the White House was draped simply in black, with white roses placed on a table beneath it. Immediately the mechanisms established long in advance were put into operation and the five day obsequies unfolded.

Andrew Jackson's Constitution Carriage

MARSHA MULLIN

*W*hen Andrew Jackson accompanied Martin Van Buren to his inauguration at the U.S. Capitol on March 4, 1837, it marked the first time that the outgoing and incoming presidents of the United States traveled to the inauguration ceremony together. The two men rode in a remarkable conveyance, a phaeton presented to Jackson by the Democratic-Republicans of New York City as a retirement gift. A phaeton was a light, open carriage made for pleasure driving, and this particular phaeton had a unique history, for it was constructed of wood salvaged from the refurbishment of the USS *Constitution*, the famous eighteenth-century warship better known as "Old Ironsides." Although Jackson had never been in the navy, the connections between Andrew Jackson and the *Constitution* made it a particularly appropriate gift from some of the staunchest Democrats in the country to the founder of the Democratic Party.

The USS *Constitution*

Authorized by Congress and President George Washington in 1794, the USS *Constitution* was launched by the United States Navy from Boston Harbor under the command of Thomas Truxton in October 1797. The ship represented an effort to improve U.S. security on

Calvert Brothers of Nashville photographed the phaeton in a studio setting with a strange iceberg-like background. This very detailed view reveals the phaeton's former splendor with heavy fringe and other details on the upholstery.

the seas, particularly against the Barbary pirates of North Africa and the British Royal Navy.[1] Between 1798 and the 1820s, the *Constitution* fought in one undeclared war and two official wars. Its military record was perfect; it was never defeated or boarded. Perhaps the ship's most famous military victory came in the early days of the War of 1812, when it defeated the HMS *Guerrière*. The *Constitution* acquired its nickname "Old Ironsides" in this engagement because shots from the *Guerrière* bounced off its seemingly impenetrable sides. The success of the *Constitution* forced the Royal Navy to abandon the practice of one-on-one encounters between their frigates and the larger U.S. frigates for fear of losing more men-of-war.

Tactically, the naval battle provided the Americans with a victory in a war that up to that point had seen mainly demoralizing defeats. The *Constitution* served ably throughout the rest of the war and engaged British ships in other spectacular victories. After the War of 1812 ended with General Andrew Jackson's miraculous victory at the battle of New Orleans on January 8, 1815, the navy mothballed "Old Ironsides" for several years. In the 1820s, it put the *Constitution* into service as part of the Mediterranean fleet for a short time and then mothballed it again. In the early 1830s, during a routine survey of mothballed ships, a rumor arose that the navy would be scrapping the venerable *Constitution*. Oliver Wendell Holmes, then a Harvard student, wrote his famous poem "Old Ironsides," which gave voice to public sentiment against its demolition. In response to the public outcry, in 1833 Congress approved funds for its restoration, and the navy sent the ship to dry dock in Boston for refurbishing.

While the ship was in dry dock, it was fitted with a new figurehead on its prow, a carved wooden figure of President Andrew Jackson. Captain Jesse Duncan Elliott, commander of the Boston Navy Yard and a great admirer of Andrew Jackson, commissioned the figurehead.[2] Although such a figurehead was apparently against navy policy, Elliott had it installed anyway, over the objections of the outraged Bostonians. At the time, Boston was generally displeased with President Jackson's order to remove the deposits from the Second Bank of the United States, which threw banking into upheaval. On the night of July 2, 1834, a merchant seaman managed to row across Boston Harbor during a driving rainstorm and cut the head off the Jackson figurehead. Eventually workers installed a replacement head on the ship, but not before the figurehead became something of a national cause célèbre. Two anti-Jackson political cartoon prints featured the incident.[3]

While the ship was in dry dock, Isaac Hull, who had been commander of the *Constitution* during the War of 1812, initiated the custom of making souvenirs of pieces of wood and metal removed during the refurbishing process. Hull gave away many canes and, later, snuff-boxes made of live oak removed from the ship.[4] In fact, Hull presented Andrew Jackson and Martin Van Buren with canes when Jackson was on his tour of the Northeast in 1833.[5] Later, in 1900, members of the Woodbury family of New Hampshire donated an "Old Ironsides" chair originally presented to Jackson's secretary of the navy, Levi Woodbury, to Jackson's Tennessee home, The Hermitage.[6] This custom of making souvenirs from salvaged pieces of wood and metal continues today at the USS Constitution Museum.[7]

The Carriage

Undoubtedly, the phaeton given to Andrew Jackson in 1837 was one of the most elaborate "Old Ironsides" souvenirs ever created. Who was the instigator of the project? Did the carriage company decide to make the phaeton on speculation, or did the political men from New York commission it? No one knows for sure.

In 1833, Andrew Jackson had purchased a barouche, an elegant open summer carriage with a collapsible top valued at $1,400, from Knowles & Thayer of Amherst, Massachusetts. In the fall of 1836, Lyman Knowles

Figurehead of Andrew Jackson, carved for the Constitution *by Laban Smith Beecher in 1834. (The head is a replacement, c. 1835.)*

At least two period political cartoon prints criticized Andrew Jackson by making fun of the decapitation of his figurehead on the USS Constitution. *Top: "The Decapitation of a great Block head by the Mysterious agency of the Claret coloured Coat," attributes the deed to demons and a secret agency. It was later found to have been a seaman who undertook the exploit on a bet. Bottom: An 1834 cartoon entitled "Fixing a blockhead to the Constitution or putting a wart on the mast of old Ironsides."*

wrote to Jackson offering to trade him a new coach of "selected materials and finished in the most splendid manner (but not gaudy)" for the old carriage and $600 in cash.[8] There is no recorded response from Jackson regarding the offer, but he had purchased the barouche in a similar manner. Was the carriage that Knowles & Thayer offered in 1836 the "Old Ironsides" phaeton? The carriage was completed by June 1, 1836, when three Knowles & Thayer craftsmen signed an affidavit certifying that the timber came from the Boston Navy Yard. In April 1836, George Budd, commandant of the Navy Yard,[9] certified that the white and live oak sold to Knowles & Thayer of Amherst, Massachusetts, for making a small carriage had been removed from the *Constitution.* John Southwick, a carpenter at the yard also certified the origins of the wood. These affidavits are now in Andrew Jackson's papers at the Library of Congress. The craftsmen's affidavit describes the carriage as "a light two horse Phaeton with a Patent Leather Top. A square open front body. Seat and body paneled with live oak, full hammer cloth drivers Seat trimmed with Silver drab Taborette, Not Painted, hung on four lobster tail Elliptic Springs and Cross Mounted."[10]

Knowles & Thayer, a carriage-making business operated by Lyman Knowles and Asahel Thayer, had opened in Amherst, Massachusetts, in 1827. It did an extensive business in Boston, but it also sold a number of vehicles in Washington. Indeed, the letter offering the trade-in references a large shipment the company was readying for the opening of the next session of Congress. With a customer base among Washington politicians, the Amherst carriage makers probably thought they would have a ready market for such a unique item. Unfortunately, none of the company's papers survive that might document how the idea for the carriage originated.[11] When Asahel Thayer died in 1877, he was credited in his obituary for making the famous carriage and presenting it to Andrew Jackson.[12]

The *New York Post* reported in December 1836 that several gentlemen of New York were planning to present a coach made of wood from the *Constitution,* built in Amherst, Massachusetts, to Andrew Jackson as a New Year's present.[13] The official presentation letter from the New York Democratic-Republicans was dated January 8, 1837 (January 8 being the twenty second anniversary of Jackson's great victory over the British at New Orleans). The actual presentation took place instead on George Washington's birthday, February 22, 1837, on the morning of the last great entertainment Jackson gave at the White House. This was the party best known for the distribution of the giant cheese,

another unusual gift to Jackson.[14] Daniel Jackson, of the New York merchants Suydam, Jackson & Co., one of the leaders of the Democratic-Republicans of New York, made the presentation. The *Washington Globe* published the committee's letter of presentation and Jackson's reply.[15] The Democratic-Republicans stated: "It appeared fitting that this remnant of the noble ship which had so often borne in triumph the flag of our country, should be appropriated to the service of the distinguished individual who in war, gloriously asserted, and in peace firmly maintained and defended, the rights of the nation to which she belonged." Andrew Jackson replied warmly: "[I] rejoice in the thought that, if the broken ribs of the renowned vessel which bore our gallant tars to victory, are now destined to bear the wreck of an old soldier to his repose, it has been my good fortune to give new and stout timbers to the ship, as the *renovated Constitution*, which I hope may conduct, under her fortunate name and destiny, other naval heroes to future triumphs."

The *Globe* pronounced the carriage "a most appropriate present from republicans to the most beloved veteran republican living."[16] The *New York Mirror* described it as

> the elegant phaeton made of the wood of the old frigate *Constitution*. It has a seat for two, with a driver's box, covered with a superb hammer-cloth, and set up rather high in front; the wheels and body are low, and there are bars for baggage behind; . . . The material is excessively beautiful—a fine grained oak, polished to a very high degree, with its colours delicately brought out by a coat of varnish. The wheels are very slender and light, but strong, and, with all of its finish, it looks a vehicle capable of a great deal of service. A portrait of the *Constitution*, under full sail, is painted on the panels.[17]

The coachman's seat was an unusual feature, for most phaetons were meant to be owner-driven. The top was patent leather, the upholstery fringed, and all of the metalwork polished bright. The *Globe* estimated that the phaeton should have cost $3,000, an incredible price when the much larger barouche Jackson purchased from the same company a few years before cost $1,400.[18]

The list of the gentlemen who presented the carriage varies between published reports and the original signed letter, but altogether about sixty-three men appear on one list or another.[19] They included Churchill Cambreleng, Daniel Jackson, Cornelius Lawrence, Daniel Tallmadge, Enos Throop, and Prosper Wetmore—men who had been New York governors, mayors, and congressional representatives. Indeed the list of presenters reads like a virtual "who's who" of early Tammany

Opposite: Nashville photographer C. C. Giers photographed the Constitution *phaeton along with Andrew Jackson's Brewster carriage in 1867. The earliest known image of the phaeton, it shows the wear and tear commented on a decade earlier by Jackson biographer James Parton. The wheels were probably replacements.*

Right: The side panels of the phaeton body survived the fire and retain their decorative image of the USS Constitution *under full sail.*

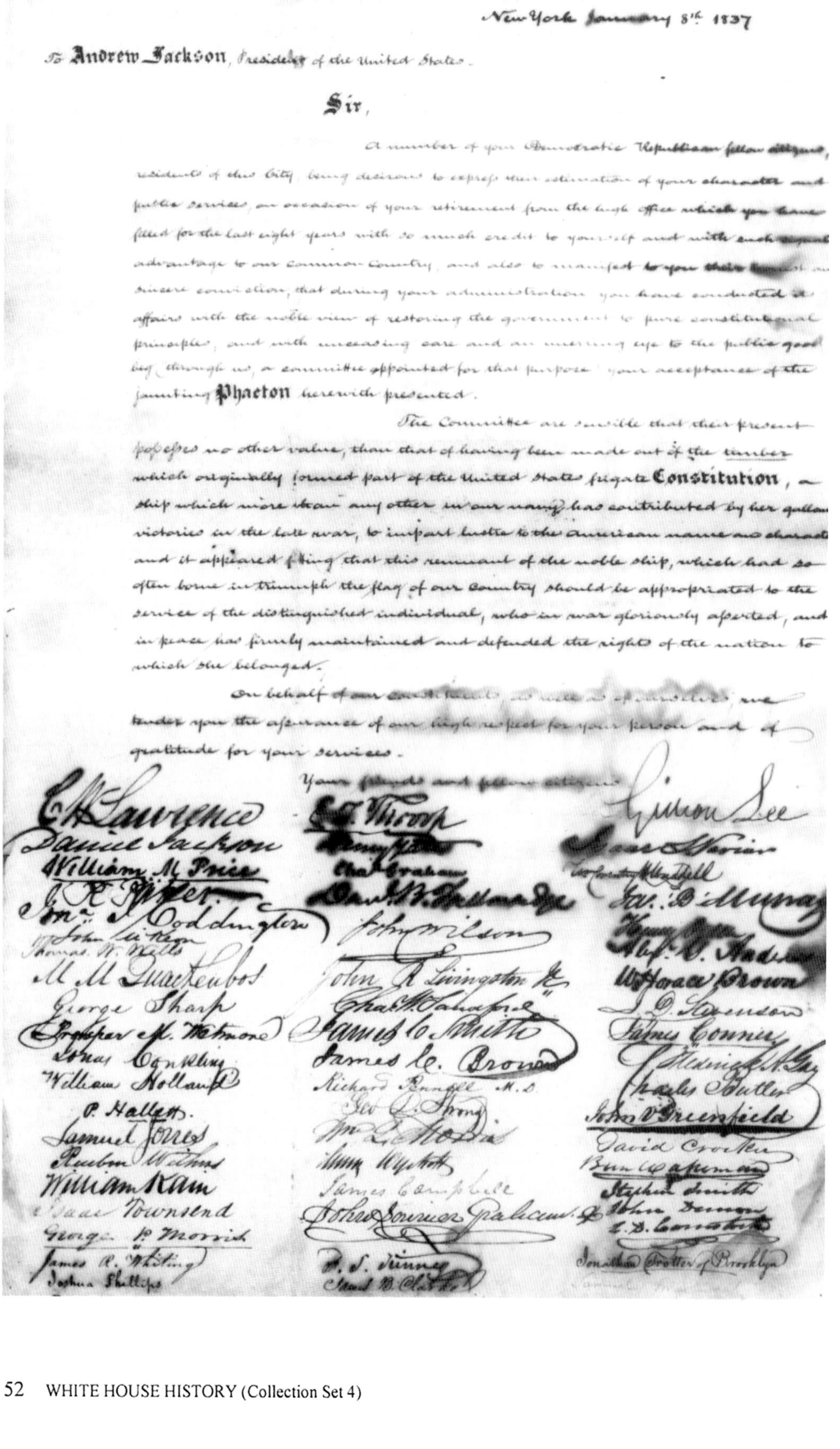
New York January 8th 1837

To Andrew Jackson, President of the United States.

Sir,

A number of your Democratic Republican fellow citizens, residents of this City, being desirous to express their estimation of your character and public services, on occasion of your retirement from the high office which you have filled for the last eight years with so much credit to yourself and with such signal advantage to our common Country, and also to manifest to you their [illegible] sincere conviction, that during your administration you have conducted its affairs with the noble view of restoring the government to pure constitutional principles, and with unceasing care and an unerring eye to the public good beg, through us, a committee appointed for that purpose, your acceptance of the jaunting Phaeton herewith presented.

The Committee are sensible that their present possesses no other value, than that of having been made out of the timber which originally formed part of the United States frigate Constitution, a ship which more than any other in our navy has contributed by her gallant victories in the late war, to impart lustre to the American name and character and it appeared fitting that this remnant of the noble ship, which had so often borne in triumph the flag of our Country should be appropriated to the service of the distinguished individual, who in war gloriously asserted, and in peace has firmly maintained and defended the rights of the nation to which she belonged.

On behalf of our [illegible] we tender you the assurance of our high respect for your person and of gratitude for your services.

Your friends and fellow citizens

THE HERMITAGE, HOME OF PRESIDENT ANDREW JACKSON

Opposite: This photograph, taken just prior to the Jackson family's departure from The Hermitage, shows the deterioration of both the phaeton and the mansion itself, where the phaeton was being stored in the dining room.

Left: Letter presenting the Constitution *phaeton to Andrew Jackson signed by a group of Democratic-Republicans of New York City. The three top row signers were the mayor of New York, a former governor of New York, and a former mayor of New York.*

Hall insiders. They had strongly supported Jackson in both of his winning presidential elections and had close ties to Martin Van Buren. Several of these men also had an interest in one of Jackson's own pet interests—Texas—and, a few years earlier, some of them had participated in a committee to raise funds for Texas independence.[20] Jackson had been in correspondence with many of them over the years, most frequently about political appointments, and his relationship with some continued after he left office. In April 1837, Daniel Jackson offered to assist Andrew Jackson with his financial needs in the North, and in 1842 Andrew Jackson approached Daniel Jackson concerning a loan for Andrew Jackson Donelson, the former president's nephew and secretary.[21]

The Van Buren Inauguration and After

Andrew Jackson and Martin Van Buren rode in the *Constitution* carriage pulled by four matched gray horses to Van Buren's inauguration at the U.S. Capitol on March 4, 1837. The pair of distinguished American leaders presented quite a sight to the gathered crowd.

The outgoing and incoming American presidents arrived with heads uncovered and proceeded through the huge throng up to the platform. The *New York Mirror* reported that Jackson had "emerged from a sick chamber which his physician had thought it impossible he should leave." Jackson bowed graciously to the crowd, and then Van Buren gave his inaugural address and took the oath of office. After the ceremony, Van Buren and Jackson "mounted the constitution carriage together, and the procession returned through the avenue, followed by the whole population of Washington."[22]

Andrew Jackson apparently intended to have the carriage driven back to Tennessee, and he purchased a pair of horses expressly for this purpose. He was dissuaded from this plan, probably because of the potential damage that could occur to the carriage on such a long trip over rough roads. In May, President Van Buren personally wrote to Jackson that the carriage had been shipped and on the same boat was a cask of sherry and an engraving of King William IV of England. The carriage was crated and sent from Alexandria, Virginia, to Philadelphia and then shipped by coastal steamer to New Orleans, where

The iron frame of the phaeton is on exhibit today in the Hermitage Visitor Center, nearly all that remains of the unique carriage given to Andrew Jackson. This view dates to the early 1980s when the carriage was in storage.

Jackson's agent, Maunsel White, accepted it and paid the shipping costs. Then the carriage was shipped up the Mississippi, Ohio, and Cumberland rivers to Nashville. Jackson wrote White in July lamenting the cost of the shipping and over being so much trouble to White. He also instructed White to take reimbursement for the shipping costs from the Nashville merchants Johnston and Rabun, who also had business in New Orleans.[23] Finally the carriage reached The Hermitage by September 1837, when a Mr. Lester saw it. Lester, one of Jackson's many retirement visitors, wrote of his Hermitage visit in a letter published in the *Nashville Union* in which he called the phaeton "a beautiful specimen of American mechanism."[24]

The Jackson family apparently used the *Constitution* phaeton heavily after it arrived in Tennessee, for in 1858 Jackson biographer James Parton saw it on a visit to The Hermitage and described it as "faded and dilapidated."[25] In 1867, Nashville photographer C. C. Giers produced a stereopticon view of the phaeton and Jackson's Brewster carriage, and the phaeton does appear well worn. It was photographed several more times in the late nineteenth century—once while it was being stored in the dining room of The Hermitage

mansion. Sometime after the 1867 Giers photograph, the heavy fringe was removed from the hammercloth on the driver's seat.

When Andrew Jackson's grandson, Andrew Jackson III, moved from The Hermitage in 1893, he took the phaeton with him along with the rest of the family's personal possessions. In 1897, while Jackson III was living in Cincinnati, Ohio, the barn where the carriage was stored burned. Only the metal frame remained intact, along with several fragments including the panels with the paintings of the USS *Constitution* under full sail. The Ladies' Hermitage Association acquired the remnants of the "Old Ironsides" phaeton in 1898 for its collections at The Hermitage. Eventually the association acquired, from the same source, nearly all the original Jackson furnishings.

In the 1920s, the legendary *Constitution* was restored at Boston and opened as a museum, although it remains a commissioned vessel of the U.S. Navy. In the late 1980s, the Ladies' Hermitage Association hoped to have the historic carriage reconstructed, but a lack of appropriate materials as well as detailed information about fabric and trims halted the project. In 1989, the association opened a new visitor center and museum, with a special display area designed for exhibiting the "Old Ironsides" phaeton and Jackson's Brewster carriage. An exhibit case contains other pieces of the "Old Ironsides" phaeton, such as the carriage lamps and painted side panels. Today the remarkable phaeton remnants are on exhibit and interpreted for The Hermitage's nearly 200,000 annual visitors.

NOTES

1. The chronology of the USS *Constitution* has been taken from the navy's official website devoted to the vessel; www.ussconstitution.navy.mil/historyupdat.htm. Jackson's best-known racehorse was named Truxton after the ship's first commander.
2. Late in Jackson's life Jesse Duncan Elliott offered Jackson a Roman sarcophagus for his burial. Jackson declined, and the sarcophagus went to the Smithsonian Institution, where it remains. Photographs and information about the sarcophagus are in the collections of the Ladies' Hermitage Association at The Hermitage.
3. James Barber, *Andrew Jackson: A Portrait Study* (Washington, D.C.: National Portrait Gallery, Smithsonian Institution, 1991), 164–66.
4. See the website of the USS Constitution Museum, www.ussconstitutionmuseum.org/faq/souvenirs.html.
5. Samuel Adams Drake, *Old Landmarks and Historic Personages of Boston* (Boston: James R. Osgood and Company, 1875), 192. Jackson was also given a penholder made of the famed ship's wood that is now in the Ladies' Hermitage Association collections. An internet search reveals that John C. Calhoun had a sideboard, Henry Wadsworth Longfellow had a pen, and the New London, Connecticut, U.S. Customs House (now the New London Maritime Museum) has front doors, all made of wood from the USS *Constitution*.
6. Ladies' Hermitage Association collections records.
7. The USS *Constitution* Museum's website, www.ussconstitutionmuseum.org/shop/special.html, features copper medallions for sale.
8. Lyman Knowles to Andrew Jackson, September 10, 1836, Papers of Andrew Jackson, Library of Congress, Washington, D.C.
9. www.navalregister1836.html.
10. Knowles & Co. to Andrew Jackson, June 1, 1836, Jackson Papers.
11. Daniel Lombardo, Director of Special Collections, Jones Library Inc., Amherst, Massachusetts, to Sharon Macpherson, The Hermitage, November 15, 1988. Ironically, Knowles & Thayer, also known as Knowles & Co., went out of business in 1837 during the financial panic following Jackson's war with the Second Bank of the United States. Asahel Thayer moved to Illinois.
12. Asahel Thayer obituary, *Waverly* (Illinois) *Journal*, November 3, 1877.
13. *New York Post*, December, 1836, reprinted in *Niles' Weekly Register*, December 31, 1836, 228.
14. The cheese, a gift to Jackson, was four feet in diameter and weighed 1,400 pounds. Like the party after Jackson's first inauguration, the party to distribute the cheese was attended by Washingtonians of every walk of life and turned into a near riot. Robert Remini, *Andrew Jackson and the Course of American Democracy, 1833–1845* (New York: Harper & Row, 1984), 393–94; N. P. Willis, "Closing Scenes" of the Session at Washington *New York Mirror*, March 25, 1837.
15. "Jackson's Phaeton," *Washington Globe*, February 23, 1837, reprinted in the *Nashville Union*, March 11, 1837.
16. "Presentation of the Phaeton," *Washington Globe*, February 23, 1837.
17. Willis, "Closing Scenes."
18. Presentation of the Phaeton, *Washington Globe*, February 23, 1837.
19. The compiled list of presenters includes Alexander Anderson, James C. Brown, W. Horace Brown, Charles Butler, Churchill C. Cambreleng, James Campbell, James B. Claxton, Jonathan Coddington, E. D. Comstock, Jonas Conkling, J. D. Conner, David Crocker, John Demon, Frederick Gay, Charles Graham, John Lorimer Graham Jr., John V. Greenfield, B. P. Hallett, J. D. Hamilton, William Holland, Daniel Jackson, Samuel Jones, F. S. Kinney, William Kain, L. Knowles (Amherst), Cornelius W. Lawrence, Gideon Lee, John R. Livingston Jr., John McKeon, George P. Morris, William L. Morris, James B. Murray, Ben Norman, Henry Ogden, Richard Pennel MD, Joshua Phillips, William M. Price, M. M. Quackenboss, Richard Riker, Charles W. Sanford, George Sharp, James C. Smith, Stephen Smith, S. C. Stambaugh (Pennsylvania), J. D. Stevenson, George D. Strong, Daniel Tallmadge, Asahel Thayer (Amherst), Enos Throop, Isaac Townsend, Jonathan Trotter (Brooklyn), Isaac S. Varian, William Coventry Waddell, Burr Wakeman, Rubin Watkins, Thomas Wells, Prosper Wetmore, James Whiting, John Wilson, Reuben Withers, Henry Wyckoff, Frank Wymeth, and Henry Yates.
20. James E. Winston, "New York and the Independence of Texas," *Southwestern Historical Quarterly Online* 18, no. 4 (1915): 368–85, www.tsha.utexas.edu/publications/journals/shq/online/v018/n4/article_2_print.html.
21. Daniel Jackson to Andrew Jackson, April 28, 1837, and Andrew Jackson to Daniel Jackson, July 12, 1842, Jackson Papers.
22. Willis, "Closing Scenes."
23. Martin Van Buren to Andrew Jackson, May 23, 1837, and Andrew Jackson to Maunsel White, July 13, 1837, *The Correspondence of Andrew Jackson*, ed. John Spencer Bassett (Washington, D.C.: Carnegie Institution of Washington, 1929), 484, 499.
24. "Interesting Letter," N. Lester to T.A.S. Doniphan, September 28, 1837, reprinted in the *Nashville Union*, November 30, 1837.
25. James Parton, *Life of Andrew Jackson* (New York: Mason Brothers, 1860), 3:628.

This photograph of President Theodore Roosevelt on Bleistein was one of a series of twelve taken in 1902 as he took the horse over a variety of jumps. Roosevelt declared that the photograph was "the best picture I ever had taken or expect to have taken," and he gave copies to members of his cabinet.

Ten Notable Horses

GWENDOLYN K. WHITE

*I*t is difficult to imagine that just one hundred years ago horses were still the primary means of transportation. For some presidents, horses were not just a necessity but also a part of their image. Before photographs, the military presidents, especially, were often portrayed in paintings on horseback. Numerous portraits of George Washington in his role as general during the American Revolution depict him on a horse. Andrew Jackson's equestrian statue climaxes Lafayette Park, across the street from the White House. Other presidents known for their military exploits include William Henry Harrison, who rode on horseback to his inauguration.

Horses that belonged to the presidents often achieved fame in their own right. The public was interested in knowing what horses and what style of carriage the president had. Zachary Taylor's horse from the Mexican War, Old Whitey, accompanied him to Washington and enjoyed a pampered retirement on the White House grounds. Ulysses S. Grant, well known for his interest in horses, visited the White House stables daily. Cincinnati, Jeff Davis, and Egypt were three of the horses that had served with him during the Civil War and also traveled to the capital with the president. Newspapers and magazines fueled the public's fascination with the president's horses and carriages. An article from an 1887 issue of the *Magazine of American History* detailed the equestrian interests of the presidents and passed judgment on their abilities as horsemen.[1] In 1902 Theodore Roosevelt and his horse Bleistein were featured in a full-page spread in the *Washington Times*, with photographs of the president and the jumper fearlessly going over a course at Chevy Chase.[2]

Some of the earlier presidents were interested in horses for sport. George Washington, an avid foxhunter and a founding member of the Alexandria Jockey Club, was admired for his horsemanship. Thomas Jefferson also frequently attended horse races at the National Race Course, which was established at the new capital even before the White House was completed. Andrew Jackson was passionately involved in horse racing and even kept some racehorses at the White House stables for a time.

Later presidents were more interested in pleasure riding. Theodore Roosevelt and his family frequently went out riding together. William Howard Taft was the first president to make the transition to automobiles, although he and many presidents after him kept horses for exercise. It was common for residents of Washington, D.C., to see the president riding down the street. Even after the White House stables were demolished, Warren G. Harding and Calvin Coolidge took up horseback riding in an effort to escape the pressures of the Oval Office. While John Kennedy was in office, a temporary stable was erected on the South Lawn for Macaroni, a pony given to his children by Lyndon Johnson. Most recently, Ronald Reagan and First Lady Nancy Reagan enjoyed horseback riding at their ranch in California.

NOTES

1. Frank G. Carpenter, "Our Presidents as Horsemen," *Magazine of American History* 17 (June 1887): 483–93.
2. "The President on Horseback," *Washington Times,* June 8, 1902.

Above: President Zachary Taylor, a general known as "Old Rough and Ready" during the Mexican American War, appears on his war horse Old Whitey in this Currier and Ives print. The scene depicted is the battle of Buena Vista in 1847.

Right: Archie Roosevelt on his pony Algonquin, one of many pets owned by the lively Roosevelt children. In his most famous adventure, Algonquin was taken on the elevator up to the second floor of the White House to visit Archie when he was confined to his room with the measles. This photograph was taken outside of the new West Wing in 1903.

Left: Andrew Jackson raced horses for most of his adult life. While he was in the White House he often entered his horses in races under the name of his nephew and private secretary Andrew Jackson Donelson, to avoid negative public opinion about the sport. Bolivia, depicted here in a painting by Edward Troye, was one of Jackson's most successful racers. Oil on canvas, 1836.

Below, left to right: This stereograph of Ulysses S. Grant's horses was taken at Cold Harbor, Virginia, on June 14, 1864. From left, the horses were Egypt, named for the district in Illinois where he was bred, Cincinnati, and Jeff Davis, captured from the plantation of the brother of Confederate President Jefferson Davis.

Opposite, top: William Howard Taft's riding horse Sterrett stands outside the White House stables with a groom in 1909. The six-year-old horse was described as a golden sorrel and stood over sixteen hands high.

Opposite bottom: President Theodore Roosevelt pictured in the newspaper riding Bleistein on Pennsylvania Avenue in Washington, D.C. Note the embroidered "R" on the saddle blanket.

Right: President John F. Kennedy standing outside the Oval Office in June 1962 with his children Caroline and John Jr. and their pony Macaroni.

Below: President Ronald Reagan feeding his white Arabian El Alamein at his California ranch Rancho Del Cielo in 1986.

WHITE HOUSE HISTORY

White House Historical Association
Washington

WHITE HOUSE KITCHENS AND COOKING • NUMBER 20
PUBLISHED SPRING 2007

Foreword

Good Cooks and
Cooking for the Presidents

The basic unit of entertainment at the White House, be it for political purposes, reasons diplomatic, or just for fun, is the dinner table. This was so with the presidency even before there was a White House. George Washington brought to his dinner table the best of foods prepared by the hotel keeper and Washington's slave cook Hercules.

Presidential customs already established first in New York, then Philadelphia, were brought to Washington in 1800 by John Adams, whose housekeepers John and Esther Briesler began the succession of cooks that continues today. This issue of *White House History* is about cooks, cooking, and kitchens at the White House. We have the recollection of a former pastry chef, who served from Carter to the present Bush; today's chef tells us about how she prepared one of her most challenging dinners; well-known cooks and cooking scholars give us tastes of White House—and other American—food customs of years gone by. A picture history of White House kitchens sets the stage for a little archaeology, in which removal of one of FDR's refrigerators reveals some early and forgotten history about how things once were at the White House.

It is a full plate of a subject our readers have asked for.

William Seale
Editor, *White House History*

A presumed portrait of George Washington's cook Hercules by Gilbert Stuart.

Kitchen Past: Thoughts on Open Hearth Cooking for the Presidents

ALICE ROSS

When George Washington's Creole chef Samuel Fraunces set out to prepare a meal for his president it was cooked at the hearth, but it was not served in the White House, as the imposing edifice was not yet finished and suitable for inhabitance. The Washingtons' successors, John and Abigail Adams, the first to occupy the White House, arrived in November 1800. During their four-month residency, Mrs. Adams used the 40-foot basement kitchen, located directly under the main entrance above. Half submerged, with barred windows, the kitchen had little natural light, and stood directly beneath the First Floor Entrance Hall.

Later a secondary kitchen accommodated small-scale daily cooking and baking, and the main kitchen was put to its primary purpose as the banquet kitchen. With two great cut-stone fireplaces, and cooking utensils "of all kinds in abundance,"[1] this mammoth kitchen more than served the simple demands of the second president. The number of servants was not adequate for a large household, and only a few people chopped wood, hauled water, and prepared meals on the hearth for Abigail Adams.

When Mrs. Adams wanted to prepare a ragout (stew), for example, she had a number of choices in her pots, for the White House inventory she left indicates a substantial supply.[2] She might have elected to use a French stewing pot made of iron or bronze, a covered frying pan, a Dutch oven, a small seasoned iron cauldron, a ceramic covered pot, or a heavy cast-bronze pot. These had three-legs that held the pot as much as 5 inches high over a pile of coals shoveled out on the hearth. Pots were also suspended from a bail handle, suspended on a hanging adjustable trammel. Or a swinging crane could be set at the proper angle to the fire, and the height up or down controlled with a series of S-hooks. And roasting, one of the most successful of all hearth processes, was accomplished by Mrs. Adams's cook by means of spits and tin reflecting ovens.

Adams's successor Thomas Jefferson, who had major concern for his table, added

The eighteenth-century hearth, a re-creation at the Alice Ross Hearth Studios in Smithtown, New York, is an accurate copy of the one at Obediah Smith House, 1705. It was typical of cooking fireplaces, complete with authentic equipment, until the widespread use of the cookstove, c. 1850.

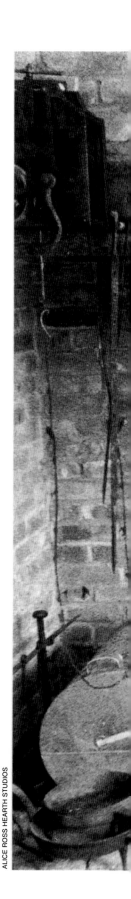

some interesting variations. To the large room he added stew stoves—a bank of masonry cooking sites built in against a wall adjacent to the hearth and its chimney—and, most important, the first coal-burning iron range complete with spits and crane, installed in one of the two large fireplaces. And in the other fireplace he placed hob-grates (meaning "coal grates")—tall, wide, and thin constructions of iron piping, to receive burning coal. These cooking grates worked much the same way as standard hearth cooking, apart from the use of hooked trivets that attached to the grates at the desired height and held the pots. The 1809 inventory of Jefferson's pots and pans includes a wide array of equipment, suggesting the range and depth of his hearth-cooked cuisine: "6 Pots of copper, 1 large skillet for preserves, 2 round casseroles with lids, 1 oval ditto, 1 English fish kettle, 1 French ditto, 4 pots ("marmites"–earthenware or metal), 2 copper ditto, 2 ditto deep, 4 Oval Pudding dishes, 1 Dripping Pan, 2 skimmers, 2 tea kettles, 1 Great boiler, 1 grid iron for oysters, 2 ditto for meat, 2 Dutch Ovens, 2 Frying Pans, 1 cleaver, . . . 1 bake Iron, 1 Coffee toaster, 1 Roasting stand, 1 marble mortar. "[3]

This gargantuan kitchen could handle roasted meats done to a turn on spits or within tin reflecting ovens before a hot fire, while the side dishes, sautéed and potted meats, and cool dishes were prepared in the other, cooler fireplace 40 feet across the room. The area was not heated to such a degree that cold preparations (puff pastry, gelled desserts, or even ice cream) were precluded; considering the limitations of the brick oven—a simple "igloo" of brick—meals were prepared that would seem incomprehensible today. Honoré Julien, the chef, and his staff cooked daily for ten to fourteen people. They prepared a number of different dishes and presented them as a seated buffet in the contemporary style à la français. It really was not so hard for those who knew no other cookery style.

Congressman Manasseh Cutler, of Massachusetts, noted the highlights of the menu of such a dinner at Jefferson's White House on February 6, 1802: "Dined at the President's—Rice soup, round of beef, turkey, ham, loin of veal, cutlets of mutton, fried eggs, fried beef, a pie called macaroni." For dessert there were, among other delicacies, "ice cream very good, crust wholly dried, crumbled into thin flakes, and a dish somewhat like a pudding—inside white as milk or curd, very porous and light, covered with cream sauce—very fine. Many other jimcracks, a great variety of fruit, plenty of wine."[4] This menu listed only the main dishes and did not mention the breads, preserves, side dishes, nuts, and cheeses that were served at the same meal. For a cook who knew how, clearly it was possible to cook very ambitiously on the hearth.

Common China.

- 8. Tea cups and saucers.
- 3. Blue china Terrines
- 34. blue china Dishes
- 74. blue china Soup plates.
- 76. flat plates. blue china
- 78. blue china Dessert Plates.
- 76. Do... smaller.
- 18. Do. Custard cups.
- 5. Do. Sauce terrines.
- 5. Oval sauce bowls.
- 4. round Pudding dishes
- 9. Chamber Pots.
- 8. Water Pitchers & Basons.

Earthen Ware -

- 9. Chamber Pots.
- 12. Common Plates.
- 7. Deep Pudding dishes
- 42. Common Plates.
- 30. Do. Smaller.
- 10. Wash Basons.

Kitchen Furniture

69 - different Pieces.

- 5. Iron Pots.

- 1. Iron Boiler
- 3. Spits with their skewers.
- 5. Chevrettes - (hand irons).
- 1. Coal Shovel.
- 2. Large Tongs
- 1. bake Iron.
- 1. ..... Grate Do.
- 1. Coffee toaster
- 1. Coffee Mill -.
- 1. Poker.
- 1. Roasting stand
- 1. marble mortar
- 1. Kitchen Screen
          fire Jack —.

The largest cooking issue in hearth cooking from our perspective today appears to be managing the heat, as the recipes themselves were not so very different from ours. While it seems at first difficult and awkward to us, accustomed as we are to thermostatic settings on our stoves and ovens, all cooks (and certainly all chefs) were trained since their early years and knew the tricks for controlling temperatures. In some instances they used the glowing embers on the hearth directly, sometimes covered or mixed with insulating ash, to broil meats or bake vegetables. They moved the pots in and out, or up and down (on trammels and cranes), to accommodate changes in the fire and the embers that produced the cooking heat. And they moved the fire, kicking or poking the logs to get the heat where it was needed. Skillets, grills, griddles, posnets (legless saucepans), and kettles, standing over a pile of embers a foot or more from the front of the fire, received heat from below and, in addition, back heat (that which hit the back of the pot). This heat was not nearly as scorching as it would have been had the pot been closer, but it sometimes required turning the pot 180 degrees to keep the cooking even. Cooks knew the wood —what kind would give specific intensities of heat. They knew, for example, that hard oak, apple, or hickory burned evenly, gave a moderate heat, and lasted for a fairly long time, while locust burned very hot and lasted for a longer time, and coal burned the hottest and lasted the longest; and they chose accordingly. The temperature was easily regulated, presuming that the chef and chef's assistants kept their eyes on the fire, as the pile of embers was easily replenished from the accumulation being formed by the large fire at the back of the hearth.

The dangers of open hearth cooking to cooks are not what we might think. The chefs and their assistants wore fabrics made of wool, linen, and later cotton, which when hit by sparks, did not flare up but only suffered small smolder holes. The chief danger lay in tipping a large cauldron of hot liquids and the subsequent scalding. The heat of the hot fire did make it necessary, however, to use long-handled utensils—spoons and ladles, meat forks, turners, spatulas, and frying pans. Perhaps the most beautiful were the waffle and wafer irons, which were handsomely patterned iron plates on long scissored handles. The waffle irons shaped small, familiar, three-dimensional forms; the wafer irons produced exceedingly thin, melt-in-your-mouth cookies made from a rich batter that was baked pressed between the two preheated, decorated plates.

Cooking on the hearth was not the only way. Better equipped kitchens like those of the White House also contained stew stoves—built-in banks of masonry containing individual "raised hearths"—often constructed against the walls adjacent to the fireplace or even a window, as one can see today in the old kitchen at historic Montgomery Place near Rhinecliff, New York, for the smoke's easy escape. They offered places to hold small fires or embers, over which were built-in grates. They held posnets, fry pans, or kettles, one on each grate. In effect, they were precursors to the cookstove of iron and indeed the range in modern times.

And then there were bake ovens, sometimes built into the back of the hearth wall, and sometimes freestanding, domed structures, large enough to hold several loaves of bread in one baking, and then pies, meats, cakes, puddings, and cookies. These dishes were inserted one category at a time, according to the dropping temperature of the oven. The fire was built inside the oven, and when it was determined that the temperature of the bricks had reached the proper height, the oven floor was raked and swabbed out, the breads placed inside by means of a long-handled peel, and the door placed over the opening. The oven temperature dropped gradually, and when the breads came out, in went the pies and meats (according to the heat level). The last to be baked were cookies and custards.

A few improvements were made during the course of the probably thousands of years during which the open hearth reigned. The rebuilding of the White House (following its burning during the War of 1812) saw the construction of new stew-holes and the installation of smoke jacks, a fanlike apparatus that hung high in the chimney and was caused to spin by the movement of smoke and, connected by gears, thereby turned the spitted meats on the hearth. And Jefferson's "Kitchen Raing" (range) was repaired and equipped anew with "spits and slyding plates & Hooks."[5]

Some of James Monroe's kitchen equipment, stored in the "Steward's Back Room," included "1 large copper soup kettle, 1 Small ditto ditto, 1 Large ham boiler, 1 Small ditto ditto, 1 large preserving kettle, 1 Ditto fish kettle, with drainers, 1 small ditto ditto, 1 Large coffee boiler, 1 2nd size ditto, 1 Brass stew pan, 3 Large sauce pans, 19 Of different sizes, 4 Oval sauce pans, 2 ditto dripping pans, 6 Ladles, spoons, and skimmers." The kitchen itself held "1 Large copper boiler, 1 Large brass kettle . . . 2 Griddles, 1 Toasting iron, 1 Frying pan, 5 Jack spits, 3 coffee mills, 1 Old dripping pan, 2 Spit stands, 4 Trivets, 1 Marble pestle and mortar, 4 Sheet iron cake bakers."[6] It would seem that hearth cooking continued to provide ample variety.

Andrew Jackson's presidency saw the use of Rumford iron roasters installed in the chimney walls and heated with coal. Clean-washed river sand was spread on the floor to absorb grease and moisture, and the walls were whitewashed once a year. During the Jackson administration, the high level of cuisine was lowered in favor of more common styles. A letter from Maryland congressman John R. Montgomery to Letitia A. Montgomery suggests that "although French dishes were put aside in preference for American country fare," the cooking and serving procedures were the same. Montgomery described a cozy dinner at the White House where he ate "ample portions served of soup, beef bouille, wild turkey ('boned and dressed with brains'), fish, chicken, and tongues, salad, canvasback duck, and celery, partridges, sweet breads, and 'old Virginia ham.'"[7] This "cozy" dinner seems hardly modest.

President Martin Van Buren's accounts for April 6, 1837, suggest that he replaced worn-out articles: "1 12 gallon pot, 1 oven and lid, 1griddle, 1 biscuit baker," and, on June 14, 1839, along with a good load of dishware and flatware, "2 pairs of lemon squeezers, 1 Britannia coffee pot, 1 ditto tea pot." Perhaps from a desire for frugality he paid for repairs: in 1839 he had fixed a "tea boiler, new handles to coffee and tea pots" and in 1838 he had ninety pieces of copper tinned.[8] These expenses were nothing, however, compared with those for the quantities of dishware and flatware he purchased.

Millard Fillmore, president from 1850 to 1853, ordered the first true cookstove placed in the White House kitchens, thus beginning of the end of the reign of the hearth. It would seem likely that his cookstove did not replace existing customs entirely, for as anyone who barbecues will attest, roasted meats on the hearth are far superior to those done in the cast-iron or even electric ovens. Stew stoves continued to provide the White House with additional cooking space. Eventually the gas cookstove was to replace the hearth in its entirety. In 1902 a total makeover of the basement kitchens eliminated hearth cooking completely.

In retrospect, it would seem that during the fifty years or so of hearth cooking in the White House, the presidents' demands on the kitchen varied only according to their tastes and desires. From Thomas Jefferson's simple but elegant standards to John Tyler's disdain for eating, from James Monroe's "most stylish dinner I had been at"[9] to the brawl of Andrew Jackson's inauguration reception, from Martin Van Buren's reticence at opening his table to the general public in favor of small, intimate dinners for select friends, to Mrs. John Quincy Adams's weekly levees—these reflected the potential challenge of hearth cookery at the early White House. Giving it up, however, was not an entirely simple matter. Indeed, when Millard Fillmore eliminated the hearth,

the old cook who had served many years at the White House was greatly upset when a range of small hotel size was brought to his quarters. He had managed to prepare a fine State dinner for thirty-six people every Thursday in a huge fireplace, with the cranes, hooks, pots, pans, kettles, and skillets; but he could not manage the draughts of the range, and it ended in a journey of the President to the Patent Office to inspect the model and restore peace in the kitchen.[10]

The art of cooking at the White House hearth had loyal experts.

NOTES

1. William Seale, *The President's House: A History* (Washington, D.C.: White House Historical Association, with the cooperation of the National Geographic Society, 1986), 1:86.
2. John Adams Inventory, February 27, 1801 *Legislative Records Sixth Senate,* 1801.
3. William Claxton, "Basement," Inventory of the President's House, February 19, 1809, Papers of Thomas Jefferson, Library of Congress, Washington, D.C.
4. Manasseh Cutler, quoted in Margaret Brown Klapthor, *The First Ladies Cook Book: Favorite Recipes of All the Presidents of the United States* (New York: GMG Publishing, 1982), 36.
5. James Martin to Sam Lane, Washington, May 1, 1817, Miscellaneous Treasury Accounts, National Archives, Washington, D.C.
6. Inventory 1825, "Basement story—Steward's Back Room" and "Kitchen."
7. John R. Montgomery (a Philadelphian) to Letitia A. Montgomery, Washington, D.C., February 20, 1834, in "Documents 1834: Letter of Robert C. Caldwell, Contributed by George M. Whicher," *American Historical Review* 27 (January 1922): 271–81.
8. John Thomas to Martin Van Buren, Baltimore, May 14, 1837, Miscellaneous Treasury Warrants, Comm of Parbu, National Archives.
9. Mrs. Benjamin Crowninshield, December 1, 1815, written two years before Monroe's presidency. Cited in Esther Singleton, *The Story of the White House* (New York, McClure Company, 1907), 1:135.
10. Ibid., 2:15.

A Look at the White House Kitchens

LYDIA BARKER TEDERICK

*T*he kitchen is usually the center of activity for any household. The same can be said for the President's House. As the site of daily meal preparation for presidential families and cuisine for more formal entertaining, the main kitchen of the White House is rarely quiet. The kitchen, as with other service areas in the Executive Mansion, is not often shared with the public. Views of this important room during the nineteenth century are rare. During the twentieth century, it was photographed on occasion, sometimes to document the appearance of the room and other times to feature the culinary staff. It is never on tour.

Originally the kitchen for the President's House was located at the center of the Ground Floor, underneath the Entrance Hall and the same size, with a great stone fireplace at each end. Prior to the addition of the North Portico in 1829–30, the windows to the kitchen could be seen from the bridge that led to the north door. Although it was an area that saw continuous activity, descriptions of this room are sketchy. In 1796, a correspondent described it as "large enough to hold the house of representatives of the Congress, and that the Senate may find room to sit in the chimney corner."[1] During the presidency of Thomas Jefferson, one of the fireplaces was fitted with a coal-fueled iron range that had stew holes, or water heaters, spits, and a crane.[2]

At some point during the mid-nineteenth century, the kitchen moved to two adjoining northwest corner rooms, where it can be found today. The reason for the move and the exact year have not been determined. Journalist Abby Gunn Baker wrote in 1904 that the central room, lacking exterior light after the construction of the North Portico, remained the kitchen until Mary Todd Lincoln moved it.[3] A floor plan drawn by architect Thomas U. Walter in 1853 to show proposed heating systems clearly designated the northwest corner rooms as "Kitchen," "Scullery," and "Pantry." The central room was identified as a cellar. Because some elements of the Walter plan were never executed, the room designations are thought to be proposals.[4] Historian William Seale has also suggested that the principal kitchen remained in its central location, but under President Andrew Johnson, a second kitchen, probably used for baking, was placed in the northwest corner.[5]

Two separate kitchens first appear in the inventories beginning in 1869, the first year of the Ulysses S. Grant administration. One room is identified simply as "Kitchen," and the other is listed as "Small Kitchen." The location of the rooms and whether they were adjacent to each other, or not, are unknown. The next inventory, taken in 1875, also lists the contents of two rooms; one was labeled "Large Kitchen" and the other "Small Kitchen." In this case, they follow each other on the same page of the document, suggesting that they were located next to each other on the Ground Floor.[6]

A plumbing plan from 1881 that was included with a report from the Committee for Sanitary Improvement of the Executive Mansion,[7] illustrates the two kitchens

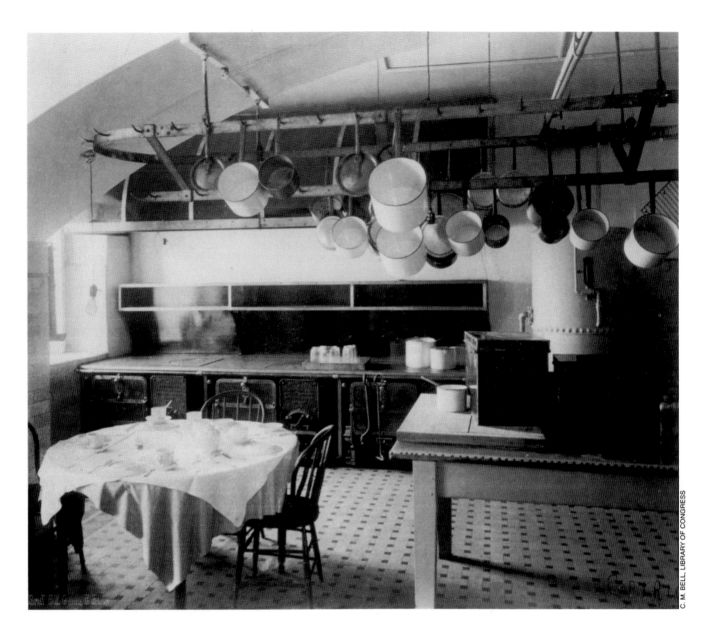

A view of the kitchen in 1901. The large kitchen was used for main events and more formal entertaining. The round table at left is set for a staff meal. The presence of electricity, introduced to the White House in 1891, can be seen by the surface-mounted electrical wiring placed along the ceiling. Single light bulbs hang from the ceiling to illuminate the room; one appears over the round table.

adjacent to one another in the northwest corner. Of special interest are the locations of the ranges and sinks, which are marked in each room. A dumbwaiter is also identified in the small kitchen.

Located directly below the State Floor Butler's Pantry, the so-called small kitchen was used to prepare everyday meals for family and staff. The earliest photograph of this room may have been taken by photojournalist Frances Benjamin Johnston. The revealing image, dated c. 1890, shows a coal range and shelves laden with pans, various cooking utensils, and tableware. Also featured is the Benjamin Harrison family cook, Dolly Johnson.

Washington, D.C.— The White House Kitchen—
Preparing Dinner, *after C. Bunnell (dates unknown),
from* Frank Leslie's Illustrated Newspaper, *April 6,
1889. This wood engraving, published not long after
Benjamin Harrison became president, includes an
early image of the main kitchen, located in the
northwest corner of the Ground Floor since the
mid-nineteenth century; a view of the original
kitchen in Andrew Jackson's time (inset above
left), which was located at the center of the
Ground Floor beneath the Entrance Hall;
and a portrait of Hugo Ziemann, a chef for
President Chester Arthur (inset above right).*

*Opposite, top: Plan of Executive Mansion, 1853.
Architect Thomas U. Walter drew this plan
to show proposed heating systems. Because
some elements of the plan were never
executed, the various room designations
may also have been proposals.*

*Opposite: Detail from plumbing plan of the White
House, 1881. The Ground Floor plan, although in
a few respects conjecturally, shows the two kitchens
located in the northwest corner of the building.
Sinks, ranges, and a dumbwaiter are also indicated.*

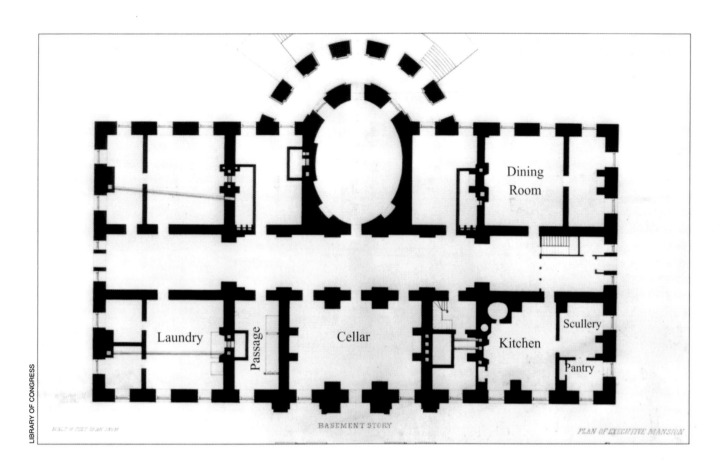

Dining Room

Laundry

Passage

Cellar

Kitchen

Scullery

Pantry

BASEMENT STORY

PLAN OF EXECUTIVE MANSION

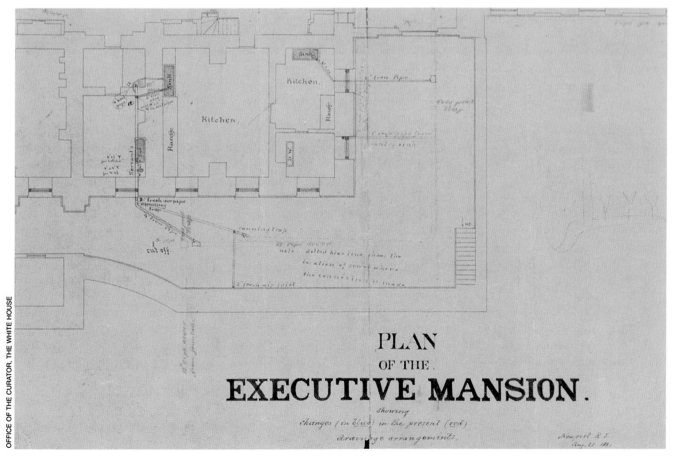

Kitchen

Kitchen

Range

Sink

Servants

cut off.

PLAN
OF THE
EXECUTIVE MANSION.

Showing
changes (in blue) in the present (red)
drainage arrangements.

Dolly Johnson, the family cook for President Benjamin Harrison, was photographed in the small, or everyday kitchen in the northwest corner of what was then called the basement, by Frances Benjamin Johnston, c. 1890. In addition to a dish rack, visible in the background, and various everyday utensils and pans, a soup tureen (on exhibit today in the China Room) from the Ulysses S. Grant rose-band service can be seen at left on the top shelf. Ordered in 1870 from Haviland & Co., this porcelain dinner service was utilized for less formal occasions.

The neighboring larger kitchen, today's main kitchen, was utilized only for major occasions when more workspace was required. Because it was used less frequently, it also served as a dining area for the domestic staff. In 1889, *Frank Leslie's Illustrated Newspaper* published a wood engraving of this room that is one of the earliest images. A similar view was photographed by C. M. Bell in 1901, showing a large gas range and a table set for a staff meal.

In 1902 under President Theodore Roosevelt, the White House underwent a major renovation overseen by Charles F. McKim of the architectural firm McKim, Mead & White. While the kitchens were not altered dramatically, the arrangement of the Ground Floor service areas was changed. Visitors and guests would now enter the White House through the newly constructed East Wing at the east end of the Ground Floor Corridor. Service functions were, therefore, shifted to the west end of the floor and extended into the West Terrace.

Subsequently, groceries and other items, previously delivered on the east side, were instead received on the west side, closer to the kitchens and storerooms and concealed from the president's guests.[8]

Photographs of the large kitchen taken following the renovation reveal few noticeable changes. Lighting was improved when the entire electrical wiring system for the building was redone. Modifications were also made to the ventilation system. Alterations made in the small kitchen were more significant. A doorway was added to the south wall that led into the Ground Floor Corridor. This provided easier access to the storeroom and a new walk-in refrigerator, located across the hall in the southwest corner of the building, and to incoming deliveries. A new stairway enabled direct access to the Butler's Pantry on the State Floor. To further assist the kitchen staff, a new "electric" dumbwaiter was installed that ran from the kitchen to the newly created mezzanine level of the Butler's Pantry.[9] Although housekeeper Elizabeth Jaffray complained that it was "often out of order," it was of great assistance to the kitchen staff and butlers when food was transported to the dining areas located above on the State Floor.[10]

The central room that had been the original kitchen, located under the Entrance Hall, was turned into a furnace room in 1902 and was used for that purpose until the Truman renovation, 1948–52. In 1935, the machinery was repositioned within the space to partition rooms for use as a staff dining room and a store pantry. During the Truman renovation, the furnace was placed underground and the old kitchen became the Broadcast Room. Since the Kennedy administration, the room has again been partitioned into smaller spaces, one of which is now occupied by the Office of the Curator.

Although the first electric refrigerator was installed in 1926, it was not until 1935, during the Franklin D. Roosevelt administration, that the kitchen would again undergo significant changes.[11] Upon her arrival in 1933, housekeeper Henrietta Nesbitt toured the White House with First Lady Eleanor Roosevelt. Describing her initial impression of the kitchen, Mrs. Nesbitt wrote:

I can't work up any charm for cockroaches. No matter how your scrub it, old wood isn't clean. This was the "first kitchen in America," and it wasn't even sanitary. Mrs. Roosevelt and I poked

around, opening doors and expecting hinges to fall off and things to fly out. It was that sort of place. Dark-looking cupboards, a huge old-fashioned gas range, sinks with time-worn wooden drains, one rusty wooden dumb waiter. The refrigerator was wood inside and bad-smelling. Even the electric wiring was old and dangerous. I was afraid to switch things on.

She then reported Mrs. Roosevelt saying, "There is only one solution—we must have a new kitchen."[12] Describing the kitchen before the renovation, a newspaper correspondent of the time wrote, "It looks like an old-fashioned German rathskeller, with a great deal of ancient architectural charm."[13]

Engineers from General Electric and Westinghouse conferred with staff at the White House to plan the modernization of the entire culinary department. The size of the kitchen, approximately 23 x 28 feet, was relatively small for the quantities of food prepared in it. The new layout would encompass contemporary ideas about grouping equipment into workstations to keep the different functions moving along in a smooth sequence during the preparation of meals.[14] The doorway that had led from the main kitchen to the Ground Floor Corridor was removed, and additional cabinet space was provided along the south wall. The small kitchen became a pantry with new, more efficient dumbwaiters to assist with transporting food to the State Floor dining rooms. Underground storerooms and refrigerated areas were also constructed under the north driveway, helping to alleviate cramped storage conditions. This transformation was funded with money allocated by the Public Works Administration and was referred to as Public Works Project No. 634. At President Franklin Roosevelt's request, relief workers were used as much as possible.[15]

Demolition and construction took place during the summer and fall of 1935. To accommodate the number of new electric appliances, the entire electrical system was changed from direct current to alternating current.[16] As with any major renovation, unforeseen problems arose. While changing the wiring, it was discovered that the plumbing had badly deteriorated. To replace all of the rusted pipes, the floors and walls were disturbed more than originally planned. Amazingly, with the room under excavation, wooden planks on the floor, and tunnels placed throughout, food service was provided when it was needed for the president, whose summer departure was delayed, and his guests. Large dinners were especially problematic for the staff. Mrs. Nesbitt recalled:

> Finally I had to scrap the menus and get in things that required just heating through. I had to co-operate with Ida by changing the menus that took too much trouble. She would be over the cooking, surrounded by a dozen men with wheelbarrows full of dirt. You couldn't tell if the place was the White House kitchen or a quarry. The world and its work kept pouring through the White House, and we balanced on boards over a bottomless pit.[17]

Photographs taken by the National Park Service documented the appearance of the kitchen prior to construction and the dramatic end result. The "New Deal Kitchen," as it was nicknamed by the staff, now had the latest equipment in stainless steel and was capable of providing a full-course meal for more than one thousand people. Electric appliances included a 16 foot long stove, six roasting ovens, warming ovens, eight refrigerators, new dumbwaiters, a meat grinder, all sorts of mixers, five dishwashers, waffle irons, a soup kettle, a 30 gallon ice cream storage box, and a deep fry pan that could hold 5 gallons of fat. Aluminum utensils, so shiny and new "they looked like a display window in Tiffany's," were also purchased.[18] New fixtures provided indirect lighting to the room. Walls of Carrara glass bordered with strips of black glass, floors of green and cream linoleum, and sinks and work surfaces of stainless steel also added to a clean, modern look. Special attention was given to selecting equipment with rounded corners to help prevent dust from accumulating and surfaces that would be easy to clean. Mrs. Nesbitt recalled:

> The Roosevelts thought it wonderful. But we had a funny situation with the help. They wouldn't use the new electric equipment. Our kitchen was a dream come true with its stainless steel and tinted walls, but the help used dishrags and towels when they could, ignoring the new dishwashers, and did their slicing and chopping by hand

although the electric company sent a man in to show them how to work things.[19]

The first major meal prepared in the new kitchen was Thanksgiving dinner. On December 16, 1935, Mrs. Roosevelt led press members on a tour, which she said would be "the first, last, and only tour of this part of the Executive Mansion."[20]

During the Truman renovation, the interior of the White House was gutted, with the exception of the Third Floor, and rebuilt to include basement levels that provided additional space for staff, storage, and machinery. Along with the replacement of some of the appliances, the kitchen area was reconstructed with a few noticeable changes. No longer needed structurally in a house newly framed in steel, the great ceiling arch was removed and replaced with a flat ceiling. Ranges and ovens were moved to the south wall, and stainless steel sinks and draining racks were placed along the east wall. New metal cabinets also lined the room. In addition to dumbwaiters and a spiral staircase in the neighboring pantry area, a staff elevator was added that has proved invaluable with the movement of staff, food items, and equipment to other floors of the house. Several photographs taken by National Park Service photographer Abbie Rowe captured views of the kitchen before, during, and after the renovation.

The main kitchen was again renovated during August 1971, while President Richard M. Nixon and his family were away for a summer vacation. The project was undertaken primarily to make more efficient use of the limited available space and improve the ventilation and fire prevention systems. In addition, most of the equipment that dated to the Truman renovation, as well as two ranges and a food warmer from 1935, was obsolete and needed to be replaced.[21] The renovation also eliminated foot traffic through the food preparation area by sacrificing a small part of the north end of the kitchen for a narrow hallway, created by the addition of a partial wall covered with tile, that led around the kitchen, into the pantry, and to the staff elevator. The White House Photo Office was on hand to photograph various stages of the work.

From 1988 to 1992, the Historic American Building Survey (HABS) produced measured drawings, field notes, and photographs of the White House, including the kitchen area, to show the changes that had occurred since the Truman renovation. Since 1971, few alterations have been made to the main kitchen. The general layout of equipment and workstations has remained the same, and appliances have been replaced only when necessary. Work space for the main kitchen staff increased slightly in 1993 when the pastry department was moved to the new pastry kitchen installed in the mezzanine level of the Butler's Pantry. In 1997, the kitchen was completely enclosed with the addition of glass and stainless steel doors and a floor-to-ceiling partition, replacing the partial wall along the north end of the room, to further remove outside distractions.

The main kitchen has occupied the same location on the Ground Floor of the White House since the mid-nineteenth century. While early views are rare, later photographs have shown modifications made to the room throughout the twentieth century. In recent years, photographs, especially those taken by White House photographers, have provided the public with perhaps the best "behind-the-scenes" look at one of the mansion's busiest areas. This documentation process will continue with upcoming administrations as technology advances and adaptations are made to meet the demands of the future.

NOTES

1. *Columbian Museum and Savannah (Ga.) Advertiser,* May 31, 1796, cited in "Clues and Footnotes," ed. Eleanor H. Gustafson, *The Magazine Antiques,* September 1977, 522.
2. William Seale, *The President's House: A History* (Washington, D.C.: White House Historical Association, with the cooperation of the National Geographic Society, 1986), 1:102. Jefferson's range was recovered from the wreckage left by the 1814 fire, repaired by a blacksmith, and reinstalled in the kitchen after it was rebuilt in 1817.
3. Abby Gunn Baker, "The New White House Kitchen," *Harper's Bazar,* November 1904, 1075–76.
4. William Seale, "The White House: Seat of the Presidency," in *Capital Drawings: Architectural Designs for Washington, D.C.,* ed. C. Ford Peatross (Baltimore: Johns Hopkins University Press, 2005), 100.
5. Seale, *President's House,* 1:438.
6. Clark, Edward. "Inventory of the Furniture of the Executive Mansion, December 14, 1869, Exclusive of Plants in the Conservatory," *Inventory of Public Property about the Capitol,* House Miscellaneous Document, no. 45, 42nd Congress, Third Session, Vol. VII, no 1572, 32–33, 36. Edward Clark, *Inventory of Public Property in the President's House,* Inventory of Public Property, House Miscellaneous Document, #39, 44th Congress, 1st Session, vol. 1, no. 1698, January 4, 1876, 27. Until recent times, inventories were not taken annually. Because of the gaps, it is difficult to pinpoint the exact year a change may have taken place.
7. Report from the Committee for Sanitary Improvement of the Executive Mansion, 1881, Office of the Curator, The White House.
8. Seale, *President's House,* 1:663–64.
9. Theodore Roosevelt, *Restoration of the White House: Message of the President of the United States Transmitting the Report of the Architects* (Washington, D.C.: Government Printing Office, 1903), 30.
10. Elizabeth Jaffray, *Secrets of the White House* (New York: Cosmopolitan Book Corporation, 1927), 120. Mrs. Jaffray held the position of housekeeper from 1909 until 1926.
11. "White House Ice Box Is Now Equipped with Modern Electric Refrigerator," newspaper clipping, August 17, 1926, files, Office of the Curator, The White House. See also "Mrs. Roosevelt's New Kitchen," *Delineator,* November 1935, 70.
12. Henrietta Nesbitt, *White House Diary* (Garden City, N.Y.: Doubleday, 1948), 30. Mrs. Nesbitt, a neighbor of the Roosevelts in Hyde Park, New York, held the position of White House housekeeper from March 1933 until May 1946. Her husband, Henry Nesbitt, also worked at the White House as a custodian or steward from March 1933 until his death in 1938.
13. Quoted in ibid.
14. Ruth Van Deman, "U.S. Kitchen No. 1," *Journal of Home Economics,* February 1936, 28:94.
15. Federal Writers' Project (Works Progress Administration), *Washington: City and Capital* (Washington, D.C.: Government Printing Office, 1937), 301.
16. "Mrs. Roosevelt's New Kitchen," 70.
17. Nesbitt, *White House Diary,* 143. Ida Allen, who cooked for the Roosevelts in the Albany governor's mansion, worked at the White House from March 1933 until December 1940.
18. Ibid., 146–47.
19. Ibid., 149.
20. Van Deman, "U.S. Kitchen No. 1," 93.
21. "1st Renovation since 1949: White House Gets New, $97,000 Kitchen," *Chicago Sun-Times,* September 24, 1971, 67.

July 20, 1902.
During the 1902 renova-
tion, the space that had
been the original kitchen,
under the Entrance Hall,
was excavated for a
boiler pit. One of the
early kitchen fireplaces
is visible at right, still
with fragments of an
early turning spit.

SAGAMORE HILL NATIONAL HISTORIC SITE, NATIONAL PARK SERVICE

c. 1909.
The kitchen as renovated
in 1902 by Theodore
Roosevelt used modern
equipment. Electrical
lighting was improved with
reflectors and brackets.
Next to the gas range and
hot water heater is a radia-
tor, heated by coal, which
provided heat to the room
especially during those
times when the range was
not in use. Two worktables
are shown; the one in the
foreground includes a
coffee grinder at one end.
Note the remnants of
carpeting, removed from
the East Room during the
renovation, that eased feet
on the hard tile floor.

HARRIS AND EWING, LIBRARY OF CONGRESS

June 20, 1935.
The kitchen and pantries
were photographed prior
to remodeling in 1935.

June 20, 1935.
Note the galvanized steel
countertop, an idea that
would be carried over
into FDR's New Deal
kitchen.

*June 20, 1935.
The smaller family
kitchen was equipped
with a dumbwaiter. The
1902 device, seen on the
right, was electrically
operated, where its pred-
ecessor had been hand
operated with pulleys,
rope and counter-
weights. The box with
the drip pan centered in
the window well appears
to be an ice chest. In the
corner next to the chest
is an electric coffee
percolator.*

*June 20, 1935.
This photograph shows
the southwest corner
of the kitchen of 1902 as
it appeared almost
unchanged before
remodeling. The door at
left leads into the
Ground Floor Corridor.
The doorway at right
opens into a pantry. This
kitchen was not all
of one design but was
an accumulation of
improvements beginning
in 1902. The linoleum
floor for example may
not have been especially
old.*

1935.

The southwest corner of the kitchen, photographed during construction. Through the doorway at right is a glimpse of the staircase added to the adjoining pantry in 1902. Note the pot rack still hanging overhead and in the walls, evidence of the old arching system that supported the house. Today this structural work is replaced by steel.

1935.

After the renovation project was completed, the southwest view was again photographed showing the revised streamlined kitchen. The door that led into the Ground Floor Corridor was removed and replaced with cabinets. One of several new refrigerators can be seen in the service pantry, through the doorway at right.

1935.
FDR's "New Deal" kitchen had the up-to-date appointments of America's best hotels— except the space, which always at the White House is limited. The renovated space contained new stainless electric appliances including ranges, ovens, and food warmers. A new doorway was added at left, which led to the preparation pantry, the store pantry, and access to various storerooms, a wine cellar, and refrigerated areas that were also built under the north driveway in 1935.

NATIONAL PARK SERVICE, OFFICE OF THE CURATOR, THE WHITE HOUSE

December 16, 1935.
A special warming and delivery cart was acquired for food prepared for President Franklin Roosevelt. It had two drawers for hot dishes and one drawer for cold and enabled the president's meals to be transported from the residence kitchen to the West Wing at an ideal temperature.

HARRIS & EWING, NATIONAL ARCHIVES

1935.
In the central room that had been the original kitchen and, after 1902, a furnace room, space was partitioned off for a staff dining room and the store pantry, seen in this photograph. Stainless steel food cabinets appear at left, and, at right, is a stainless steel fish box. The main kitchen can be seen in the background through the doorway.

1935.
The service pantry, the room that had been the everyday kitchen, was reconfigured in 1935 to include built-in refrigerators, under the arch, and two new dumbwaiters. The ice cream storage box appears at left.

*January 21, 1948.
Abbie Rowe
photographed the
White House interior
prior to the Truman
renovation. The main
kitchen and the service
pantry still reflect
the 1935 remodeling,
dented and scratched
from many years of
wear.*

*January 21, 1948.
Dumbwaiters in the reno-
vated kitchen of 1935 as
they appeared just before
demolition.*

June 12, 1950. During the Truman renovation, the interior of the White House was removed with the exception of the Third Floor. The kitchen was rebuilt in its previous location in the northwest corner of the building, seen in the background at center.

February 14, 1952. In addition to documenting the demolition of the building's interior, Abbie Rowe also photographed rooms while they were being reassembled. In February 1952, appliances and other fixtures were installed in the main kitchen.

*February 21, 1952.
The new Truman kitchen
shown here being
installed was tailored
precisely to White House
needs, with every mod-
ern culinary conven-
ience. The ovens and
ranges that had been
against the east wall
were now positioned
along the south wall
of the room.*

*March 21, 1952.
Staff clean and reset
the kitchen in prepara-
tion of President Harry
Truman's return to
the White House,
March 27, 1952.*

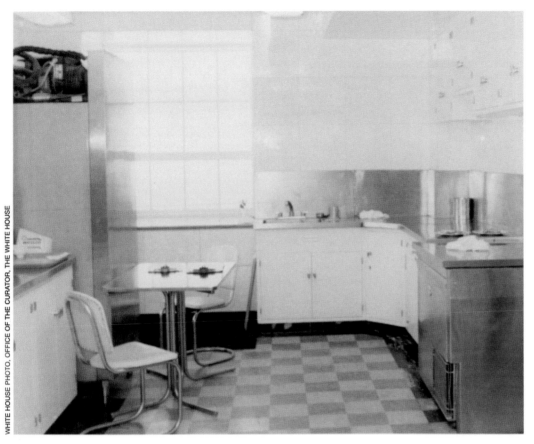

August 3, 1971. The north end of the service pantry is seen prior to remodeling work that occurred during August 1971 under President Richard M. Nixon.

September 22, 1971. This southeast view of the kitchen was taken after the project was completed. Much of the equipment installed nearly twenty years earlier during the Truman renovation, including two ranges and a food warmer from 1935, had become obsolete and was replaced. Work areas were rearranged to make better use of limited space.

September 22, 1971. In 1971, a partial wall, seen at right, was installed along the north end of the kitchen to create a hallway to help restrict foot traffic through the food preparation area.

c. 1990–92.

The Historic American Building Survey (HABS) produced measured drawings, field notes, and photographs of the White House, 1988–92, to show the changes that had occurred since the Truman renovation. This image reflects the appearance of the main kitchen as it is today. The placement of the sinks, ranges, ovens, and work spaces has not changed since the Nixon administration. Equipment installed in 1971 has been replaced when necessary.

c. 1990–92.
During the Truman reno-
vation, a spiral staircase
and a staff elevator were
placed next to the dumb-
waiters in the pantry
area to enable easier
movement of food from
the kitchen to the State
Floor dining rooms.
This arrangement
remains to the present
day.

1982.
First Lady Nancy Reagan
views a swan made of
spun sugar while visiting
the White House kitchen.
Chefs from left to right,
Roland Mesnier (pastry
chef, 1980–2004); Henry
Haller (executive chef,
1966–87); and Frank Ruta
(assistant chef, 1980–87
and 1988–90).

My White House Years

ROLAND MESNIER

*T*wenty-five years is a long time and
a short time. These are the number of years I spent in
the White House at the discretion of five first families.
I consider myself very blessed and honored. Sometimes
I cannot even believe that, being a kid from a very small
province in France, I landed at the White House: is it a
dream, or did it really happen?

I was hired in 1979 and started to work in early
1980. Jimmy Carter was then president of the United
States. The country was going through some very bad
times, with interest rates soaring, lines at the gas pumps,
hostages in Iran. The press was talking about a malaise
in the White House. Nevertheless, when Mrs. Carter
hired me, I thought I was very privileged and honored.
I was about to enter a very different zone, a zone that
very few people have experienced. I was going to get to
know how this great and beautiful mansion at 1600
Pennsylvania Avenue worked, operated, and functioned.
I was going to get to know the first family, their children
and friends. One of my first thoughts was, how could I
formulate my own policy on how I should function, act,

*Opposite: Chef Mesnier poses with one
of his creations in the State Dining Room.*

*Above right: Chef Mesnier with President
and Mrs. Jimmy Carter, 1980.*

and react, when addressed by the first lady or possibly
the president or their children? It was an enormous
challenge. Would I be clever enough to last? I did
not know, but I would certainly try my best and my
hardest. Another question was, how could I best serve
the family? I would pay close attention to many details
about the likes and dislikes of the first family. I would
create desserts according to the mood of the day, the
weather, the politics of the day, the happy and unhappy
moments of the family. I decided to formulate my own
code of conduct and ethics. The very first point was that
I would not be seen but would stage myself in only certain areas of the house. In other words, I would remain
where I was supposed to be, and that was in my pastry
shop. If the first family wanted to see me they would

Scenes from Chef Mesnier's early years in the White House kitchen. Presentation of food is important at the White House and Chef Mesnier's innovations brought a lavishness to decorations not seen since the era of Theodore Roosevelt. Desserts, salads, and main courses often followed themes in food, such as the lobster seen here.

The White House chefs during a lunch break (left) and preparing for an event (below).

COURTESY OF THE AUTHOR

COURTESY OF THE AUTHOR

know where to find me. I decided I would never go to the private areas unless accompanied by another staff member. Instead of trying to expose the family, I decided my role was to protect the family. If the family was ever in danger, would I be able to do what was necessary to help? Of course I would. Now that I had answered those crucial questions, I had a clear vision of the course on which I had embarked.

The executive chef at that time was Henry Haller, Swiss-born, classically trained in French and other cooking. The assistant chef (sous chef), Hans Raffert, was German-born, classically trained as well. A third chef, Frank Ruta, had the title of assistant chef; he was a young man just starting his career. When I first started the pastry shop was in the White House kitchen, and it was manned by me as the pastry chef. In that kitchen there was just one other person, who did the cleaning. When we got really busy we called on outside help, who were called part-timers or SBAs: service by agreement.

The kitchen was very small compared to hotel and restaurant kitchens. That the pastry shop occupied part of that same room sometimes caused great frustration, as when I needed cool temperatures for my work with ice

creams, chocolate, or sugar and the chef needed a hot kitchen for work on the stove. So there were times when a few sparks would fly. But executive chef Haller was very good at keeping the kitchen under control, and when tempers flared, he put an end to it very quickly. He also made sure that the kitchen was kept spotless. If you spilled anything on the floor it had to be cleaned up right away. When the kitchen was not in use—when the first families would spend a few days at Camp David, for example, or be away on official state visits—the kitchen looked like a show kitchen. We the cooks would spend the time scrubbing and cleaning. All machines had special covers. Everyone took great pride in keeping the presidential kitchen almost a sacred place. The equipment was not the most elaborate but it was sufficient for the production we had. We had to keep in mind that the White House kitchen is not a hotel or a restaurant kitchen but rather the kitchen of a private home.

I had a lot of joy to bake in such a clean environment. We were all very proud to be working in the number one kitchen in the United States of America, where the president and his family's food was prepared as well as all official dinners and receptions. I never lost sight

Left: President and Mrs. Bill Clinton view dessert tables with Chef Mesnier at an elaborate Easter reception in 1998.

Right: President and Mrs. Reagan prepare to take the first slices of a cake made by Chef Mesnier for the president's seventieth birthday party in 1981, as John Ficklin looks on.

COURTESY OF THE AUTHOR

of where I was and for whom I was cracking an egg, or weighing my ingredients, or peeling, chopping, and slicing the fruit that would end up on the president's plate; it had to be the best.

Pressure was on at all times. Preparing food for the first family usually came from a weekly menu that the first lady would review and then accept or reject some of the proposed dishes. The menu would consist of a small appetizer, main course of different meat, seafood, or pasta dishes, pot pies, pizzas, sometimes food with an oriental, Mexican, or southern influence, depending on which first family was in residence. The menu would also feature different salads and, of course, a dessert. I tried always to keep the desserts interesting, as I realized from the beginning that I was going to be making desserts for the same people for four or eight years. I did not want them to get bored with my desserts. I was constantly creating new recipes, and on many occasions I would personalize the dessert. After finding out if we had guests dining with the first family, I would find out who they were, if they had hobbies, and what their jobs were, so I could introduce something "touching" to the creation of the day. Desserts became increasingly popular during my twenty-five years at the White House. The Carter family at the beginning of my tenure wanted desserts only when they were having guests. That changed very quickly, however, after they saw some of my desserts.

The Reagan administration really put desserts at the White House at the center of attention. I realized that right away when I met with Mrs. Reagan one afternoon during a tasting of a raspberry mousse in the residence

kitchen. President Reagan had already showed up, changed into his blue jeans and checked shirt. He was very jovial and charming. When he saw the raspberry mousse he became almost frantic as he could not find a spoon so he grabbed my huge kitchen spoon, took a big serving, and proceeded to move the spoon to his mouth but he missed, and most of the mousse ended up on his shirt. Mrs. Reagan was not too pleased with this display—but all during the remainder of my time with them President Reagan pretended to scrape the mousse off his shirt, telling Mrs. Reagan, "Don't worry honey, I got it all and it was delicious!" After that episode I knew what this administration was going to be all about—lots of sweets!

When the George H. W. Bush administration came I had to change the style of many of my desserts for several reasons. The family had a lot of children, and last-minute guests were many. Some of the grandchildren had allergies, and in that case I would create a dessert that everyone could enjoy, as I did not want to make the person with the allergy feel different or be the object of unnecessary attention. Remember that this President Bush had been the vice president for eight years, and he

COURTESY OF THE AUTHOR

Chocolate tango dancers created for dessert
for a State Dinner honoring President Carlos
Menem of Argentina in 1999.

knew the style of the Reagans. I decided to do more "family-styled" desserts for the Bushes, as opposed to small, tiny plated desserts that consisted of a lot of sorbet, ice cream, and fresh fruit. For the Bush family I made more custard types of desserts—more cakes, pies, and tarts. Of course for the spaniel Millie's birthday we always made a special cake shaped like a dog biscuit. During this administration we had a lot of birthday parties for the grandchildren and for Mrs. Bush's staff. Mrs. Bush did not care to celebrate her own birthday. She always managed to be out of the White House. But on one occasion we caught her having lunch in the residence on her birthday. So I made a tiny cake shaped like a gift box, wrapped with a sugar ribbon and a beautiful bow and a long-stemmed red rose coming out of the bow, all made of sugar. On the dessert plate, in chocolate, I printed the musical notes to "Happy Birthday." She was very touched, and as it was not a birthday cake per se, she was very happy.

Another administration arrived, President Bill Clinton with First Lady Hillary Clinton, daughter Chelsea, and Socks, the "first cat." Chelsea did not eat many desserts, as, like most girls her age, she was watching her figure. President Clinton made up for her, however, as he loved his cherry pie with honey vanilla ice cream and his low-calorie strawberry cake and, of course, the family carrot cake. Mrs. Clinton liked very much the mocha cake that I designed especially for her in a grand presentation for her book, *An Invitation to the White House.* The cake was decorated with the "Hillary Rose" created for her. The Clinton administration became known for a lot of entertaining. The State Dinner numbers went way up from the traditional 140 people, climbing gradually to 220, 350, 600, with 800 being the largest. Only the Clinton family took their meals in the private kitchen on the Second Floor of the White House. They enjoyed the relaxed family atmosphere, also leftover food, especially the desserts. In January 2001, when all the staff had gathered in the State Dining Room to wish the Clinton family well, there was not a dry eye in the room. Family departures were for me my most difficult times during my twenty-five years. From the Carter family to that of President George H. W. Bush, I totally detested to have to say good-bye. I enjoyed serving every family during my time at the White House.

In a few hours we were to meet the new president. I already knew a lot about the younger Bushes for they visited the White House often when his father was president. I remember hearing the majority of the staff saying it is going to be a "piece of cake," as they thought it was going to be just like the senior President Bush. I, for one, was not that sure. Just in case, I thought, I will assume that I do not know them. If they give me some sign that they know me it will be the icing on the cake for me, but as far as I was concerned this was an entirely new family so everything had to be reviewed and reinvented. With the Bush family you could count on one thing: the house is going to be lively with their brothers, sisters, children, pets, and lots of family gatherings; and I did not want to forget their parents, former President and Mrs. Bush as well as Mrs. Welch, the mother of First Lady Laura Bush.

The Bush family always gave me the impression of being a very close-knit unit who enjoyed each other.

Every Bush reunion sounded and looked like the same thing that happens in any other home in America. Entertaining changed a lot during my years of the George W. Bush administration. There were fewer State Dinners but many more working luncheons and dinners. A tremendous number of heads of state were invited to those luncheons and dinners.

The Bush family love their pets. I remember the first Mrs. Bush with her dog Millie, a very smart dog who wrote a book that became a best seller! Millie gave birth to quite a few puppies, which were adorable. Two of them I remember were Ranger, who was full of life, and Spot, who was adopted by George W. Bush. I played with Spot as a puppy and I said good-bye to Spot the day she died. It was a very difficult day for all the staff at the White House and particularly the first family. It was as if we all had lost a family member.

President George W. Bush makes sure he has the strength to assume his responsibilities by staying very fit. He is one of the fittest presidents I have ever seen. Mrs. Bush has a wonderful eye for color and style. Everything has to be streamlined, not clogged up by lots of trinkets. The look totally reflects her personality, all over the house.

State Dinners at the White House

The Carter administration took a bad rap from the press when it came to entertaining at the White House. Reporters often asked if we were feeding them "peanuts"! I will respectfully disagree with the press on this issue. The Carter family had as much taste as any other family. I was only one year with the Carter administration. I did not participate at many State Dinners, but one comes to mind. It was the kosher dinner for Prime Minister Menaham Begin of Israel. That occasion was the only time I saw the White House kitchen become kosher—top to bottom. Cooking tables were burned with a gas torch and then covered with tinfoil. Dishes and silverware were boiled in large water kettles, and we had the pressure of a rabbi in the kitchen making sure we did not use the wrong ingredients. Prime Minister Begin sent through the butler his compliments on the dessert, which made me extremely happy.

During the Reagan administration Mrs. Reagan liked to do a tasting of the dinner prior to an occasion such as a State Dinner, which was great, so you knew exactly what to do the day of the event. Mrs. Reagan wanted the desserts to make a statement or have an impact on the guests. Desserts had to draw "oohs and ahs." If they did not she saw that as a failing grade. Mrs. Reagan wanted the White House to be the very best, featuring the most beautiful food with elegance and fabulous taste. Because of Mrs. Reagan's striving for excellence, I worked harder and researched more. The challenges given to me by the first lady made me a better pastry chef, for which I will always be very grateful. But I needed help so I turned to embassies, first of all for correctness but to also have access to brochures and literature that I could read and learn about the visiting countries. During the Reagan administration it was not uncommon to have two State Dinners a month.

During the George H. W. Bush administration State Dinners remained pretty much the same as during the Reagan years. Since my coming to the White House we had a third executive chef, Hans Raffert. He had been the sous chef to Henry Haller for about seventeen years, so the cooking remained pretty much the same. Frank Ruta was now his sous chef. Ruta came to the White House in 1979 as an assistant chef. He had left the White House during the Reagan administration to go to Italy to perfect his cooking and came back during the last couple of years of the Reagan administration. Frank Ruta was a very energetic, fast-learning chef who gave a lot of support to the executive chef, Hans Raffert. When Chef Henry Haller retired during the 1980s, the Reagan administration hired an executive chef who lasted only a few months. Frank Ruta left the White House again during the early years of the Bush administration, so the door was opened for Pierre Chambrin to come in as sous chef to Hans Raffert. Toward the end of the Bush administration Hans Raffert retired and Pierre Chambrin was named executive chef to the Geroge H. W. Bush family.

Then in 1994 it was time for a new first family at the White House. I was not ready for this one! I thought I had seen everything! After all I had been at the White House for thirteen years; how could it get more demanding? Wrong! At first events started out small, and I kept hearing that the Clintons were "in training." It was great having small, intimate dinners. It did not last long, however. The Democrats were back! When I saw the pavilion being erected on the White House lawn I knew what was coming.

First Lady Nancy Reagan slices President Reagan's birthday cake at Camp David.

Chef Mesnier presents Chelsea Clinton with a cake as she celebrates her birthday with friends in the White House.

Above: President Clinton and Tipper Gore pose with a cake decorated with sorbet roses made by Chef Mesnier for their shared birthday celebration.

Right: A cake made for the third birthday of Marshall Bush, the granddaughter of President George H. W. Bush.

Right: Chef Mesnier poses in front of the White House Christmas tree with President and Mrs. George H. W. Bush in 1992.

Below right: During the White House two hundredth anniversary celebrations in 2000, Chef Mesnier and First Lady Hillary Clinton pose with a special Christmas gingerbread display of replicas of American buildings including the Washington Monument and Mount Vernon.

COURTESY OF THE AUTHOR

COURTESY OF THE AUTHOR

COURTESY OF THE AUTHOR

Right: President Bill Clinton examines a gingerbread replica of his childhood home in Arkansas created by Chef Mesnier for Christmas 1994.

COURTESY OF THE AUTHOR

Right: Chef Mesnier in the chocolate shop during the creation of Christmas decorations based on Willie Wonka and the Chocolate Factory.

Below: Chef Mesnier watches as a gingerbread house is carried inside through the North Portico. Too large to be moved to the State Floor on the elevator, the gingerbread house was taken outside from the Ground Floor kitchen and carried in the North Door, in 2000.

But I stayed on. And the eight years to come were going to be rocking right up to the end with unbelievable numbers. The State Dinner for Japan: six hundred people. The State Dinner for India: eight hundred people. The NATO dinner: nine hundred people. Receptions were up to twelve hundred people. The Millennium dinners and receptions: four thousand people. We worked twenty-four hours without stopping.

Meanwhile I was still visiting embassies for advice about more than food. I was looking not to reproduce desserts from the home countries of White House guests but rather looking to reproduce a way of decorating the dessert platters that would be meaningful for them. On one occasion I was visiting the Embassy of Argentina when I was told the ambassador wanted to meet me. That was a little bit unusual. He was a very nice, likable man, and he proceeded to invite me to his memorable barbeques, for the beef in Argentina is very well known as outstanding. He then proceeded to tell me what I needed to do to decorate my dessert platters. His suggestion was to have the head of a cow on each platter! Everyone, he said, will recognize this as Argentina! Needless to say, I thanked him profusely and left with my brochures of his beautiful country knowing that there would not be any cow heads on my dessert platters because I knew then my head would end up on a platter! Instead, after reviewing the brochures, I discovered in a corner a tiny picture of a couple dancing the tango. This was it—the theme for the dessert—the tango dancers! Everyone knows that the tango is the steamy dance of Argentina. I made a stage out of chocolate and placed on it a couple dancing the tango. The whole scene was decorated with chocolate palm trees to give the platter some depth. The dessert was presented in front of the magnificent showpiece, which was greatly appreciated and well received that night, especially as after the dinner Robert Duvall danced the tango as an entertainer in the East Room. I thought that evening was absolutely perfect in every way, and I know both heads of state and their families were amused by the tango dancer theme. Because of those special five minutes at the end of a meal, I believe it was a job well done, not only by me but by all my staff in the pastry shop, as we were all truly devoted to any idea I came up with for State Dinners during my twenty-five years.

The Best Ingredients

Of course every first lady has to approve State Dinner menus. The executive chef writes the menu, and the Usher's Office types it and sends it to me to add my dessert. I make sure there are no flavors in conflict or duplicate, especially if the executive chef is including fruit in any of the dishes. The menu then goes back to the Usher's Office for review and then to the first lady's office as well as the Social Office, where changes are made as necessary. Shortly after that a tasting takes place with the president, first lady, and guests. The first lady gets a critique from the president and the guests and asks for the changes she desires.

The main problem in creating a menu is being able to get the best ingredients possible, the freshest fruits, and to get what we need at the time we need it. One cannot take a chance after the menu is printed, so we have to make sure we have what it takes to execute it. For example, my biggest problem was to get the best and freshest fruit—ripe and tasty—and to have everything arrive on time. It was not always easy to do. I worked with several suppliers. I would talk to them every day after an order was placed, checking on my order's progress. I did that until my order arrived at the White House. The cases would be opened immediately and each fruit checked, one by one, and placed on a baking sheet covered with foam so it would not bruise. Each fruit was checked for ripeness, and, as needed, it would be refrigerated or left outside until ready for use.

The rest of the ingredients would be purchased by the store room in local grocery stores and picked up with an unmarked vehicle and an agent driving as well as a store room employee on board. To ensure the safety of the food, the food was never purchased using the White House name. Different names and addresses are used, and I am not at liberty to disclose them. The White House does not have tasters for poison; choices are made at the discretion of the store room and the chefs. Sometimes food is sent to the first family by individuals outside the White House who want to make a gift to the first family. Unless it comes from a very close friend, it is destroyed for the sake of the safety of the first family.

Christmas at the White House

Christmas is a magical time of the year, when the White House becomes a fairyland. Each first lady puts her own stamp on how to make every year a special Christmas. My first Christmas at the White House during the Carter administration made me realize how special a place the White House is. The opulent decorations in every room, so many trees all over the house, wreaths and garlands and in particular the tree in the Blue Room —all made the fairyland. The National Tree that year was decorated with antique dolls—a stunning array. I did not know at this point that I was going to see twenty-four more Christmases at the White House. The food throughout the years was pretty much traditional— turkey, ham, beef with side dishes, shrimp, cheese trays, holiday breads, and lots of pastries including Yule cakes, cookies, gingerbread, fruitcake, and, of course, the famous gingerbread house that in those years was created by the assistant chef, Hans Raffert. He started the tradition of the gingerbread house when he came on board during the Nixon administration. He made it every year until he retired in the third year of the George H. W. Bush administration. At that point I took over the making of the gingerbread house, and I did it until my retirement. The house was pretty much the same every year— shaped like an A-frame house with Hansel and Gretel decorations and lots of traditional cookies. Mrs. Reagan had Hans make a second house to be taken to the Washington Children's Hospital.

My first gingerbread house was for the last year of the George H. W. Bush administration. I decided to change the format and design by doing a village in a winter scene with Mrs. Bush and Millie passing around a tray of Christmas cookies. Of course, Mrs. Bush's pearls were very prominent. Mrs. Bush was very particular about continuing to make the White House as the gingerbread house. The outside of the house would change every year, decorated with the theme of the holiday chosen by Mrs. Bush. One year we did children's literature and a lot of characters from children's books. One year the gingerbread house was so big it could not be carried up the stairs from the China Room, where it was always built. We had to place it in a van and drive it to the front portico on Pennsylvania Avenue.

When the Clintons came in, I decided to do buildings that had something in common with their lives. So I decided to do houses where they were born and grew up. First I did the president's house. When he looked at it he had tears in his eyes. The following year I did the first lady's house. In the third year for Chelsea we did a house that was open showing a scene of *The Nutcracker* ballet, as Chelsea at that time was big into ballet and, in particular, *The Nutcracker.* One of the characters happened to look just like Chelsea all done out of sugar. The following year we started doing the White House, which grew bigger with each year. Of course, we always displayed the family pets. One of the houses was turned into the House of Socks with black cats everywhere. Of course they were all dressed up for the Holiday Season. Then came the Millennium when Mrs. Clinton requested that we feature four Washington monuments—the White House (the early years), the Washington Monument, the Jefferson Memorial, and Mount Vernon with the river passing by it with fireworks in the background, all made of sugar.

Through each administration, the Christmas desserts changed, but always maintained a modern look and taste. During the George H. W. Bush administration a dessert buffet was added in the East Room of the house. During the George W. Bush administration a chocolate showpiece was added to the East Room buffet. One year the dessert table was graced by a huge chocolate eagle. The following year the showpiece was *Willy Wonka and the Chocolate Factory.* During the Christmas holidays I would use about 120,000 pieces of cakes and cookies. Christmas production would start in June, as everything was made and baked in the House. It was my biggest pride that many of my cookies ended up on people's Christmas trees. These are all great memories. Happy Holidays!

Bad Times in the White House

Every administration had its challenges, and most of the time the staff is not spared from them, as the bad and good times reflect on the mood of the house and its occupants. Many times my menu would change according to the mood of the day. The desserts would also reflect on the world events of the day. I was particularly attentive to that. I think those moments were more important than the good times. In the bad times you had to double your effort in order to please. In these times I always would create "homey" desserts, something easy to digest and that tastes really good, for example, a good baked apple served warm with a nice little sauce or custard. I always liked to use honey as a sweetener, as it is comforting. A great hot soufflé would always be welcome. I would definitely avoid acetic or heavy desserts.

My first experience of bad times came at the time of the hostage rescue mission late in the administration of President Carter. We knew something was up when we were ordered to make big trays of sandwiches and lots of cookies to be sent to the West Wing. The president was always on time for meals, but during this time he would be very late or not show up at all. When we found out about the mission, it had already happened and the entire world knew the results. It was a very hard time for the president, from then to the end of his term. I felt very bad about it; at such a time you feel totally helpless. The only thing a cook can do is to give total attention to the food to give him a sense of comfort.

The next bad time was when President Reagan was shot on March 31, 1981. This was a day like every other: the president got to the Hilton Hotel in the afternoon and my day's work was over around 3:00 p.m. I proceeded to go to the third floor of the White House where I had a small office that I shared with the executive chef and the sous chef and got changed into my street clothes. I would usually put my pass around my neck so it would be visible. I did not do so that day; I kept my pass in my pocket. I did not wear my pass during work because it was dangerous to do so when operating the machines, and that was okay, as everybody knew me in uniform. But nobody would recognize me in street clothes.

After changing I came out of my room and suddenly heard a lot of commotion, doors opening and a whole lot of Secret Service agents dressed in black carrying guns yelling at me to get against the wall and shouting, "Who are you and what are you doing here?" After I replied to their questions, they told me to put "your god damn pass around your neck; you should never be without your pass when you are in the residence." After verifying my pass, they left. I still did not know what it was all about. I left the building to go to my car and turned the radio on and heard for the first time what had happened. That gave me a chill through my entire body. I was on my way to teach a class at L'Academie de Cuisine. I followed what was going on all the way to

Bethesda, as Mike Buchanan was reporting on WMAL with his very distinctive voice. The president was being operated on, and his life was in suspense—the world was in suspense. What were we to think? Is our president going to make it? If he makes it will he be the same man? Is his presidency over? Will we have a new "boss" in the White House? Mrs. Reagan must be devastated. Of course, we could not tell her how we all felt because of the protocol.

For days after that day, we kept glued to the radio and television to follow the president's health. Mrs. Reagan would visit him every day, bringing some treats from the White House pastry shop. One treat was peeled grapes in white wine jelly using Gewürztraminer, a good white wine from the Alsace region of France. I also sent one of his favorites—coconut ice cream. Both were approved by his doctor. As the president got better it was time for him to come home. On that day the entire staff of the White House and the Old Executive Office Building stood on the steps of the OEOB with a huge banner saying "Get Well Soon, Mr. President" and down below, "Jim, Tim and Tom," the others who also got hurt in the shooting incident. Here I was standing tall, happy and proud and very grateful to God that our president had been spared. That episode was an inspiration in courage and strength to the entire world. I will never forget it.

In January 1991, the evening before the war started in Kuwait, the Reverend Billy Graham dined with the Bush family. I noticed throughout the years that something was in the making when the Reverend Graham was invited to dine with the first family. Sure enough, a few hours later, after turning the television on you could see the scud missiles flying over Iraq and Kuwait. Not only scuds were flying but rumors, too. I was due to go to France on January 20 for the World Cup of Pastry competition, as I am the president of the American team. My wife Martha was very scared for me to fly. There were rumors that planes might be shot down or bombed in the airports. She begged me not to go, but it takes more than that to stop me. I do not give up that easily to terrorists. As we know President Bush came out of this war a hero with a tremendous approval rating.

During the Clinton administration, I was the last one to know about a little bomb ticking in the White House

GET WELL SOON!
Mr. President
Jim, Tim, and Tom

Staff members assembled on the steps of the Old Executive Office Building to welcome President Ronald Reagan back to the White House from the hospital after he was wounded in an attempted assassination, 1981.

called Monica Lewinsky, which went off in January 1998. I had no idea. I have not much to add to the story, as everybody has had more than one occasion to read and hear about it. I can only say that for these years the White House was plunged into uncertainty and deep sadness. We knew how painful it was for the first family. I was so proud of Chelsea, how she sometimes took over in front of the press showing great poise and strength of character.

It was for me probably the worst of times, but it proved one thing: that you can build castles on top of ashes.

September 11, 2001! The sky is bright blue over Washington, D.C., not a cloud to be seen. I am walking on the South Lawn, watching the crew moving picnic tables—a lot of them, as we are preparing for the congressional barbeque for the entire Congress and the government, about three thousand people. I am thinking this is going to be a glorious day. Mr. Tom Perini and his staff are busy setting the barbeque pit. A close friend of the Bush family and a caterer specializing in barbeque, he has come all the way from Texas. In the early hours former President and Mrs. Barbara Bush departed the White House after a short visit. President Bush had already left to go to Florida, and the first lady would be shortly departing for Capitol Hill. A lot of chefs and butlers were doing the preparations for the afternoon event.

*Following a White House tradition, President Clinton
says goodbye to the assembled White House residence
staff shortly before leaving the house to attend the
inauguration of his successor, George W. Bush, 2001.*

I was working with an assistant in what we call the
Chocolate Room, which is located near to the exit door
on the Ground Floor. The pastry shop, on a mezzanine
two floors up, was in full action with another six or
seven chefs. Around 9:00 a.m. the assistant with me in
the Chocolate Room told me that a plane had gone into
a tower in New York City. I dismissed it by saying, "Oh
well, just another crazy playing around." But then I was
told that another plane had gone into the second tower.
I knew it was no longer a joke. I started to panic, knowing that the barbeque would no doubt be canceled. A

few minutes later Claire Faulkner from the Usher's
Office rushed into the Chocolate Room and practically
dragged us out yelling, "You have to get out. Get out
now! There is a plane coming for the White House in
ten minutes." At first I thought it was a joke. I was not
at all ready to leave but then she rephrased it so that
everyone knew it was not a joke. I picked up the phone
to call the pastry shop to let the staff there know to
evacuate. The line was busy. I wanted to go back to the
shop to let them know, but no way, the agent would not
let me through. On my way out I asked half a dozen
officers to call the pastry shop to give the staff there the
message. I was really very upset, as I felt responsible
for all my staff. I got out of the building running in my
chef uniform complete with my tall hat so I knew that
when the other assistants were out they could find me in
the crowd, which they did.

We met up in Lafayette Park, watching the sky for incoming planes. By then we all had learned about the Pentagon. A great feeling of uncertainty had overtaken all of us: what is next? After a few hours we decided to follow one of our co-workers to her home in Arlington. We had to walk quite a few miles through the streets of Washington and Georgetown, where we could see the commotion of people trying to get home. After reaching the house our co-worker was nice enough to fix us a little lunch with a couple of beers. We were then able to watch the drama on television as it unfolded in New York. No one could believe what we were seeing. Later on during that day we were taken to a meeting point where members of each family could pick up their loved ones. I could not imagine in my wildest dream being witness to the destruction of the most powerful home in the world—the White House.

Leaving the White House

Leaving the White House is very hard to do: watching history in the making and being in the middle of it and having had the privilege and the honor to work in that great, powerful mansion—serving the elites of the world—what a thrill! If you are staff or president, it is the same feeling when you leave the White House. If you are the president you have had, for four or eight years, many people catering to all your needs. You are completely looked after. The eyes of the world are on you. Then comes that day when the staff will get together in the State Dining Room to bid good-bye to the first family, the people who have been the center of your life for four or eight years. For me it was the single most difficult moment—extremely sad. There were always a lot of tears. I have seen presidents just melting into tears and then not being able to say good-bye. Some were quite jovial.

Then came the day I had to say good-bye to all my co-workers and the first family whom I had known for a very long time. I decided to give six months' notice so I could decompress slowly. I also needed to work out how I was going to conduct my life after the White House. I planned for a book I had written to be released shortly after I retired, which gave me something to fall into after my White House years. My last day was very much like any other day. I came to work on time and left on time after turning off the light for the last time: twenty-five years had passed. I was leaving behind a lot of emotions and a lot of feelings. When I left that day all the staff at the White House lined up on the long hallways leading to the parking lot to wish me well. What a surprise, and it drew some tears of joy. I felt warm all over to be recognized in this way by my co-workers, whom I am honored and proud to call my friends.

Final Chapter

Here we are in early March 2006 going into my second year of retirement. I have just returned from France after a two-week blitz tour to promote my new book, *Sucre d'Etat* (Sweet Thing of the State). This book received a great reception in France. I am still working on a "cake book," and I continue to tour the United States promoting *Dessert University*, my first book since leaving the White House. I go around the nation giving demonstrations and lectures, consulting, and in general enjoying life and retirement with my wife, Martha, and our son, George.

On March 9 I have an appointment to see about a consulting job at a Georgetown cafe, to try to improve its pastry and cake lines. It is a great meeting, and I am tempted to do it. I am just thinking about how very happy I am with my life right now and that I am finally able to totally disconnect myself from the White House. After all, the White House had been my life for many years, and it felt very good not to have that feeling anymore. I had totally decompressed and had returned to a more normal, peaceful life.

On March 11 the day promises to be a beautiful morning, sunshine and all. I am up at 7:00 a.m. and after a cup of coffee and reviewing the newspaper I go to the office to respond to my e-mail and phone messages. Around 10:00 a.m. the phone rings, and my wife answers, as I am outside in the courtyard working on my roses. My wife tells me that Lea Berman, the White House social secretary, has called and asks that I call her back, which I do. She is very nice on the phone, and she is telling me that the new pastry chef is on his way out after being at the White House for a short time. Mrs. Bush has asked Lea to contact me about coming back until a new pastry chef is hired. My reply is, "Of course!" Besides, I had promised Mrs. Bush at the time I gave my notice (Christmas 2003) that if she ever needed me, I would be just a phone call away. So the call has come, and I am very honored to help out on a limited basis.

A pastry shop, separate from the main kitchen, was created in 1999. Many of Chef Mesnier's special creations are displayed in the case above the marble counter.

On Monday, March 13, I receive a call from the chief usher, Gary Walters, working out the security details. On the following day I begin a series of meetings in my house with assistant pastry chef, Suzie Morrison, to talk about reorganizing the staff situation, making sure all shifts are covered, revising menus, and designing new desserts and recipes. I want Suzie to brief me about all the events going on so I can take action.

Saturday, March 18, is my first day back into the White House compound. At lunchtime the butler informs the president and first lady that I am back in the pastry shop. Right away they ask to see me in the Dining Room, where they are having lunch with daughter Jenna and two other guests. My heart starts to beat really fast, as it has many times before. It occurs to me

that what is happening is what I have lived many times before. Déjà vu all over again! I had been called into that Dining Room by other presidents and first ladies. I had entered and everyone stood up and applauded me. I felt so nervous and humble. I still cannot forget where I am coming from. On this occasion the first lady gives me a hug and the president shakes my hand. He reminds me that he had told me before I retired that I would be back in the White House someday. I reply that I did remember. Yes, it is correct, and it is nice to see the family once again. I tell him that I will do my best to please, and I then thank them and leave the room.

After leaving the Dining Room I felt as if I had never left the White House. Now it was up to me to swing between my commitments and the White House events. In the next several days I met on several occasions with Lea Berman and Gary Walters. It is the first time I have met Lea Berman, and I found her very nice and easy to work with. I liked her style. I also began to work very closely with the assistant pastry chef, Suzie Morrison, starting to design a dessert for the retiring Justice Sandra Day O'Connor using the scales of justice

Chef Mesnier meets with First Lady Laura Bush in the Map Room in 2004 to announce his plans for retirement.

fresh cherries filled with a kumquat puree. Of course, on July Fourth we observed the president's birthday for two hundred guests. We created a huge chocolate cake with chocolate decorations celebrating his entire life right up to the presidency.

Many things had changed since my departure in July 2004. A huge turning point was that a new executive chef has been appointed by Mrs. Bush. This is Cristeta Comerford, with whom I had worked for nearly ten years, and I am a great fan of her cooking as well an admirer of her as a human being. I was pleasantly surprised after my return to see how she had totally changed the main kitchen. She had brought back the integrity and stability of this great place. Her staff seems to be very happy, and her management style is all about quality work and serving the first family well. Her organization is superb.

After securing for the Usher's Office a list of potential candidates for the pastry chef position and as the summer rolls in with a decrease in work, for the family is on vacation, I begin planning my second retirement from the White House. It begins on July 15, 2006, as time does not permit me to work there any longer. It has been quite an honor to serve again and to see all my friends at the White House. I would like to wish my successor the best of luck, and may he or she have as much fun as I have had serving the great leaders of the world.

as a part of the presentation for the dessert. We designed a special Napoleon for Lebanon. We worked on a State Luncheon with 160 from China, making a three-melon sorbet with orange rind and toasted sesame seeds presented on ice carving in a carved melon, for the Chinese love melons, in particular watermelon. After that there was a State Luncheon for Ghana, and we had been told to make it extra special as President and Mrs. Bush had just visited there and had been very well received. There were many other lunches and dinners until May 16, when we had a State Dinner for Australia. There were close to two hundred people for dessert. The dessert, called "The Australian Black Pearl," was served inside a white chocolate seashell with chocolate seaweed in the background with a lot of small chocolate fishes attached to the seaweed. Following that was the congressional barbeque for one thousand people, and on June 29 there was a State Dinner for Japan. The title of the dessert was "Sweet Serenity—Bonsai Garden," and the composition was a sour cherry sorbet filled with almond mousse with tiny macaroons and pieces of nougat, fresh peaches, and

To

The Right Honorable Earle of Errol

My Lord,

The honour conferred on me in being permitted to dedicate the following pages to your Lordship presents an opportunity, of which I gladly avail myself, to express publicly my grateful acknowledgments for the liberal encouragement and uniform kindness I have ever experienced, since I had the good fortune to come under your Lordship's notice.

If my anxious endeavour to produce a useful treatise on the art I profess, worthy of public favour and of the distinguished patronage I have received, shall be successful, the satisfaction this will give me will ever be associated with a grateful recollection of the many facilities afforded me for acquiring additional practical knowledge and experience, while in Her Majesty's service as Chief Cook and Maitre-d'Hotel, in which office I had the advantage to act under the liberal and judicious directions of your Lordship, when Lord Steward of the Household.

I have the honour to be,
My Lord,
With the greatest respect,
Your Lordship's most obedient and very humble servant,

Charles Elme Francatelli

Dedication quoted from Charles Elme Francatelli, *The Modern Cook: A Practical Guide to the Culinary Arts* (London: Richard Bentley, New Burlington Street, 1846), 2.

Preparation of the Menu for the Prince of Wales Dinner in 2005

CRISTETA PASIA COMERFORD

*C*harles Elme Francatelli was a maitre-d'hotel and chief cook to Queen Victoria in the mid-1800s. His book, *The Modern Cook: A Practical Guide to the Culinary Arts*, was a great blessing for me to have at those times in my profession when I had a very important dinner to prepare. The dedication he wrote to the Earl of Errol resonates with what every true culinarian's soul and spirit possess: a penchant for dedication, availability, and service.

Two months after I was installed in August 2005 as the new executive chef of the White House, a premiere challenge lay ahead. Britain's Prince Charles and his wife, Camilla, the Duchess of Cornwall, were to visit the United States in the fall. The knot in my stomach was more than anyone might readily imagine. December, too, lay ahead with its promise of ninety-five hundred guests and twenty-five events altogether, not including the daily meals, planning, and staffing with which I have had to contend. With the clear understanding that pleasing the first family is my utmost priority, pleasing their guests, including the royal couple is just as important. *The Washington Times* headline on November 2 read:

COMMANDER IN CHEF
Female Head of the White House Kitchen Debuts
with a Royal Menu

As with any official visit or social event, the planning and preparation require a very careful process. When the calendar is blocked for a State Dinner, usually at least a few months ahead, everyone's mind starts gearing up, and ideas, visions, and plans begin to develop. With previous experience and knowledge of the president and the first lady's entertaining style and preferences, the next step is to balance that information with the royal couple's preferences. The season of the year that the dinner is scheduled will also be considered and have a great impact.

The dinner was scheduled for early November 2005. With the fall season at its peak, the menu leans toward a "game"-oriented theme. And as Prince Charles is known for his hunting activities, a menu that would highlight American game was envisioned. Also taken into consideration was the abundant availability of good-quality regional produce that would enhance the "seasonal, American, and game-oriented" menu that entered its planning stage.

When a first menu proposal is submitted to the White House social secretary, it normally follows a set format, providing at least three choices for each of the four courses: the first course, the main course, the salad course, and the dessert course. It might seem to be a laundry list of wonderful, savory, and succulent ideas so that it is now just a matter of choosing what would best represent the first family. The challenge, however, is to prepare a proposal in which no ingredients are redundant so that no matter what courses are selected nothing is repetitive.

I made the first proposal on September 6, a good two months before the actual event. Pheasant, squab, and quail were the three choices for the first course, prepared with ingredients that are reflective of the fall season. A black-eyed pea accompaniment for the squab would highlight a wonderful legume from the South. The main course proposal consisted of American buffalo, venison, and

Lunch
Wednesday, November 2, 2005
location tbd
12:00 pm serving time
10 Guests

Menu 121A/ 2005
Generated on 8/8/05
Main courses added 9/15/05

Lunch for Prince Charles

First course: Please choose from the following:

___Roasted Buttercream Squash Bisque
Brown Butter and Sage Crisps
___Watercress Soup with Applewood Smoked Bacon
Espelette Cream
___Leek and Chestnut Soup with Pineapple
Pancetta Fleurons

Main course: Please choose from the following:

___Lemon Sole with Herb Crust
Warm Salad of Chicory, Petite Asparagus and Black Cherry Tomatoes
___Poussin with Morels and Red Swiss Chard
Black Eye Peas with Parsley Vinaigrette
___Texas Gulf Shrimp with Shredded Filo
Dilled Cucumber "Linguini" with Lemon Yogurt Sauce

Salad course: Please choose from the following:

___Bowtie Arugula, Roasted Beets and Navel Oranges
Walnut Oil Vinaigrette
___Salad of Sorrel, Purslane and Peppercress
Silton Cheese Tartlette
___Composed Salad of Butter Lettuce, White Cucumbers and Golden Pea Tendrils
Champagne Dressing

Dessert: please choose one of the following:

___"Autumn Harvest"
Pumpkin Ice Cream and Crispy Leaf Cookies

___"Fall Festival"
Apple Sorbet, Spiced Fruit Compote and Brandy Snaps

Lunch
Wednesday, November 2, 2005
location tbd?
?? pm serving time
10 Guests

Menu 121A/ 2005
Generated on 8/8/05

Lunch for Prince Charles

please choose one of the following:

"Autumn Harvest"
Pumpkin Ice Cream and Crispy Leaf Cookies

"Fall Festival"
Apple Sorbet, Spiced Fruit Compote and Brandy Snaps

Alaska Hudson Bay duck breast. These were paired with vegetables and garnitures that would be very complementary in textures and flavors. The salad courses presented highlighted a number of wonderful heirloom varieties of young lettuces and vegetables grown in Ohio paired with some nutty and creamy artisanal (handcrafted in small batches) American cheeses that are as excellent as the European varieties. Pastry chef Thaddeus DuBois proposed three desserts showcasing all the best fruits of the season. These were later changed to desserts that were to be passed and required a more elegant presentation.

When the "first" final menu was chosen, the first course selected was pheasant consommé with dry sherry, apple quenelles, and vegetable brunoise. The main course was medallion of buffalo tenderloin with roast corn sauce, glazed parsnips and young carrots, and wild rice pancakes. The salad course consisted of crisp romaine lettuce with blood orange vinaigrette paired with a blue-veined cheese from Point Reyes, California, and spiced walnuts from the South. The dessert course was autumn chrysanthemum petit four cake served with chartreuse ice cream and a red

and green grape sauce. The wines were added by October 5. It is during this time that a chef's ability to connect with the right purveyors to procure the best meat, produce, and specialty products will be most important to the success of the menu itself.

The next step is for the social secretary to schedule a workable date for menu-tasting. The tricky part of this process is to find a date that the president and the first lady's schedule will allow and that is also early enough to tweak a few changes, if necessary. If it is too early, however, certain products may not be at their peak of seasonality. Another menu revision was created on October 20, as it was decided that the consommé would be too challenging to serve properly. Therefore, two new first courses were presented: One was a celery broth with crispy rock shrimp; the other was a roasted quince and sweet carrot soup.

When the menu tasting was finally scheduled, about a week and a half before the State Dinner, the vision became more definite, as the presentation and dishing up aspects are all carefully thought out. There were twelve

Lunch
Wednesday, November 2, 2005
location tbd
12:00 pm serving time
12 Guests

Menu 121B/ 2005
Generated on 8/8/05
Main courses added 9/15/05
Revised 9/16/05

Lunch for Prince Charles

Watercress Soup with Applewood Smoked Bacon
Espelette Cream

Lemon Sole with Herb Crust
Warm Salad of Chicory, Petite Asparagus and Black Cherry Tomatoes

Composed Salad of Butter Lettuce, White Cucumbers and Golden Pea Tendrils
Champagne Dressing

Spiced Autumn Fruit Compote in Brandy Snap Baskets
Lady Apple Sorbet (shaped in apple molds) with Sugar Leaves
Warm Berry Sauce

Lunch
Wednesday, November 2, 2005
location tbd
12:00 pm serving time
12 Guests

Menu 121C/ 2005
Generated on 8/8/05
Main courses added 9/15/05
Revised 9/22/05
Wine added 10/03/05

Lunch for Prince Charles

Watercress Soup with Applewood Smoked Bacon
Espelette Cream

Lemon Sole with Herb Crust
Warm Salad of Chicory, Petite Asparagus and Black Cherry Tomatoes

Composed Salad of Butter Lettuce, White Cucumbers and Golden Pea Tendrils
Champagne Dressing

Lady Apple Sorbet
Brandy Snap Basket
Spiced Autumn Fruit Compote

Peter Michael "L'Apres Midi" 2004

Dinner
Wednesday, November 2, 2005
State Floor
7:00 pm serving time
100 Guests

Menu 144A/ 2005
Generated on 10/13/05

Passed Canapes for Prince of Wales

Please choose from the following:

___Slow Poached Lobster with Vanilla Cream, Peppercress and Polenta Crisp

___Yukon Potato "Chips" with Truffles and Chive

___Applewood Smoked Duck with Leek Fondue, Fried Shallots and
Arugula Pesto

___Maryland Blue Crab Fritters with Lemon-Parsley Aioli

___Fontina Risotto Crisps with Porcini Mushrooms and Thyme Oil

---

Dinner
Wednesday, November 2, 2005
State Floor
7:00 pm serving time
100 Guests

Menu 144A/ 2005
Generated on 10/13/05
Revised 10/13/05

Passed Canapes for Prince of Wales

Slow Poached Lobster with Vanilla Cream, Peppercress and Polenta Crisp

Yukon Potato "Chips" with Truffles and Chive

Applewood Smoked Duck with Leek Fondue, Fried Shallots and
Arugula Pesto

Right and below: Drafts of the dinner menu detail the decision making process for each course and the additions of wine and dessert.

Dinner
Wednesday, November 2, 2005
State Floor
7:00 pm serving time
100 Guests

Menu 132A/ 2005
Generated on 9/6/05
Dessert added 9/8/05

Dinner with Prince Charles

First Course: Please choose from the following:

___Pheasant Consomme with Dry Sherry
Apple Quennelles and Vegetable Brunoise
___Smoked Squab with Black Muscat Vinaigrette
Black Eye Pea Pilaf and Pancetta Bacon Crisps
___Grilled Quail with Figs and Prosciuto Ham
Peppercress and Walnuts

Main Course: Please choose from the following:

___Medallion of Buffalo Tenderloin with Roast Corn Sauce
Glazed Parsnips and Young Carrots
Wild Rice Pancakes
___Venison Loin with Roasted Pears and Chantrelles
Braised Spinach and Sweet Potato Polenta
___Tamarind Glazed Duck Breasts with Sweet Onion Relish
Red Cabbage Vinaigrette and Leg Confit

Salad Course: Please choose from the following:

___Painted Oak Leaf, Lolla Rosa, and Mache with Blackberry Dressing
Vermont Artisanal Cheddar Tart
___Tom Thumb Bibb Lettuces with Champagne Vinaigrette
Cucumber, Vine Ripened Tomatoes and Artichokes
___Crisp Mint Romaine Lettuce with Blood Orange Vinaigrette
Point Reyes Blue Cheese and Spiced Walnuts

Desserts: Please choose from the following:
___Apple and Plum Crumble with Honeycomb Ice Cream (plated)
English Custard Sauce
___English Bread and Butter Pudding with Rum Raisin Ice Cream (plated)
Stewed Apricot Brandy Sauce
___English Trifle Cake with Raspberry and Black Currant Sorbet (platter)
Lemon Curd Sauce

Dinner
Wednesday, November 2, 2005
State Floor
7:00 pm serving time
100 Guests

Menu 132B/ 2005
Generated on 9/6/05
Dessert added 9/8/05
Revised 9/9/05

Dinner with Prince Charles

First Course: Please choose from the following:

___Pheasant Consomme with Dry Sherry
Apple Quennelles and Vegetable Brunoise
___Smoked Squab with Black Muscat Vinaigrette
Black Eye Pea Pilaf and Pancetta Bacon Crisps
___Grilled Quail with Figs and Prosciuto Ham
Peppercress and Walnuts

Main Course: Please choose from the following:

___Medallion of Buffalo Tenderloin with Roast Corn Sauce
Glazed Parsnips and Young Carrots
Wild Rice Pancakes
___Venison Loin with Roasted Pears and Chantrelles
Braised Spinach and Sweet Potato Polenta
___Tamarind Glazed Duck Breasts with Sweet Onion Relish
Red Cabbage Vinaigrette and Leg Confit

Salad Course: Please choose from the following:

___Painted Oak Leaf, Lolla Rosa, and Mache with Blackberry Dressing
Vermont Artisanal Cheddar Tart
___Tom Thumb Bibb Lettuces with Champagne Vinaigrette
Cucumber, Vine Ripened Tomatoes and Artichokes
___Crisp Mint Romaine Lettuce with Blood Orange Vinaigrette
Point Reyes Blue Cheese and Spiced Walnuts

Desserts: Please choose from the following:
___Autumn Chrysanthemum Petit Four Cake (platter)
Chartreuse Ice Cream and Red and Green Grape Sauce
___Warm Blueberry Financier (platter)
Lemon Verbena Ice Cream with Burnt Orange Sauce
___White Chocolate Espresso Mousse Demitasse (platter)
Cocoa Sorbet and Fresh Oranges with Almond Cookie "Spoons"

Dinner
Wednesday, November 2, 2005
State Floor
7:00 pm serving time
100 Guests

Menu 132C/ 2005
Generated on 9/6/05
Dessert added 9/8/05
Revised 9/16/05
Wines 10/05/05

Dinner with Prince Charles

Pheasant Consomme with Dry Sherry
Apple Quennelles and Vegetable Brunoise

Newton Chardonnay (year TBD)

Medallion of Buffalo Tenderloin with Roast Corn Sauce
Glazed Parsnips and Young Carrots
Wild Rice Pancakes

Peter Michael Pinot Noir "Le Moulin Rouge" 2003

Crisp Mint Romaine Lettuce with Blood Orange Vinaigrette
Point Reyes Blue Cheese and Spiced Walnuts

Autumn Chrysanthemum Petit Four Cake (platter)
Chartreuse Ice Cream
Red and Green Grape Sauce

Iron Horse "Wedding Cuvee" 2002

Dinner
Wednesday, November 2, 2005
State Floor
7:00 pm serving time
100 Guests

Menu 132D/ 2005
Generated on 9/6/05
Dessert added 9/8/05
Revised 10/20/05
Wines first added 10/03/05

Dinner with Prince Charles

please choose from the following:

___ Celery Broth with Crispy Rock Shrimp
Cinnamon Basil
or
___ Roasted Quince and Sweet Carrot Bisque

Newton Chardonnay "Unfiltered" 2002

Medallion of Buffalo Tenderloin with Roast Corn
Glazed Parsnips and Young Carrots
Wild Rice Pancakes

Peter Michael Pinot Noir "Le Moulin Rouge" 2002

Crisp Mint Romaine Lettuce with Blood Orange Vinaigrette
Vermont Camembert Cheese and Spiced Walnuts

Petit Four Cake (platter)
Chartreuse Ice Cream
Red and Green Grape Sauce

Iron Horse "Wedding Cuvee" 2002

*The White House serving staff gather
for a reading of the dinner menu with Chef
Comerford and pastry chef Thaddeus DuBois.*

Dinner
Wednesday, November 2, 2005
State Floor
7:00 pm serving time
100 Guests

Menu 132E/ 2005
Generated on 9/6/05
Dessert added 9/8/05
Revised 10/25/05
Wines first added 10/03/05

Dinner with Prince Charles

Celery Broth with Crispy Rock Shrimp
Cinnamon Basil

Newton Chardonnay "Unfiltered" 2002

Medallion of Buffalo Tenderloin with Roast Corn
Glazed Parsnips and Young Carrots
Wild Rice Pancakes

Peter Michael Pinot Noir "Le Moulin Rouge" 2002

Crisp Mint Romaine Lettuce with Blood Orange Vinaigrette
Vermont Camembert Cheese and Spiced Walnuts

Autumn Petit Four Cake (platter)
Chartreuse Ice Cream
Red and Green Grape Sauce

Iron Horse "Wedding Cuvee" 2002

TASTING DINNER REQUISITION
SUBMITTED

Qty	Unit	Item	Size	Requsition Date	Shopping List

Dairy Products

Qty	Unit	Item	Size	Requsition Date	Shopping List
1	Each	Cheese, Brie Camembert Vermont/2 wheels	Kilo	10/18/05	SL05-23808

Fresh Fruits

Qty	Unit	Item	Size	Requsition Date	Shopping List
12	Each	Organic, orange	Each	10/18/05	SL05-0238106
6	Each	Apple, Honey Krisp	Each	10/18/05	SL05-023810

Fresh Vegetables

Qty	Unit	Item	Size	Requsition Date	Shopping List
1	Each	Squash, Acorn	Each	10/18/05	SL05-023780
1	Each	Squash, Butternut	Each	10/18/05	SL05-023780
1	Lb	Squash, Kuri	Lb	10/18/05	SL05-023780
1	Lb	Squash, Zucchini	Lb	10/18/05	SL05-023780
1	Lb	Squash, Yellow	Lb	10/18/05	SL05-023780
20	Each	Corn by the Ear yellow or mixed	Each	10/18/05	SL05-023780
10	Lb	Parsnips	Lb	10/18/05	SL05-023780
1	Case	Carrot, Mixed Baby	Case	10/18/05	SL05-023780
2	Lb	Shallots	Lb	10/18/05	SL05-023780
1	Lb	Garlic	Lb	10/18/05	SL05-023780
4	Bunch	Leeks by the Bunch	Bunch	10/18/05	SL05-023780
1	Case	Leeks, Baby	Case	10/18/05	SL05-023780
2	Bunch	Chives by the Bunch	Bunch	10/18/05	SL05-023780
2	Bunch	Chervil by the Bunch	Bunch	10/18/05	SL05-023780
1	Bunch	Parsley, Italian	Bunch	10/18/05	SL05-023780
1	Lb	Brussel Sprouts baby green and red 4 1/2 pints	Lb	10/18/05	SL05-023780
1	Clam	Celery, Micro, Baby	Clam	10/18/05	SL05-023780
1	Each	Lettuce, Romaine mint romaine, 2 50 count pkg	Each	10/18/05	SL05-023780
1	Bunch	Basil by the Bunch 1 clam/basil sampler	Bunch	10/18/05	SL05-023780
1	Clam	Microgreens, Thanksgiving blend	8 oz Clam	10/18/05	SL05-023780
1	Case	Turnip, Baby Scarlet red	Case	10/18/05	SL05-023780

Meats/Seafood

Qty	Unit	Item	Size	Requsition Date	Shopping List
6	Lb	Pheasant whole	Lb	10/18/05	SL05-23767
2	Each	Buffalo tenderloin	Lb	10/18/05	SL05-23767

dinner guests, and service was at 7:30 p.m. The choice for the first course had yet to be made, and after service, the celery broth with crispy rock shrimp was the overwhelming choice. The buffalo tenderloin was crusted with four types of peppercorns—tellicherry, pink, green, and white—and three types of salt—fleur de sel, kosher, and English Maldon salt. The tenderloin was then seared in butter and continuously basted and scented with lemon thyme and garlic cloves until was roasted to a medium-rare stage and allowed to rest. A purveyor was able to find some chanterelle mushrooms, which are among Prince Charles's favorites. Browning them in butter with finely minced shallots and incorporating them with roasted creamed corn would complement the buffalo with an ample sweetness, texture, and depth. Wild rice pancakes were accented with sweated (cooked over low heat in a small amount of fat, softening without browning) mirepoix and a trio of peppers and served alongside the buffalo slices. The platter was then presented in a very traditional, yet contemporary style. I thought it would be appropriate to juxtapose some unusual Indian corn, multicolored husks, and chanterelles for a very artsy centerpiece. The vegetable platter was just a simple mélange of fall vegetables including parsnips and carrots, slightly glazed with Turbinado sugar and Vermont butter. The salad course was very straightforward.

When the dessert was served, it was almost demure. The centerpiece was made out of pulled sugar, mimicking the opulent flowers on the table. The petit four cakes, portioned individually, looked almost like miniature wedding cakes. They were garnished with a very intricate and minuscule green grape bunch fashioned out of marzipan. The chartreuse ice cream was decadent yet light enough for indulgence. A bowl of warm red and green grape sauce was served alongside, and the tartness of the sauce toned down the sweetness that was prevalent in the petit four cakes.

When the tasting was over, Mrs. Bush requested that the pastry chef, Thaddeus DuBois and myself be present. An integral aspect of being a chef is listening intently and

Opposite: Chef Comerford's requisition shows the quantities of food ordered to prepare the dinner.

Chef Comerford explains how to assemble the slow poached lobster with vanilla cream, peppercress, and polenta crisp.

WHITE HOUSE PHOTO

understanding that all comments and critiques are for the best. The first lady gave a very reassuring smile. The best part about executing a tasting menu is that it is a very good guideline for what is to come. It's just a matter of multiplying the workload, preparation time, and the dish-up time. This tasting gives the chef the chance to think through strategies and plan logistics. It also allows ample time for the purveyors to search for the best produce, meats, seafood, and specialty products.

Two days prior to the dinner, the kitchen starts abuzz with the basic *mise en place* that we will be using for the event. Chicken stock, about one hundred pounds worth of chicken carcasses, is a very dominant aroma. The oven is full of veal bones and tenderloin trims that will be used for the demi-glace. Tommy Kurpradit, one of my assistant chefs, is carefully filleting the tenderloins so that they can be tied prior to roasting.

The two "Suzie's" in the pastry shop, Suzie Morrison

Opposite: The dish-up of the vegetable platters and first course, November 2, 2005.

Right: Chef Comerford photographs the centerpieces.

Below: Roasted Vidalia onion stuffed with glazed fall vegetables.

The White House culinary staff posed in the Family Dining Room beneath the portrait of First Lady Edith Roosevelt prior to the event. From left to right: Patrice Olivon, Eileen Cortese, Thaddeus DuBois, John Revelle, Andrew Rucker, Guillermo Fernando, Susan Morrison, Chris Philipps, Susan Limb, Tommy Kupradit, Chef Cris Comerford, Adam Collick, Denzil Benjamin, Paula Patton-Moutsos, Lance Mion, Kathleen Willis, and John Moeller.

and Susan Limb, are constantly pacing in and out of the kitchen to retrieve their own equipment and retreat back to their mezzanine shop to finish the intricate pieces for their platters. Tuesday is when most of the fresh produce is shipped overnight, and now kitchen space becomes prime. Space in the White House kitchen is extremely limited. We have at least six part-time cooks in the main kitchen and the pastry shop. The key word for the day is "organization." Everything goes to a certain space and everything is accounted for—amounts of ingredients and equipment. This "prep" day will come to a halt only when everything on the work list is checked and rechecked. The goal is to prepare up to the point of cooking and dishing-up the day of the dinner.

Wednesday, November 2, 2005: this date has been specially marked on the calendar for more than two months. All the planning and execution are now coming to fruition. I thank God for mentors such as Chef Roland Mesnier, who had passed on a lot of his wisdom to me. "Your work will speak volumes about you," he said. With this statement resonating in my head all day, the two months of preparation is now coming to its culmination.

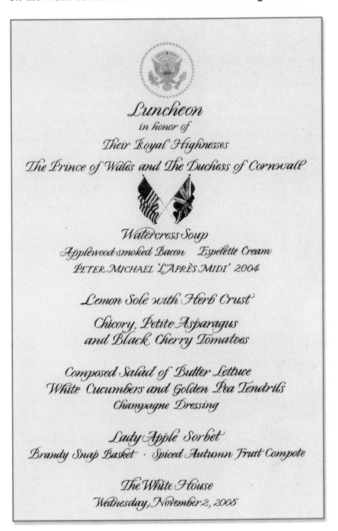

Luncheon
in honor of
Their Royal Highnesses
The Prince of Wales and The Duchess of Cornwall

Watercress Soup
Applewood-smoked Bacon · Espelette Cream
PETER MICHAEL 'L'APRÈS MIDI' 2004

Lemon Sole with Herb Crust
Chicory, Petite Asparagus
and Black Cherry Tomatoes

Composed Salad of Butter Lettuce
White Cucumbers and Golden Pea Tendrils
Champagne Dressing

Lady Apple Sorbet
Brandy Snap Basket · Spiced Autumn Fruit Compote

The White House
Wednesday, November 2, 2005

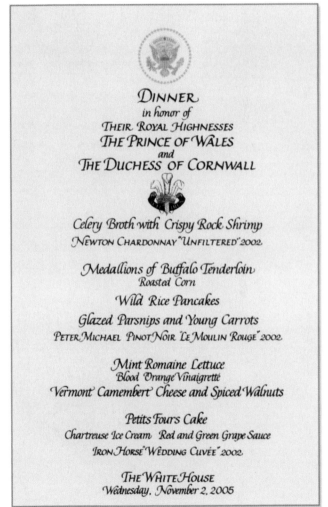

DINNER
in honor of
THEIR ROYAL HIGHNESSES
THE PRINCE OF WALES
and
THE DUCHESS OF CORNWALL

Celery Broth with Crispy Rock Shrimp
NEWTON CHARDONNAY "UNFILTERED" 2002

Medallions of Buffalo Tenderloin
Roasted Corn
Wild Rice Pancakes
Glazed Parsnips and Young Carrots
PETER MICHAEL PINOT NOIR 'LE MOULIN ROUGE' 2002

Mint Romaine Lettuce
Blood Orange Vinaigrette
Vermont Camembert Cheese and Spiced Walnuts

Petits Fours Cake
Chartreuse Ice Cream · Red and Green Grape Sauce
IRON HORSE 'WEDDING CUVÉE' 2002

THE WHITE HOUSE
Wednesday, November 2, 2005

Opposite: President and Mrs. George W. Bush welcome Britain's Prince Charles and Camilla, Duchess of Cornwall, on the North Portico of the White House, November 2005.

Above: The final luncheon and dinner menus.

White House Wines

DANIEL SHANKS

*S*erving wine at table has been a custom continually at the Executive Residence from 1800—with the exception of an abstemious President Rutherford B. Hayes from 1877 to 1881. Early presidents wrote of the role wine played in social entertaining at the White House, telling us that social menus focused on European wines and recognizing that the American wine industry was nascent. Menus and letters are replete with mentions of Claret, Sauterne, Port, Madeira, Tokay, and Champagne—though two hundred years ago the term Champagne referred to a desired still white wine, not the naturally carbonated beverage of today. Transporting and storing wine for the White House table in 1800 formed significant obstacles. Wine frequently spoiled over the long journey by sea from Europe. Those with higher alcohols and residual sugars handled the abuse with more grace and stamina than would the more ethereal, dry-finished still wines we currently enjoy at the table. White House menus today feature wines closer at hand, all of them American and equal to any in the world.

The president's place is set for a dinner in honor of the National Medal of Arts and the Charles Frankel Prize Awards, 1993. The use of wines at official dinners is a long White House tradition, borrowed from the customs of the diplomatic community.

Some of the influences that have shaped White House wine protocol are times of service, numbers of guests, and array of wines served. Early nineteenth-century dinner schedules were dictated by the light of the day, often beginning in late afternoon to take advantage of the light of the setting sun and continuing only into early evening. Today the time chosen reflects a combination of presidential scheduling and current social norms, not setting suns. Early dinners would seat as few as ten guests, rarely more than forty. Today's guest lists are limited only by room size and the historical confines of the White House. In recent years the temporary construction of large tented pavilions and use of the Rose Garden and the East Garden adjacent to the residence have been ways of accommodating larger numbers as well as varying the venues for entertaining. The number of wines poured also mirrors the times. When activities were fewer and the streets of Washington empty at night, a menu could offer a choice of eight to twelve wines at a single meal. Cider and lager were common for cocktails, and after dinner the male guests adjourned for cheese, port, and cigars while the ladies enjoyed sherry with their conversation separately, in the other parlors. Today tight schedules and the increased pace of meal service allow a standard of three wines at the most formal of events and frequently just a single wine served at what would be considered a "working meal."

In the modern White House, many factors dictate the structure of an event. One of the most significant is the

time allocated. Schedules are very stringently maintained at the White House. It is not uncommon for a formal meal of four courses, three wines, and toasts to be allocated approximately an hour from beginning to end, rather than President Thomas Jefferson's three to four hours. What might be a harried pace seems quite otherwise, however, for order, formality, and graciousness of service help make the pace seem unhurried.

Dinner service begins after the guests are seated, with the entry of the butlers, two to a table. Dinner concludes with service of the dessert course, for which a dessert wine or sparkling wine is poured. The president then invites the company to join him in the East Room for entertainment, which will last from fifteen to twenty-five minutes. Dancing and champagne in the foyer begin, and the visiting dignitaries take their leave.

For this most formal of White House events, the entire scheduled duration is often no more than three and a half hours. Social dinners, where the meal is the primary focus of the evening, may be more leisurely and smaller; intimate dinners take their cue from the first family as the dinner unfolds. Even so, the time is strictly managed. A rigid clock is a necessity at the President's House.

How does a wine steward adapt his selections to these time limitations in a manner that bodes well for both the wine and the evening? As industry professionals, most of us have been trained in fine restaurants, where wine lists are large and designed to focus on small groups of diners in a relaxed, unhurried environment. The wines that are offered are usually aged to produce a "flavor profile" to fit the moment. We have all had a perfectly aged bottle of a great Cabernet or Pinot Noir and enjoyed the nuances as if they were the reason for getting together that night.

Take that thought and transport yourself to the State

Opposite: President Theodore Roosevelt toasts guest of honor Prince Henry of Prussia, brother of Kaiser Wilhelm II, at a White House dinner held in the East Room, 1901.

Above: President Gerald Ford toasts Great Britain's Queen Elizabeth II during the dinner at the White House in 1976 celebrating the two-hundredth year of American independence.

Dining Room, where you see around you 130 fellow guests, seated at round tables laden with elegant and vibrant centerpieces, formal napery, or linens, three foot tall candlesticks, and a table full silver and glassware, all choreographed to perfect visual harmony. This setting is the stage on which the wine steward plays in his selections. What a steward wishes for are wines of youth and vigor that carry a strong impression of their presence, yet balance and purity on the palate. Aromatic wines, such as Pinot Noir, Syrah, Zinfandel, Viognier, Riesling, and Pinot Gris lend an advantage by filling the space above the glass with a "wine presence," not just in the glass. These criteria help the wine maintain an identity at the table, the first focus of a good steward. The first course wine, almost always a white wine, has to withstand the vagaries of schedules, because it is poured before the guests enter the Dining Room. At the White House we strive to have staff in the Dining Room only to exchange plates and service the table. Otherwise, with the exception of a butler present to attend each of the head tables, no other staff members are in the room.

The white wine needs to be a wine of balance that will still give good expression as awaits the guests. The

WHITE HOUSE HISTORICAL ASSOCIATION

red wine, or main course wine, looks to the entrée for definition. Heavier, more richly flavored dishes call for Cabernet or Cabernet blends, or perhaps and occasional Cabernet Franc or Syrah. The wine steward determines whether the wine will benefit from airing to enhance its flavor profile. With our modern winemaking techniques, decanting is rarely demanded because of sediment in the bottle. We decant to give the wine its best expression. Recently we have dared to take liberties with traditional service, which saw the red wine poured in conjunction with the main course, by allowing the butlers to pour the wine toward the end of the first course to give guests a moment to enjoy the wine on its own during the changing of the courses. The meal concludes with the service of either a dessert wine or a sparkling wine, again a decision reflecting the purpose of the event, the dessert chosen, the time of year, and whether entertainment follows, as it usually does for a State

Dinner, thus giving another opportunity to offer sparkling wine to accompany the entertainment and dancing. All these elements create good theater but also a very unique stage upon which the wine steward plies his craft.

When selecting the right wine for an event the steward also looks to the history of the moment and the intent of the event. What have we served to the guests at past meals? Just as the chef researches past menus, the wine steward likewise recognizes history and continuity and relishes playing to it. If the event is a visit from the prime minister of Great Britain and we previously had served a Peter Michael wine from the world-quality California winery dreamed into existence by Englishman Sir Peter Michael, then the continuity expressed in pouring another Peter Michael wine can symbolize the continuity of the history of relations between the two countries. The wine steward will use the vast resources of the American wine industry to draw such parallels.

Consider yourself the wine steward of the White House with an impending visit by the president of France. During his last visit to the White House you had featured winemakers from France that had established wineries of high quality in this country. They wanted their wineries to be a synthesis of New World fruits and the Old World techniques and they had used successfully in their home country. Thus that particular dinner you offer Chateau Woltner Chardonnay from Napa Valley, Domaine Drouhin Pinot Noir from Oregon, and Roederer sparkling wine from Mendocino, California. It was a great success but, alas, too recent to replicate. Taking another tack, you might decide to feature French traditional grape varietals that have recently made a strong appearance in the vineyards of America, again putting the spotlight on the continuing ties between the nations. Finally you select a newly released experimental Viognier from Beringer Vineyards and the Zaca Mesa Syrah from the central coast of California, again creating the supporting role wine can play for our country. Your pairings were very well received!

Religion can also play a part in the wine decisions and menu choices in the Executive Residence. We are a sectarian government, created so that religion is a private, not a state matter. But throughout the world, many nations do choose a religion as the basic tenet of their culture. Fellow nations must respect that choice, especially in the cultivation of cordial relations. A visit by the prime minister of Israel or, on another occasion, the dinner in celebration of the opening of the Anne Frank Exhibit at the United States Holocaust Memorial Museum called for selecting appropriately sanctified kosher wines, of which we have several excellent producers nationally. When we host a country where Islam is the official religion of the country we omit wine service as a sign of respect and understanding (juice is served instead). In entertaining other countries with

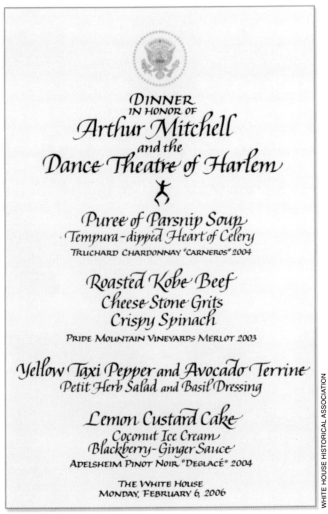

DINNER
IN HONOR OF
Arthur Mitchell
and the
Dance Theatre of Harlem

Puree of Parsnip Soup
Tempura-dipped Heart of Celery
TRUCHARD CHARDONNAY "CARNEROS" 2004

Roasted Kobe Beef
Cheese Stone Grits
Crispy Spinach
PRIDE MOUNTAIN VINEYARDS MERLOT 2003

Yellow Taxi Pepper and Avocado Terrine
Petit Herb Salad and Basil Dressing

Lemon Custard Cake
Coconut Ice Cream
Blackberry-Ginger Sauce
ADELSHEIM PINOT NOIR "DEGLACÉ" 2004

THE WHITE HOUSE
MONDAY, FEBRUARY 6, 2006

The menu for a dinner honoring the visionary classical dancer Arthur Mitchell in February 2006 included three wines: a Chardonnay, a Merlot, and a Pinot Noir.

Dinner
Honoring Her Excellency
The President of Ireland
and Mr. Nicholas Robinson

Seared Salmon & Yukon Gold Potatoes
Marinated Leeks and Savoy
Dill, Mustard, and Scallion Sauces

Grilled Rack of Lamb with Vidalia Onions
Butternut and Ginger Flan
Spring Vegetables
Spiced Peach and Lamb Reductions

Field Greens, Endive & Roasted Tomatoes
Layered Goat's Cheese and Portabello
Shallot Balsamic Dressing

Amaretto Castle
Fresh Bing Cherries
Murphy Goode "Sonoma" Chardonnay 1995
Mahoney Estate "Carneros" Pinot Noir 1994
Flynn Vineyards "Oregon" Brut 1988

The White House
Thursday, June 13, 1996

The menu for a dinner honoring the president of Ireland in 1996 included a Chardonnay, a Pinot Noir, and a Brut.

sizable Muslim populations but sectarian governments, we inquire beforehand about the wishes of the visiting head of state and, if possible, respect those choices.

The last aspect of wine selection in the White House is recognition of the abundance of viticultural areas where great wine is produced in our country. Every state in the nation has a bonded winery, including Alaska and Maine, and Hawaii. We have witnessed almost universal interest in regional cuisines, each telling the story of their area in the flavors and preparations of food. The same is true for wine. So many areas, as of yet unknown, have a winemaker who has selected the right site and chosen the right varietal and is producing truly great wine that speaks of a region and of its people. We at the White House take great pleasure in matching the occasion, the guests, the menu, and the wines.

The White House holds a wide range of events over the course of the year, from State Dinners to the relaxed

congressional picnic on the south grounds. Wines purchased during the year reflect that diversity, from the white wine selected to be served at the bars during large receptions, where fresh forward fruit is appreciated, to older, more mature wines to accompany intimate dinners, wines frequently cajoled from the cellars of winery owners themselves. Often the location of the event, whether a room, garden, or constructed pavilion, calls for the style of wine that best fits that place. The larger the environment, the more robust the wine's presence must appear. A Syrah in the East Room might be a better selection than a Pinot Noir, which would better grace the Red Room, and Zinfandel, with its higher alcohols and aromatics, might do justice best for a four-hundred guest sit-down dinner on the south grounds. These variations call for perception on the wine steward's part but also add a playful aspect to the task of wine buying.

What does the wine steward look for in a wine? First is balance–a harmony of all the parts of the wine. Alcohol must be in proportion to the weight of the wine. Fruit flavors should be accompanied by length on the palate and equally impressive aromatics. Acids need

The wine is poured in the State Dining Room in preparation for an event.

to keep the wine fresh and alive but not announce themselves along the way. "Closed wines" that need time to evolve in the glass have no chance of showing their worth with the time limitations set by schedules, yet sometimes possess a magic that should not be missed. The wine steward will use his training and past knowledge of similar wines enjoyed during his career to determine if decanting and aerating the wine will bring out this magic and to determine how far ahead the decanting should occur and how vigorous it should be. Of equal importance is the ongoing dialogue between the steward and the kitchen staff. Great food can be made greater by the wines that support it, and great wine can only experience its full potential alongside great food. Both interplay in the course of the dinner. Elegance in a wine will melt away in the company of spicy foods, cream-based sauces sensually break up when assaulted by bracing acidity, and residual sugar will grow ponderous with delicate dishes. A large part of the enjoyment of the position of wine purchaser is being part of the team that creates the moment, long remembered by the guests at the president's table.

Financial expenditures are a part of any reasonable purchaser's daily life, and it is equally important with wine. We at the White House are given a public trust that we will be prudent in executing our duties. Many of us in the profession learned long ago that in wine high prices do not guarantee high enjoyment. For that reason, some "trophy wines" may never appear on the president's table. One will argue that some of the penultimate wine experiences to be savored have been with truly expensive wines, but most of us can also recall countless more surprises with more reasonably priced selections. It always must be remembered that the wine must fit the moment. One reason you see many of these famous wines on restaurant wine lists is the return on investment they provide the restaurant from their perceived scarcity. It is not always because they provide the best company for the menu.

Service is the hallmark of White House hospitality. This is true of the service of wine. The glassware must be appropriate to the beverage, free from prints and dust, at the proper temperature, and presented with grace. Wines need correct storage, handling, opening, and presentation. Wine butlers are taught to hold the bottle with the front label showing to the guests. For many of our guests, the name of the wine as printed on the menu may not be familiar, but when they have had a chance to see the label as it is poured, they develop an association with the wine that lasts. On more than a few occasions a local wine shop will call to tell us about customers who asked to purchase a specific bottle of wine they liked at a White House event, where they took note of the name on the label.

Temperature is a very important consideration when serving wine. White wine should be quite cool, but not cold, and with the wide range of white wine varietals and styles of winemaking available, from Chardonnay to Riesling to Pinot Gris, temperature becomes a personal decision. However, remember that the old practice of chilling white wines to near slush grew from drinking poorly made wines. They were wines that had little in the way of flavor and were unbalanced with acidity. Chilling mitigated the flaws and left the wine approaching the territory of ice water. Red wines need to be slightly cool to the palate. With the tremendous fruit and varietal purity of today's wines, one of the most damaging mistakes to make is to serve a red wine too warm. "Room temperature" is a misnomer coined when homes were less well insulated and cooler. We can all remember sitting in a fine dining room, ordering a long anticipated wine, and having it arrive the temperature of bath water due to bad storage conditions. The wine presented muddled flat flavors, astringent with acid and devoid of life. We want the wine to speak to us of fresh fruit and crushed berry, not leaf and herb mulch.

At one time or another all of us have had to select wine for our own special occasion. It gives cause for thought. To the wine steward at the White House that challenge is multiplied by about a thousand, when the most important dinner in the world is to receive its crowning touch.

Home Cooking in the White House

BARBARA HABER

$\mathcal{A}$mericans want and expect their presidents to live in the formal and decorous style suitable to heads of state, but we also want them to be like us. We want to know all about White House ceremonial meals, but we also want to know what our national leaders eat for breakfast, how they like their steaks, if they eat all their vegetables, and what flavor ice cream they prefer. Bill Clinton's frequenting of fast food restaurants endeared him to countless Americans, a connection they could not get from descriptions of his State Dinners. His predecessors, Ronald Reagan and George H. W. Bush displayed their common touch by liking jelly beans and hating broccoli, respectively. And earlier, descriptions of Franklin D. Roosevelt's angry objections to dishes on White House menus—what Mrs. Roosevelt termed his "tizzy-wizzies"—humanize him, for Henrietta Nesbitt was certain that his wife understood them to be displacements for his worries about the war in Europe.

Opposite: First Lady Mamie Eisenhower inspects the stock of canned goods in the White House pantry, 1958.

Above right: President William Clinton exits a McDonald's Restaurant, 2000. Below right: A White House cabinet meeting in 1981, President Ronald Reagan reaches for his jelly beans.

REUTERS / CORBIS

RONALD REAGAN LIBRARY

No American president took a greater interest in food and its preparation than Thomas Jefferson, the second of our leaders to occupy the White House. In addition to his notebooks on gardening and farming, he left behind a manuscript book of recipes compiled at home and abroad that was passed on to generations of his family and eventually published.[1] Letters he wrote to close friends and colleagues often included observations about food mixed in with political commentary. These writings reveal eating preferences that were unusual, even peculiar, for an American statesman in that time.

In the years that he was minister to France, Jefferson recorded recipes he planned to incorporate into meals back home, eventually realizing this ambition by hiring those who could provide French cooking to work in his White House kitchen. Patrick Henry said of Jefferson that he "came home from France so Frenchified that he abjured his native victuals."[2] But Jefferson belied the accusation by maintaining his fondness for such native products as sweet potatoes, corn, black-eyed peas, turnip greens, and shad, which he regularly incorporated into meals served at the White House. So fond was he of locally grown vegetables that he kept a schedule of when each appeared in local Washington markets so that he could fulfill his desire for the tastes of the season. This preference gave rise to the false notion that Jefferson was a vegetarian. In fact, even by our standards, he was a nutritionally sensible eater and preferred small portions of meat relative to vegetables at a time when most Americans consumed large quantities of meat at every meal. He imported exotic vanilla and the more humble macaroni for the enjoyment of his countrymen, and he unsuccessfully tried to grow olive trees in Virginia, having developed a taste for olive oil when he was abroad, another example of his remarkable aptitude for tasty and healthy foods.[3]

Invitations to dine with Jefferson were prized. Most nights he served up to fourteen guests informally without the pomp usually associated with a head of state, for Jefferson philosophically abhorred displays of ceremony. Because he was a widower, without a wife to serve as hostess—and also because his entertaining was

President Thomas Jefferson's handwritten recipe for ice cream, one of his favorite desserts.

usually political—his dinners tended to be male affairs. He was likely to include anyone who might pique his many interests as well as the usual political cronies. To secure privacy, he initiated fashionable European practice by eliminating the presence of servants with dining room contraptions the diners could operate themselves.

His good friend, Margaret Bayard Smith, author-wife of the pro-Jefferson editor of the *Washington Intelligencier,* described an ingenious turntable Jefferson introduced that functioned somewhat like a dumbwaiter: "There was in his dining room an invention for introducing and removing the dinner without the opening and shutting of doors. A set of circular shelves were so contrived in the wall, that on touching a spring they turned into the room loaded with the dishes placed on them by the servants without the wall, and by the same process the removed dishes were conveyed out of the room."[4] What was new to her was fairly common in fashionable Paris and London.

A French cook, Honoré Julien, prepared the cuisine of his country along with the native Virginia dishes Jefferson favored so that a *pot-au-feu* might follow okra or catfish soup and the meal topped off with either a *gateau de pomme de terre* or a huckleberry pudding.[5] Whatever the menu, guests were served excellent and abundant wines that complemented the dinners.

Though she often served as a hostess for Thomas Jefferson when James Madison was secretary of state, Dolley Madison's own dinner table under her husband's presidency was a sign of her warm hospitality. She served French-inspired dishes as well as native fare and, prompted by her reputed sweet tooth, covered her buffet tables with an assortment of ice creams, macaroons, preserves, cakes, nuts, and fruit. One of her bountiful meals was criticized when Mrs. Anthony Merry, the priggish wife of the British minister, said that the dinner she had attended at the Madisons was "more like a harvest home supper than the entertainment of a Secretary of State." To this sort of criticism Mrs. Madison replied: "The profusion of my table so repugnant to foreign customs arises from the happy circumstance of abundance and prosperity in our country."[6]

With James Madison's presidency, Dolley Madison was beloved in an otherwise dull capital for her Wednesday evening receptions soon dubbed "Mrs. Madison's levees," to note their non-Republican royal tone. But her White House festivities ended abruptly in 1814 during the War of 1812 when the British marched on Washington. The usual dinner for forty was left untouched as Mrs. Madison, assisted by her able and loyal steward, Jean-Pierre Sioussat, hurriedly packed up papers and valuables before fleeing Washington. The British arrived shortly thereafter and burned the mansion, but not before taking advantage of Dolley Madison's unintended hospitality. While the sailors prepared the house to burn, the officers consumed the abandoned meal!

Sioussat's tenure as a steward for the Madisons started a long line of individuals who have served the White House in that role from that time to the present. Responsible for keeping the quality of dining high as well as culinary expertise in the kitchen, this functionary also supervises the maintenance of the building, the care of its contents, and management of the domestic staff that keeps the White House going. In the 1850s, the steward gained the name usher. In earlier times it was chief doorkeeper or steward; the official reports directly to the president and his wife and is indispensable to the smooth running of the establishment.

Irwin "Ike" Hoover, a legendary usher who served the White House from 1891 until his death in 1933, said that in consultation with the president and his wife chief ushers made plans for every sort of entertainment and had to be physically present sometimes sixteen- to eighteen-hours running to see that the plans were carried out. They are always on call.

Hoover's devotion to the White House was clear from the start: on his first tour of the basement, he noted that the floor was covered with slimy brick and that everything was black and dirty, yet he was moved when he came across the remains of the old kitchen, observing:

> the old open fireplaces once used for broiling the chickens and baking the hoecakes for the early Fathers of our country, the old cranes and spits still in place. Out of the door to the rear there yet remained the old wine-vault, the meathouse, and the smokehouse . . . you could still almost smell the wine odors and the aroma from the hams and bacon that must have been so deliciously and painstakingly prepared here.[7]

Hoover found poetry in what another might have found offensive, revealing his appreciation for the history and spirit of the old mansion and for the meals that relic of a kitchen had obviously turned out.

In addition to the more typical salaried kitchen staff, many early meals had been cooked by slaves brought to the White House by antebellum southern presidents. Expert slaves likewise may have been employed in many other early administrations as cooks. The remnants of the kitchen Ike Hoover describes remind one of similar descriptions of plantation kitchens. In *The Virginia Housewife,* published in 1824, Mary Randolph—sister-in-law of Jefferson's daughter Martha—gives a sense of the work involved in preparing meals in such facilities. Though she wrote the book to inform homemakers of her time, the author makes it fairly clear that the lady was not doing all the work herself, and her directions include sensible tips for managing kitchen servants. She advises the housewife to pay close attention to the foodstuffs and serving pieces in her possession, for "we have no right to expect slaves or hired servants to be more attentive to our interest than we ourselves are."[8] The White House being in a sense a public house, this domestic responsibility fell to the chief usher. In 1867 he was bonded.

Mrs. Randolph's recipes and her household tips further shed light on the White House of her day, where animals were also slaughtered and often cured right on the spot, and kitchen gardens grew where the West Wing now stands. Her lengthy recipe for curing bacon is eye-opening, for it begins with fattening the live pigs that, she advises, "should be fed with corn, six weeks at least, before they are killed." She goes on to describe butchering the carcass, how to handle the hams and other choice cuts, and ends with instructions for dealing with the lesser parts: "You should cut off the feet just above the knee joint; take off the ears and nose, and lay them in a large tub of cold water for souse."[9] While these pickled bits of the animal were often what the servants received as rewards, they were popular foods with all classes as well. No part of an animal was discarded and any part might appear on the dinner table in America and other countries.

Intelligent and informed about cooking and food, Mary Randolph dispels old wives' tales, telling her readers that "ancient prejudice has established a notion that meat killed in the decrease of the moon will draw up when cooked. The true cause of this shrinking may be found in the old age of the animal, or in its diseased state, at the time of killing."[10] Some of her recipes are surprisingly modern: string beans cooked in the French manner by boiling them in a big pot of water until just tender; delicate puff pastry; and foreign dishes such as polenta, vermicelli, and macaroni, that favorite of Thomas Jefferson.

Mary Randolph may have owned a kitchen range, an appliance that was replacing open hearth cooking in America in the nineteenth century. Characteristically ahead of his time, Thomas Jefferson had an iron range, thought to be imported from England, installed in one of the two fireplaces in the White House kitchen, then located directly below the Entrance Hall.[11] That kitchen, like everything else in the White House, had to be rebuilt after the fire of 1814, a task completed by 1817 when President James Monroe was in residence. The Jefferson range was fished out of the ashes by Souissat and reused. Repairs, expansions, and accommodations to advancing technology took place over the years, and by the time William Howard Taft took office in 1909, the White House had an additional smaller kitchen for everyday "family" cooking. Expansion in Taft's time also brought to the kitchen glass-front cabinets, four gas ovens, and two hotel-size gas ranges, the largest, a 12 foot French Coal Range that was purchased by Taft in 1912.[12] It was a kitchen well-proportioned to this giant of a presidential gourmand.

Renovations of the basement where the kitchens were located went on throughout the 1930s. When Franklin D. Roosevelt indicated that new electric ranges would be enough of an improvement, Lorenzo Winslow, the architect involved in the project, informed him "that the whole Kitchen should be done over in order to clean out the vermin, filth and grease of more than 50 years." A follow-up tour of the kitchen convinced FDR that both the small and large kitchens needed remodeling.[13] By this time, home efficiency experts like Christine Frederick were doing time-motion studies and persuading American consumers to modernize their kitchens. (The term "modern," much in use in the 1930s, evoked sleek surfaces and electrical appliances.) The uncluttered new White House kitchen with its fresh paint and hotel-size electric ranges and ovens was right in vogue, and the tradition continues today.

The style in which the presidents entertained is always telling. Early day levees were presentations where the public had the opportunity to see the nation's

The Virginia Housewife *collected many recipes popular in the mid-nineteenth century, including Turtle Soup.*

FOR THE [TURTLE] SOUP.

At an early hour in the morning, put on eight pounds of coarse beef, some bacon, onions, sweet herbs, pepper and salt. Make a rich soup, strain it and thicken with a bit of butter, and brown flour; add to it the water left from boiling the bottom shell; season it very high with wine, catsup, spice and cayenne; put in the flesh you reserved, and if that is not enough, add the nicest parts of a well boiled calf's head; but do not use the eyes or tongue; let it boil till tender, and serve it up with fried forcemeat balls in it.

If you have curry powder, (see receipt for it,) it will give a higher flavour to both soup and turtle, than spice. Should you not want soup, the remaining flesh may be fried, and served with a rich gravy.

TO MAKE POLENTA.

Put a large spoonful of butter in a quart of water, wet your corn meal with cold water in a bowl, add some salt, and make it quite smooth, then put it in the buttered water when it is hot, let it boil, stirring it continually till done; as soon as you can handle it, make it into a ball, and let it stand till quite cold--then cut it in thin slices, lay them in the bottom of a deep dish so as to cover it, put on it slices of cheese, and on that a few bits of butter; then mush, cheese and butter, until the dish is full; put on the top thin slices of cheese and butter, put the dish in a quick oven; twenty or thirty minutes will bake it.

MACARONI.

Boil as much macaroni as will fill your dish, in milk and water, till quite tender; drain it on a sieve sprinkle a little salt over it, put a layer in your dish then cheese and butter as in the polenta, and bake it in the same manner.

leader in person. At the thickly crowded events, they were seldom able to do more. The custom of holding public receptions on New Year's Day and the Fourth of July—and for a span of two decades January 8—proved a wearisome convention whose handshaking and greetings exhausted chief executives, but it lasted for 132 years. Other official entertaining evolved, soon creating a social season structured around White House events starting from early in December until the last in May. Until Theodore Roosevelt's administration, State Dinners were held only for the Supreme Court, members of the cabinet, and diplomats. To smooth political feathers, Roosevelt added a Speaker's Dinner and a dinner for the vice-president.[14] Today State Dinners are scheduled from time to time, mainly to honor important visitors from abroad.

The reception of the king and queen of England at the Franklin D. Roosevelt White House in 1939 was the most famous event of an international character up to then, for no reigning British monarch previously had touched American shores. Much was made at the time of the royal couple being served hot dogs at the White House. News of this menu was carefully tailored to reach the front page of the *New York Times* and many other papers. In fact, the hot dogs were served at Hyde Park, well after a properly formal White House State Dinner had taken place at the White House the night before.

Other fare for the royal couple at Hyde Park included Virginia ham, smoked turkey, cranberry jelly, green salad from the Hyde Park garden, and strawberry shortcake.[15] Another anecdote about this occasion has come down to us from Eleanor Roosevelt. Awaiting the arrival of the king and queen, the president, who enjoyed sparring with his proper mother, told her that he was going to offer cocktails to the royal couple when they arrived. Firmly believing this a misstep, his mother insisted that, since they were English, they would prefer tea. When they arrived, the president said, "My mother thinks you would rather have a cup of tea after your tiring trip, but

A Washington Post *article reporting on the royal visit to the United States included this photograph. From left to right: First Lady Eleanor Roosevelt, King George, Sara Delano Roosevelt (the president's mother), Queen Elizabeth, and President Franklin D. Roosevelt.*

I wonder if you'd like a cocktail." With a smile, the king replied, "My mother would say exactly the same thing. I'd frankly prefer a cocktail."[16]

Royalty and heads of state have continued to be entertained by presidents, but usually within the confines of the White House State Dining Room. Jacqueline Kennedy broke with this tradition by holding an alfresco State Dinner and concert on the grounds of Mount Vernon in honor of the president of Pakistan. Guests arrived by yacht up the Potomac and were served a meal prepared by René Verdon, President Kennedy's French chef: an avocado and crabmeat cocktail for an appetizer; *poulet chasseur* with molded rice for an entrée, and raspberries and whipped cream for dessert. This menu, simple yet elegant, reflected the sophisticated style Mrs. Kennedy cultivated at the White House.[17] She loosened up State Dinners by

retiring the traditional horseshoe-shaped table in favor of round tables that seated just eight or ten, an off-and-on tradition begun by Theodore Roosevelt in 1902. She preferred relaxed flower arrangements reminiscent of great Flemish still lifes over the usual formal ones that she said reminded her of funeral parlors.

Of the private events held in the White House, weddings have garnered the most attention from the public and the press. Several daughters of presidents have been married in formal ceremonies there, including Nellie Grant, Alice Roosevelt, Lynda Bird Johnson, and Tricia Nixon; but President Grover Cleveland's wedding in 1886 attracted the most attention of all. A forty-nine-year-old bachelor at the time, the president had been rumored to be romantically involved with the widow of his late law partner when in fact he had been courting her twenty-two-year-old-daughter. Though their wedding was intimate, limited only to relatives, close friends, and cabinet officers and their wives, it had glamour. The Blue Room was lushly decorated with tropical plants and flowers, and John Philip Sousa conducted the Marine Band's rendition of Felix Mendelssohn's "Wedding March." Washington's top caterers prepared a buffet of terrapin, breast of spring chicken, cold meats, salads, *paté de foie gras,* and molds of ice cream, bonbons, and fruit, and of course, the wedding cake.[18]

One pauses over mention of stewed terrapin, a dish that has all but disappeared from the American table but knew great popularity in the capital throughout the nineteenth century. It was a perennial favorite at the White House, together with turtle soup. A member of the reptile family and not some form of seafood, as some would have it, terrapin required the hands of a brave and skillful cook, judging from a 1902 cookbook written for servants who, after killing the turtles by beheading with a meat cleaver, are instructed to "select live female terrapins, cover them with boiling water, and cook for ten minutes. Remove from the fire, and when sufficiently cooked, scrape the skin and pull out the toe nails."[19] Those brave enough to read further learn that the next steps involve breaking open the shell and removing the meat, eggs, and liver without breaking the gall sac, only after which is the dish ready to be stewed. Recipes call for egg yolks, butter, and cream and sometimes sherry, which perk up what has been described as a bland and stringy meat. Terrapin was an acquired taste much enjoyed by Grover Cleveland and Franklin Roosevelt and featured on menus at private men's clubs around the country. Few these days would know how to cook terrapin.

Keeping food costs down was a major responsibility in management of the White House, and one of great interest to presidents who paid family food bills from their own pockets. Elizabeth Jaffray, employed by the Tafts in 1909, was the first housekeeper given that title, putting her in charge of cleaning, mending, and general care of the rooms as well as maids and butlers; and food matters. The use of caterers was abolished. A genteel widow who had fallen on hard times, the Canadian Mrs. Jaffray earned her living by supervising household staffs in respectable homes and was delighted when her agency sent her to Mrs. Taft. A methodical woman, Mrs. Jaffray calculated that between the president's family and the servants, she was responsible each month for 2,610 meals that added up to $868.93.[20] Making great savings, she had the food for receptions prepared by the three cooks employed there under her direction. Charles Dumonet, a fashionable Washington caterer, told her that before she came he had been receiving as much as $20,000 a year for White House events. Like other employees of the rich or powerful who presume to write memoirs, Mrs. Jaffray was outspoken on many matters others discreetly leave unsaid. She revealed, for instance, that President Taft weighed 332 pounds before he announced he was going on a diet, but a year later looked to her to be 400 pounds. He loved salted almonds and about every other kind of food except eggs, Mrs. Jaffray reported, and ate a twelve-ounce steak for breakfast every day, which he cut to six-ounces when he went on his unsuccessful diet.[21]

Being prepared for emergencies and rising to the occasion when they take place are themes that recur in the memoirs and other writings of White House staff. Ava Long, the housekeeper for the Hoovers, describes being told a half hour before a scheduled lunch that the guest list had increased from four to forty when all she had purchased for the meal were a dozen lamb chops. Undaunted, she and the head cook raided the ice box for every bit of leftover meat and vegetable they could find, brought out the food grinder, and wound up with croquettes that they embellished with a mushroom sauce and a sprinkling of chopped parsley. When a distinguished foreign guest later requested the recipe, Mrs. Long struggled to recall the ingredients of her impromptu dish, which she christened "White House Surprise Supreme."[22]

Because of their frequency, unexpected meal preparation was a way of life in the FDR White House. Numerous children and grandchildren came and went with little notice, friends and staff moved in for extended visits, and last-minute guests were routinely invited to meals. Figuring out what and how much to prepare and serve was a constant problem for those in charge of the kitchen. Famously indifferent to keeping house and cooking, Eleanor Roosevelt brought along Henrietta Nesbitt, a Hyde Park neighbor with no professional experience, to serve as the official housekeeper. Accustomed to her tidy kitchen back home, Mrs. Nesbitt was stunned to find that "the first kitchen in America" was dark and unsanitary with a huge old-fashioned gas range and a foul-smelling refrigerator. "Mrs. Roosevelt and I poked around," she said, "opening doors and expecting hinges to fall off and things to fly out."[23]

That kitchen, which was soon renovated, was only the first of the challenges Mrs. Nesbitt was to face in the next thirteen years. She writes in her memoirs that she felt obliged to keep meals simple through the

Ham'n' Kraut's Scarce, Even At White House

By Margaret Kernodle
Associated Press Feature Writer

A hamhock hasn't flavored sauerkraut at the White House for eight months!

That was the exclamation of the Nation's No. 1 housekeeper, Mrs. Henrietta Nesbitt, as she stared at the new point rationing lists issued yesterday.

"I haven't even seen a hamhock," the housekeeper at the Executive Mansion said, explaining that she's kept account of all meat used in the first family's Capital kitchen for a year.

Folks at the White House face meatless days, too, she insisted, because it's the best way to work meat rationing.

First, she'll stretch meat as far as she can. But even in advance of meat rationing, White House cooks have skidded against the scarcity which caught other kitchens occasionally. Until recently they couldn't get corned beef. There's been less and less poultry lately, and the size of chickens changed from an average of four and five pounds to 3½ pounds. No broilers were available lately, and roasting chickens were used for fried chickens at the White House. For the past few days no ham or bacon at all came into the No. 1 kitchen.

Butter, Breakfast Only

Besides butter for breakfast only these days, the White House no longer has food sauteed in butter. It substitutes bacon fat. Coffee's been kept to one cup a day for everybody but foreign visitors, Mrs. Nesbitt asserted.

Days for desserts dwindle. If a White House eater has dessert, he gets no salad or the other way around. Not even formal dinners go beyond three courses since last fall. Pies and ice creams are favored desserts, but fruit ice creams take precedence over creamy ice creams and are better anyhow, Mrs. Nesbitt said.

Last month the first larder of this land checked its sugar coupons back where they came from because the White House had a surplus of sugar. Not a pound more than the regular allowance was used, the housekeeper explained proudly.

Her shopping has to be the same "catch as catch can" as any other American housekeeper's. She does put a little aside now and then to build that backlog she must have for visitors, even though the number of visitors had been cut. She admits she's inclined to be "tight" in insisting on having some aside for "special foreign guests."

No More Caviar

The days of caviar are over at the White House for the duration, it seems. Even if it's only seven points a pound, she estimates the cost at about $35 a pound. The only time the White House will have caviar will be when somebody gives some to the President (and that has happened.)

Even with all her careful systematizing of the White House kitchens, on rationed schedule, Mrs. Nesbitt refuses to cut down on the President's food if she can help it. Others will have to sacrifice at the White House, she said, because she does not intend for food to worry him. She admitted she doesn't always give him all he likes.

Here are favorite foods which will be White House meat-stretchers:

Stuffed peppers, stew, ham scallop, noodles and mushrooms with chicken scraps, spaghetti with meat cakes cut down from the "good old American size" to mere marbles, curries or omelets with meat tidbits;

Croquettes for a sustaining meal in themselves; minestrone soup or fish chowders, "both good meals in themselves," creamed cheeses (soft ones aren't rationed) for a satisfying light meal, gumbo z'herbes (good light meal even for children if less spiced); stuffed eggs (meat bits for stuffing), baked beans with any kind of beans, deviled meats and casseroles.

Here's How

And here's how several of the foods are fixed:

1. Fry tiny cubes bacon until rendered, 1 teaspoon each pepper. Skim out and set aside.
2. Fry minced onion in part of above fat until golden brown, 1 teaspoon for each pepper.
3. Boil rice until tender, strain.
4. Add rice and onions. Add bacon, season with black pepper and salt. Add chives, 1 teaspon for each pepper (cut fine), and stuff peppers.

Gumbo Z'Herbes (Cheapest Soup)

2 tablespoons lard
2 tablespons flour
1 bunch each of spinach, mustard greens, green cabbage, beet tops, watercress, radishes, chopped onion, parsley, thyme, bay leaf, green onion top, salt, pepper, red pepper pod or drop of tabasco. Bacon strip, veal or pork brisket or ham bone.

Wash well the greens, bacon strip, put in hot water and boil well. Drain off water and save it. Fry meat in 1 teaspoon lard, chopping up the while the greens with the onion and seasoning. Take out the meat and fry the greens, stirring. When well fried, all the four, stir.

Season well. Add the meat and the treasured wate. of the boiled greens; leave all to simmer for an hour or so.

Croquettes (Can Be Done Day Ahead)

Make thick heavy cream sauce, let it get cold. Use left-over fish made into regular croquettes. Dip in fine bread crumbs, then into

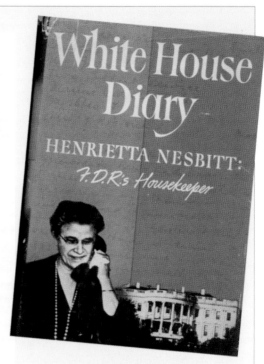

eggs, and back into bread crumbs. Cover with cloth if you want to keep until next day to cook.

Ham Scallop

1 cup dry bread crumbs.
1½ cup minced ham.
1 teaspoon dry mustard.
⅛ teaspoon nutmeg.
2 eggs.
2 cups milk or more.
Mix and place in casserole and bake until set. Oven 350 degrees.

Lismore Stew (Serves Six)
2 pounds lean chuck in cubes.
12 onions size of walnuts or quarter.
2 bunches carrots cut.
Tops of bunch celery cut in short lengths.

Use Dutch oven or iron pot. Braise meat in some fat until nicely browned on all sides so as to have a nice gravy. Add vegetables and water, salt and pepper to taste. Add a clove of garlic, then one-fourth teaspoon of stew herbs. Simmer over low fire several hours, watch and stir. Before serving add teaspoon of Worcester or similar sauce. Simmer few minutes.

Minestroni (Serves Six)

1 cup dry beans
2 onions sliced
½ minced clove of garlic
1 sprig parsley
1 stalk celery
4 pounds soup meat
Salt and pepper
¼ cup bacon fat
1 cup stewed tomatoes
1 cup chopped spinach
1 cup chopped cabbage
Parmesan cheese
Put meat in six cups cold water and cook slowly until it is tender, season to taste. Heat fat and saute onion, celery, garlic, parsley until lightly browned. Add everything to the soup stock. Cook until vegetables are tender and serve in a soup tureen sprinkled with Parmesan cheese.

Depression and war years as an example to the American public, but, truth to tell, lavish dishes were just not part of her repertoire. Favoring less costly parts of animals like brains, sweetbreads, and beef tongues, she had the habit of serving them to the first family in a limited and continuous rotation. In a memo to his wife, President Roosevelt said about Mrs. Nesbitt's monotonous food: "I am getting to the point where my stomach positively rebels and this does not help my relations with foreign powers. I bit two of them today."[24]

Her taste in food—Mrs. Nesbitt left behind a cookbook[25] as well as her memoirs—epitomizes the shortcomings of home cooking in general in America in the 1930s and 1940s: no seasoning, a reliance on canned goods, and a propensity for fad dishes that included fussy congealed salads and the overuse of marshmallows to doll them up. Her recipe for Ashville salad is typical, consisting as it does of canned tomato soup, chopped vegetables, gelatin, cream cheese, and mayonnaise. Holding to the conviction that men did not know what was good for them, since they disdained salads and vegetables, Mrs. Nesbitt felt it her duty to coax them down, and she had the irritating habit of serving the president platefuls of foods she knew he disliked. Before she was through, "old lady" Nesbitt and her cooking became the butt of countless jokes by FDR, his friends and associates, his children, the White House staff, and the national press. She has, in fact, been immortalized by Elliott Roosevelt in his series of White House mysteries that star his mother as sleuth. In one book, a dead body is found in Mrs. Nesbitt's refrigerator and in another she is the victim of the president's humorous speculation that she will use up in mediocre sauces his precious case of Château Lafite Rothschild.[26] Despite all the criticism, Mrs. Nesbitt prevailed in the FDR White House for twelve years, with Mrs. Roosevelt the only ally she needed.

When Eleanor Roosevelt moved out of the White House after her husband's death in 1945, Mrs. Nesbitt

stayed behind as the Truman housekeeper, but not for long. She came close to being fired when, acting out her conviction that men must be forced to eat vegetables, she served Brussels sprouts three nights in a row to the president, little caring that he hated them. But it was a stick of butter that sealed her fate. Bess Truman, on her way to a potluck luncheon with her Senate wives' bridge club, stopped by the White House kitchen for some butter, only to be told by Mrs. Nesbitt that it was rationed and would not be leaving her kitchen. Instead, Mrs. Nesbitt was asked to leave it, once and for all, and her long reign finally ended.[27]

Of the many stories about those who cook, serve, and eat in the White House, there is one told by Colonel Edmund Starling, a Secret Service man on White House detail during the Hoover years, that captures many of the meanings Americans attach to food consumed by the first family and their guests. The people of Bangor, Maine, had sent a fresh salmon to President Herbert Hoover and were expecting to see it photographed with him and one of their congressmen. The lawmaker appeared at the White House ready to pose with the president and the fish only to learn that the salmon was in the kitchen with its head cut off being cooked. A halt was called. Colonel Starling, with needle and thread, sewed back the head of the fish, making it presentable enough for the photograph, and the congressman left happy.[28]

For the people of Maine, the salmon represented their New England state; they were giving something of themselves to the president. For the White House staff, expediting that fish into the kitchen and quickly decapitating it epitomized their efficiency. For Colonel Starling, the headless fish was a challenge, a problem to be solved like many other problems he faced as a security officer. For the president and the congressman, the fish was a political opportunity, a way to connect with the voters of Maine. As for the White House cook, the fresh salmon was a desirable ingredient to be cooked, served, and eaten. Sometimes, even in the White House, a fish is just a fish.

A Washington Post *article from 1943 includes several recipes from Henrietta Nesbitt, the Roosevelt's housekeeper. Mrs. Nesbitt published her memories of working in the White House in* White House Diary *in 1948.*

A shelf of White House cookbooks. Over the years many books about White House cooking have been published— some are written by former chefs such as Henry Haller and René Verdon, and others are collections of recipes related to the White House.

NOTES

1. Marie Kimball, *Thomas Jefferson's Cook Book* (Charlottesville: University Press of Virginia, 1976).
2. Jean Harvey Hazelton, "Thomas Jefferson, Gourmet," *American Heritage,* October 1964, 104.
3. Kimball, *Thomas Jefferson's Cook Book,* vii, ix, 10.
4. Margaret Bayard Smith, *The First Forty Years of Washington Society in the Family Letters of Mrs. Samuel Harrison Smith* (Margaret Bayard), from the Collection of Her Grandson, J. Henley Smith, ed. Gaillard Hunt (New York: Frederick Ungar, 1965), 387. See *White House History,* no. 17 (Winter 2006): 45–49.
5. Kimball, *Thomas Jefferson's Cook Book,* 45, 46, 50, 99.
6. Both quoted in Margaret Brown Klapthor, *The First Ladies Cook Book: Favorite Recipes of All the Presidents of the United States* (New York: GMG Publishing, 1982), 44.
7. Irwin Hood Hoover, *Forty-Two Years in the White House* (Boston: Houghton Mifflin, 1934), 5.
8. Mary Randolph, *The Virginia Housewife* (Reprint, Birmingham, Ala.: Oxmoor House, 1984), 49.
9. Ibid.
10. Ibid., 25.
11. William Seale, *The President's House: A History* (Washington, D.C.: White House Historical Association, with the cooperation of the National Geographic Society, 1986), 1:102.
12. Ibid., 1:754.
13. Ibid., 1:958.
14. Hoover, *Forty-Two Years in the White House,* 293–94.
15. Klapthor, *First Ladies Cookbook,* 194. Eleanor Roosevelt had served hot dogs at the postinaugural lunch in 1933.
16. Both quoted in Eleanor Roosevelt, "I Remember Hyde Park: A Final Reminiscence," *McCalls,* February 1963, 71–73, 162–63.
17. Letitia Baldrige, *In the Kennedy Style: Magical Evenings in the Kennedy White House* (New York: Doubleday, 1998), 48–65.
18. Seale, *President's House,* 564–66; Ona Griffin Jeffries, *In and Out of the White House* (New York: Wilfred Funk, 1960), 240.
19. Lida Seely, *Mrs. Seely's Cookbook: A Manual of French and American Cookery* (New York: Macmillan, 1902), 141–42.
20. Elizabeth Jaffray, *Secrets of the White House* (New York: Cosmopolitan Book Corporation, 1927), 15.
21. Ibid., 24.
22. Ava Long, "Presidents at Home," *Ladies' Home Journal,* September 1933, 8.
23. Henrietta Nesbitt, *White House Diary* (Garden City, N.Y.: Doubleday, 1948), 30.
24. J. B. West, *Upstairs at the White House: My Life with the First Ladies* (New York: Coward, McConn and Geohegan, 1977), 81–5.
25. Henrietta Nesbitt, *The Presidential Cookbook: Feeding the Roosevelts and Their Guests* (Garden City, N.Y.: Doubleday, 1951).
26. Elliott Roosevelt, *The Hyde Park Murder* (New York: St. Martin's, 1985) and *The White House Pantry Murder* (New York: St. Martin's, 1987).
27. Margaret Truman. *Bess W. Truman* (New York: Mcmillan, 1986), 284–85.
28. Edmund W. Starling, *Starling of the White House* (New York: Simon and Schuster, 1946), 285.

FURTHER READING

Baldrige, Letitia. *In the Kennedy Style: Magical Evenings in the Kennedy White House.* New York: Doubleday, 1998.

Fields, Alonso. *My 21 Years in the White House.* New York: Coward-McCann, 1961.

Furman, Bess. *White House Profile.* Indianapolis: Bobbs-Merrill, 1951.

Haller, Henry. *The White House Family Cookbook.* New York: Random House, 1987.

Helm, Edith Benham. *The Captains and the Kings.* New York: G. P. Putnam's, 1954.

Hoover, Irwin Hood. *Forty-Two Years in the White House.* Boston: Houghton Mifflin, 1934.

Jaffrey, Elizabeth. *Secrets of the White House.* New York: Cosmopolitan Book Corporation, 1927.

Jeffries, Ona Griffin. *In and Out of the White House.* New York: Wilfred Funk, 1960.

Kimball, Marie. *Thomas Jefferson's Cook Book.* Charlottesville: University Press of Virginia, 1976.

Klapthor, Margaret Brown. *The First Ladies Cook Book.* New York: GMG Publishing, 1982.

Long, Ava, "Presidents at Home," *Ladies' Home Journal,* September 1933.

Nesbitt, Henrietta. *The Presidential Cookbook: Feeding the Roosevelts and Their Guests.* Garden City, N.Y.: Doubleday, 1951.

Nesbitt, Henrietta. *White House Diary.* Garden City, N.Y.: Doubleday, 1948.

Randolph, Mary. *The Virginia Housewife,* 1824. Reprint, Birmingham, Ala.: Oxmoor House, 1984.

Roosevelt, Eleanor, "I Remember Hyde Park: A Final Reminiscence," *McCalls,* February 1963, 71–73, 162–63.

Seely, Lida. *Mrs. Seely's Cookbook: A Manual of French and American Cookery.* New York: Macmillan, 1902.

Smith, Margaret Bayard. *The First Forty Years of Washington Society in the Family Letters of Mrs. Samuel Harrison Smith* (Margaret Bayard), from the Collection of Her Grandson, J. Henley Smith. Ed. Gaillard Hunt (New York: Frederick Ungar, 1965).

Starling, Edmund W. *Starling of the White House.* New York: Simon and Schuster, 1946.

Truman, Margaret. *Bess W. Truman.* New York: Macmillan, 1986.

Verdon, René. *The White House Chef Cookbook.* Garden City, N.Y.: Doubleday, 1968.

West, J. B. *Upstairs at the White House: My Life with the First Ladies.* New York: Coward, McCann & Geoghegan, 1973.

A Bit of Architectural History Comes in from the Cold

WILLIAM G. ALLMAN

Supplying the White House kitchens with quality ingredients for formal and family meals is not a once-a-week shopping trip. Nonetheless, milk, meat, fruits, and other perishable foodstuffs are stored, if only briefly, in a "Cold Storage" room created under the North Portico during the 1935 modernization of the White House kitchen by President Franklin D. Roosevelt. In early 2006 the replacement of the 1970s' lining of this nearly 11 foot square refrigerator exposed elements of White House architectural history of much longer duration than the sixty years during which White House chefs and cooks have been seen emerging from behind its stainless steel door.

The part of the White House in question involves rooms partitioned off nearly two centuries ago in the masonry passageway beneath the North Portico. The passage itself is built in a moat-like, deep areaway that crosses the north front of the house, out of sight from Pennsylvania Avenue and meant to give light and air to basement domestic work rooms that are below grade. Thomas Jefferson built a bridge across the passage to the main entrance door; in Andrew Jackson's time this bridge was widened considerably and became the foundation of the new North Portico, appropriately arched and vaulted to allow market wagons to pass through the

The entrance to the cold storage area seen from the passageway after the liner was removed in 2006.

areaway beneath it. At some point early on, the vaulted space under the portico was reduced in width when three rooms were built on the north wall. After serving many functions, the room on the east was converted to a cold room or refrigerator, and late last year, when it was remodeled, we got a look at the early construction that had been hidden for so long.

The removal of the white metal panels that had constituted the sides and ceiling of the refrigerator's lining revealed part of the stone and brick vault of the below-grade areaway long known as the "Tradesmen's Entrance." This included not just brickwork from the foundations of the North Portico created for President Andrew Jackson in 1829–30 but part of the north entry that preceded it, built in 1807–8 for President Thomas Jefferson by Benjamin Henry Latrobe. Capitalizing on a brief window of opportunity, the Historic American Buildings Survey, long involved in documenting the structure of the White House, was invited to draw and photograph quickly the exposed materials.

To beautify the north entrance of the President's House, Benjamin Henry Latrobe, Jefferson's appointee as the surveyor of the public buildings, built in 1807–8 a vault-supported "platform" to replace the wooden bridge that had spanned the deep areaway that provided access and some light to the Ground Floor kitchen. Latrobe's plan and sections (now in the Library of Congress) show a 20 foot wide passageway and a central parabolic vault that eliminated parts of the handsome keystone and quoins of James Hoban's original

North view of the President's House in the City of Washington (detail), aquatint after an 1811 drawing by Benjamin Henry Latrobe. Access to the north door was improved by Latrobe's 1807–8 staircase bridging the below-grade areaway, enlarged in 1829–30 to form the base for the North Portico. The old arch was exposed temporarily during the replacement of the refrigerator lining in 2006.

kitchen doorway. The east and west ends of this structure were stone arches supported by 7 foot square-capped pilasters. The southern half of the arches and their southern supporting pilasters have always been exposed to view within the passageway, although under a painted coating. Exposed in the emptied Cold Storage, however, were the long-hidden northeast pilaster, smeared with cork insulation, the remainder of the eastern arch, and a 2 foot wide strip of the original Latrobe brick vaulting inset with a few unexplained blocks of sandstone.

With the creation of the North Portico in 1829–30 by James Hoban, the original architect of the President's House, the covered passageway was lengthened to accommodate the broad porch above it. The entries and the interior of the passageway were narrowed to accommodate curved foundations for the walkways above that led to pedestrian stairs set between the side columns of the new portico, which served as a sheltering *porte cochere.* Two small windowless rooms and a corridor were walled away beneath the portico across the passage from the house. One of these the "North Pier" room remained behind the central corridor, with doors opening into the two new flanking rooms. The 5 foot width of arched brick ceiling exposed in the eastern room dates to the portico construction, Hoban's last work at a White House he had completed 1831.

By 1881, the eastern room had become a bathroom, with a bathtub and water closet along its south wall. No specific function for its western counterpart was record-ed. In 1902, as part of the Theodore Roosevelt renovation, both rooms became "coal storage" to fuel a new furnace installed below the floor of the nearby original kitchen. In 1935, in coordination with the creation of underground spaces extending to the east and west, the north corridor and flanking rooms were reconfigured into five spaces. The corridor was now used for "Wood Storage," while the eastern part of the old vestibule and part of the eastern room became, with only a modest change of letters, the new "Cold Storage." The western part of the vestibule became "Fruit Storage," with the room to the west a "Receiving Room." During the Truman renovation, the central passageway would be lengthened once more, beneath new space dug out beyond the North Portico footprint, and a second cold storage unit was created beside the original 1935 room.

In 2006 after a brief moment of exposure to interested examination by Laura Bush, White House staff, and HABS architects, components of the surviving structures of Jefferson and Latrobe, of Jackson and Hoban, have been concealed again behind a new refrigerator lining. And once more, the residence staff, going about its work, and the staff of the East and West Wings, crossing through the residence, may be surprised when a White House chef laden with groceries pops out from a Cold Storage sheltered partly by masonry nearly two hundred years old.

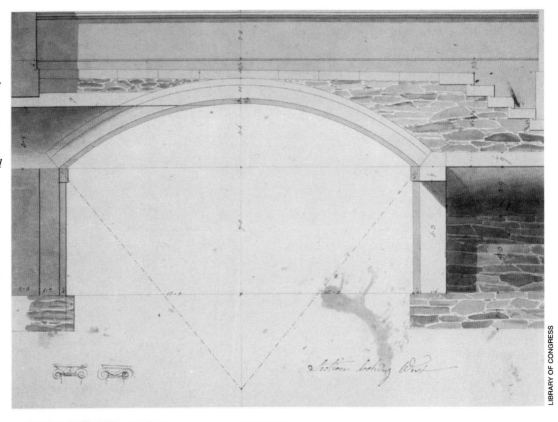

Benjamin Henry Latrobe's sectional drawing of the stone arch that spanned the service areaway to support a pre-portico entry platform. The simple square-capped pilaster and about half of the arch at right were exposed inside the space occupied by Cold Storage since 1935.

The "Tradesman's Entrance," a Ground Floor vaulted passageway running below the North Portico. The two central arches were created in 1807–08, during the administration of President Thomas Jefferson; the farthest arch and the shadowed trace of its counterpart at the upper edge of the photograph were built in the 1829–30 construction of the North Portico during the administration of President Andrew Jackson. "Cold Storage" created in 1935 is accessed through the stainless steel door at the near right.

Left: The more uniform brickwork to the east of the arch, mostly alternating courses of stretchers and headers, was built in 1829 as part of the foundations of the North Portico. An original end wall beneath the stone arch presumably preserved part of the fluted stone underside. This vaulting is seen exposed in the Cold Storage.

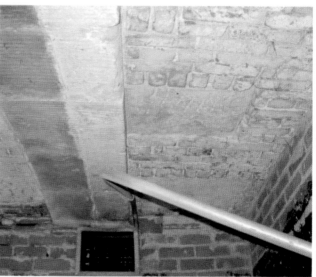

Above: The exposed vault showing the stone arch that marked the eastern limit of Latrobe's platform. The mixed masonry of brick and sandstone to the right is also part of the Jeffersonian structure.

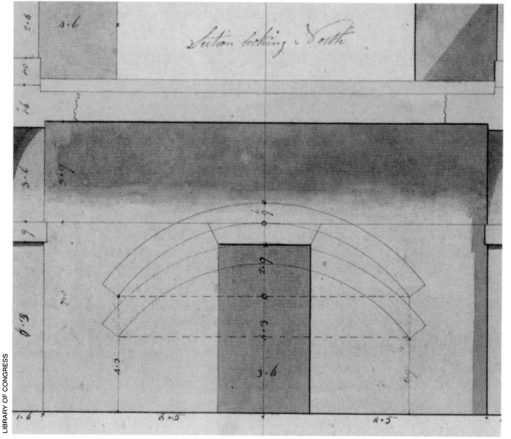

Left: Latrobe's north-facing section of the pier built into the North Lawn to support the entry platform. Two small rooms and a central corridor were built here, the Cold Storage on the right.

Above: Interior of Cold Storage after the removal of its liner in 2006 revealed the vaulted ceiling. The northern pilaster and half of the sandstone arch were built for Benjamin Latrobe in 1807–08. The brickwork to the left (west) of the arch was built for Latrobe: that to the right (east) for James Hoban in 1829. The walls and part of the ceiling are blackened by the residue of a layer of cork insulation.

Right: Cold storage with the new interior, 2006. The historic structural elements are preserved but out of sight once more.

WHITE HOUSE HISTORY

White House Historical Association
Washington

PRESIDENT EISENHOWER'S WHITE HOUSE • NUMBER 21
PUBLISHED FALL 2007

Foreword

The Eisenhower White House

President Dwight D. Eisenhower by J. Anthony Wills, 1967.

Dwight D. Eisenhower was inaugurated president of the United States on Tuesday, January 20, 1953, and served eight years. He was the most recent military hero to serve in the office, in the line descended from Washington through Jackson, Harrison, Taylor, and Grant. Others had served notably, James Garfield, for example, and Theodore Roosevelt, but none so significantly as those, and with Eisenhower, as with the others, one always hesitated whether to address him General Eisenhower or Mr. President.

As the White House is always a mirror of its times, it was a mirror of the 1950s, but the fifties outran it. Social change and the upsurge of transformation that began in that decade were hardly reflected in the tranquil White House, where the president and his extremely popular first lady presided during the week but on weekends hurried to Gettysburg, where adjacent to the battlefield they had a farm with a rambling old house, the first and only home they ever owned. The White House was very much "the office," and while Mrs. Eisenhower brought forth the idea of furnishing rooms museum-style, the president had a golf green on the south grounds, and they created a very personal barbecue patio on the roof, home was still always Gettysburg.

Everyone liked Ike and everyone wanted to see him. He invited more people to dine at the White House than had ever been there before—state dinners, formal evening affairs, stag dinners, and breakfasts. He approved the guest lists, having his own purposes, and she very emphatically planned the flowers, entertainment, and menus, once gently reprimanding a chef for giving the president a menu to review. The White House was her job. The presidency was his.

White House History visits the Eisenhowers this issue showing various angles on their lives at the White House. Eisenhower the painter; Mrs. Eisenhower "making maturity glamorous," a look at the Eisenhower legend after his time in the creation of a memorial room at Blair House, and not least the president's at first cautious, then very certain acceptance of television as a fact of life for the presidency. Our publication in this issue of a previously unknown and recently discovered photograph of President Polk and some of his cabinet members cannot be explained in terms of Eisenhower, only our excitement at *White House History* about the find.

First Lady Mamie Eisenhower by Thomas Edgar Stevens, 1959.

WHITE HOUSE HISTORICAL ASSOCIATION

William Seale
Editor, *White House History*

Dwight David Eisenhower:
The First Television President

MARTHA JOYNT KUMAR

*E*arly in the Truman administration, New Yorkers had their first chance to view live scenes from Washington, televised by means of a recently laid coaxial cable. What they saw on February 12, 1946, was arguably the most popular American placing a garland at the base of the presidential statue at the Lincoln Memorial.[1] That American was a hero of World War II, General Dwight D. Eisenhower. Though the general was uneasy with the new medium then, and continued to be uneasy with it when he became president seven years later, Eisenhower was good for television and television was good to him.

As president, Eisenhower regularly communicated with citizens about their government, his actions and thoughts, his illnesses and subsequent recoveries, and his travels throughout the world. Through television Americans saw Eisenhower regularly—when he took the oath of office in 1953 and again in 1957, when he gave his annual State of the Union messages before a joint session of Congress, and, beginning in January 1955, when reporters queried him at his twice-monthly

General Dwight D. Eisenhower was televised as he received news of his nomination for the presidency at the Republican National Convention, July 11, 1952.

press conferences. Each year of his presidency, Americans saw the family side of the president when he and First Lady Mamie Eisenhower lit the national Christmas tree on the Ellipse between the White House and the Washington Monument. The new medium brought to a growing number of citizens a pastiche of images that together provided an unvarnished view of their president.

During Eisenhower's years in office, television was significant as a channel from the president to the public, but also important as a vehicle for delivering images of news events. Those images sometimes brought pressure on the administration for action—civil rights disorders in New Orleans, for example, where high schools under court order to desegregate, brought images of adults attacking children into American homes. In October 1957, pictures of the Soviet space capsule, *Sputnik,* underscored the reality that the U.S. space program was behind that of the Soviet Union. These pictures affected what citizens expected of the president and what they thought their government ought to emphasize and achieve. Eisenhower's statements also determined which issues received public attention. During his years in office Eisenhower learned that television could be an important tool for presidents, but he also found that it could take on a life of its own.[2]

Eisenhower's successful use of television rested on a combination of factors, including a growing television audience and technological advances in the medium, the president's high standing with the public as a military and political leader, and his own interest in using video to expand the president's ability to make news. He was served and encouraged by a cadre of publicity advisers schooled in the ways of television, including a press secretary, James C. Hagerty, who understood the strengths of his president and could anticipate the potholes that might lie ahead for him. From his first days in office, the new president and his team planned to integrate television into established presidential public presentations, including what were previously off-the-record news conferences.

Growth of Presidential Television

During Eisenhower's years in office, the Americans who could view their president expanded beyond a narrow band of set owners in major cities on the East Coast to include an audience overseas. President Eisenhower himself grew in his use of television just as the medium matured on his watch. In 1950, only 9 percent of American households had a television set, while ten years later, at the end of the Eisenhower administration, 67 percent did.[3] The president and his staff took full advantage of this expanding audience and developed a

variety of strategies for using television for campaigns, major addresses, and informal events.

Presidents Calvin Coolidge, Herbert Hoover, and Franklin D. Roosevelt had spoken to the public by way of radio. Roosevelt was the first president to appear on television. Television cameras recorded the president arriving in his car at the 1939 New York World's Fair and then as he sat with his family members and dignitaries. The images were carried to receivers within a 50-mile radius of the Empire State Building, where the National Broadcasting Company's television transmitter was located. "It was estimated that from 100 to 200 receivers were in tune and that possibly 1,000 persons looked in on the pageant," reported the *New York Times*.[4] It did not take long for television to move from broadcasting presidential images to broadcasting presidential speeches. In the final stages of the 1940 presidential campaign, when President Roosevelt spoke at a Democratic rally at Madison Square Garden, an estimated 40,000 people located at 4,000 receivers in the New York metropolitan area had tuned in the event. But television in this era could give little more than a general impression of a scene. "Only the most well-known persons at the rally were recognizable," reported the *Times*,

BETTMAN / CORBIS

Above: President Eisenhower delivers his first televised State of the Union address, January 7, 1954.

The number of American homes with televisions increased dramatically during the Eisenhower administration. A crowd is seen gathered to watch a World Series game on a television set in the window of bank building in New York City in 1950 (opposite). By May 1956, many more families had televisions in their homes (right).

"and faces were very hard to discern on the screen."[5]

During the Truman administration the use of television expanded beyond the broadcasting of political addresses in major cities to serve as a way to link the president and the public. On October 5, 1945, President Harry S. Truman spoke from the White House to ask American citizens to observe meatless Tuesdays and Thursdays—no poultry or eggs either—to conserve food in order to help meet the needs of postwar Europe. While news organizations reported the contents of the president's speech over radio and television, at the time they did not recognize it as precedent-setting. Not until the fifteenth paragraph of the *New York Times* report was the speech noted as the first presidential speech televised from the White House.[6]

It was not until the end of his administration that Truman received good reviews for his television appearances. In May 1952, Truman took viewers on an hour-long television tour of the newly renovated White House. "His poise, his naturally hearty laugh, and his intuitive dignity made for an unusual and absorbing video experience," said *New York Times* television critic

Jack Gould. "In short, thanks to television, the person at home had an intimate, friendly and personalized lesson both in history and the meaning of the Presidency that the individual is not likely to forget quickly."[7] Succeeding presidents valued the medium for its same combination of personal and official benefits.

One of the stops Truman made on that White House tour was the recently created Broadcast Room, fashioned from the original kitchen. During the three and one-half year renovation, Truman had given his televised speeches from a variety of settings, including the Oval Office and Projection Room E.[8] From that experience, he recognized that presidents needed dedicated broadcast space, and he used this new space for the remainder of his presidency.

When Eisenhower became president, he knew he wanted to reach the public directly with pictures as well as words, and this new broadcast studio stood ready for him to use. He felt comfortable giving addresses from the Broadcast Room because there he was free to lay out his information cards. "With respect to the Radio-Television-Newsreel statement, such things I ordinarily

Left: The north center room on the Ground Floor of the White House was set up as the Press Room, by President Harry S. Truman in 1952 and used for a period by Eisenhower, until it proved too small to admit the necessary television equipment. The room is subdivided today into offices and storage space.

Right: First Lady Mamie Eisenhower poses for photographers in the Press Room in 1953 prior to the start of her first White House press conference. Newsmen as well as newswomen attended the session.

BETTMAN / CORBIS

make in the broadcasting room of the White House with no one present," he wrote to Secretary of State John Foster Dulles. "By doing it in this way I can use aids, such as cards and so on to help in keeping me on the right track."[9] The Broadcast Room was also attractive for telecasting because it was substantially larger than the Oval Office, was camera-ready whenever the president wanted to use it, and had some seating space for reporters invited to observe the president. With the *Resolute* desk as its centerpiece, the room had an official look.[10]

With the president's support for the studio and First Lady Mamie Eisenhower's interest in using it for her news conferences, the White House staff set about to make the studio work well. It was a large room, and on March 11, 1953, it accommodated the thirty-seven female and forty-one male journalists who attended the first press conference by a first lady since Eleanor Roosevelt.[11]

But television technology was developing quickly, and just a week later Press Office Assistant Murray Snyder wrote to Chief of Staff Sherman Adams about adapting the Broadcast Room to meet current needs.

"Since the first week after the inauguration we have been studying means of improving the facilities of the radio-television room in the White House," he wrote. "Our first objective was to eliminate the necessity of having the President deliver short prepared addresses twice; in other words, make it possible for newsreel and television cameras to work side by side and, simultaneously, transmit or record the message for radio."[12] The issue of preparing multiple recordings of the same presidential remarks was solved by installing curtains, paid for by newsreel, television, and radio organizations, that absorbed the sound of the newsreel cameras.[13]

A Popular President Interested in Communications

Eisenhower was popular with the public long before he ran for office, and he retained his popularity throughout his presidency. In his first term in office, his job approval rating slipped under 60 percent only once. While his second term had more leadership challenges than his first, even then his ratings only once fell under 50 percent.[14] With high poll ratings, there was every reason to keep the president in front of the public.

A VERY BIG SUBJECT
THIS GREAT COUNTRY OF OURS
A QUICK SURVEY OF
    STRENGTHS
    PROBLEMS
    WORRIES
    FUTURE

UNDERSTAND P
STRENGTH AND
    STRENGTH
    SPIRITUAL
    INSTITUTION
    UNDERSTAND
    ECONOMIC P
    MILITARY
    INTERNATIONA
TOTAL STRENGTH

Opposite: President Eisenhower delivered televised remarks from various locations in the White House during his presidency. Robert Montgomery is seen from behind working on the camera setup for a speech in the Press Room in 1954 (top). President Eisenhower is seated in the Oval Office (bottom left) to read a statement from handwritten notes in 1959. And he answers questions at a press conference in the Executive Office Building (bottom right).

Above: Dwight and Mamie Eisenhower are televised in a relaxed pose on the set of a television program as the president appeals to viewers to "get out and vote," 1954.

During the 1952 presidential campaign Eisenhower had established a strong television presence, and he and his advisers came to the White House committed to the idea that television would be a significant carrier of the president's words and images. "We are in a day of a new medium—television," observed Press Secretary Hagerty on January 21, 1953. He told reporters: "I would like to work out with television representatives and with you gentlemen, a system whereby the President could give talks to the people of the country—possible press conferences to the country—on television."[15]

Eisenhower himself was concerned about the direction of his publicity and, in a memorandum he sent to his staff, demonstrated his intention to think through the best way of communicating the accomplishments of his administration: "In the first problem, that involving the relationships of the Administration with one hundred and sixty million people, we have a task that is not unlike the advertising and sales activity of a great industrial organization. It is first necessary to have a good product to sell; next it is necessary to have an effective and persuasive way of informing the public of the excellence of that product."[16]

WHITE HOUSE HISTORY (Collection Set 4)   163

Over the years Hagerty and Eisenhower worked through technical issues related to television coverage of presidential press conferences, and Eisenhower experimented with a variety of speaking formats and forums. While he used the Oval Office for his national addresses and generally appeared alone, he sometimes spoke from other places and with one or more officials from his administration. An April 1954 report to the nation on the progress of his administration was, Gould observed, the president's most successful television appearance to date. Eisenhower "was shown sitting on the edge of a desk, his arms folded and a quiet smile on his lips," and the format allowed him "to achieve relaxation and immeasurably greater freedom of movement. The result was the attainment of television's most desired quality—naturalness." "His warm human qualities came through on the home screen," Gould concluded, "as they have not done since he entered the White House."[17]

Eisenhower's highly successful televising of presidential press conferences meant that he had to make a basic change in their format, notably from off-the-record to on-the-record. From their inception in 1913, during the administration of Woodrow Wilson, press

A newsman covers the arrival of President Eisenhower and his doctor at the Gettysburg farm following the president's stroke, 1957.

conferences were governed by rules requiring reporters to report what the president said only indirectly and to obtain permission for a direct quotation. If a president said something he regretted, he could refuse to let reporters quote him. But no filmed press conference could honor this rule. It was an additional year before these sessions were made more comfortable for the president. Hagerty worked with the Kodak company, for example, to develop film allowing for a reduced amount of light.[18]

On January 18, 1955, Eisenhower held his first on-the-record televised session. It was a hit. The session was filmed in the morning and played on television that night. Gould commented: "In last night's film President Eisenhower was just himself, doing things in his own way, speaking extemporaneously and, for all practical purposes, forgetting about the presence of the television cameras." "As a result," Gould continued, "his own personality and forcefulness came to the fore. The press conference proved, if further proof was needed, that in television no staged program can compare with actuality itself."[19] Risk of error aside, press conferences paid off for the president because people could see him personally describe his policies and his goals. This first televised press conference set the pattern for his subsequent ones.

Not all of Eisenhower's publicity experiments were successful, however, especially those in which the president shared the stage with members of his administration. In one such incident, the president introduced Secretary of State John Foster Dulles for a discussion of a two-week trip during which Dulles had met with European leaders to discuss issues such as Germany's membership in the North Atlantic Treaty Organization and a summit meeting including the Soviet Union.[20] Gould commented: "When the President appears on television, he inevitably is the star: in the audience's mind he receives top billing even if he does not wish it. Yet on Tuesday night the star was cast as a supporting player and, to make matters more awkward, a supporting player with hardly any lines to say."[21]

In the course of his presidency, Eisenhower's ideas evolved about whether he should or should not appear on television. At first he tailored a distinction between what was appropriate for television and when radio worked best. At a press conference on May 14, 1953, he explained the differences he saw between radio and television as tools of presidential communications: "I personally would hope to be able to talk very informally on the television. I think when you have to be exact and talk formally, I would rather be on the radio," he told reporters.[22]

As his presidency progressed, however, and the majority of Americans had TV sets, Eisenhower found the situation reversed. Television proved best for the important events. In September 1957 he addressed the nation about the Supreme Court decision calling for the integration of Central High School in Little Rock, Arkansas, and carefully explaining his decision to federalize the Arkansas National Guard to enforce the court order.[23] To enhance the gravity of the situation, Eisenhower spoke from his office at the White House:

For a few minutes this evening I want to speak to you about the serious situation that has arisen in Little Rock. To make this talk I have come to the President's office in the White House. I could have spoken from Rhode Island, where I have been staying recently, but I felt that, in speaking from the house of Lincoln, of Jackson and of Wilson, my words would better convey both the sadness I feel in the action I was compelled today to take and the firmness with which I intend to pursue this course until the orders of the federal court at Little Rock can be executed without unlawful interference.[24]

Television was as important in carrying the president's images as it was his words. As major illnesses raised continuing questions throughout Eisenhower's presidency, television, which conveyed the president's appearance, proved very important for addressing the public's concerns. By the time the Little Rock crisis broke, Eisenhower had already had a serious heart attack (September 24, 1955) and an ileitis attack and operation (June 8, 1956), with a mild stroke (November 25, 1958) ahead of him. His robust looks were important news. "The President appeared fit and vigorous when he stepped into his White House office tonight," said Anthony Lewis in his *New York Times* article reporting the Little Rock speech.[25] But it was Eisenhower's words that drove the news. In that era of 15-minute news programs once each evening, an appearance by the president relating to a topic of the day made a difference. Gould remarked on the aggressive treatment the Little Rock crisis received on the air after the president's speech. "Beyond their regular news periods and an occasional week-end feature the TV networks have not delved too deeply into the Little Rock story nor given it the expanded coverage it so clearly warranted many days ago. Last night there were signs of an awakening."[26]

In less dramatic instances than Little Rock, the presence of the chief executive on television reminded people what he was doing and where he fit into the news from other parts of the government. With all of his televised talks, Eisenhower provided pictures for news programs as well as a copy of the speech that he gave live to the public. Hagerty, who understood that the news programs were eager for newsreel footage and video, also made sure to provide a regular stream of presidential appearances to both NBC and CBS for their newscasts.[27]

Publicity Advisers

Gradually the president came to recognize the planning talents of his press secretary. A year and a half into his administration, Eisenhower told William Edward Robinson, a friend and a publicity adviser, of his intention to add a person in Hagerty's shop to help "in the day-to-day operation" as well as to "extinguish the constantly recurring fires. This would free Jim—who daily proves himself to be of real caliber—to think about all these important matters and do the necessary planning."[28] Eisenhower appreciated Hagerty's qualities and the fit

sultant was Hollywood producer and 1930s film star Robert Montgomery, who advised the president from his own office in the Executive Office Building. During Eisenhower's first two years, Montgomery was credited for theatrical innovations such as raising the reading stand by 3 inches for the 1954 State of the Union address to allow the television camera to get more of the president's face and less of the bald spot on the top of his head.[30] Montgomery also devised clever ways of putting the president at ease (admonishing him for battering a golf ball) and acquainting him with the "myriad

Right: President Eisenhower addresses the press in the Executive Office Building, 1958. Press Secretary James C. Hagerty is seated to his left.

Opposite: In the Oval Office, Robert Montgomery consults with President Eisenhower prior to his televised announcement of his decision to run for a second term.

TIME AND LIFE PICTURES/GETTY IMAGES

they represented for the responsibility of handling press relations. "Possessed of an agile mind, a canny capacity for judging people, political shrewdness, and a healthy Irish temper, he had the respect of the White House correspondents as a 'real pro,'" reflected Eisenhower after he left office.[29]

Hagerty also had a strong sense of where television fit into the Eisenhower presidency and how to use outside consultants as well as White House staff members to help design his television appearances. The public relations people who were involved in the Citizens for Eisenhower operation during the 1952 campaign were involved in the early years of his presidency. One con-

mysteries of electronic theatre." "His suggestions on lighting, appearance, delivery and format," said Gould, "all receive the President's attention."[31]

Another very important adviser was Eisenhower's close friend Sigurd Larmon, who headed the New York agency, Young and Rubicam Advertising. An organizer of Citizens for Eisenhower, Larmon kept up a correspondence with the president during his White House years, writing with publicity suggestions and answering questions from the president about communications strategy. In his second year in office, Eisenhower put to Larmon a criticism he had heard from friends, that "the accomplishments of this Administration are

simply unknown to the people." "My question to you is—Do you agree with this general view? If you do, have you any specific ideas as to how to correct the situation?"[32]

Eisenhower knew what kind of information he wanted the public to have and wanted his advisers to help ensure a positive rendering of the administration's actions. "What I am talking about is more of publicizing our factual record, in which each of the items would be so well dressed up and presented that it would be news. Consequently it would be sought after rather than pushed upon a resisting public."[33] Eisenhower was interested in sharing administration accomplishments by

taking advantage of the news interview programs. His officials and supporters would get out the administration's message by appearing on such shows as NBC's *Meet the Press*, which had been on the air since November 1945, and CBS's *Face the Nation*, which began in November 1954. In his diary, the president described his charge to Republican Party chairman Leonard Hall: to provide information to officials appearing on the "press programs" on the facts of what the administration was doing in a variety of foreign initiatives and relationships.

Nine months after leaving office, President Eisenhower appeared on the cover of TV Guide, *preparing for the October 12, 1961,* CBS Reports *interview, filmed over a five day period at the Gettysburg farm. Interviewer Walter Cronkite said the monumental Eisenhower seemed to him like a "grandfather."*

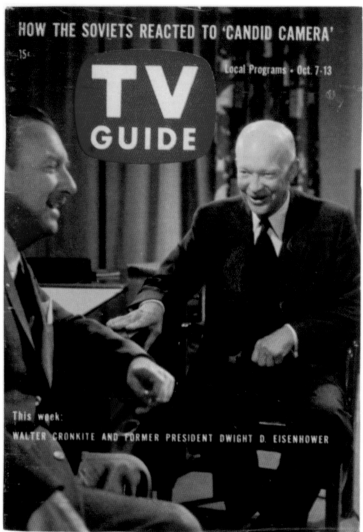

HOW THE SOVIETS REACTED TO 'CANDID CAMERA'

15¢

Local Programs · Oct. 7-13

TV GUIDE

This week:

WALTER CRONKITE AND FORMER PRESIDENT DWIGHT D. EISENHOWER

I urged Len Hall to obtain from the State Department the briefest kind of review of world developments since January, 1953, and then to furnish that review to all Republicans in the Congress, to all Governors, and to every other Republican who could conceivably be asked to appear on the television networks in the so-called press programs. I told him that he should send out nothing elaborate—merely the briefest kind of statement with respect to Korea, Indo China, Iran, Mid East, Trieste, Guatemala, and progress in NATO, SEATO, Northern Tier and the like. My belief is that if such a record is made too elaborate, it will not be read. Moreover, I cautioned him against claiming too much in the way of credit for the Administration—we should put out the bald facts and let them speak for themselves.[34]

President Eisenhower never lost his appreciation for the value of television coverage. At a rally in November 1960 he asked his audience to be patient with the technical crew. "I know that some of you are blanketed by the television cameras, but I would hope this is some little inconvenience with which you can put up for the simple reasons that these men also have a job, and they are trying to record these proceedings for the public. So while I recognize that you would like to throw a bulb at them, or something of that kind, I do plead that they are performing a service for the public and for this meeting and its proceedings."[35] Television also provided a service that worked well for President Eisenhower. For the first time, citizens could regularly watch their president explain his views and actions even as they witnessed the very events in the United States and in the world that had brought him before them.

NOTES

1. "Capital Exercises Are Telecast Here," *New York Times*, February 13, 1946, 22.

2. For a fine work on President Dwight D. Eisenhower and the media, see Craig Allen, *Eisenhower and the Mass Media* (Chapel Hill, N.C.: University of North Carolina Press, 1993).

3. Harold W. Stanley and Richard G. Niemi, *Vital Statistics on American Politics, 2005–2006* (Washington, D.C.: CQ Press, 2006), 173, table on growth and reach of selected media, 1950–2006.

4. Orrin E. Dunlap, "Ceremony Is Carried by Television as Industry Makes Its Formal Bow," *New York Times*, May 1, 1939, 8.

5. "Roosevelt Rally Sent by Television, First Use of New Medium as 'Vote Getter' Is Made at Gathering in Garden," *New York Times*, October 26, 1940, 14.

6. See Samuel A. Tower, "All To Aid Europe, Anderson, Harriman, Luckman, and Marshall Join in Radio Plea," *New York Times*, October 6, 1945, 1.

7. Jack Gould, "Radio and Television, President Makes Poised Appearance on Video as He Conducts Tour of White House," *New York Times*, May 5, 1952, 30.

8. Truman Library archivist Randy Sowell believes Projection Room E "may be a reference to a portion of the movie theater in the West Wing." Letter to author, November 7, 2006.

9. Dwight D. Eisenhower to John Foster Dulles, January 12, 1957, in *The Papers of Dwight D. Eisenhower*, ed. Louis Galambos and Daun van Ee (Baltimore, Md.: Johns Hopkins University Press, 1996), doc. 2170, facsimile of the print edition by Dwight D. Eisenhower Memorial Commission, at http://www.eisenhowermemorial.org/presidential-papers/first-term/documents/2170.cfm.

10. By the time President John F. Kennedy came into office, technological developments had shrunk the size and increased the mobility of television cameras. The Broadcast Room was disbanded and the *Resolute* desk went out to the Oval Office in the West Wing.

11. Bess Furman, "Mrs. Eisenhower Enjoys New Job; Reports on White House Changes," *New York Times*, March 12, 1953, 1.

12. Murray Snyder to Sherman Adams, March 17, 1953, Records as President, 1953–1961, White House Central Files, Official File, box 395, folder 101-B-8 White House Radio-Television Room, Dwight D. Eisenhower Presidential Library, Abilene, Kans.

13. See correspondence between Snyder and the Decorating Shop at B. Altman & Co. in New York, ibid.

14. Michael Nelson, ed., *Congressional Quarterly Guide to the Presidency* (Washington, D.C.: Congressional Quarterly, 1996), 1698–99, reporting Gallup Poll surveys.

15. Quoted in Anthony Leviero, "Eisenhower Widens Talks with Press," *New York Times*, January 22, 1953, 1.

16. Eisenhower, personal memorandum to Sherman Adams, Henry Cabot Lodge, Leonard Wood Hall, George Magoffin Humphrey, Thomas Edwin Stephens, and Arthur Ellsworth Summerfield, November 23, 1953, in *Papers of Eisenhower*, ed. Galambos and van Ee, doc. 555, at http://www.eisenhowermemorial.org/presidential-papers/first-term/documents/555.cfm.

17. Jack Gould, "Television in Review: New 'Format' Brings Out the President's Warmth and Charm Before Camera," *New York Times*, April 6, 1954, 41.

18. Allen, *Eisenhower and the Mass Media*, 59–60.

19. Jack Gould, "Television in Review: President's Press Conference an Example to Millions of Democracy at Work," *New York Times*, January 20, 1955, 39.

20. Eisenhower, "Remarks of the President During Secretary of State Dulles' Television Report on His European Visit," May 17, 1955, in *The Public Papers of the Presidents: President Dwight David Eisenhower*, American Presidency Project, University of California Santa Barbara, a collaboration by John Woolley and Gerhard Peters, at http://www.presidency.ucsb.edu/index.php.

21. Jack Gould, "TV: Matter of Technique, Viewer Distracted from Secretary Dulles' Message by President Eisenhower," *New York Times*, May 20, 1955, 51.

22. Eisenhower, "The President's News Conference of May 14, 1953," in *Public Papers of the Presidents: Eisenhower*, American Presidency Project, at http://www.presidency.ucsb.edu/index.php.

23. Jack Gould, "TV: President Speaks, Eisenhower Address on Little Rock Crisis Brings Home Seriousness of Situation," *New York Times*, September 25, 1957, 59.

24. Eisenhower, "Radio and Television Address to the American People About the Situation in Little Rock," September 24, 1957, in *Public Papers of the Presidents: Eisenhower*, American Presidency Project, at http://www.presidency.ucsb.edu/index.php.

25. Anthony Lewis, "Eisenhower on Air, Says School Defiance Has Gravely Harmed Prestige of U.S.," *New York Times*, September 25, 1957, 1.

26. Jack Gould, "TV: President Speaks, Eisenhower Address on Little Rock Crisis Brings Home Seriousness of Situation," *New York Times*, September 25, 1957, 59.

27. Both networks moved to 30-minute evening news programs in September 1963, CBS on September 2 and NBC on September 9. Both network programs were in black and white until 1966, when they moved to color. ABC did not develop its news programming until after the end of the Eisenhower administration, when James Hagerty became the head of its news division.

28. Eisenhower to William Edward Robinson, August 4, 1954, in *Papers of Eisenhower*, ed. Galambos and van Ee, doc. 1006, at http://www.eisenhowermemorial.org/presidential-papers/first-term/documents/1006.cfm.

29. Dwight D. Eisenhower, *Mandate for Change: The White House Years, 1953–1956* (Garden City, N.Y.: Doubleday, 1963), 1:117.

30. Associated Press, "President's TV Adviser Gives Message a Lift," *New York Times*, January 6, 1954, 20.

31. Jack Gould, "TV Techniques on the Political Stage," *New York Times Magazine*, April 25, 1954, 12. For the golf ball, see Associated Press, "Little Things Often Put President at Ease on TV," *New York Times*, February 11, 1954.

32. Eisenhower, personal and confidential to Sigurd Stanton Larmon, February 1, 1954, in *Papers of Eisenhower*, ed. Galambos and van Ee, doc. 699, at http://www.eisenhowermemorial.org/presidential-papers/first-term/documents/699.cfm.

33. Ibid.

34. Eisenhower, diary, March 13, 1956, in *Papers of Eisenhower*, ed. Galambos and van Ee, doc. 1786, at http://www.eisenhowermemorial.org/presidential-papers/first-term/documents/1786.cfm.

35. Eisenhower, "Rally in Garden City, New York," November 2, 1960, in *Public Papers of the Presidents: Eisenhower*, American Presidency Project, at http://www.presidency.ucsb.edu/index.php.

"She's Making Maturity Glamorous": Mamie Eisenhower's White House Style

EDITH MAYO

Since the nation's beginning, White House style has been no minor factor in the popularity and acceptance of a presidential administration by the people. George and Martha Washington—the only president and first lady who did not live in the White House— were aware that they were setting precedents, and they realized that presidential style would help define the nation. The president sought advice from his cabinet and advisers about how he and his wife should comport themselves in public—what "style" would best become the leaders of the new republic. Gouverneur Morris, an American statesman then in Paris, offered them this wisdom: "It is of great importance to fix the Taste of our Country properly . . . everything about you should be substantially good and majestically plain."[1] It is frequently the first lady—through her personal style and her public entertaining—who "sets" the style for the administration.

The American public first became aware of Marie Geneva Doud Eisenhower as a public figure during the 1952 presidential campaign. Mamie, as she was popularly known, was an outgoing woman who genuinely loved people. She had a midwestern openness

about her; she smiled easily and was friendly. Often described as "breezy," she was perceived as genuine and unpretentious. She appeared, especially to women (who, by the 1950s, were voting in equal numbers with men) as an average woman. Although personally she did not fit that designation, she did present herself as a level-headed, plainspoken spouse who had been exalted to a high position by the circumstances of her husband's military and political career but who did not "put on airs." Both visually and in print, she appeared as the adoring wife whose entire identity was defined by husband and family. Because she epitomized the popularly held conventions of femininity in the 1950s, the women of America perceived her as "one of their own."[2]

A major aspect of Mamie Eisenhower's public image was her trademark bangs, which became a widely copied fashion among women. Bangs were thought to give a youthful insouciance to a woman then in her fifty-sixth year. In reality, she had worn bangs for many years. Bangs became an integral part of her hairstyle in the early 1920s when the tragic death from scarlet fever of the Eisenhowers' first child, three-year-old Doud Dwight, known as Icky, had caused a crisis in their marriage. The wife of Eisenhower's commanding officer in Panama, Virginia Connor, mentored the young wife and impressed upon her that the marriage was at a crossroads. Mrs. Connor counseled Mrs. Eisenhower that she must take the initiative in rescuing the relationship. Part of this new beginning was that Mrs. Eisenhower took a renewed interest in her appearance, which included the

---

In January 1953, First Lady Mamie Eisenhower poses in her pink inaugural gown embroidered with two thousand glittering stones, which she felt added that "little extra flair." The gown was designed by Nettie Rosenstein and purchased through Neiman-Marcus in Dallas.

ATTENTION : CHARLES   INSTRUCTIONS FOR MRS. EISENHOWER'S HAIR

N° 1   All The hair must be well brushed back

N° 2   The bangs divided in the middle

N° 3   A parting at ear level, separate short
        hair from long hair.

N° 4   Shape the hair and form the curls in the
        shaping

N° 5   Curls on the nape of the neck four cms. long

N° 6   Accentuate the wave. Curls one row in one
        direction, the others in the opposite
        direction

N° 7   Comb the fringe loosely with one row of
        loose curls

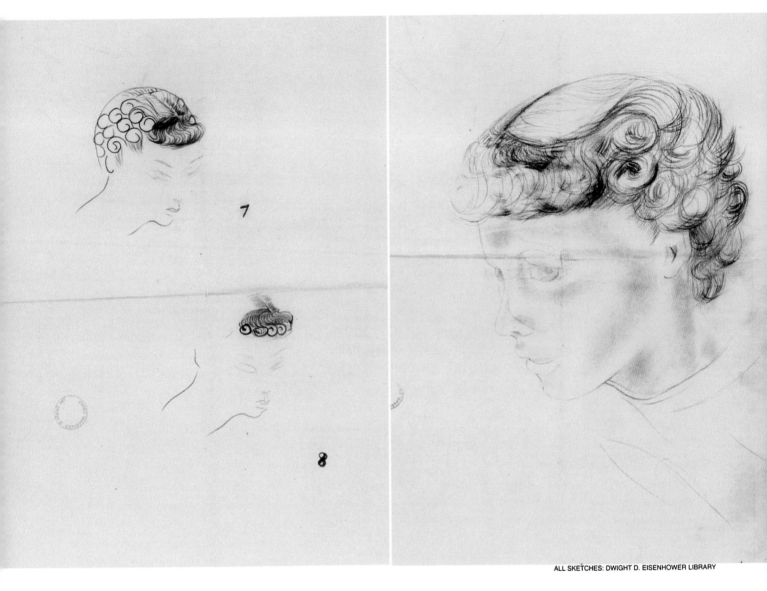

Stylists at Elizabeth Arden's salons all over the world followed these illustrated step-by-step "Structural Drawings" to achieve Mrs. Eisenhower's well-known bangs and curls without variation. It was a style Mrs. Eisenhower had worn since the 1920s.

introduction of her now-famous bangs. The bangs reminded both Eisenhowers of that period of rapprochement in their marriage, and so became symbolic of their relationship.[3]

Of more recent vintage, however, was the particular version of the bangs. After the war, when Eisenhower was stationed in Paris as American chief of staff, Mrs. Eisenhower began to frequent the Paris salon of Elizabeth Arden, under the proprietorship of Arden's sister, Gladys. The ultimate arbiter of fashionable beauty for elite American women both at home and abroad, Elizabeth Arden boasted more than forty salons around the world by the 1940s.[4] According to Elizabeth Arden's biographers, "Elizabeth first met Mamie Eisenhower, when the general was president of Columbia University [1948], and she came into the New York salon. . . . Upon being introduced to Miss Arden, she [Mrs. Eisenhower] smiled and said, 'So you're Gladys' sister.' It was the first time that Elizabeth had ever received that sort of billing." Despite Mamie Eisenhower's breezy reference to the self-absorbed Arden as "Gladys' sister," the two women instantly liked each other, and Arden became an early supporter of Eisenhower for president.[5]

In January 1953, after the Eisenhower victory, Elizabeth Arden wrote to Mamie Eisenhower expressing her happiness over "the thrilling election results!" She then went on, "A letter received today from Gladys tells me you are having difficulty finding the right hairdresser for your precious, 'much discussed' bangs," and she offered to send a hairdresser from New York.[6] Mrs. Eisenhower replied that what would truly be of assistance would be someone who could do her hair in Washington. Arden sent a hairdresser from her Washington salon to do Mrs. Eisenhower's hair for the inauguration. The new first lady wrote to thank Arden "for all the wonderful courtesies your Salon extended to me the day before Inauguration. It would have been impossible for me to leave my hotel . . . to have my hair done or my nails manicured, so your prompt and excellent services were blessings indeed and helped me look my best and feel my most confident."[7]

Arden attended the inaugural festivities and continued to render services to the first lady through her Washington salon. In February 1953, Arden wrote, "It is our pleasure to grant your every wish whenever possible." She continued:

When you first returned from Paris I thought your hair looked really beautiful, but it did not seem quite the same in subsequent newspaper photographs . . . so I suggested that Gladys have Stanislaus draw a structural diagram, with complete instructions. The sketch has just arrived, and I am asking the young woman who does your hair to study it very carefully . . . until she has your special hair-do down perfectly! . . . I am inclosing a diagram for your personal use, thinking it might be helpful during your travels.[8]

Now the first lady could travel the world assured that her famous bangs would turn out perfectly at any Arden salon she chose to patronize!

The two women continued their friendship throughout the Eisenhower years, and the first lady also purchased suits and dresses from Arden's couture collection. In addition, the first lady and other Eisenhower administration wives patronized Arden's Maine Chance Spa in Phoenix, Arizona. In one exchange, Arden admonished the first lady, "You must not gain back a single ounce you have lost. Your wonderful loss is really your gain."[9] Despite periodic calls in fashion circles to "update" her hairstyle, Mamie's bangs, as "designed" by Elizabeth Arden, became such a symbol of her public persona that she continued to wear her hair in that style for the rest of her life.

Since fashion functions as an extension of self and a presentation of personality, the first lady's wardrobe was also scrutinized as part of her style. Her suits, dresses, gowns, and accessories were closely watched. The historian of popular culture in the 1950s, Karal Ann Marling, describes how Mrs. Eisenhower's style was greatly influenced by the postwar popularity of Christian Dior's 1947 fashion line. Dubbed "The New Look," by *Life* magazine, this line set the style for the "look" of the 1950s in the United States by celebrating femininity. Suits were sensuous, full in the skirt, nipped in at the waist, with rounded hips and bustline. The wartime skimping on fabric was a thing of the past. Peplums on jackets and petticoats under skirts were the rage. Shoes, bags, and other accessories were carefully coordinated. It was a postwar aesthetic of deliberate artfulness, complexity, acquisition, and unabashed consumerism.[10]

Mamie Eisenhower preferred "The New Look" as filtered through the less extreme American adaptations of Dior's originals. She equated the idea of "new" with a youthfulness of attitude. "An unrepentant clothes-horse," says Marling, "Mamie wanted to be stylish, forever young, wholesomely, girlishly sexy, and well turned out on all occasions. Since she was constantly in the public eye [she was] known for her delight in her well-stocked closets."[11] In a biographical campaign piece done by *Collier's* magazine, Mrs. Eisenhower was photographed wearing "a sleeveless halter-top sundress with a billowing skirt that made her look more like a girl than a mature woman." Mrs. Eisenhower made it clear that "I hate old-lady clothes. And I shall never wear them." During the Eisenhowers' whistle-stop tour of the nation, says Marling, her sense of style soon became familiar to anybody who followed the campaign."[12]

Mrs. Eisenhower brought an extensive wardrobe to Washington and had one of Bess Truman's sitting rooms made over as her large clothes closet. Though she had little interest in one-of-a-kind designer dresses, she patronized the top American designers of the period—Mollie Parnis, her favorite, as well as Hattie Carnegie, Nettie Rosenstein, lines from Elizabeth Arden, and Sally Victor hats. "Mamie Eisenhower liked Parnis's clothes because, she explained, they had that 'little extra flair.'"[13] Marling adds that Parnis's clothes "stake[d] out a middle ground between Paris and Levittown."[14] Marling describes Mrs. Eisenhower's favorite style as "a one-piece dress (sometimes a suit) with a full skirt . . . made up in a fabric with a reflective or slightly iridescent surface—like silk taffeta. The dress itself was a fancy, ornamental variation on the shirtwaist."[15] Parnis, clearly delighted that Mamie Eisenhower purchased so many of her designs, praised the first lady: "She's making maturity glamorous."[16]

The first lady often personalized her fashion statement with matching shoes, purse, and gloves. She sometimes accessorized with dyed-to-match stockings purchased from Paris. Her biographical bracelets held charms that recounted significant "steps" in the president's successful career, crowned by a White House charm—successes to which she had contributed and that were hers as well. Together with her famous bangs, this ensemble came to be known as "the Mamie look."[17] The "Full Mamie" consisted of the above elements, often worn with a double or triple strand of pearls with matching or coordinating earrings, a brooch or large pin on one lapel of her suit with a corsage pinned to the other and, topping all, a mink stole or a full-length mink coat.

These trappings of acquisition were a statement that "success" had been well-earned.

Having scrutinized every article of clothing during the 1952 campaign, fashion mavens and the public alike awaited Mrs. Eisenhower's choices for an inaugural wardrobe, and they were not disappointed. A press release from Eisenhower headquarters announced:

> The description of Mrs. Eisenhower's gown and suit was prepared for the press by the fashion experts of the Neiman-Marcus store. . . . Both her town suit for the Inaugural ceremonies and parade and her gown for the traditional ball came from the internationally famous Texas specialty store, Neiman-Marcus. Mr. Lawrence Marcus, vice president of the store, commissioned Nettie Rosenstein, New York designer, to execute the ball dress and Hattie Carnegie, the suit.[18]

The commission to design the new first lady's inaugural wardrobe originated with Stanley Marcus, who headed the fashionable Dallas store. An early proponent of and Texas fund raiser for the Eisenhower for President movement, "Mr. Stanley" had told Eisenhower that Neiman-Marcus would be honored to make the first lady's inaugural clothing. He followed up on his offer after the Eisenhower electoral victory.[19]

The inaugural ball gown was quite a Mamie confection. "For color," the press release explained, "Mrs. Eisenhower selected a delicate yet definite Renoir pink [her favorite color] in a beautiful quality of *peau-de-soie*. Mr. Marcus said that in designing the gown, Mrs. Rosenstein took into account Mrs. Eisenhower's graceful neck and shoulders."[20] As was to become her custom, Mamie Eisenhower demanded that "little extra flair." "Mrs. Eisenhower personally specified a wide skirt," explains Marling, "chose the color, and insisted that Nettie Rosenstein supply additional glitter in the form of 2,000 hand-sewn rhinestones in four sizes and several shades of pink. . . . The stones drew attention to the lavish use of material . . . exaggerated by stiff taffeta underskirts."[21] The press release provided more detail: "The more than 2000 stones used in decorating the gown . . . [were] sewn on by hand. The bodice is snugly fitted . . . the top of the bodice is gathered . . . at the shoulder line. The skirt is set on a small yoke just below the waistline and the top of the skirt is crowded with clusters of stones." The inaugural ball gown ensemble

Patricia Nixon, wife of the vice president, joins Mrs. Eisenhower at the Cherry Blossom Fashion Luncheon at the Mayflower Hotel in 1958. Their outlandish floral hats were described in detail by the press.

A model displays seven new hats created by milliner Sally Victor for Mrs. Eisenhower's spring wardrobe in 1956. She is wearing a flower pillbox of forget-me-nots and holding a white sailor with a single pink rose and another white sailor with a lace edge. On the table left to right are a cotton lace pillbox on black velvet; a four-leaf clover pillbox covered with yellow mimosa; a small cap of white straw in rouching effect; and a black straw hat.

Mrs. Eisenhower enjoys a piece of a cake (decorated to look like the front page of a newspaper) on her sixty-third birthday in 1960 at a celebration that also marked the fortieth anniversary of the Women's National Press Club. She is seen with reporter Helen Thomas, who was then president of the club and early in a career with the White House Press Corps that would continue for nearly fifty years more.

The Eisenhowers celebrated their forty-third wedding anniversary with a procession into the East Room in October 1953. "Dress up" as brides and grooms was an example of the sort of theme party in which Mrs. Eisenhower took delight.

was completed with above-the-elbow matching gloves, a purse encrusted all over with colored rhinestones, Delman evening shoes covered with material to match her gown, and sapphire hose to blend with her dress.[22]

The inaugural suit worn to the swearing-in ceremony and the parade was a "daytime ensemble in a soft gray dressmaker suit with a nipped in jacket and semifull skirt," designed by Hattie Carnegie.[23] With this, the first lady wore, says Marling, a Sally Victor hat "shaped like a shallow, inverted bowl or an iced cupcake . . . made of soft gray felt, contoured into four scalloped layers and slashed to show flashes of a bright green lining." Completing her costume was a charm bracelet, a single strand of choker pearls and matching earrings, and a mink coat worn with an enormous orchid corsage.[24]

In terms of style, these inaugural ensembles anticipated most of the elements of Mrs. Eisenhower's clothing style during the White House years. "Mamie Pink" became a fashion rage and a staple of clothing and household color schemes throughout the 1950s. When details of the first lady's inaugural wardrobe were published in newspapers, "the New York Dress Institute," says Marling, "named Mamie to its list of the world's twelve best-dressed women. . . . She made the lists every year."[25]

As first lady, Mamie Eisenhower considered her most important role to be that of hostess for her husband and the nation, entertaining guests from charitable organizations and women's clubs to world heads of state. It was a role she relished and took seriously, one she had played during her entire married life. During her husband's military and diplomatic career, the couple's quarters were known as "Club Eisenhower." Accustomed to official circles, Mamie Eisenhower ushered in a new era in Washington's social scene. After a long period of curtailed activities due to the Great Depression, World War II, and the Truman renovation, she brought formal, large-scale entertaining to the White House.[26] Nona Brown Washington reported for the *New York Times,* "She says that the First Lady's role represents very little change from her life of the past eleven years, since Dwight Eisenhower became a public figure . . . [with] protocol-encrusted dinners and receptions." Mrs. Eisenhower noted that she counted her "years of training" as a military wife to be a "definite asset."[27]

The Eisenhowers maintained a full White House social schedule. During the social season of 1954 the president and first lady held fourteen formal State Dinners, four formal evening receptions, and nine State Luncheons, and they attended six embassy dinners and six press dinners. In addition there were numerous informal receptions, dinners, teas, and public tours that the Eisenhower White House hosted for charitable groups, philanthropies, women's clubs, and traditional organizations such as veterans, the Girl Scouts, and the Red Cross.[28] In addition, in the early years of the administration, President Eisenhower had introduced a "Knife and Fork" series of breakfasts, luncheons, and dinners for members of Congress, and he hosted small stag dinners (these probably could not have taken place in the following decade) for male leaders in every field, to which guests usually wore white dinner jackets.[29] In the 1970s, when White House head usher J. B. West published *Upstairs at the White House,* society reporter Isabelle Shelton quoted West's description of Mamie Eisenhower's no-nonsense approach to entertaining: "She knew exactly what she wanted and how it should be done. She could give orders like a five star general. . . . [She had] a spine of steel forged by years of military discipline."[30]

Having experienced the finest of international entertaining during his years as head of the North Atlantic Treaty Organization, the president insisted that White House menus and protocol be elaborate and formal. Evening dress was white tie. Assisting Mrs. Eisenhower with entertaining duties was her social secretary, Mary Jane McCaffree, and a French chef, François Rysavy, who prepared formal dinners. Mamie Eisenhower herself oversaw the selection of food and the preparation of the menus. State Dinners consisted of seven courses, with the menu printed in English. The first lady introduced an E-shaped table to her formal state dinners so that she and Ike could sit side by side and face their guests, rather than use the U-shaped table where the presidential couple were seated across from each other and the first lady's back was to her guests.

Mrs. Eisenhower took a particular interest in the White House china collection, and, although the Trumans had purchased an elegant state dining service as part of the mansion's 1948–52 renovation, the first lady wanted to leave her own mark on the china collection. She ordered service plates to seat a dinner of 120

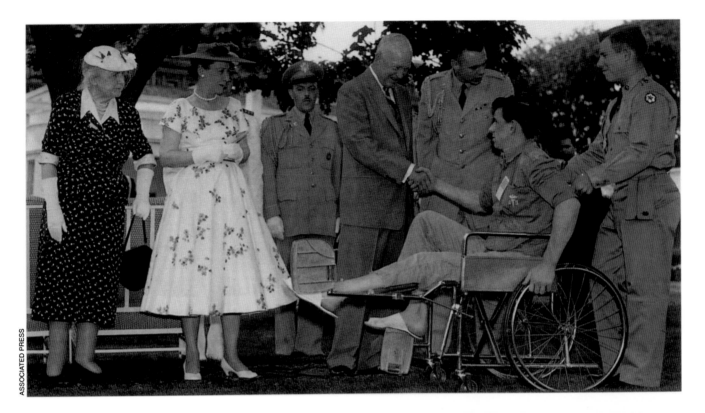

President and Mrs. Eisenhower greet guests at a White House garden party hosted for Korean War veterans in May 1954.

Mrs. Eisenhower was known for her elaborate White House holiday decorations. Corn stalks and black cats were featured at Halloween in 1958.

guests. The rims of the plates were covered with pure coin gold in an embossed gold medallion pattern, with the presidential seal in gold in the center. These service plates, made by Castleton, a subsidiary of Shenango China Company of New Castle, Pennsylvania, at a cost of $3,606.40, were delivered to the White House on October 25, 1955. Mrs. Eisenhower most often mixed the service plates with the Truman state dinnerware of celadon green plates.[31]

The White House State Dinner for the Soviet Union's Nikita and Nina Khrushchev on September 15, 1959, serves as an example of the Eisenhowers' formal entertaining style, as the menus and events remained remarkably similar throughout the eight-year administration. The first course of melon with prosciutto ham was followed by curry soup with whole wheat melba toast, celery hearts, and queen and ripe olives. A third course con-

By Douglas Chevalier. Staff Photographer

An Eisenhower Waits for Halloween

Mary Jean Eisenhower is almost 3, so she's not afraid of Halloween ghosts, goblins, witches, black cats and owls which are now hanging in the usually sedate marble foyer of the White House. The President's granddaughter sits on a pump- kin in front of a shock of golden corn stalks and waits to do a little haunting herself. Tourists who visit the White House today and Saturday can see the decorations. Story on Page C1 and another picture on Page C2.

President and Mrs. Eisenhower pose with Soviet Premier Nikita and Madame Nina Khrushchev on the Ground Floor prior to a State Dinner. The doors that form the background were made from pine beams extracted from the White House during the Truman renovation. Though reflecting classic 1950s taste, the exposed pine is now painted.

The menu for the State Dinner held in honor of the visit of the Khrushchevs on September 15, 1959, showcased classic American foods such as roasted turkey with dressing.

DINNER

Melon with Prosciutto Ham

Dry Sack — Curry Soup / Whole Wheat Melba Toast / Celery Hearts — Queen and Ripe Olives

Chateau Climens 1950 — Molded Crab Louis / Coleslaw in Tomato Basket / Boston Brown Bread Sandwiches

Beaune Greves 1952 — Roast Young Turkey / Cornbread Dressing / Gravy / Whole Cranberry Sauce / Scalloped Sweet Potatoes and Pineapple / French Green Beans Almondine / Bread Sticks

Pol Roger 1952 — Tossed Bibb Lettuce Parmesan / Green Goddess Dressing / Toasted Sesame Crackers

Lime Glacé / Ladyfingers

Nuts   Candies   Coffee

THE WHITE HOUSE
Tuesday, September 15, 1959

sisted of molded crab Louis, with coleslaw in a tomato basket and Boston brown bread sandwiches. The main course was probably meant to showcase a classic American favorite: roast young turkey with cornbread dressing and gravy, whole cranberry sauce, scalloped sweet potatoes and pineapple, French green beans almondine, and bread sticks. The fifth course of tossed bibb lettuce Parmesan was served with green goddess dressing and toasted sesame crackers. Dessert of lime glacé and lady fingers was followed by a final course of nuts, candies, and coffee. The after-dinner musical entertainment was provided by that middle-American

favorite, Fred Waring and the Pennsylvanians "in a program of Best Loved American Songs."[32] Although the president and Mrs. Eisenhower were formally attired in "white tie" and evening gown for the 8:00 p.m. evening dinner, Premier Khrushchev appeared in a dark business suit and Mrs. Khrushchev wore a plain blue-teal gown.[33] No doubt the Khrushchevs wished to avoid wearing "decadent" capitalist clothing.

Other types of entertaining for which the first lady was renowned included garden parties for senior citizens at public retirement facilities, teas on the White House lawn, large receptions for wounded veterans, holiday luncheons and teas, receptions for White House staff, and luncheons for congressional and Senate wives, women reporters, and wives of chiefs of state. Mamie Eisenhower especially liked theme parties and holidays. An example of her informal entertaining was the Halloween party given for the wives of the White House staff on October 30, 1958, which featured "eight spooky skeletons hung from wall lights" in the State Dining Room while miniature witches on broomsticks perched on white tablecloths. Yellow jack-o'-lanterns and shocks of corn stalks were banked in the corners of the room. Black cats, disembodied witch heads, black owls, and goblins peered from among the fall foliage mounted on the chandeliers in the foyer. Spaced along the table were miniature goblins, ghosts, owls, and cats. Orange light bulbs in the chandeliers lent an eerie glow.[34]

These extremes of formal and informal White House entertaining showcased the first lady's expertise and knowledge of the best the nation had to offer in food, presentation, and musical entertainment for diplomatic and international circles, while her humorous—sometimes "hokey"—informal theme parties demonstrated her skill in making the most average American citizen feel welcomed and at home in the White House. Mamie Eisenhower's personal style in hair, fashion, and entertaining both reflected and set American taste in the postwar era and engendered a popularity that endeared the Eisenhower administration to the nation.

NOTES

1. Quoted in Carl S. Anthony, *First Ladies: The Saga of the Presidents' Wives and Their Power, 1789–1961* (New York: William Morrow, 1990), 45.

2. Edith P. Mayo, "Mamie Eisenhower and the Campaigns of the 1950s," in *Mamie Eisenhower—Wife, Mother, First Lady: Her Impact and Influence on Her Time* (Gettysburg, Pa.: Eisenhower Seminar, 1998), 16–27.

3. Martin Teasley, " Mamie (Geneva Doud) Eisenhower," in *American First Ladies: Their Lives and Their Legacy,* ed. Lewis Gould (New York: Garland Publishing, 1996), 468.

4. Edith P. Mayo, *Enterprising Women: 250 Years of American Business,* script for a traveling exhibition of the same title sponsored by the Schlesinger Library, Radcliffe Institute for Advanced Research, Harvard University, 2002–4.

5. Alfred Allan Lewis and Constance Woodworth, *Miss Elizabeth Arden* (New York: Coward, McCann & Geoghan, 1972), 282.

6. Elizabeth Arden to Mamie Eisenhower, January 3, 1953, Mamie Dowd Eisenhower Papers, 1894–1979, White House Series, box 2, folder Elizabeth Arden, Dwight D. Eisenhower Presidential Library, Abilene, Kans.

7. Mamie Eisenhower to Elizabeth Arden, January 26, 1953, ibid.

8. Elizabeth Arden to Mamie Eisenhower, February 20, 1953, ibid.

9. Elizabeth Arden to Mamie Eisenhower, March 25, 1959, ibid..

10. Karal Ann Marling, *As Seen on TV: The Visual Culture of Everyday Life in the 1950s* (Cambridge, Mass.: Harvard University Press, 1994), 9–19.

11. Ibid., 19.

12. Ibid., 24, quoting Mamie Eisenhower.

13. Ibid.

14. Ibid., 26.

15. Ibid., 25.

16. Quoted in ibid., 26.

17. Ibid.

18. Eisenhower inaugural press release, January 13, 1953, Mamie Doud Eisenhower Papers, 1894–1979, White House Series, box 22, folder Inauguration 1953 (1), Eisenhower Library.

19. Stanley Marcus to Mrs. Dwight D. Eisenhower, July 23, 1952, and Lawrence Marcus to Mrs. Dwight D. Eisenhower, December 1, 1952, file Personal Data—Wardrobe N–Q, box 381, White House Social Office, Eisenhower Library.

20. Eisenhower inaugural press release, January 13, 1953, box 22, White House Series, Mamie Doud Eisenhower Papers, 1894–1979, folder Inauguration 1953 (1), Eisenhower Library.

21. Marling, *As Seen on TV,* 35.

22. Eisenhower inaugural press release, January 13, 1953. The inaugural gown, purse, gloves, and shoes are now housed in the First Ladies Collection, Division of Politics and Reform, National Museum of American History, Smithsonian Institution, Washington, D.C.

23. Ibid.

24. Marling, *As Seen on TV,* 33.

25. Ibid., 35.

26. Edith P. Mayo, *First Ladies: Political Role and Public Image,* script for an exhibition at the National Museum of American History, Smithsonian Institution, 1992–2006, and the traveling exhibition of the same title, 2004–7.

27. Nona Brown Washington, "Being First Lady Is a Man-Sized Job," *New York Times,* May 10, 1953, 1, 3, clipping file, Office of the Curator, The White House, Washington, D.C.

28. Betty Beale, "Eisenhowers in the White House," *Washington Sunday Star,* March 30, 1969, E–2, clipping file, Office of the Curator, The White House..

29. Ona Griffin Jeffries, *In and Out of the White House* (New York: Wilfred Funk, 1960), 379–80.

30. Isabelle Shelton, "J. B. West, 'Upstairs at the White House,'" *Washington Star-News,* July 22, 1973, F–3, clipping file, Office of the Curator, The White House.

31. Margaret Brown Klapthor, *The First Ladies Cook Book: Favorite Recipes of All the Presidents of the United States* (New York: Published for *Parents' Magazine Press* by Home Library Press, 1965), 203–6; Margaret Brown Klapthor, *Official White House China: 1789 to the Present* (Washington, D.C.: Smithsonian Institution Press, 1975), 162–63.

32. Menu and musicale program, scrapbook, Tuesday, September 15, 1959, Office of the Curator, The White House.

33. Jeffries, *In and Out of the White House,* 392.

34. Marie Smith, *Entertaining in the White House* (Washington, D.C.: Acropolis Books, 1967), 228–29.

President Eisenhower: Painter

SISTER WENDY BECKETT

*T*he only true response to art is to look with an eye like that of a child: unprejudiced, unbiased, clear, and uncommitted. When it is the art of a celebrity, this ideal, always almost unobtainable, becomes progressively difficult. Can we see the work in the dazzle of the artist's aura? When the paintings of Noel Coward come to auction, they do well enough, but are the buyers interested in Coward himself rather than in his work, bright, confident, and attractive though it is? When Prince Charles, who is a seriously good painter, sends his work to the Royal Academy Summer Exhibition, where it shows to great effect, he sends it under a nom-de-plume, precisely so as to allow the selectors to choose or reject only on artistic merit. The prime example is Winston Churchill, a man whom history has already anointed as great. Is it really possible to make an objective judgment of his pictures?

Churchill the painter, of course, is the closest equivalent we have of Dwight D. Eisenhower as painter. It may well have been seeing his friend at work, lost in the joy of his pigments, that first turned Eisenhower's mind to the possibility of painting himself. His immediate spur, we know, was observing the artist Thomas E. Stephens painting a portrait of Mamie Eisenhower during their all

---

President Eisenhower at his easel at Camp David (opposite). Sir Winston Churchill (above) may have been one inspiration that led him to painting.

too brief stay at Columbia University. The future president, at the time only president of the university, was intrigued, and his mind, ever restless and emulative, became fascinated by the challenge of himself "copying" what was before him. One of the little-realized facts about Eisenhower was the intensity of his need to excel. Ike looked laid-back and affable, and indeed he was, a delightful man. But at heart he was determined always to be in command, never to be bested. This ambition showed with painful rawness in his boyhood, challenging his elder brothers. He learned to hide it under his easy smile and genuine charm, but one can quite imagine him studying Mamie's portrait and feeling determined to see if he could find within himself skills to match the artist's.

Before Stephens made his visit to the Eisenhowers, the president seems to have had no encounter with art except as the hobby of Winston Churchill. Since golf was Eisenhower's hobby, and always would be, his interest in Churchillian landscapes was benignly detached. After the war though, with time on his hands, this strange activity entered significantly into his own space, as it were. While Mamie and Stephens toured the house to find the best place to hang her portrait, Eisenhower got his aide, John Moaney, to help him stretch a white dust cloth for a canvas to the bottom of a box. Then—one can imagine his puzzled but dogged expression—he tried to copy the picture. He showed the group what he had done, he says, describing his efforts as "weird and wonderful to behold," adding that "we all laughed heartily."[1] Stephens asked for this attempt as a keepsake, and was given it without hesitation. Eisenhower, for all his pride, had no false pride.

Painting was not something Eisenhower wanted to be good at or, perhaps, thought he could be good at. Stephens sent him a complete painting kit, which Ike appreciated but thought a "sheer waste of money," something the boy from a poor home could never accept comfortably. Maybe it was this innate frugality—the desire not to waste a gift—that spurred him to practice. Eisenhower was convinced that to become a painter, he lacked the one thing necessary, "ability."[2] But he was interested: he enjoyed experimenting. He would not dream of painting, of course, if there were a chance for golf or, for that matter, if he could find bridge partners or set up a poker game. (His legendary skill at poker, said to have added appreciably to his military earnings throughout his career, meant there were few partners to hand.) But at 58, the age in which painting became a part, however tenuous, of his life, the physical demands of golf and his weakening heart made his idle hours more frequent. The Kennedy successors said that Eisenhower had never read a book, which annoyed Mamie, who knew how assiduously he had pored over military history. But that was reading with a purpose: information a soldier needed. Those days were over, and as president, he read little more than Westerns. Painting, with its inbuilt challenge, its very status of being something he was not naturally good at, was a far more attractive option.

Writing to Churchill in 1950, Eisenhower said, "I have a lot of fun since I took it up, in my somewhat miserable way, your hobby of painting. I have had no instruction, have no talent, and certainly no justification for covering nice, white canvas with the kind of daubs that seem constantly to spring from my brushes. Nevertheless, I like it tremendously, and in fact, have produced two or three things that I like enough to

keep."[3] This is language rather different from Churchill's own, which speaks about art in exalted terms: "Soul," "Contemplation of harmonies," "Joy and glory."[4] But for Churchill, painting genuinely mattered. He had an outdoor hobby, bricklaying, but that satisfied him far less than the aesthetic stimulus he derived from gazing at something beautiful and trying to make visible his personal reaction to it. For Eisenhower, the excitement was in the manual skill in producing a copy, usually of a photograph or a magazine reproduction. (If the weather was fine enough to sit and paint, it was fine enough for golf: no contest!) It was simply the intellectual puzzle of it, how to make on his own canvas what another artist or photographer had captured. His favorite subject was his daughter-in-law with his two grandchildren, but he branched out freely into depictions of landscape, however secondhand, and buildings, with the occasional portrait (remember, copied). He described his portrait paintings as "magnificent audacity," and burned most of them.[5] Churchill valued what he had created. Eisenhower did not. It was the making that Eisenhower enjoyed, rather akin to achieving a birdie at golf, and what was made was a means, not an end.

Eisenhower was reticent about his deep emotions. (Of the supreme sorrow of his life, the death in babyhood of his son Icky, he never spoke.) We catch a rare glimpse of his inner nature when we read, in a letter of late adolescence, how he felt about the loss, through injury, of the football career that had been his driving passion. "Life seemed to have little meaning. A need to excel was gone."[6] The "need to excel" grew back again, now not rooted in football or boxing—another skill—but in the army and, eventually, in politics. I think it was this same need that drove him in his painting. He would have scorned any thought of objective excellence. He called his works "daubs": was he right? Or was he overly modest? The dictionary defines a "daub" as a painting that is clumsy or crude, with implications of carelessness. This is not true in Eisenhower's case. He took infinite care, sometimes, he confessed, spending two hours in getting a color "right."[7] Nor was he so unskilled. His first encounter with a professional artist, at Columbia, led to his being given the tools for serious work in this field. Obviously, though he may have laughed with Ike, Stephens was impressed.

What Eisenhower was to produce in the last short third of his life is work that still gives the impartial onlooker pleasure. A daub irritates; these paintings, simple and earnest, rather cause us to wonder at the hidden depths of this reticent president. Notice the scenes to which he was drawn: they are all of the peaceful countryside, a symbol of the unspoiled America in which he had grown to manhood. Naturally, experienced traveler that he was, there are foreign scenes, too: Ann Hathaway's Cottage in England, a French garden, or an Alpine scene. But he concentrates on views like *Rolling Wooded Hills,* painted in Denver in 1955. He had a special affection for hills, and here they gently rise and fall. He had an affection, too, for tall trees, often the subject of presidential doodling in the Oval Office. In this work we see two, green and gold, and surging toward them a bright pool of bluebonnets, dazzling in the sunshine. He admitted to a great love of color, and it is delightfully apparent in all his best pictures. I have a fondness for the *Mountain Fall Scene,* where it is not hills but mountains that seize his attention, splendid peaks, rising in icy splendor, blue and shadowed, while the foreground is alive with the brightness of an American fall. Two small trees are a gleaming yellow, while behind them another two, equally spindly, are deep pink, tipped with crimson. If we really look at this mountain path framed with evergreens, we begin to notice, as the artist did, many stray touches of color, yellows and pinks, that tie the whole picture together tonally. Who but the artist himself would dare call this a "daub"? Not great art, needless to say, but pleasing art, art that has a lyrical sweetness to it, however unassumingly expressed.

Eisenhower was interested in undamaged nature—perhaps the effect of years as a soldier?—and in people. To me, the nature studies are more effective, but sometimes he gets a face exactly right. One of Mamie's favorite pictures was *Mexican,* which Ike painted in 1953 from an advertisement. He has caught the man's vigor, the masculine radiance of his smile, the swagger of his sombrero, the dazzling flash of his teeth against the sunburn of his face. He is interesting, too, on Abraham Lincoln, not so much in the traditional bearded Lincoln, well depicted though it is. He gave this image to the White House staff as their 1953 Christmas card, and I imagine it is still cherished. But there is a more imaginative projection in *Melancholy Lincoln,* taken from a photograph of the young lawyer, clean shaven and yet inexplicably sad. Eisenhower did not paint to "express" his inner self; he curbed his imagination and resolutely imitated the reproduction before him. Yet there seems to me a personal note in this work, as if

he were subliminally seeing in Lincoln's melancholy a distant awareness of the burden of the presidency.

Because we are so conditioned to overreact to celebrity, most of us will have come to Eisenhower's paintings with a readiness to scoff. But try to be impartial, and you will be very pleasantly surprised. One final irony. President Eisenhower was a conservative, in art as in many other areas, and he had no time at all for the avant-garde. He felt modern art was morally wrong. Speaking on May Day, 1962, he grieved that "our very art forms [are] so changed that we seem to have forgotten the works of Michelangelo and Leonardo da Vinci" and went on to excoriate, with unusual eloquence, works like "a piece of canvas that looks like a broken-down Tin Lizzie, loaded with paint, has been driven over it." "What has happened to our concept of beauty and decency and morality?"[8] Here comes the irony. Take up any magazine of contemporary art, or look through a Christie's or Sotheby's catalog of such a sale. You will find that, for some of the best-selling contemporary artists, their aim seems to be to create what looks like a "daub."

The effect of clumsiness that Eisenhower so fought against, untrained and inexperienced as he was, is now sought after by men and women, highly trained and deeply experienced. Their works adorn the walls of galleries that would laugh at the very thought of hanging an Eisenhower. Yet who is the truer artist, these mischievous painters who play with their skill, or Eisenhower, thrilled by color, eager to understand how to create, humble but persevering?

NOTES

1. Dwight D. Eisenhower, *At Ease: Stories I Tell to Friends* (Garden City, N.Y.: Doubleday, 1967), 340.

2. Ibid.

3. Dwight D. Eisenhower to Winston S. Churchill, September 21, 1950, Pre-presidential Files (16–52), Churchill, W (2), DDE to WC, box 22, Dwight D. Eisenhower Presidential Library, Abilene, Kans.

4. Winston Churchill, *Painting as a Pastime* (New York, Cornerstone Library Publications), 23–24.

5. Eisenhower, *At Ease,* 341.

6. Ibid., 16

7. Kenneth S. Davis, *The Eisenhower College Collection: The Paintings of Dwight D. Eisenhower* (Los Angeles: Nash Publishing,) 147–49.

8. Dwight D. Eisenhower, Eisenhower Library Dedication speech, May 1, 1962, Post-presidential Papers, 1961–69, Speech series, box 2, Eisenhower Library.

Winter Birches, *oil, 1955.*

Snow Capped Mountains, *oil, c. 1955.*

Untitled waterfall, oil on canvas, 1949. Inscribed on the canvas at the lower edge, "For my friend, Howard Young, Dwight D. Eisenhower."

George Washington, *oil, 1954. Eisenhower's portrait of George Washington is based upon Gilbert Stuart's "Athenaeum" portrait of Washington painted in 1796, popularly known as the "unfinished" portrait. A copy of this picture hung in tens of thousands of American schoolrooms, perhaps Eisenhower's as well, when he was boy.*

Eisenhower Family Home, *Oil, mid-1950s, after a painting by Margaret Sandzen Greenough.*

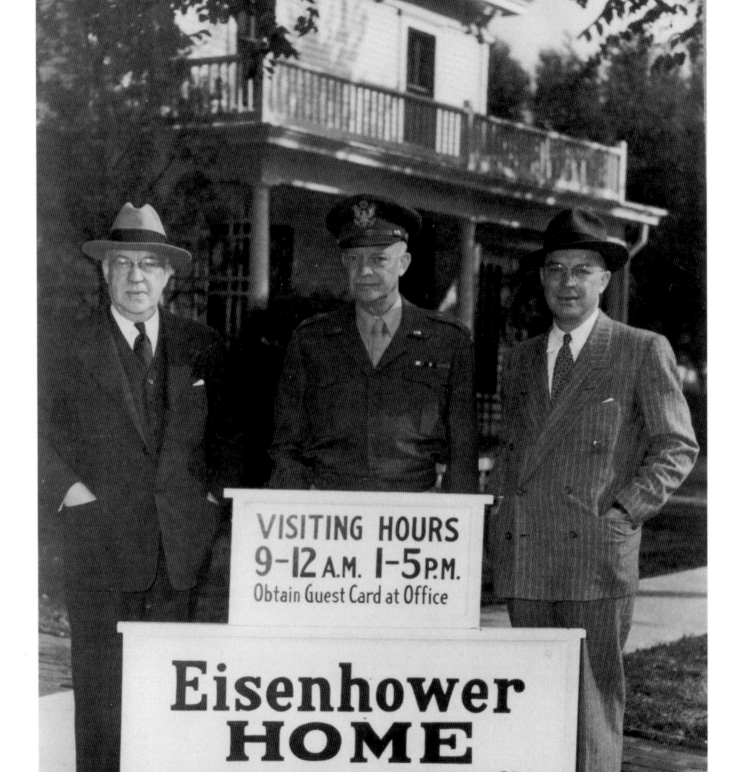

The Eisenhower Family Home in Abilene, Kansas

DENNIS MEDINA

The Eisenhower Family Home is located in the heart of the Midwest—Abilene, Kansas—and is part of the complex known as the Eisenhower Center. The 23 acre center includes the Dwight D. Eisenhower Presidential Library, a repository for the papers of the thirty-fourth president of the United States; the Eisenhower Museum; the Visitors Center; and the Place of Meditation, where Dwight David Eisenhower and Mamie Doud Eisenhower are buried. Also buried here is their first-born son, Doud Dwight, affectionately nick-named Icky by his maternal grandmother; the child died at the age of three in 1921, more than thirty years before the start of the presidency and originally had been buried in Denver. The Eisenhower Center is administered by the National Archives and Records Administration (NARA) and is one of twelve libraries in the Presidential Library system. The Eisenhower Family Home is the only historic home in the NARA system. Many of the presidential homes and birthplaces are operated by the National Park Service or a state agency.

Much has been written about the history of the town of Abilene, Kansas. It is known from 1867 to 1885 for

Brothers Arthur, Dwight, and Milton Eisenhower in front of the family home, 1947, where they were reared with their brothers Edgar, Roy, and Earl.

its cattle trail days as "The End of the Chisholm Trail"; a Wild West town that had a famous U.S. marshal, Wild Bill Hickok; a community of fine Victorian homes; and Eisenhower's boyhood home. In fact, on I-70, as one approaches Abilene from the east or the west, billboards advertise Abilene as the town of "History, Mansions, and Heroes."

A large part of the history of the Eisenhower Family Home was collected by J. Earl Endacott, a retired schoolteacher and the executive secretary of the Eisenhower Foundation and curator of the Eisenhower Home and Museum, which was operated privately by the foundation. In the early 1970s, Charlotte Clark, education specialist, and I assisted Endacott in developing a more comprehensive history of the house and the grounds for use as a training guide for the docents in the Eisenhower Family Home. In the mid-1970s the museum staff began an archaeological dig of the grounds to locate several outbuildings that had been removed in the 1930s.

The Eisenhower family migrated to Dickinson, Kansas, from Lancaster, Pennsylvania, in 1878. Three generations of the Eisenhower family made the trip; they were in the first group to come to this community. Frederick Eisenhower (the president's great-grandfather), the senior member, was accompanied by his son Jacob Frederick and several of Jacob Frederick's children, including David, Ike's father. They settled in a community southeast of Abilene known as Belle Springs. Another group came to this area a year later.

This migration was part of a close-knit religious group known as the River Brethren that was devoted to its religious beliefs and also to the economics of the community. Eventually these newcomers formed the Belle Springs Creamery, an outlet for selling dairy products from their farms to consumers. In later years, Eisenhower's father worked at the creamery along with all of his sons while they were in high school.

The Eisenhower Family Home, according to records found in the Dickinson County Courthouse, was erected on lot 9, block 8, of the J. M. Fisher Addition, Dickinson County, Abilene, Kansas. This original structure at 201 Southeast Fourth Street was built by Ephraim Ellis, a schoolteacher, in 1887. The property returned to the ownership of J. M. Fisher for nonpayment of property taxes. On May 11, 1894, Anna B. Eisenhower, wife of Abraham Lincoln Eisenhower, Dwight's uncle and a lay preacher, purchased the house from the estate of J. M. Fisher for $200. In 1898, Abraham entered the ministry on a full-time basis in Oklahoma; he and his wife, Anna, sold the home to Ida Stover Eisenhower, Dwight's mother, for $1,000, as recorded in the Dickinson County Courthouse, Office of the Register of Deeds, on November 4, 1898. On August 24, 1907, the deed was changed to reflect joint ownership of both Eisenhower's parents, David J. Eisenhower and Ida S. Eisenhower.

The location proved ideal for the fast-growing family of Eisenhower boys. Ida and David, married in 1885, had seven sons: Arthur Bradford (1886–1958), Edgar Newton (1889–1971), Dwight David (1890–1969), Roy Jacob (1892–1942), Paul Abraham (1894–1895), Earl David (1898–1968), and Milton Stover (1899–1985). Along with the residence, the nearly three acres of land contained a vegetable garden planted by the Eisenhowers. Lincoln Grade School was located on the west,

across the street, and several somewhat similar residences stood on the south.

In architectural terms, the Eisenhowers' house would have been called a "cottage" for sure. The style was probably the "chalet" mode, or perhaps Queen Anne. The cubical two-story form was made interesting by an asymmetrical arrangement of a small entrance porch and an uncovered deck railed in wooden fretwork. Odd peaked pediments surmounted the pair of windows of the parlor, which was also enhanced by a bay window. It was a charming cottage with a decorative flair. Sometime after 1900, the Eisenhower family added a new one-story south porch, the entire width of the house. Three round Doric columns supported the flat roof, which was crowned by a wooden balustrade. With this change the Victorian cottage took on the look of a more modern Colonial Revival house.

The structure was wood balloon frame, two stories, painted white, with three very small rooms on each floor. On the first were the front and back parlors, divided by a long, narrow entry hall and stairwell that terminated in a combined dining room–kitchen. The hallway was also used as a room for sewing and storage for quite a number of books. Upstairs were two bedrooms plus a small bedroom known for a while as the nursery but later always the bedroom for the oldest boy living at home. The house was constructed of white pine clapboard siding with a cedar shingle roof. The interior walls were lath and plaster trimmed with pine woodwork that was variously stained or painted. The original piers and footings were stones held together by mortar. Dug out beneath the house was a storm and root cellar with dirt walls and floor, but the rest of the area was a crawl space.

Prior to the move in 1898, the Eisenhowers had lived at 112 Southeast Second Street, a block and a half north

of the structure today known as the Eisenhower Family Home. Ike later recalled:

> The move from the little cottage on Second to the new house was a step up in the world! A two-story step, for the new house seemed a mansion with its upstairs bedrooms. There were two fairly large bedrooms, with a miniature bedroom at the end of the hall. The first of the large ones was occupied by Father and Mother with the baby, Earl, in a cradle. Three boys slept in the adjoining room, Roy and I in one bed, Edgar in the other. Arthur, the eldest, was awarded the little room at the end of the hall. Its dimensions were 6½ feet by 6½ feet. Whether considered as an underdeveloped bedroom or a generous closet, the rest of us envied his splendid isolation. He was the only person in the house with a room of his own.[1]

After a visit to Abilene in 1962, Edgar wrote to Ike, "Earl, Milton and I visited the home and again I was struck by the smallness of the rooms and I wondered how eight people could ever have lived in such small quarters. In fact, we three brothers were unable to determine exactly where Earl and Milton slept."[2] But Eisenhower also recalled his mother's delight in the new house: "For the first time we have a home where my children will have room to play. I am most thankful."[3]

In 1900, the living space was increased by the addition of two bedrooms and a small connecting closet to the east side of the house. This addition provided space for Grandfather Jacob Frederick Eisenhower, who moved in with his son after the death of his wife, Rebecca, and later the death of his housekeeper-caregiver. The bedroom Grandfather Eisenhower occupied was also the room in which young Dwight passed through one of the most difficult episodes of his early years. Stricken with blood poisoning at age 16, Dwight refused to allow the doctor to amputate his badly infected leg. Two of his brothers guarded the door, which the patient had barricaded from within. A local physician later consulted a Topeka physician, and with the drastic treatment, "the painting of a belt of carbolic acid around my body, the progress of the disease was stopped,"[4] Eisenhower later recalled. Recovery was complete, but young Dwight lost so much time from school that he was forced to repeat his freshman year of high school. A few years after

Opposite: The Eisenhower boys at the 112 Southeast Second Street residence, where the family lived from 1892 to 1898, a small one-story house, their first Abilene home.

Right: The Eisenhower home as the Eisenhowers bought it prior to the south porch addition. Parlor windows look onto an uncovererd deck or terrace.

Below: The Eisenhower Family Home, c. 1900, with the added south porch and crowning balustrade crossing the front, providing shade and a comfortable outdoor living room.

DWIGHT D. EISENHOWER LIBRARY

DWIGHT D. EISENHOWER LIBRARY

Left: Dwight and Mamie Eisenhower on their wedding day, Denver, Colorado, July 1, 1916.

Opposite, top: First Lieutenant Dwight D. Eisenhower (seated on the steps) with his family on the south porch in 1926. From left to right: his brothers Roy, Arthur, Earl, and Edgar, his father David, his brother Milton, and his mother Ida.

Opposite, bottom left: President Eisenhower's parents, Ida and David Eisenhower, on their south porch, about the beginning of World War II.

Opposite, bottom right: The widowed Ida Eisenhower with Eisenhower Foundation members on the west side porch, 1945. After her death, her sons donated the house to the foundation, specifying that it be kept exactly as she left it.

Grandfather Eisenhower's death in 1906, when city water and sewer connections arrived in the south side of Abilene, this bedroom was converted into a bathroom.

In 1915 a new kitchen and pantry were built on the north end of the house. Prior to this addition, the cooking took place in the largest room of the house, the combined dining room and kitchen on the back of the first floor. A large coal-burning stove was located in this room until 1919, when gas was finally brought into the area and the kitchen was moved into the 1915 kitchen space.

In 1911, Eisenhower left his family and Abilene for the United States Military Academy, West Point, New York. Upon graduation in 1915 as a second lieutenant, he was assigned to Fort Sam Houston in San Antonio, Texas. There in the fall of 1915, he met Mamie Geneva Doud, and, after a brief courtship, they became engaged on Valentine's Day, 1916. They originally planned a

November wedding, but with war raging in Europe, the young couple decided to marry on July 1, 1916, in Denver. No Eisenhower relations were present at the wedding. Therefore, after a brief honeymoon the newlyweds left Denver by train for Abilene to see Ike's family for a matter of hours before heading back to San Antonio. They arrived very early in the morning. "My Mother was determined that we would have at least one fine meal in her house," Eisenhower recalled, "and so instead of the normal breakfast, our meal that morning was a monumental fried chicken dinner."[5]

The bride's memories of the Eisenhower family home, on the few visits she made, were not always pleasant. She later explained that soon after she and her husband arrived in Abilene for family visits, Ike would leave and go into town and play cards with his male friends, leaving her at the house with her in-laws. Ida and David Eisenhower were stern River Brethren who

Left: Merrill Eisenhower Atwater, the president's great-grandson, speaks from the front porch of the Eisenhower Famly Home at a program marking the fiftieth anniversary of President Eisenhower's great project, the National Defense Highway Act that created the interstate highway system.

Right: A recent aerial view of the Dwight D. Eisenhower Presidential Library and Museum.

did not condone smoking, much less drinking, in their house. Mamie would slip upstairs, sit by an open bedroom window, and have her cigarette, blowing the smoke through the window screens.[6]

The Eisenhower boys grew to manhood in this simple house and nurturing home. Their success in life is remarkable. Arthur, a banker, lived in Kansas City; Edgar, a lawyer, lived in Tacoma, Washington; Dwight was supreme commander, Allied Expeditionary Forces, during World War II, president of Columbia University, and thirty-fourth president of the United States; Roy, a pharmacist, lived in Junction City, Kansas; Earl, an electrical engineer, lived in Illinois and Indiana; and Milton was president of Kansas State University, Pennsylvania State University, and Johns Hopkins University, and was an indispensable special adviser to the Eisenhower administration. The boys' father died in 1941, and Ida Eisenhower continued to live in the house with the assistance of a caregiver until her death in 1946. The Eisenhower sons donated the property to the newly created Eisenhower Foundation with the understanding that the furnishings must remain as left by their mother and no major changes could be made to the home with-

out their consent. The foundation opened the Eisenhower Home to the public on June 22, 1947, and since that time it has been seen by more than 3 million visitors.

In July 1951 Smoky Hill River, just south of Abilene, and Mud Creek, to the west, rose to flood stage and crested 3 feet higher than the record set in a 1903 flood. Floodwaters did not damage the first floor of the Eisenhower Home, but the basement was engulfed in water and its rock foundation was ruined. Because of cost, temporary measures only were undertaken. In 1955, however, Edward J. and Katherine Bermingham, friends of Eisenhower from his days as president of Columbia University, were visiting from Wyoming and worked out an agreement to assist financially with the needed repairs. A contracting firm prepared a full condition report of the structure and outlined the work needed to stabilize it and to improve the grade above the floodplain. Following completion of repairs, the home was rededicated on November 27, 1956. Routine maintenance, replacement of climate and security systems, the replication of the first floor interior wall coverings, and occasional exterior painting and reroofing have ensured that it looks the same now as it did then.

In a January 12, 1962, letter to his brothers, Eisenhower described a proposal from Harry Darby, chairman of the Eisenhower Foundation, that the home be turned over to the federal government.[7] This transaction was not completed until 1966, when the Eisenhower Foundation turned over ownership of the home and the Eisenhower Museum buildings to the federal government to operate them as part of the Presidential Library system. The governing agency was originally the General Services Administration. In 1985, Congress created an independent agency within the federal government, the National Archives and Records Administration, and within this administration the Office of Presidential Libraries.

On January 25, 1971, State Historic Preservation Officer Nyle Miller signed the documents placing the Eisenhower Family Home on the National Register of Historic Places. The home has been the site of several Eisenhower-Doud family reunions, and most recently Merrill Eisenhower Atwater, great-grandson of the president, gave remarks on the porch of the home for the fiftieth anniversary of President Eisenhower's signing of the National Defense Highway Act creating the interstate highway system. He said,

> Abilene holds a special place in our family's heart. This is where our roots are. My great-grandfather lived right here where I am standing. It is amazing to me and eerie at the same time knowing that he played right where I am standing. . . . That is absolutely fantastic.[8]

NOTES

1. Dwight D. Eisenhower, *At Ease: Stories I Tell to Friends* (Garden City, N.Y.: Doubleday, 1967), 72.

2. Edgar Newton Eisenhower to Dwight D. Eisenhower, May 8, 1962, 1962 Principal File, box 33, Eisenhower (Family Correspondence), Dwight D. Eisenhower Presidential Library, Abilene, Kans.

3. Quoted in Eisenhower, *At Ease,*1.

4. Ibid., 97.

5. Ibid., 123.

6. Mamie Doud Eisenhower, conversation with the author, October 1970.

7. Dwight D. Eisenhower to Milton Eisenhower, January 12, 1962, 1962 Signature File, box 33, Eisenhower (2), Eisenhower Library.

8. Merrill Eisenhower Atwater, Speech on the Fiftieth Anniversary Highway Act, June 21, 2006, EL-VT-329-1, film, Eisenhower Library.

The Eisenhower Home is open seven days a week, except for Thanksgiving, Christmas, and New Year's Day. For further information on the Eisenhower Center, visit the website, at www.eisenhower.archives.gov.

"Proud Housewife": Mamie Eisenhower Collects for the White House

MELISSA NAULIN

Every presidential family that resides in the White House leaves a mark on the building and its traditions. The extent of a family's influence on the physical White House depends usually on its length of residence and its inclinations to take the trouble to make changes. History plays a part as well. While major additions to the White House and its grounds have usually been directed by the presidents themselves, changes to the interior furnishings have typically fallen to the first ladies. Mamie Eisenhower's impact in this regard has been underappreciated, especially in the light of the campaign of her successor, Jacqueline Kennedy, to "restore" the White House with antiques to the idea of its earliest years. Yet working less publicly within the parameters of a more traditional role of housewife, Mamie Eisenhower also made significant contributions to the White House interiors during President Dwight D. Eisenhower's eight years in office. Indeed, by asserting her authority over all aspects of housekeeping, entertaining, and decorating in the White House, Mamie Eisenhower made the Executive Residence her home in every sense.

Mamie Eisenhower poses in the China Room of the White House with new additions to the collection from the administrations of President Calvin Coolidge and President Herbert Hoover.

President and Mrs. Eisenhower moved into the White House at an unusual time in its history. Less than ten months earlier, President Harry S. Truman had returned to the house following a three and one-half year renovation. In its July 1952 color spread showing the newly renovated White House interiors, *Life* magazine declared that "whatever family moves in next January will enjoy practically brand-new quarters."[1] This was not an overstatement; during the Truman renovation, the White House had been completely gutted. Besides the exterior stone walls and a few selected interior architectural elements, the house had been reconstructed with modern materials. Although rebuilt on the same general plan as the earlier building, the house was dramatically different. Changes included two new basement levels, seventy or so new rooms, and a comprehensive air-conditioning system. The Executive Residence staff was still adjusting to the new building and the increased costs associated with its updated technologies when the Eisenhowers arrived in January 1953.

The Commission on the Renovation of the Executive Mansion, which had overseen construction, had also been charged with the interior furnishing of the restored house. For this purpose, $200,000 had been appropriated to cover all interior work, from painting the walls and restoring old furniture to buying new furnishings. Accepting severe limits of time and money, B. Altman & Co., a New York City department store, took the contract for the interiors. Altman's had recently provided upholstery services for both the State Floor and the West

Wing, so when he was forced to quickly empty the White House in the fall of 1948, Chief Usher Howell Crim turned to Altman's to supervise packing, moving, and storage services. Pleased with the company's work, Crim recommended that it receive the exclusive furnishings contract for the renovation. Altman's proposal, which committed the company to complete all work at cost, receiving no publicity, was accepted in the fall of 1950. Approximately one year was allowed to complete the work.

Charles Haight, director of Altman's design department, told the Commission on the Renovation that although he believed the White House should be furnished with "antiques of the period," there was not nearly enough money even to consider such an undertaking. President Truman had already effectually silenced the other proponents of this approach. His anger at the Commission of Fine Arts for its reaction to his addition in 1948 of a balcony on the South Portico limited its influence with him and thus any impact it might have had on the furnishing plans. Most important, Truman had barred from the renovation the Commission of Fine Arts subcommittee on White House furnishings, which had been working since the Coolidge administration under the leadership of Harriet Barnes Pratt to add period antiques to the State Floor. "There is going to be no special privileged people allowed to decide what will be done with the refurnishing of the White House," Truman commanded.[2] Without a strong advocate for using antiques to furnish the house or the funding sources to secure them, Haight decided to seek reproductions of period chairs, tables, and the like that he felt were appropriate for the house.[3] The reproduction furnishings selected, which tended to be more characteristic of the English Georgian style than American Federal, reflected the upscale furniture market of the time.

Changes made to White House interiors during the Truman renovation were met with almost universal acclaim. The White House's "original 18th Century style of decoration has been restored, [and] anachronistic details eliminated" proclaimed *Life* magazine.[4] "Every one of the . . . White House rooms is adequately and tastefully furnished," wrote Bess Furman for the *New York Times*. Furman also went on to anticipate the pros and cons of Mrs. Eisenhower's challenge:

Precisely because the White House is so spick-and-

span, Mrs. Eisenhower will step into fewer household headaches than any of her predecessors. She will move into the best-looking White House since Abigail Adams crossed its threshold. . . . At the same time, the new First Lady will have the least self-expression in White House interior decoration. She can't order a paint job when everything is fresh as paint—not a thrifty soul like Mamie Eisenhower.[5]

After the government had just spent almost $5.8 million renovating the White House, it was evident that neither Congress nor the general public would be in the mood to spend any significant amount of money to change the interior decorations to suit the new first family's tastes. Thus, although Chief Usher Crim requested it, the Eisenhowers did not receive the traditional $50,000 congressional appropriation given to each administration upon election (and reelection) to be used for purchasing and repairing furnishings for the White House. Crim's budget covered only routine operating expenses of the house and could not absorb any furnishing costs, so he continued to push for dedicated furnishing funds after the appropriation request was denied. Finally Crim was instructed to use leftover money from a large appropriation made in 1946 to meet the Eisenhowers' furnishing requests.

The 1946 appropriation, originally $680,000, had been intended to fund a variety of improvements to the Executive Mansion and its grounds, including a renovation of the East Wing, a study of the historical furnishings of the White House, and updates to the elevators.[6] The unexpected Truman renovation and its subsequent appropriation had eliminated the need for some of the line items of 1946 such as replacing the floor in the private quarters and installing a new heating system. Other projects funded in 1946, including work on the East Wing and landscaping, had been postponed indefinitely. Approximately $200,000 remained from the 1946 appropriation when President Eisenhower took office. During the Eisenhower administration, this account paid for all expenditures that the Usher's Office deemed nonroutine, from new tableware and curtains to plants, scaffolding, and mechanical equipment. In 1958, the 1946 appropriation was finally exhausted, and a new appropriation of $100,000 was secured for "extraordinary alterations, repairs, furniture, and furnishings" for fiscal year 1959.[7]

The Eisenhowers watching television in the Library of the White House with their only son John and his family. One of Mrs. Eisenhower's primary objectives was to make the house comfortable for her family.

Mamie Eisenhower therefore had some cash in hand for redecorating, but her options were largely reduced to inexpensive necessities such as reupholstering worn furniture and painting walls. The life span for such components of White House interiors is very brief. As someone who considered herself a professional homemaker and who loved to decorate houses, the limitations at the White House upset Mrs. Eisenhower. Assistant Usher J. B. West recalled that Mrs. Eisenhower was "terribly disappointed that she couldn't transform the entire mansion" when she arrived.[8] However, as a long-time military wife, she had literally decades of experience in creating a suitable home for her and her husband with quarters and furnishings that were provided for them rather

than those they had chosen themselves.[9] By her count, the White House was their thirty-sixth residence.[10]

Mamie Eisenhower's first decorating objectives in the White House were to make the private quarters comfortable for both her and her husband and for their grandchildren, who would visit often. Less than twenty-four hours after President Eisenhower's inauguration, it was clear that Mrs. Eisenhower had already been contemplating how she could rearrange things to meet her tastes. Her first objective, as it had been in their many previous homes, was to establish a comfortable master bedroom. West recalls that during her first morning in the White House, she directed that Bess Truman's former sitting room would serve as the Eisenhowers' bedroom.[11]

Mamie Eisenhower's limited budget forced her to be creative in accomplishing her decorating goals. She created the master bedroom she desired by rearranging existing White House furnishings. By requesting to use the draperies, carpet, and chairs from Margaret Truman's

Above and left: Two photographs of Margaret Truman's sitting room taken in July 1952 show the draperies and chairs that were used to furnish the White House bedroom for President and Mrs. Eisenhower (opposite), seen here in 1960.

former sitting room for the Eisenhower bedroom, expenses were limited to creating a new upholstered headboard, dust ruffle, and bedspread to match the borrowed furnishings. Mamie Eisenhower's thrift was also demonstrated in her efforts to provide window hangings for the Third Floor. She secured parachute silk from a local army base at 10 cents a yard and instructed the White House seamstress to fabricate curtains.[12]

West also reports that one of Mrs. Eisenhower's first inquiries upon her arrival was about the historic furnishings in the White House:

> Looking around at the bland department-store reproductions, she asked brightly, "Can't we bring out the real antiques?" When I answered that we had none stashed away anywhere, she was crestfallen. "But isn't there any way we can get historic furniture for this house?"
>
> "Donations only," I answered, pointing out the few genuine pieces.

"Well, I guess I'll just have to make do!" she said, marching resolutely off.[13]

According to her granddaughter, Mamie Eisenhower "loved quality—fine antiques, rich silks and brocades, and the best china and sterling silver money could buy."[14] Growing up in a wealthy family, she had been surrounded by fine furnishings. Although money was tight early in her marriage, she still insisted on buying high-quality goods, collecting sets of china and sterling silver slowly over a period of many years. Just prior to moving to the White House, the Eisenhowers had lived at the Villa Saint-Pierre, a historic mansion 10 miles outside of Paris. There Mrs. Eisenhower had had her choice of antique furnishings from French government storage along with the advice of leading French interior designers to furnish the house. The warehouses yielded a bed used by Napoleon at Fontainebleau and a historic French tapestry, but she also insisted as well on modern and comfortable furniture.[15]

Mrs. Eisenhower's appreciation for history was later seen in the Gettysburg Farm, the first home the Eisenhowers had ever owned. In his memoirs, Dwight Eisenhower recalls that Mamie "started off by deciding to restore the old farmhouse located on the ground we had bought." However, an engineering survey revealed that the house was an eighteenth-century log cabin faced with brick and that the wood was in such poor condition that it could not be saved. "So anxious was Mamie to retain even a fragment of the original structure, that when she found one portion of the wall and a Dutch oven in which no logs had been used [in what had been the original summer kitchen], she built a complete house around them," the president proudly wrote.[16] Ceiling beams used in the den were also milled from the original wood of the house.

Mamie Eisenhower might have had the desire to furnish the White House with "real antiques," but there were few to select from and there were no available resources to buy more. Even if she had wanted to personally solicit donations of funds or antique furniture, she probably understood that, coming on the heels of the Truman renovation, there would be little public support for such an effort. Her husband's political ideology also worked against her in this regard, as Republican President Eisenhower was intent on reducing government budgets after two decades of Democratic control in which the federal government had expanded exponentially.

Eisenhower was unwilling to push Congress for even the traditional $50,000 furnishing appropriation.[17] Mamie Eisenhower clearly expressed her desires to her husband, however, as West reported that the president "met me in the hall one day, and explained that he had a 'little money' left over from his office appropriation. 'Couldn't we use it to do some of the things Mrs. Eisenhower wants to do in the White House?' I had to explain that it would be fiscally impossible and illegal to transfer funds from the President's office to the President's house."[18]

Mamie Eisenhower reluctantly accepted that donations would be the only way to add antiques to the White House. Potential acquisitions during the Eisenhower administration were evaluated primarily on their historical importance, particularly to the White House; their suitability to the continued goal established in the 1920s of decorating the house to reflect its earliest era; and their practicality of use. Mrs. Eisenhower was eager to accept gifts associated with the White House or its former occupants. Her first opportunity arose in late 1953 when English lawyer John C. Witt offered a rococo revival sofa, slipper chair, and two armchairs with the provenance of having been among "Abraham Lincoln's private additions to White House furniture" that had been "sold on the lawn by the White House after Lincoln's assassination."[19]

After having secured the recommendations to accept the donation from both Stanley McClure, a National Park Service employee who had been studying the historic White House furnishings since the Truman administration, and the Commission of Fine Arts, Mrs. Eisenhower gave her approval. Mary Jane McCaffree, her social secretary, communicated her decision, writing, "Mrs. Eisenhower is very much interested in obtaining the furniture . . . and asks that a formal acceptance be transmitted. Space for these pieces has been found in the Lincoln Room and The First Lady is delighted to know that the furniture is being restored to The White House."[20] Mrs. Eisenhower accepted a number of other important gifts relating to President Lincoln for the White House during her tenure, including a massive bronze bust of Lincoln by Mount Rushmore sculptor Gutzon Borglum, a bronze statuette of Lincoln by Hungarian artist Jeno Juszko, and most significant, one of only five known copies of the Gettysburg Address written by Lincoln himself.

Mrs. Eisenhower eagerly approved the donation of a classical mahogany sofa said to have been used in the White House by President James Monroe. As was her custom with gifts of historical significance, she insisted upon writing personally to thank the donor. Thus in September 1956 she wrote to Colonel Theodore Barnes Jr.:

> The mahogany French couch which you have graciously given to America by placing it again in the White House is a source of deepest pleasure to all of us who are aware of the importance of such a gift. The sofa will be placed in the Monroe Room where it will highlight furnishings that are also products of the former President's selection. Because of the beauty and historical significance of this gift, the President and I join the countless people who will profit from your generosity in expressing our most sincere gratitude.[21]

After it was reupholstered, Mrs. Eisenhower fulfilled her promise to place the sofa in the Monroe Room, a sitting room on the Second Floor of the White House (now called the Treaty Room) established by Lou Hoover and decorated with furnishings associated with the Monroes.[22]

Mamie Eisenhower's desire to add antique furnishings to the White House is demonstrated by her acceptance and subsequent use of three large collections donated by brothers William and Shirley Burden, Josephine Boardman Crane, and Margaret Thompson Biddle. She used these new acquisitions to supplement the sparse furnishings of the Truman renovation and sometimes to replace them. In March 1955, the Burdens donated more than sixty items, including furniture, prints, fireplace equipment, and lighting fixtures, that they had inherited from Florham, their grandparents' c. 1895 New Jersey estate. Because the majority of the donated items were in the style of the late eighteenth century, the Burden gifts may very well have been accepted with the belief that they fit the goal of furnishing the White House in the period of its

A view of the Monroe Room (now called the Treaty Room) showing furniture acquired during the Eisenhower administration: James Monroe sofa, Burden tray-top table in front of the sofa, Burden upholstered-back armchairs in the front of the window, and Crane blue-and-white jars on the chest on the south wall.

earliest occupancy. However, most of the objects are late nineteenth-century English adaptations of earlier styles. Mrs. Eisenhower put many of the Burden gifts into immediate use in both the public rooms and the private quarters.

Shortly after the Burden gifts arrived, Josephine Boardman Crane (Mrs. Winthrop Murray Crane) donated twenty Chinese porcelain jars and vases from the estate of her sister, Eleonor Boardman that dated from the seventeenth to nineteenth centuries. Mrs. Eisenhower placed most of the Crane gifts on the Second Floor.

WHITE HOUSE HISTORICAL ASSOCIATION

WHITE HOUSE COLLECTION

WHITE HOUSE HISTORICAL ASSOCIATION

Top left to right: The large vermeil collection donated by Margaret Thompson Biddle included a wine ewer with satyr and grapevines (by Richard Sibley, London, 1817–18). A copy of John Trumbull's The Declaration of Independence, *created in crochet, was a donation that Mamie Eisenhower accepted from Mary Peck Dwyer simply because she liked it. A pair of English satinwood armchairs in the Adam style were among the large collection donated by brothers William and Shirley Burden. A covered jar displayed in the Red Room during the Eisenhower administration was one of twenty Chinese porcelain jars and vases donated by Josephine Boardman Crane.*

Left: A large bronze bust of Abraham Lincoln by Mount Rushmore sculptor Gutzon Borglum was one of many Lincoln objects accepted into the collection by Mrs. Eisenhower.

Right: A fruit basket used during the John Tyler administration was donated by the family of Mrs. Alfred E. Bates in 1957. A French curio cabinet, c. 1890 was donated by Esther Clark Rider.

In sheer numbers and monetary value, the largest single donation ever given to the White House is believed to be the result of President and Mrs. Eisenhower's friendship with Margaret Thompson Biddle.[23] In 1956, Mrs. Biddle bequeathed her collection of almost 1,600 pieces of vermeil to the White House. The collection of gold-plated silver consists largely of English and French examples dating from the eighteenth and nineteenth centuries, many of which were made by the finest silversmiths of the period, including Paul Storr and Jean-Baptiste-Claude Odiot. The tight White House budget is revealed in the negotiations over transporting the Biddle collection from her residence in France to Washington, D.C. To avoid paying duty on the $100,000 collection, and because Mrs. Biddle's executors were not allowed to spend estate funds on shipping, the White House arranged for one of the president's military aides, Colonel Robert Schulz, to transport the collection on behalf of the president. It was even difficult to secure the $250 in packing charges that were required. While many of the vermeil pieces were quickly pressed into service to hold either food or flowers, a large sampling of the collection was put on display in the Ground Floor Conference Room, now called the Vermeil Room.[24]

Mamie Eisenhower was famous for the great interest she took in the personal lives of everyone she knew, and this proclivity toward personal connections inspired her collecting choices. While she requested that the Commission of Fine Arts advise on what Crim termed the "acceptability" of large or historically significant gifts such as those offered by the Burdens, Mrs. Crane, or Mrs. Biddle, Mrs. Eisenhower approved certain gifts without seeking the commission's counsel. For example, when Esther Clark Rider, a self-described "great admirer" of Mrs. Eisenhower, wrote the first lady directly to offer one of her family heirlooms, a c. 1890 French curio cabinet, Mrs. Eisenhower accepted it for the White House. In her thank you letter to Mrs. Rider, Mrs. Eisenhower wrote, "This cabinet is a little jewel and will bring much pleasure and happiness to us."[25] She placed the cabinet in the private sitting room. In accepting this gift, Mamie Eisenhower was not concerned with notions of historical appropriateness but reacted on a very personal level. Similarly, she accepted a large crocheted handiwork rendering of John Trumbull's painting *The Declaration of Independence*

from Mary Peck Dwyer in 1959 simply because she liked it.

The most influential factors in Mrs. Eisenhower's collecting decisions appear to have been the decorative appeal of an offered gift and its potential use rather than its value as a work of art or conformation to an ideal of a suitable style for the White House. Correspondence between Howell Crim or J. B. West and David Finley, chairman of the Commission of Fine Arts, about potential acquisitions almost always centered on where the item could be placed. If a suitable location could not be identified, the object was declined, sometimes to the regret of the Commission of Fine Arts. Thus offered donations such as an eighteenth-century English corner cabinet, a suite of mid-nineteenth-century American furniture, and a Louis XVI salon suite were all rejected. In another instance, the White House declined the offer of a museum-quality eighteenth-century bed complete with period hangings due to the fragility of the textiles. Finley often worked to place donations rejected by the White House into other suitable museums or buildings in Washington.

While Mamie Eisenhower was involved in all White House furnishing decisions during her tenure as first lady, she was most interested in the White House china collection. In her 1974 foreword to the book *Official White House China*, she wrote, "My interest in beautiful tableware began in childhood. I can remember my grandmother's lovely Haviland china, which she used on formal occasions. My mother's well-appointed table was a source of pride to her and a pleasure to her family." As she "began to think of what I could do to add to the enjoyment of those who might pass through" the White House, Mrs. Eisenhower decided to order new ceramics.[26]

Because she had limited funds and because the Trumans had ordered a large dinner service near the end of their administration, Mrs. Eisenhower ordered only service plates that could be used in conjunction with the Truman pieces. Obviously pleased with the service plates provided by Castleton, a subsidiary of the Shenango China Company of Pennsylvania, which featured a coin gold border with raised medallions and the presidential seal at center, Mrs. Eisenhower also commissioned Shenango to produce new tableware for the *Columbine,* the president's plane.

During President Eisenhower's second term the first lady shifted her attention to studying the historic White

Right: The Eisenhower service plate.

Below: A view of the State Dining Room set for dinner during the Eisenhower administration showing the furnishings they acquired, including pier mirrors on the south wall from Josephine Crane, Castleton service plates, and vermeil from the Biddle collection.

NATIONAL GEOGRAPHIC. PHOTO BY B. ANTHONY STEWART

House china and rearranging its exhibition in the China Room. "Shortly after I decided on this project, I realized that professional advice was needed to assure proper identification," Mrs. Eisenhower recalled.[27] Learning that Margaret Brown Klapthor, a curator at the Smithsonian Institution, had recently been researching that museum's collection of presidential china for exhibition in the First Ladies' Hall, Mrs. Eisenhower solicited her assistance for the White House collection. Klapthor's research corrected many misattributions and identified gaps in the collections of both the Smithsonian and the White House. Reciprocal loans between the two institutions filled some of these voids,

but five administrations remained unrepresented. Mrs. Eisenhower remarked in her foreword to *Official White House China*, "It seemed sad that these names [Presidents Andrew Johnson, William Howard Taft, Warren G. Harding, Calvin Coolidge, and Herbert Hoover] were missing in the White House collection; but since several other presidents were represented by their personal china, I felt that the collection would be enhanced by the addition of china owned by these presidential families."[28]

Hoping to attract donations from the unrepresented administrations, the White House alerted the press of the project.[29] That September, President Herbert Hoover,

214   WHITE HOUSE HISTORY (Collection Set 4)

This photograph of the refurbished Diplomatic Reception Room was included in the January 1961 issue of National Geographic. *This was the first room in the White House to be furnished exclusively with antiques and served as an important model for future room refurbishments.*

the first to respond, donated a set of six plates from family Wedgwood services that had been used at the White House. Donations from the Taft, Coolidge, Harding, and Johnson families arrived in 1959. Mrs. Eisenhower wrote to each family member expressing personal thanks for the contributions to "my favorite White House China Room," she wrote to Helen Herron Taft Manning.[29] "The completion of this room has been very close to my heart," she wrote to Margaret Johnson Patterson Bartlett, a descendant of Andrew Johnson who traveled to the White House to personally present Mrs. Eisenhower with the Johnson china,[30] the donation that completed the collection. Mrs. Eisenhower's desire to represent each first family in the collection further reflects her personal approach to historic furnishings.

The press's coverage of Mamie Eisenhower's work with the White House china collection highlights the cultural expectations of the role of first lady. Her activities were repeatedly couched in terms of women's traditional responsibilities. "Like housewives throughout the country, Mrs. Eisenhower wanted her 'china closet' in order," the *Washington Star* explained.[31] Mrs. Eisenhower's activism on behalf of the White House china collection was portrayed as an extension of her role as a woman and wife, thereby allowing American women to identify with her. Mamie Eisenhower also understood the importance of keeping a relatively low profile in relation to her interest in furnishing the White House. "The dictates of protocol would hardly permit Mrs. Eisenhower to go about begging china from the descendants of these Presidents, or even the President himself, in the case of President Hoover" explained one reporter.[32] Mrs. Eisenhower maintained her positive public image in her furnishing work by being seen as contributing to the history of the White House without interfering with its revered traditions or stepping outside her expected role.

The most significant and enduring change made to the White House interiors during the Eisenhower administration was the refurbishing of the Diplomatic Reception Room with fine early nineteenth-century antiques. This project nearly failed before it got under way. The project was the brainchild of Michael Greer, the gifted decorator, then chairman of the Board of Directors of the National Society of Interior Designers (NSID). Greer wrote to Cabinet Secretary Maxwell Rabb in April 1958 proposing "to furnish appropriately

the Oval Lobby on the first floor of the White House."[33] His offer was forwarded to Chief Usher J. B. West, who was not sure if Greer meant the Blue Room or the Diplomatic Reception Room. Undoubtedly after conferring with Mrs. Eisenhower, West asked Finley to inform Greer that they felt the furnishings in both rooms were "quite adequate."[34]

When the Eisenhowers arrived at the White House, the Diplomatic Reception Room was minimally furnished with newly purchased reproductions from the Kaplan Furniture Company. Mrs. Eisenhower added a number of objects of various styles donated during her tenure, resulting in a less unified effect than its post-renovation appearance. This mélange of style inspired Michael Greer to identify it most in need of the NSID's decorating assistance. From his first interactions with the White House, it was clear that the aggressive Greer was not going to take no for an answer. A little more than a year after his first attempt, he contacted the cabinet secretary, Robert Gray, to press his case again. This time, Finley expressed interest in talking to him if he meant the Diplomatic Reception Room and not the Blue Room. Greer finally got his desired meeting with Finley and West on February 1, 1960.

Finley was encouraging of the proposal, and Greer was clearly eager to get started. However, West left a message for Finley a few days after their meeting to report that he had discussed Greer's proposal with Mrs. Eisenhower. "Since it is so near the end of the president's term of office, she would prefer to have nothing done at this time. She thinks that any changes should be left for the next First Lady," West reported. Finley and possibly West appear to have disagreed with the first lady, as Finley noted on the bottom of this message, "Mr. West will talk further with Mrs. Eisenhower."[35]

West and Finley succeeded in convincing Mrs. Eisenhower to accept the NSID's proposal. When he wrote to Greer on March 3, 1960, West felt the need to remind Greer that "all plans and furnishings must be approved by the White House and the Commission of Fine Arts." Greer's presumptions and ambitious timetable had apparently already upset West and Finley, as West continued, "It might therefore save future embarrassment if all plans were submitted to the Commission in the preliminary stages for tentative approval."[36] Greer thus began attending the commission's monthly meetings to report on the project.

*The unveiling of the refurbished Diplomatic Reception
Room, June 29, 1960. Beneath the portrait of Angelica
Singleton Van Buren, which came to the White House
in 1890, and among antique furniture newly acquired,
President and Mrs. Eisenhower join Michael Greer and
Dora Brahms of the National Society of Interior Designers.*

Tensions grew throughout the spring as the broad project progressed and the scope of Greer's ambitions became clearer. At the end of April, West called the commission offices to express his concern for the "magnitude which Mr. Greer's plan for the decoration of the Diplomatic Reception Room is taking." West felt that "Mr. Greer is going too far and too fast" and was worried that Mrs. Eisenhower "might not be pleased with the elaborateness of the plans, which in their initial stages gave no indication of involving so much." He indicated that "there is also a great danger of getting the room too splendid for its place in the White House routine."[37]

Design struggles also emerged as Greer resisted suggestions from both the Commission of Fine Arts and Mrs. Eisenhower. In April, David Finley wrote Greer of the commission's doubt about the chandelier that Greer had proposed, questioning whether a chandelier was necessary with such a low ceiling. Nevertheless, in his May 2 proposal addressed to the President and Mrs. Eisenhower, Greer included plans for a chandelier. Ultimately, no chandelier was installed. Mrs. Eisenhower personally objected to the "French gray" paint sample that Greer had submitted for the walls and instead requested a "bone white" color.[38] Greer never accepted this decision, continuing to press his case for French gray walls well into the Kennedy administration.

Although not complete, the room was unveiled to the press on June 29, 1960, with President and Mrs. Eisenhower, Michael Greer, and Dora Brahms of the NSID all in attendance. Greer had placed the elegant Federal-era furnishings, primarily made in New England and New York, into small conversation groupings. The photographers in attendance captured Mrs. Eisenhower admiring the new furnishings and the next day the *Washington Post* published one such image of Mrs. Eisenhower captioned "Proud Housewife." While Mrs. Eisenhower was pleased to add historically appropriate antiques to the White House, she also made it clear that such additions to the White House must be practical. During the event, Mrs. Eisenhower asked Greer to move two of his carefully arranged chairs to make the room more functional for her family. As the *Post* reported, after complimenting the color of fabric on the chairs:

she turned housewife and with a few sharp glances around the room suggested to Michael Greer, presi-

dent of the professional organization, that the two arm chairs be moved away from the fireplace setting to make more room for picture-taking. "We use this side of the room more than the other," she explained, "because we often have pictures taken in front of the fireplace. So if we could put these chairs some place else to have a little more space, it would be better." Greer gallantly moved the two chairs across the room to make a conversation grouping with the sofa.[39]

Working within traditional parameters as the "housewife" of the White House, Mamie Eisenhower asserted her control over all aspects of White House furnishings during her tenure.

Betty Monkman has written about the 1960 refurbishment of the Diplomatic Reception Room, "This gift of furnishings from the period of the building of the White House and its earliest occupancy was the first successful attempt to furnish a room in the White House with American antiques of the highest quality, and it set a precedent for Jacqueline Kennedy's efforts in the early 1960s to bring a historic character to the house."[40] It is difficult to know exactly how great of an influence this refurbishment had on Mrs. Kennedy's comprehensive vision for a White House completely furnished with period antiques and whether she would have devised such a plan without this inspiration. At the very least, the project illustrated again at an important juncture the potential of using outside donors to furnish the White House with the type of high-quality antiques for which the United States government was never willing to pay. Mamie Eisenhower certainly deserves credit for supporting this important project, but her discomfort during the process and her reaction to its unveiling make it clear that, even if the project had taken place much earlier in her tenure, she never would have undertaken the type of refurbishing campaign that Jacqueline Kennedy carried out. As housewife of the White House, Mrs. Eisenhower defined the scope carefully. She believed it her responsibility to create a comfortable home and a gracious setting for the entertaining requisite to her husband's position. Thus caring for the existing White House furnishings and acquiring beautiful and historic new objects for the house were part of her job as first lady.

NOTES

1. "The White House Redecorated," *Life*, July 7, 1952, 47.

2. Quoted in William Seale, *The President's House: A History* (Washington, D.C.: White House Historical Association, with the cooperation of the National Geographic Society, 1986), 2:1040.

3. Ibid., 2:1038–45; Betty C. Monkman, "The White House Collection: The Truman Interiors," *White House History*, no. 5: 58–61.

4. "White House Redecorated," 47.

5. Bess Furman, "Keeping House at the White House," *New York Times*, December 28, 1952, SM7.

6. This $680,000 was originally part of an even larger appropriation for $1,650,000 that was to include an expansion of the West Wing, but public outcry caused Congress to eliminate funding for this project. See Seale, *President's House*, 2:1006–10; Elizabeth Beard Goldsmith, "Tempest in a Teapot: Truman's Failed Attempt at an Office Addition," *White House History*, no. 5 (Spring 1999): 13–22. The $680,000 appropriation had included the traditional $50,000 furnishings money for President and Mrs. Truman, but this money (and then some) had been spent almost immediately. The $680,000 appropriation also ended up covering costs for the Truman Balcony. Office of the Curator, The White House, Washington, D.C.

7. J. B. West to Dwight D. Eisenhower, June 25, 1958, Office of the Curator, The White House.

8. J. B. West and Mary Lynn Kotz, *Upstairs at the White House: My Life with the First Ladies* (New York: Coward, McCann & Geoghegan, 1973), 139.

9. See Susan Eisenhower, *Mrs. Ike: Memories and Reflections on the Life of Mamie Eisenhower* (New York: Farrar, Straus and Giroux, 1996), 61–62.

10. Lester David and Irene David, *Ike and Mamie: The Story of the General and His Lady* (New York: G. P. Putnam's Sons, 1981), 270. The authors write that Mamie stated that she and Ike lived in thirty-seven separate residences while they were married. If Gettysburg Farm was their thirty-seventh home, then the White House would have been their thirty-sixth. The authors note that Mamie's count reflected temporary lodgings (including hotels) and by their count, the White House was the Eisenhowers' twentieth residence.

11. West and Kotz, *Upstairs at the White House*, 130.

12. Susan Eisenhower, *Mrs. Ike*, 283.

13. West and Kotz, *Upstairs at the White House*, 139–40.

14. Susan Eisenhower, *Mrs. Ike*, 4.

15. Ibid., 257–58; David and David, *Ike and Mamie*, 175–76.

16. Dwight D. Eisenhower, *At Ease: Stories I Tell to Friends* (Garden City, N.Y.: Doubleday, 1967), 359.

17. Susan Eisenhower, *Mrs. Ike*, 283.

18. West and Kotz, *Upstairs at the White House*, 139–40.

19. Daniel Varney Thompson to Harry S. Truman, August 15, 1952, Office of the Curator, The White House.

20. Mary Jane McCaffree to R. D. Muir, February 16, 1954, Office of the Curator, The White House.

21. Mamie Eisenhower to Colonel Theodore Barnes Jr., September 11, 1956, Office of the Curator, The White House.

22. The James Monroe Law Library in Fredericksburg, Virginia, owns six armchairs that appear to match this sofa. Two additional matching armchairs and a sidechair were recently purchased at auction by Ash Lawn–Highland, Monroe's home in Charlottesville, Virginia.

23. See Susan Eisenhower, *Mrs. Ike*, 293; Betty C. Monkman, *The White House: Its Historic Furnishings and First Families* (Washington, D.C., and New York: White House Historical Association and Abbeville Press, 2000), 224. It is unclear exactly when Mrs. Biddle included the clause in her will that directed that her vermeil collection be given to the White House. A 1958 article in the *Washington Star* quotes Mrs. Biddle's daughter as saying that her mother decided to leave her collection to the White House during one of her many visits to the White House, but it is unclear whether this was before or during the Eisenhower administration. "White House Gets Famed Collection," *Washington Star*, January 17, 1958. Margaret Biddle's probated will is dated October 16, 1954, but it is not known whether any earlier versions of her will made the same bequest. Susan Tell, New York State Surrogate Court, e-mail message to author, October 6, 2006.

24. Files on the Biddle donation, Office of the Curator, the White House.

25. Esther Clark Rider to Mamie Eisenhower, October 19, 1956; Mamie Eisenhower to Esther Clark Rider, November 20, 1956, Office of the Curator, The White House.

26. Mamie Eisenhower, foreword to Margaret Brown Klapthor, *Official White House China: 1789 to the Present,* 2nd ed. (New York: Harry N. Abrams, 1999), 7.

27. Ibid.

28. Ibid.

29. Margaret Brown Klapthor, "White House China Room," June 1958, Office of the Curator, The White House.

29. Mamie Eisenhower to Mrs. Frederick [Helen Herron Taft] Manning, April 11, 1959, Office of the Curator, The White House.

30. Mamie Eisenhower to Margaret Johnson Patterson Bartlett, April 30, 1959, Office of the Curator, the White House.

31. Daisy Cleland, "The White House China Collection Is Unique, Colorful and Complete," *Washington Star*, c. May 10, 1959, Office of the Curator, The White House.

32. Daisy Cleland, "Completion of White House Collection of China Near with Offers from Presidents' Relatives," *Washington Star*, September 28, 1958, D1.

33 Michael Greer to Maxwell Rabb, April 16, 1958, Record Group 66, Records of the Commission of Fine Arts, Central Files, Series 7A, National Archives, Washington, D.C.

34. West to David Finley, June 30, 1958, ibid.

35. SEB [unidentified staff member at the Commission of Fine Arts] to Finley, February 5, 1960, ibid.

36. West to Greer, March 3, 1960, Office of the Curator, The White House.

37. Linton Wilson to Finley, April 21, 1960, Record Group 66, Records of the Commission of Fine Arts, Central Files, Series 7A, National Archives.

38. West, notes on meeting of Commission of Fine Arts in the Diplomatic Reception Room, May 17, 1960, Office of the Curator, The White House.

39. Patricia Griffith, "Mamie Accepts Antiques," *Washington Post*, June 30, 1960, C20.

40. Monkman, *White House*, 226.

"In the Goodness of Time":
Creating the Dwight David Eisenhower
Room at Blair House

CANDACE S. SHIREMAN

*A*merica's historic house interiors bear the imprint of those who create, occupy, support, and pass through them. The often-conflicting mandates of long-term preservation and periodic renewal constantly challenge benefactors and stewards, especially if organizations must operate within the walls of a historic building. Over time changing values and priorities influence decisions about room functions and meanings and thus decorating and furnishing choices. Ultimately, whether the results are lasting or transient, they are made "as much of personalities" as they are of wood, paint, and fabric.[1]

The 1970 creation of the Dwight David Eisenhower Room at Blair House by Mamie Eisenhower and a group of close friends and associates to honor her late husband brought together a small, eclectic, and very personal collection of furnishings and mementos to what is officially called the President's Guest House for dignitaries visiting the United States. While the room itself has changed with intervening years and circumstances, the objects representing President Eisenhower's life and career achievements, many donated by Mrs. Eisenhower

herself, are among the most meaningful treasures in Blair House.

Since 1942, when the federal government purchased Blair House and transformed it from the private residence of a distinguished American political family[2] into an elegant "hotel" with a unique public service mission, Blair House, like the White House, has evolved with changing presidential administrations. Operated by the State Department's Office of the Chief of Protocol, its role as home-away-from-home for foreign heads of state and other official guests of the United States government places it at the center of international events. The rooms are settings for social and ceremonial activities integral to American diplomacy. That their decorations and furnishings represent the American story from the nation's founding is part of a conscious effort to present the best of American hospitality and culture to its distinguished guests in a welcoming, comfortable, and secure atmosphere.

The country's growing involvement in World War II brought many world leaders, most frequently British Prime Minister Winston Churchill, to Washington for meetings with President Franklin D. Roosevelt and usually a first-night stay at the White House. When the strain of housing them began to wear on the first family, Eleanor Roosevelt pressed her husband for relief, and the convenient Blair House was eventually acquired and renovated for this important diplomatic function.[3]

As work began in 1942, the Public Buildings Administration hired New York interior decorator

---

Blair House, 1945. The flags are at half-staff, mourning the death of President Franklin Roosevelt. It was Roosevelt who set the house aside for preservation when by law it was to be demolished to make way for government office buildings.

Gladys Miller to assist Irene de Bruyn Robbins (Mrs. Warren Delano Robbins), chief of the State Department's Foreign Service furnishings division, with the interior finishing. Using original Blair family furnishings acquired with the house, a few loans from the White House and the National Gallery of Art, and catalog reproductions, they created a typically American, eclectic, and homey blend of function, comfort, history, and charm in a modernized version of the Blairs' Federal and Colonial Revival taste, informed by period rooms in the Metropolitan Museum of Art's American Wing, Mount Vernon, Colonial Williamsburg, and emerging museums such as Old Sturbridge Village, Historic Deerfield, and Winterthur. The largest second floor bedroom with private bath, the Ranking Guest Bedroom, and the adjacent Library together formed the chief of state "suite." Following visits by King George II of Greece and Peter II of Yugoslavia in June 1942, the bedroom became known as the King's (or chief of state) Bedroom and, with the Library as connecting sitting room/study, the King's Suite.[4]

Global change during the postwar era brought greater diplomatic requirements. In 1948 Blair House and the Lee House next door were joined into a single residence for President Harry S. Truman and his family until major White House renovations were completed in 1952. The King's Bedroom decorations remained unchanged, per the Trumans' request. The president slept in an early nineteenth-century American figured maple tester bed dressed in fringed muslin, reached for the telephone on a corresponding period worktable, walked on an early hand-hooked rug from Maine among other "historic" Blair family furnishings, and peered outside through the "George Washington toile" window draperies—including that afternoon when would-be assassins' gunshots were fired on Pennsylvania Avenue.[5]

President Eisenhower used Blair House to host fifty-five foreign leaders at various functions in his first term, testimony to the country's growing leadership in world affairs and the president's commitment to "wage peace" through diplomacy.[6] Blair House records documenting the appearance of the interiors at this time are sparse, but it seems the King's Bedroom, known post-Truman as the President's Bedroom, remained in its original uniform. Former Blair House Manager Mary Wilroy's memoirs describe how refurbishing was mainly done by the manager and staff working with the wife of the chief of protocol and a consulting decorator. The first lady typically toured the facilities in the early months of a new term, and her thoughts and preferences were noted. The General Services Administration (GSA) provided construction and maintenance. Both agencies covered the expenditures and donations of furniture, while objets d'art were accepted through the Office of the Chief of Protocol gifts process.[7]

Several factors during the Kennedy administration partly changed this solely government arrangement. Jacqueline Kennedy's ambitious White House restoration and nationally televised personal tour energized the historic preservation movement on America's cultural agenda and influenced on a national scale American taste in interior design. The aging Truman-era decor of the President's Guest House seems to have looked shabby to the new first lady. She encouraged Robin Chandler Duke, her close friend and wife of incoming Chief of Protocol Angier Biddle Duke, to organize and lead an independent, nongovernment committee to solicit and receive private donations for restoring Blair House. What she had in mind was similar to the Fine Arts Committee for the White House established in 1961. The Blair House Fine Arts Committee (BHFAC) was officially formed in early 1963, with Mrs. Kennedy as honorary chairman and Robin Duke as chairman.[8]

Mrs. Kennedy's influence encouraged the BHFAC to coordinate the Truman-Eisenhower era decorating of Blair House to a taste more in line with the new look of the White House. Incumbent Blair family pieces received much-needed conservation and were joined by museum-quality antiques and new pieces; upgraded walls and floors enlivened the rooms, together with new fabrics in color schemes inspired largely by English and French documents. Lady Bird Johnson's presence on the committee with the wives of other cabinet members ensured the project's continuation through the Johnson administration. The January 1965 issue of *House and Garden* featured some of the completed rooms in a thirteen-page full-color spread. Decorated by McMillan, Inc., New York City, and again called the King's Bedroom, the new decor of the chief of state bedroom amplified Gladys Miller's original design. The same figured maple bedroom suite had been refitted with the

The King's Bedroom at Blair House, ca. 1950 during President Truman's occupancy, showing Blair family furniture and "George Washington toile" draperies.

tester bed canopied and skirted in red-accented white-on-white linen and cotton crewel; Blair pieces of early American, English, and Bohemian glass and porcelain accented the family's fall-front desk and side tables; a contemporary hooked rug with bold red-on-black floral pattern strongly contrasted with the all-white ceiling, walls, and moldings.[9]

Four years later the major effort of connecting two adjacent row houses on Jackson Place to the guest house complex had just begun when two historical events refocused plans. The new Nixon administration meant changing leadership and agendas for the Protocol Office and the restoration committee. On March 28, 1969, a few months after Nixon's inauguration, Dwight D. Eisenhower died after a long illness. The desire to commemorate the beloved former president by his

former vice-president, at the guest house, was in keeping with the emerging trend of memorializing in historic houses, partly as a means of attracting donors for preservation and restoration funding.

Correspondence of Patricia Mosbacher, wife of President Richard Nixon's first chief of protocol, Emil Mosbacher Jr., in the collections of the Dwight D. Eisenhower Presidential Library and Blair House provides glimpses of the process that again changed the look, name, and meaning of the chief of state suite.[10] Writing to Mrs. Eisenhower on November 19, 1969,

Above and opposite: Watercolor schematics by interior designer Elizabeth Draper proposing decor for the Eisenhower Room at Blair House, ca. August 1970.

Mrs. Mosbacher expressed pleasure at having seen her and been included "with the group of your old and dear friends" at a recent social event and described the BHFAC's "wish to create a 'General Eisenhower Room' . . . to include one of his paintings and possibly his West Point chair." She also expressed her intention to ask wives of other former presidents since the advent of the President's Guest House for donations of personal mementos for display. Closing with hopes for cooperation with this "special tribute," Mrs. Mosbacher connected President Eisenhower's global appeal with the Blair House mission: "General Eisenhower was known and loved in so many countries throughout the world, it seems particularly fitting that he should be honored at Blair House, where the foreign chiefs of state and heads of government stay during their visits to the United States."[11]

The reference to foreign leaders spending the night may have inadvertently reminded the widow of the chief of state suite's primary status among the guest house rooms and so its desirability for memorializing her late husband. The extensive Truman renovations had denied her funding to redecorate the White House to any extent, a big disappointment for a first lady who appreciated history, loved design, and would become an acknowledged fashion influence for America's homemakers throughout the 1950s.[12] Mamie Eisenhower still managed to leave her imprint on its interiors with the documentation and reinstallation of the china collection and China Room, the acquisition of Margaret Thompson Biddle's magnificent vermeil collection that led to creation of the Vermeil Room, and the redecoration of the Diplomatic Reception Room with Federal period antiques—all projects she supported. These successes, and her work with New York designer Elizabeth Draper on the Gettysburg farm and the Morningside Drive house at Columbia University, bolstered her decorating confidence and experience. Jacqueline Kennedy's altering of the Diplomatic Reception Room she had seen redecorated may also partly explain the strong appeal an Eisenhower Room at Blair House had for his widow later, when she was devoted to preserving her husband's legacy in a variety of ways.[13]

On April 28, 1970, Mrs. Eisenhower and longtime friend Elizabeth Draper stopped by Blair House for the first meeting about the project. Soon after columnist

Betty Beale wrote an article announcing "Changes in Blair House Décor" for the *Sunday Star* and including a White House press photograph of a smiling Mrs. Eisenhower in the rear drawing room, seated between Mrs. Mosbacher and Mrs. Draper on a Federal-style camelback sofa and reviewing a large floor plan. Described at length is Mrs. Draper's proposed redecoration of the main dining room, another memorial project to be donated by Franklin D. Roosevelt Jr. in honor of his father. Plans for the "Eisenhower Room," although incomplete, make it clear that Mrs. Eisenhower had brought her own ideas to the earlier discussion: the chief of state suite would be redesigned to suggest the general's private quarters at the Gettysburg farm.[14]

Mamie Eisenhower's personalized, down-to-earth version of "high-class" taste perfectly suited Blair House's domesticated elegance. More correspondence and a visit to Gettysburg by Pat Mosbacher and Elizabeth Draper to see the room in question and Mamie's memorabilia selections followed over the summer. Additional donations of objects and funding arrived throughout the fall from the couple's closest friends and associates who had formed the ad hoc Friends of Eisenhower to complete the project.[15]

A commemorative photograph album prepared for the December 4, 1970, dedication preserves the results. Yellow walls, a rich red carpet, and coordinating floral-striped damaskdraperies, the General's Gettysburg rooms' color scheme, showcase some of the thirty-six objects presented by the Eisenhower family and other donations. Elizabeth Draper's "Eisenhower toile" fabric with scenes from the late president's life, first made by F. Schumacher for his Gettysburg sitting room and here copied in maroon rather than the original dark gold, covers a Blair family wing chair and an antique Martinique mahogany bed purchased with Friends of Eisenhower funds. On a cherry and rosewood desk in one corner an engraved sterling silver inkstand and cigarette box, a leather desk pad fitted with one of his inaugural medals, a gilt metal magnifying glass and case with eagle finial, all join his horn-rim eyeglasses in a monogrammed leather holder. Mrs. Eisenhower gave them all. Over the desk a framed needlepoint of the presidential seal, worked by a family friend, was another of her donations. Eisenhower's Windsor-style West Point captain's chair, an earlier gift to him by

alumni of his 1916 class, stands nearby. Two of his own oil paintings, *Sunset* and *Cottage by the Lake*, and two figurines of prized cattle including *Hereford Bull* by noted porcelain maker Edward Marshall Boehm, represent his retirement to pursue life as an amateur painter and "gentleman farmer."[16]

Among other personal effects donated by Mrs. Eisenhower were a small five-star general's flag; a table lamp with cannon shell canister base and West Point seal; a reproduction of a pedestal table used at the Capitol for Abraham Lincoln's swearing-in, given to Mamie in 1953 and reportedly used at Eisenhower's inauguration; a small Louis Mayer bronze bust of Abraham Lincoln; a framed print of the Supreme Headquarters Allied Powers Europe signed by artist Frank E. Beresford; volumes of Eisenhower's published writings, some signed; favorite books from his personal library, some inscribed to him by the authors; and a framed photograph of his wife that always stood at his bedside.

A 1945 bronze portrait bust of the president by Nison H. Tregor, donated by Ralph Becker; a pencil sketch of

Mamie Eisenhower giving remarks at the dedication of the Eisenhower Room, 1970.

Columbia University's Low Building signifying Eisenhower's tenure as president from 1948 to 1953, from William S. Paley; an 1885 bible given by retired army chaplain William Devanny; a framed needlework commemorating the couple's golden wedding anniversary, 1916–66; and additional Friends of Eisenhower gifts-in-kind augment the former first lady's contributions. A fireplace, its antique carved mantel flanked by the American and president's flags and surmounted by a replica of Eisenhower's West Point cadet sword, presented by General William C. Westmoreland, complete the room's dignified yet cozy men's club character. The total effect—simple, hospitable, conveying masculine warmth and a bit of feminine charm—expresses its creator as much as its honoree.

At the dedication ceremony held in the room, Mamie Eisenhower, visibly moved, began her remarks, "I'd like

A recent view of the Eisenhower Room. No longer used as a bedroom, the room retains the red-and-gold color scheme and serves as a comfortable sitting room for guests. It is decorated with a collection of President Eisenhower's mementos and objects related to his administration.

PHOTO BY BRUCE WHITE FOR THE WHITE HOUSE HISTORICAL ASSOCIATION

to thank everyone, all of Ike's friends . . ."; overcome, her eyes filling with tears, she quickly concluded, "All I can say is thank you so much."[17] The Reverend Dr. Edward Elson, pastor of the Presbyterian church attended by the first family while in the White House, gave the dedicatory prayer. The former first lady then received the West Point sword presented by two uniformed U.S. Military Academy cadets.

A wake-up call for more guest house improvements came in 1982, early in the Reagan administration, when a guest bedroom chandelier nearly fell. Undertaken by Chief of Protocol Selwa "Lucky" Roosevelt, plans already in progress for painting and wallpapering a few rooms were quickly expanded to include major structural and systems upgrades, the building of a new wing and gardens, and a comprehensive redecoration by designers Mark Hampton and Mario Buatta that unified the interiors and set new standards of style and efficiency.[18] Recognition of the need to balance preservation, function, and, of course, aesthetics in what was now a four-building, 119-room mixed-use modern and historic structure deemphasized commemoration in favor of practicality and current aesthetic tastes in interior decoration. A more spacious, up-to-date, and well-appointed Principal Suite in the new Garden Wing relieved the Eisenhower Room of its function and status. Some of the furnishings were deployed to new duty in other rooms and a few to storage. But many key pieces remained as the Eisenhower Room was redefined as a waiting room for higher-ranking delegation members accompanying a visiting leader.

Today the Eisenhower Sitting Room still serves as a lounge where guests can relax with refreshments and catch up on news from their homelands between meetings and special events. The red-and-yellow color scheme endures with draperies and upholstery in Fortuny fabrics replacing the Eisenhower toile, a comfortable sofa standing in for the mahogany bed, and an eighteenth-century English, Blair family secretary-

bookcase for Eisenhower's inscribed books and other mementos. The West Point cadet sword, oil paintings, and bronze portrait bust continue to invoke his memory and, with other treasures from Mrs. Eisenhower's generous bequest, are now visible to many more guests than ever before in this transitional but also contemplative space between the Principal Suite and other parts of the complex. An illuminated copy of Eisenhower's own *President's Prayer* with which he closed his first inaugural address, given by Mamie and framed on one wall, reminds all who pass through the President's Guest House of one of our nation's most esteemed presidents and his dream of America's ability to "wage peace" to bring all peoples and nations together "in the goodness of time."[19]

NOTES

1. William Seale, *The President's House: A History* (Washington, D.C.: White House Historical Association, with the cooperation of the National Geographic Society, 1986). See also John A. Herbst, "Historic Houses," *History Museums in the United States: A Critical Assessment* (Urbana and Chicago: University of Illinois Press, 1989), 110.

2. William Ernest Smith, *The Francis Preston Blair Family in Politics* (New York: Da Capo Press, 1969); Katherine Elizabeth Crane, *Blair House Past and Present: An Account of Its Life and Times in the City of Washington* (Washington, D.C.: United States Department of State, 1945); Eleanor Lee Templeman, *The Blair-Lee House: Guest House of the President* (McLean, Va.: EPM Publications, 1980); Marlene

Elizabeth Heck, *Blair House: The President's Guest House* (Washington, D.C., and Charlottesville, Va.: Blair House Restoration Fund and Thomasson-Grant, 1989). Built in 1824 by Dr. Joseph Lovell, first surgeon general of the U.S. Army, the house at 1651 Pennsylvania Avenue, NW, across from the White House, was acquired in 1837 by Kentucky newspaper publisher Francis Preston Blair, confidant of presidents from Andrew Jackson to Ulysses S. Grant and owner-editor of the local *Globe* newspaper. Blair became very influential as a member of Jackson's Kitchen Cabinet, through his insightful editorials on political issues and his first publication of the daily proceedings of Congress in his *Congressional Globe*, precursor to today's *Congressional Record*. Later breaking with the Democrats, he and sons Montgomery and Frank Jr. helped form the Republican Party and promoted Abraham Lincoln into the presidency. Montgomery served as Lincoln's postmaster general; Frank Jr. became a Missouri senator. Daughter Elizabeth and husband Samuel Phillips Lee, cousin of Robert E. Lee, lived next door to Blair House in Lee House, built 1858–59 by her father. Both houses remained in family hands to the third generation, Blair House until 1941 when the death of grandson Gist Blair's widow cleared the way for government acquisition of the property per her husband's wishes. Lee House was bought for government use in 1943.

3. Mary Edith Wilroy and Lucie Prinz, *Inside Blair House* (Garden City, N.Y.: Doubleday, 1982), 7–8; Heck, *Blair House*, 27–29. FDR's New Deal program included the Historic American Building Survey, founded in 1933. With the president's support, Blair House was designated a national historic landmark by the Department of the Interior in 1939. Gist Blair, the last family member to live in it, cited the past presidential connections and the history of political and social entertaining in his long campaign for the preservation of the house. During the Eisenhower years, the practice of visiting heads of state spending a first night at the White House ended in 1955 and Blair House received the official designation as the President's Guest House in 1957.

4. Richard Guy Wilson, *The Colonial Revival House* (New York: Harry N. Abrams, 2004), 166, 179; Gladys Miller Scrapbooks, 7 vols., Office of the Curator, Blair House, Washington, D.C.; "Blair House Has Seen So Much," *Washington Post*, July 26, 1970, 47; "List of Visits of Foreign Chiefs of State and Heads of Government to the United States 1789–1970," January 1971, 6, Historical Studies Division, Historical Office, Bureau of Public Affairs, Department of State, copy in Office of the Curator, Blair House. Gist Blair's 1910–20 renovations of Blair House and penchant for collecting and preserving family pieces and other Americana reveal his taste for the then-new Colonial Revival style and provided a treasure trove for Gladys Miller and Irene Robbins to work with.

5. Crane: Plate "Red Bedroom." During this time, discussions and decisions resulting in the Marshall Plan for postwar European reconstruction, the Truman Doctrine, the U.S. entry into the Korean War, and other historic events took place at Blair House. On November 1, 1950, two Puerto Rican nationalists attempted to assassinate the president, who was in his Blair House bedroom at the time.

6. Robert A. Grookett, "Visits of Heads of State During President Eisenhower's First Term," research paper in Government and Politics for Dr. Elmer Plischke, January 1957, 3, Office of the Curator, Blair House, Philip B. Kunhardt Jr. et al., *The American President: The Human Drama of Our Nation's Highest Office* (New York: Riverhead Books, 1999), 39.

7. Wilroy and Prinz, *Inside Blair House*, 51. Blair House records documenting Bess Truman's and Mamie Eisenhower's involvement, if any, in guest house decorating during their husbands' terms have not come to light.

8. Betty C. Monkman, *The White House: Its Historic Furnishings and First Families* (Washington, D.C., and New York: White House Historical Association and Abbeville Press, 2000), 234; Wilroy and Prinz, *Inside Blair House*, 58; Jacqueline Kennedy to Robin Duke,

9. "Only in America," *House and Garden*, January 1965, 98. The newly refurbished White House Queens' Bedroom and the 1962 visit of His Majesty Ibn Abd al-Aziz al-Saud, king of Saudi Arabia, who stayed at Blair House, may have prompted resurrection of the designation King's Bedroom for Blair House's chief of state bedroom.

10. Wilroy and Prinz, *Inside Blair House*, 193. Pat Mosbacher, like her predecessors, led the BHFAC with enthusiasm, respect for the historic Blair House, and new ideas for its ongoing refurbishing. Several rooms left unfinished during the Kennedy-Johnson years were completed in her tenure.

11. Mrs. Emil Mosbacher Jr. to Mrs. Dwight D. Eisenhower, November 19, 1969, Mamie Doud Eisenhower Papers, 1894–1979, 1970 Files Series (A73-37), box 20 Mos (1) (2) Pat Mosbacher re Blair House, Dwight D. Eisenhower Presidential Library, Abilene, Kans.

12. Susan Eisenhower, *Mrs. Ike: Memories and Reflections on the Life of Mamie Eisenhower* (New York: Farrar, Straus and Giroux, 1996), 282–83; Karal Ann Marling, *As Seen on TV: The Visual Culture of Everyday Life in the 1950s* (Cambridge, Mass.: Harvard University Press, 1994), 8–49.

13. Seale, *President's House*, 2:1053; Monkman, *White House*, 222–26; Susan Eisenhower, *Mrs. Ike*, 317–21.

14. Betty Beale, "Changes in Blair House Décor," *Washington Sunday Star*, May 10, 1970, F2, F12. In her memoirs, Mary Wilroy recalls hopes that another bedroom more in need of refurbishing would be chosen, "but Mamie Eisenhower had another idea and she was not to be budged. She was going to transform the head of state's bedroom into a monument to Dwight David Eisenhower. Her decision caused a bit of consternation behind the scenes. . . . The head of state's bedroom was full of marvelous furniture, and because it had been for so long the bedroom of former President Truman, many people thought it should become a room to honor him." With no funds forthcoming, and protocol requiring, "that one doesn't argue with a former first lady," Mamie "had her way." Wilroy and Prinz, *Inside Blair House*, 211. On her grandmother as a sometimes dominating, very detail-oriented personality, see Susan Eisenhower, *Mrs. Ike*, 292.

15. Mrs. Emil Mosbacher Jr. to Mrs. Dwight D. Eisenhower, May 8 and June 30, 1970, Mamie Doud Eisenhower Papers, 1894–1979, 1970 Files Series (A73-37), box 20, Mos (1) (2) Pat Mosbacher re Blair House, Eisenhower Library, carbon copies in BHFAC Records, Office of the Curator, Blair House. The Friends of Eisenhower included George Climpson, G. Keith Funston, Benjamin H. Griswold III, Neil J. McKinnon, Thomas S. Nichols, CBS Chairman William S. Paley, General William C. Westmoreland, Lowell Wicker, and others. Complete donor names and descriptions of gifts and other acquisitions are contained in "Appraisal of Items Given by Mrs. Mamie Eisenhower to Blair House," September 11, 1970, and other items in BHFAC Records, Office of the Curator, Blair House.

16. "Dedication of the Eisenhower Room, Blair House 1970," photograph album, BHFAC Records, Office of the Curator, Blair House; Naomi Nover, "Washington Dateline," *Denver Post*, clipping file, Office of the Curator, Blair House.

17. Quoted in M. M. Flatley, "Mamie Had to Hold Her Tears," *Washington Evening Star*, December 5, 1970, Woman's World, A13.

18. Selwa Roosevelt, *Keeper of the Gate* (New York: Simon and Schuster, 1990), 83–96; Andrea Metzger, "A Brief History of Blair House," 2004, Office of the Curator, Blair House.

19. President Dwight D. Eisenhower, Farewell Radio and Televsion Address to the American People, January 17, 1961, Section VII, Dwight D. Eisenhower Presidential Center website, at www.eisenhower.archives.gov/speeches/farewell_address.html.

President James K. Polk and cabinet members, State Dining Room, White House, February 16, 1849, from a Levin C. Handy copy photograph after a daguerreotype by Mathew B. Brady, now lost, published here for the first time. President Polk stands at center; seated, left to right, are Secretary of the Navy John Young Mason, Secretary of State James Buchanan, Secretary of the Treasury Robert J. Walker, and Attorney General Isaac Toucey.

Discovered: An Unknown Brady Portrait of President James K. Polk and Members of His Cabinet

CLIFFORD KRAINIK

Small pieces of history often find their way to remote, seldom-visited personal spaces. Attics and basements provide the traditional resting place for bundles of love letters, brittle newspaper clippings announcing the engagements and weddings, births and deaths of several generations, and the ubiquitous family photograph album. Levin Corbin Handy (1855–1932) of Washington, D.C., accumulated many such items. But as a professional photographer and nephew to the renowned Civil War photographer Mathew B. Brady (1823–1896), Handy had a cache of memorabilia that was of historic proportions. In the mid-nineteenth century, Brady was the leading portrait photographer in America, having established fashionable galleries on Broadway in New York City and on Pennsylvania Avenue in Washington, D.C., halfway between the Capitol and the White House. His carriage trade included the most famous personalities of the day from all walks of life: political, military, clerical, and artistic. There were heroes and scoundrels, the ultrarich and the notorious; even P. T. Barnum's entourage frequented Brady's galleries. In short, if you were "someone," you had your photograph taken "by Brady." It was Brady's grand vision to document the Civil War, and he sent, at his own expense, groups of photographers to capture historic scenes on the battlefields. These photographs alone would secure his place of honor in history.

Levin Handy went to work for his famous uncle at age 12 to prepare glass-plate photographic negatives. He proved a worthy apprentice, and by 1871 was listed in the Washington City directory as a photographer; he opened his own gallery in 1880. Upon Brady's death in 1896 Handy, received a vast collection of daguerreotypes, glass-plate negatives, and paper photographs from which he printed copies that he sold until his own death in March 1932. In 1954, Handy's two daughters, Alice H. Cox and Mary H. Evans, sold approximately ten thousand original, duplicate, and copy negatives as well as daguerreotypes and paper photographs to the Library of Congress. The remainder of the Brady-Handy collection was stored for decades in Handy's home on Maryland Avenue on Capitol Hill. Eventually his daughters' descendants received the collection—filing cabinets of glass negatives and cardboard boxes of photographic prints—and secured it in the basement of a modest home in Falls Church, Virginia. It was from this location that a historically important, torn and curled, slightly soiled silver-print copy photograph of a Brady daguerreotype of eleventh president James K. Polk and his cabinet members emerged.[1]

In 1849, during the final days of President Polk's administration, Mathew Brady made a formal request for a photographic sitting to the White House. He realized that the self-proclaimed one-term president would soon leave office, and he was eager to record the likeness of the chief executive and his cabinet members. This was not the first such request that President Polk had received during his four tumultuous years in office; it would, however, be his last. John Plumbe Jr. photographed President Polk in 1845 and in the spring of 1846 made a historic daguerreotype portrait of the president and his cabinet—the earliest known photograph

President Polk and his cabinet in the State Dining Room is the earliest photographic record of a White House interior and the first photograph of a U.S. president with his advisers. Seated, left to right: Attorney General John Young Mason, Secretary of War William Marcy, President Polk, Secretary of the Treasury Robert J. Walker; standing: Postmaster General Cave Johnson (center); Secretary of the Navy George Bancroft. One of President James Monroe's mantels imported from Italy can be seen in the background. Half-plate daguerreotype, approximately 4½ x 5½ inches, attributed to John Plumbe Jr., c. 1846.

Mathew B. Brady photographed every U.S. president from John Quincy Adams to William McKinley, with the exception of William Henry Harrison. Lithograph by F. D'Avignon for the Photographic Art Journal, *January 1851.*

taken inside the White House.[2] Other artists and photographers also besieged the president for sittings, including the artist George Healy, whose request to photograph President Polk in the White House was denied in the summer of 1846.

In his diary on February 14, 1849, President Polk noted that Mathew Brady was given permission to convert the State Dining Room into a temporary photographic studio.[3] Here Brady would labor for several days taking unique daguerreotype portraits of the president and his most trusted advisers. Until recently only a single portrait of President Polk had been identified as from this sitting. It was not until the beginning of the twenty-first century—more than one hundred and fifty years later—that a second likeness of James K. Polk, this time posed with cabinet members, came to light.

The background of the image is completely devoid of decorative elements or architectural details, much to the dismay of White House historians.[4] Brady's composition places the chief executive in a dominant position standing at center stage, a tall, thin, erect figure. Seated before him, viewed left to right, are four of the six members of his cabinet: John Young Mason, secretary of the navy; James Buchanan, secretary of state; Robert J. Walker, secretary of the treasury; and Isaac Toucey, attorney general. Surely the most striking of all the portraits in the group is the future fifteenth president of the United States, James Buchanan. With his high, upturned collar and a white starched stock, Secretary Buchanan departs in dress, if not in political sentiment, from his conservative colleagues. Missing are the secretary of war, William L. Marcy, and Postmaster General Cave Johnson.

This newly discovered photograph poses an intriguing question: Given Brady's desire to photograph the president, why did this portrait remain unpublished for more than a century? One explanation might be in what is missing from the photograph: two important cabinet members are absent, and the background lacks detail. Furthermore, the portrait was made in the last days of Polk's administration—a time when it would hold little interest to an audience eager to see the newly elected president and Mexican War hero, Zachary Taylor. Brady would photograph President Taylor and his full cabinet at the White House early in 1849 and reproduce that portrait as a fine lithograph.

Another possibility is that the president appears to be unwell. Polk's health was declining, and less than

five months later he would die suddenly, possibly from cholera contracted during his triumphant return home to Tennessee. Historically, the president of the United States has been portrayed as a powerful leader—from Generals George Washington to Dwight D. Eisenhower. Brady may have decided that the group portrait would do little to convey the image of a strong president. Instead, Brady chose to enhance and publish only an individual likeness of Polk—the portrait best known to posterity.

Despite the mystery behind its long concealment, the portrait will serve as an important document of early presidential history. It presents in the same image two presidents of polar abilities and accomplishments and provides a fuller picture of the beleaguered dark-horse president, James K. Polk.

NOTES

1. The author of this article recently purchased the balance of the Brady-Handy Photographic Archives. It was while inventorying this collection that he discovered the heretofore unknown image of President Polk and cabinet members. The discovered portrait is a silver-print photograph approximately 5I by 7I inches. It is a copy of a paper photographic copy of the daguerreotype taken by Mathew Brady in 1849.

2. Clifford Krainik, "A 'Dark Horse' in Sunlight and Shadow: Daguerreotypes of President James K. Polk," *White House History*, (1997): 16:22–39.

3. James K. Polk, *The Diary of James K. Polk During His Presidency*, ed. Milo Milton Quaife (Chicago: A. C. McClurg and Co., 1910), 4:334.

4. For a discussion about the architectural details in the State Dining Room revealed in the President James K. Polk and cabinet daguerreotype taken by John Plumbe Jr. in 1846, see William Seale, *The President's House: A History* (Washington, D.C.: White House Historical Association with the cooperation of the National Geographic Society, 1986), 1:254.

WHITE HOUSE
HISTORY

White House Historical Association
Washington

JAMES HOBAN: ARCHITECT OF THE WHITE HOUSE • NUMBER 22
PUBLISHED SPRING 2008

Foreword

James Hoban: Architect of the White House

More than a century before the White House was built, the English architect Sir Christopher Wren advised a prospective client how to approach constructing a building: "There are 3 ways of working: by the Day, by Means, by Great." The commissioners charged by President George Washington with setting up the new national capital faced the same alternatives in 1792 when they addressed their first building, a "suitable" house for the "accomodation" of the president. It had been called for in the 1790 Act of Congress called the "Residence Act."

"By Day" meant paying day wages, an arrangement craftsmen resented; the second, "by Means," which the upper levels of skilled workmen—bricklayers, stonemasons, joiners, and finish carpenters—preferred, called for "measuring" the work in stages and by complicated mathematical and geometrical formulas arriving at a mutually acceptable figure for payment; "by Great" turned the whole work over to one contractor, including the acquisition of materials and the securing and payment of workmen. The commissioners combined the first and second: they provided the materials and kept control.

A detail of James Hoban's 1793 elevation for the President's House.

They needed a manager to represent them. The man they selected was the architect whose plan had most pleased the president, James Hoban, who brought with him from his native Ireland experience in architectural drawing as well as the techniques of building. It is to Hoban that this special issue of *White House History* is devoted.

Building the White House was the greatest event in Hoban's life. He worked on the Capitol, but others did as well; the White House was his. Born a peasant on the County Kilkenny estate of the Anglo-Irish Cuffe family, he achieved his training in Dublin and a niche in America through hard work and luck. He had his storms with the commissioners, but he got the job done. Good, finished performance of what he set out to do was a key feature of his life.

To paint as full a picture of this man as the limited documentation will allow, we have brought together historians with interests in him and his era in Ireland and America. We see him in the context of building and architecture as he knew them.

William Seale
Editor, *White House History*

James Hoban: Builder of the White House

*J*ames Hoban died in Washington December 8, 1831. That morning, realizing the end was near, he summoned his son James, a lawyer, to write his will, distributing a not-inconsiderable inventory of real estate and possessions to his surviving family. News of Hoban's death called to the city's memory the venerable "Captain Hoban" who had been in Washington almost from its inception and had built a number of the public buildings as well as many other buildings. He had been an architect; a builder; an employer of scores of building men; a friend of many from all walks of life; the venerable captain of the militia company; an early member and continuing pillar of Saint Patrick's Roman Catholic Church.[1] Captain Hoban had been of the generation, ever thinner in number, who had forged the capital city of the great republican experiment from fallow fields and deep forests, following the wishes of the idolized George Washington.

Hoban's was an American success story of the sort that is recorded proudly in family histories, if not claiming space in the great narratives. In Hoban's case, a moment in the sun keeps his name alive: he built the

---

James Hoban was born and grew up in the agricultural world of County Kilkenny, Ireland. His birthplace, a thatch-roof whitewashed stone cottage very like the one that appears here, stood until it was demolished in the middle 1930s.

White House. A builder by trade, he put up many an edifice over his lifetime and in his Irish boyhood learned his hand at the crafts and doubtless to love the smell of mortar and new-cut timber, but no detail of him is more than incidental beside that of building the White House. He built it, returned to build it back after the British burned it, then returned twice again to give it the columned porticoes, north and south, that we are likely to see whenever we turn on the television.

The Cornerstone

For all we do know about Hoban, much more about him is a mystery. In his lifetime he was not the national figure he has since become. Except for his role in the building and rebuilding of the White House, he is one of the more promising of many eighteenth-century men who made their way to America. He was not without self-confidence, and he seems to have got what he wanted. On December 1, 1792, he wrote to the Commissioners of the Federal District charged with building the new city of Washington:

> Being universally acquainted with men in the Building line in Ireland, particularly with many able Stone Cutters in Dublin with whom I have been concerned in building, as the Royal Exchange, New Bank, and Custom house, all of which buildings were done in the same stile as the business to be done here, and nearly the same kind of Stone, to these men I would write to bring skilled tradesmen to America.[2]

Thomas Ivory, center, with his fellow Anglo-Irish architects in Dublin. Traditionally this painting is said to be a meeting of the Bluecoat School. Portrait group by John Trotter.

By that date Hoban was already a player in the Federal City. He had won the competition for the design of the President's House in July, went right to work organizing the very disorganized building site, with its crew of hired slaves, and on October 13 was present to see the cornerstone—a brass plate with his name and others upon it—mortared into place between two stones. By December he was pushing for more work, greater responsibility, a characteristic of him on every job we know of that he ever had.

Early Training and Contacts

Hoban never had difficulty dealing with the great and powerful. He ignored affronts, as best we can tell, and while he could make large numbers of men work hard, he seems to have been by most accounts gentle by nature. His predecessor, Pierre Charles L'Enfant, tried to play by his own rules and fell hard, in spite of the admi-

ration George Washington had for him. L'Enfant never learned that those he considered little people, if not of much help to him, could bring a lot of harm. Hoban, on the other hand, was a master in keeping matters calm and moving on all levels, in spite of transgressions on his part that might have created problems—such as requiring the workmen to join his militia (the Washington Artillery, of which he was captain) and docking their pay if they did not show up for drills.

Hoban's early training under his master at the Dublin Society drawing school, Thomas Ivory, served him well.[3] The buildings Hoban claimed to have been associated with were all involved with Ivory, who seems to have put his promising pupils to work on his projects.[4] Construction was then a part of architectural education. How Hoban got to Dublin and Ivory's studio at the Dublin Society is not known, although it is probably a good guess that he received help from his Hoban relatives in the county, who were marble workers, or even the Cuffe family, to whom his parents were attached, on the Cuffe estate, Desart Court, in County Kilkenny.[5] As Ivory's student, Hoban excelled and won second prize for his drawing of a country house. This was one of two medals he would win and cherish, the other being for designing the White House.[6]

Professor Edward McParland has written of Thomas Ivory: "His influence here on the training and standards of a generation of craftsmen is incalculable."[7] Ivory's taste was conservative, in the Anglo-Palladian style we see in the design of the White House. Books he ordered for his pupils were all in that genre.[8] Recognition at the school came to

Hoban as a draftsman, and while only four of his drawings survive from his long career, they are more than competent. A more valuable attribute was his knowledge of the crafts of building. Two other of Ivory's students, John Cash and Robert Pool, published a book of views of Dublin architecture, the plates for which were exhibited at the school.[9] One of those plates, a view of Leinster House, may have been held up by Hoban a few years later before his prospective client, George Washington, as a model to follow for the President's House.

Ivory, a native of Ireland, suffered the same condescension as other Irish architects when he applied for major projects. He flowered only during a hiatus between mid-century and 1780, when no English or European

Hoban's section for the North Front of the White House, 1792 (left), bears reference to the facade of Desart Court (above), the stately Irish country house intimate to his youth.

architects were on the scene. Perhaps discrimination in the profession against the Irish led Hoban to depart; perhaps Ivory encouraged it, hoping this pupil might have an easier time of it than he. That Hoban struck out for Philadelphia was not surprising, considering the kinship Dublin and that city felt for each other. The American War of Independence was over and had warm popular support in Ireland.

When Hoban set sail to America is not certain. If he worked for Ivory on the Newcomen Bank, then he left well after 1781, because Ivory started building the bank that year. It stood in Castle Street and was his finest work. By 1785 we first document Hoban as being in America, for he advertises in the Philadelphia newspaper on May 25: "Any gentleman who wishes to build in an elegant style, may hear of a person properly calculated for that purpose who can execute the Joining and Carpenter's business in the modern taste. James Hoban."[10]

Two years later, in 1787, Hoban was in Charleston, South Carolina, answering on April 21 a mathematical riddle published in the *Charleston Morning Post*.[11] He

Portrait of George Washington's friend, Henry Laurens, painted in 1781 while he was held in the Tower of London.

lived in Charleston for about five years. We know little about his life there except that he formed a partnership with Pierce Purcell and became known among the gentry for his ability at architecture and building—even though we cannot really pinpoint why. He and Purcell and their wives lived in the same house in Charleston. Hoban placed the following advertisement in the *City Gazette,* January 17, 1789: "Absented himself on Sunday the 4th instant. A negro fellow, named PETER, by trade a carpenter, about five feet seven or eight inches high, had on a brown coatee, corduroy or nankeen breeches, and a three cocked hat; being closely pursued he lost one of his shoes, and his feet being remarkably large, he cannot be easily fitted, which causes him to go barefooted." Twenty shillings reward offered.[12]

What happened to Mrs. Hoban we do not know. There is no evidence of her being in Washington, and slight evidence of her in Charleston. We can assume that she died in Charleston. Hoban was married again in Washington, as the walls of the White House were rising.

Among Hoban's references were some of the most prominent citizens of Charleston. The colorful statesman Henry Laurens, imprisoned in the Tower of London during the American Revolution and later traded for Lord Cornwallis after the American victory at Yorktown, was a close friend of Washington. Another of the references was the celebrated Aedanus Burke, an Irish judge who immigrated to America and rose to prominence in Charleston in law and politics. Flamboyant and witty, Burke castigated the Founding Fathers in the most public way for their aristocratic pretensions, and was popular with all of them as a jolly good fellow in spite of it. Both Laurens and Burke and Hoban's other references were presumably those who introduced him to Washington and later wrote letters of recommendation. All were involved in the rebuilding of the local statehouse, particularly Henry Laurens, who was the principal patron, hoping the legislature, which had moved from Charleston to inland Columbia, would return if desirable quarters were provided. Hoban may well have built that building, which stands at the corner of Meeting and Broad Streets, today a courthouse.

The Assignment in Washington

By the Residence Act of 1790, an Act of Congress, the new city of Washington was allowed ten years to be built and occupied as capital. George Washington and

Hoban's letter to the commissioners building the White House described his credentials for building monumental architecture.

others had seen this location on the Potomac River as a perfect place, more or less in the middle of the United States—this was before the Louisiana Purchase. The Potomac was navigable by sailing ships some 300 miles from the sea, one of the farthest places inland accessible by water in the United States as it was then. Moreover, a system of canals could extend the river's navigation to the Ohio River and thus open up the Old Northwest.

George Washington watched the clock's hands move and heard unhappily about the utter pandemonium at the site of the city, as the commission quarreled with builders and suppliers walked off the job. Without the public buildings by December 1, 1800, the specified decade's end, there would be no capital on the Potomac. In desperation, at some point he recalled the "practical architect" who had been introduced to him by his prominent friends in Charleston. He could not remember his name, but having some reason to think that this

might be the ticket, he wrote to Henry Laurens. Not very long afterward (factoring in the slow transportation) James Hoban appeared at the presidential house in Philadelphia, having already been to the site of the Federal City and left his partner Pierce Purcell there to take stock of the situation. These two wasted no time.[13]

It is a great loss to history that we can only surmise what transpired at Washington's several conferences with Hoban. That they got along well is clear; that some words were exchanged on architecture is certain; that Hoban returned to Washington with a letter of introduction to the commissioners is documented fact. Meanwhile, a competition had been launched for a design for a capitol and president's house. Thomas Jefferson, secretary of state, had insisted upon the competition, fearing what the president's meddling would produce. Hoban set up in the commissioners' office and drew his plan. The commissioners reported his progress to Wash-

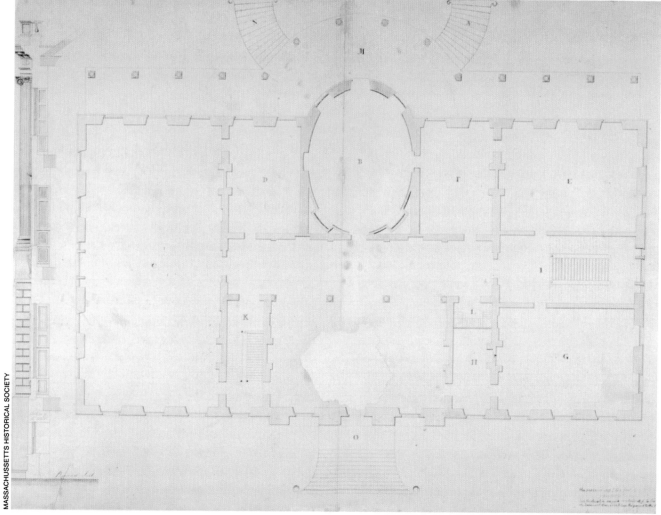

Opposite, top: Upper, final designs for the North Front of the White House, drawing by James Hoban autumn of 1793 or early 1794. Bottom: Plan of the State Floor of the White House, probably Hoban's competition drawing made in summer 1792.

Right: William Robert Fitzgerald, Second Duke of Leinster and patron of the Dublin Society when Hoban was enrolled in its drawing class.

Below: Leinster House, Dublin. When built it was known as Kildare House. Hoban's model for the White House, Leinster House was designed about 1750 by Richard Cassels (or Castle) for James Fitzgerald, who became the first Duke of Leinster in 1766, Today Leinster House is the home of the Oireachtas, Irish Dáil, or Parliament.

ington. Other competition entries appeared, including one secretly sponsored by Jefferson. In June 1792, President Washington appeared and spent some time with Hoban. He returned in July to announce the winner of the competition, James Hoban.[14]

The design of the house was based upon Leinster House, official seat in Dublin of the Duke of Leinster. Of this there can be no mistake. I suspect Hoban offered this, among other designs, and Washington liked not only it but its associations with the Fitzgerald family, of which the Duke of Leinster was a head. The duke was well known as the "First Gentleman of Ireland," and Washington thought of the president as living like "the first gentleman of the land." Lord Edward, the duke's younger brother, had been a prisoner of war confined to Washington's nephew's residence in Charleston. Hoban could show the practicality of a house of the Leinster

George Washington's library fireplace at Mount Vernon contains most of the decorative ornaments found on the White House. It is possible the president and Hoban met here when they conferred at Mount Vernon.

House sort of architecture, the attached columns, the rusticated basement above ground, the extension of wings. Washington ordered that the house be built of stone. The commissioners objected, as did Jefferson, but the president prevailed. He also wanted it ornamented, indeed scattered all over, with Palladian detailing.[15]

The Building of the President's House

Three individuals exerted powerful influence over the White House through its more than 250 years. Hoban was the first; the second was Charles McKim, the famous Beaux Arts architect of the firm McKim, Mead & White; and the last was Lorenzo Winslow, who rebuilt the house for President Harry S. Truman.

Of the three, Hoban's role must be considered the most important, for while the house he built and rebuilt survives only as a shell, with a house essentially fifty years old within it, a skeleton of steel with concrete, it was Hoban who designed the house and brought its materials together for the first time in creating the house that was to prevail through history.

Hoban had the confidence of George Washington. When Washington appeared on his tours of inspection, Hoban was there to explain the progress to him; when Washington was at Mount Vernon, Hoban met with him there. I like to observe in the library at Mount Vernon, where they probably met, nearly all the ornaments of the White House stonework—guilloche, acanthus leaves, dentil moldings, pilasters, and the like. One wonders if they were sometimes illustrations, helping Hoban explain design details.

Hoban's knowledge of building techniques and materials was excellent. He inspected the stone from its bed in the quarry, to the stone shed where it was dressed and carved, to the walls of the house. Hoban knew how to build groin vaults and load-bearing arches. He knew wood and personally traveled to distant places in Virginia and North Carolina to select trees to be cut and cured and shipped to the White House site for hewing into the huge timbers that supported the floors and roof.

The construction site of the President's House in the 1790s must have resembled one of those paintings from the Middle Ages, with the house—a great house by American standards—rising in the middle of a hive of people. At the most, 150 workmen were busy six days a week building the President's House. The structure was completed in 1798 at the close of the season in middle October, with considerable interior work remain-

Building the President's House, 1796, *oil on canvas, commissioned by the White House Historical Association from historical painter Peter Waddell in 2007, whose meticulously researched details are revealed in the crafts in progress and their equipment, including hoisting cranes. In the foreground he includes James Hoban between commissioner William Thornton and his carpenter and partner Pierce Purcell, standing on the high east wall, looking down into what would be the East Room. On the right are slave carpenters. Stonemasons build the outer walls of dressed sandstone, while brickmasons line them for support with soft clay bricks. The worker's village, brick kiln and the Potomac River are seen in the distance.*

ing to be done. At that time, the last brushstrokes were made in whitewashing the entire building to protect the soft stone from winter freezing. Meant to wear off for the most part, leaving cracks and crevices filled, the whitewash would never be allowed to wear, but would be refreshed until 1818, when at last the structure was actually painted with white lead paint. By that time it had for more than a decade already been known as "The White House."[16]

The Interior and Rebuilding of the Interior

It was during Jefferson's occupancy (1801–1809) that the secretary to the British minister in Washington wrote, "The President's house was erected by an Irish mason who gave as his own the plan of the Duke of Leinster's house in Dublin, which being shewn to Gen-

eral Washington was approved of by him, and the Irishman who had been but a journeyman under the real architect and designer of the plan, was appointed to supervise the building. He left out the upper story however and built no cellars."[17]

We only have two of Hoban's drawings of the White House proper, one the competition entry of 1792, which shows the plan and a section, and an elevation from the north as finally modified in October 1793. We have tracings of several more from a later date. These were made by Charles Bulfinch in 1829 from Hoban's drawings for the North Portico, which Hoban and Bulfinch (the public architect) took down from the wall in Hoban's house and removed from their frames, so the copies could be made. The only other drawing by Hoban himself, making three in all, is a cross-section of a sewer that conducted water from the President's House to Tiber Creek, a distance away at the foot of the hill. Into this Jefferson's water closets (built by Hoban) were channeled, and today, interrupted by steel bars, the same brick-lined tunnel serves as a chase for pipes of all kinds. With only three drawings, and one so specialized, we can only reconstruct what Hoban drew to please the president from the written record—minutes of the commissioners who built the house, letters from Washington, memorandums from James Hoban.[18]

As built first, the White House had no porches at all and no portico on the north. The interior was much more in the earlier eighteenth-century manner than it was later to be, with pediments over the doors, wainscoting, and ornamental mantelpieces. Nothing much was modern about it. The old patterns of service were brought over from earlier houses. Not even a dumbwaiter eased the work of the servants. Heat was from wood fires. John Adams added service bells in the rooms, ringing in the servants' hall below. Jefferson added water closets, although there was no running water; his devices were fed from the gutters and cisterns in the attic. He organized the many support structures necessary to such a house within wings to the east and west.[19]

The interior, compared to others in American houses, was monumental indeed. It had more or less the plan originally that we know today. The large Entrance Hall was crossed by a row of Ionic columns with arches between; beyond it a Transverse Hall, off which, as at Leinster House, was a row of parlors, those with color names, the Green Room (1818); the oval Blue Room (1838); and the Red Room (1848). At the west end was the Grand Staircase, which occupied a space now absorbed in the enlarged dining room. At the east end was the great salon known as the East Room. This room Hoban finished only when he rebuilt the house, and a decade thereafter Andrew Jackson decorated it, keeping Hoban's moldings, in bright blue and yellow, with the convenience of twenty-two spittoons.[20]

Below was a long transverse hall with rooms to its sides, all arched and vaulted to support marble floors never built to the main floor above. The second or chamber story had a long transverse hall with rooms flanking it, all bedrooms except one, an oval drawing room directly above the Blue Room. On the Second Floor Hoban manipulated placement of the windows so

that the house would come out proportionately on the outside, but the result upstairs is for the windows to all seem too low on the walls. Generations of decorators have tried to correct this impression with curtains. The floors on the east rise 4 feet to accommodate the elevated ceiling of the East Room, which doubtless would have been a solution otherwise had the original raised basement or "rustic" not been removed from the plan.

The house Hoban built was occupied as ordered in the Residence Act on November 1, 1800. It stood for thirteen years and eight months and was burned in the British invasion in August 1814. Reduced to a raw shell and much of that in bad condition, the White House, like the other burned-out public buildings, was a signal to start over. After strong effort in Congress to move the capital to Cincinnati (the new center of the nation), the government appointed two architects to "repair" the Federal City's public buildings. One was Hoban. The other was Benjamin Henry Latrobe, an Englishman of skill in architecture and engineering who had worked on both the Capitol and the White House under Thomas Jefferson and James Madison.

It is unfortunate that Latrobe detested Hoban to the extent that he did. Hoban was adept at obtaining work. The haughty, outspoken Latrobe—surely the greater talent at design—was fired about as often as he was hired. History is formed from many kinds of sources. At least some of Hoban's obscurity is probably owing to Latrobe's often insulting remarks that demeaned Hoban in the public eye, added to the fact that Latrobe left hundreds of drawings and letters, where Hoban left almost none. Hoban never fought back, to my knowledge. Latrobe's opinion of the architecture of the White House was low: "It is not even original, but a mutilated copy of a badly designed building near Dublin."[21]

When Latrobe tried to push himself on President Madison for the job of rebuilding the public buildings and shook the president's carefully assembled political scheme for "repair" of the public buildings, he was fired. Hoban stayed on to rebuild the White House that had burned and also did minimum work on the Capitol. He built the four executive office buildings flanking the White House, all of which are replaced today. A feature of the rebuilding plan for the White House was porches to the north and south with heroic columns. Hoban completed the house in 1817 but returned in 1824 to build the portico on the south for President James Monroe, and in 1829 that on the north after Andrew Jackson came to office. To the commissioners he wrote in 1816 that porticoes were part of the original plan he had agreed upon with President Washington, they had only been postponed.[22] Credit for the design usually goes to Latrobe because of drawings that might suggest it. The truth is not clear.

Hoban's Record

James Hoban thus built and rebuilt the White House. Meanwhile, he developed what appears to have been quite a business in Washington. He and Pierce Purcell kept their partnership, apart from White House work, until at least 1805 on various projects, although Purcell was let go from his last government project in 1797. They kept apprentices. In 1798, the year the White House was roofed in and the exterior finished, Purcell advertised in the papers for an apprentice named James Coghlan, who had "eloped from my employ." The advertisement noted, "As he has different suits of clothes, it is impossible to describe him by his apparel— He is supposed to be lurking in Alexandria, as he was seen attending a Billiard table there a few days since. A reward will be paid for bringing him home."[23]

Of Hoban's work, little apparently remains besides the White House. He was one of the two architects originally named on the Capitol cornerstone, set by Washington in 1793, but his work there was, if constant for some years, not notable. He is believed to have built, about 1809, the Gothic Revival–style Saint Patrick's Catholic Church, which was reminiscent of a parish church in Ireland. Oak Hill, a fine house President James Monroe built for his retirement outside Washington in Loudoun County, Virginia, seems to have been designed and was certainly at least in part built by Hoban, while Monroe was in office. Jefferson had something to do with the design process but did not design Oak Hill. Hoban's name appears in the building records. He was in the federal employ, at the president's pleasure, so cannot have overlooked an opportunity to please the chief of state.

That Hoban worked with James and Elizabeth Monroe on the design of Oak Hill seems somewhat evident in the appearance of the house. It is a lofty, handsome building of red brick, rich in form, finely executed, with a dramatic arch around the entrance and a few elegant rooms inside served by smaller rooms and passages. The lofty portico of five columns is not on the front, as was usual, but overlooks the garden and meadows rolling away in the distance. The portico functions more as a balcony or terrace, approached only from within the house. President Monroe and his wife, having lived in Paris, were very interested in houses and French decor. Their plan and some of the features are reminiscent of some of the small and elegant houses built in late eighteenth-century France, although the house otherwise has an Anglo-Irish flavor.

By legend the Seabrook House on Seabrook Island, South Carolina, was built by Hoban. Civil War photographer Mathew Brady recorded its large formal gardens, the house, and columned outbuildings. Perhaps it would look more like Hoban if we know more of what he built. The most striking feature at Seabrook House is the divided stair inside. It is like the one Hoban designed and built at the White House but had long passed into history before people began attributing Seabrook House to Hoban. Again, whatever document connected Seabrook House with James Hoban seems lost.

It is difficult to see the White House entirely as a piece of architecture. Time and occupants with different needs have altered it in many ways. Even as this journal goes to press the old West Wing rooms behind the colonnade are being gutted and rebuilt. But this rebuilding has happened there before. Herbert Hoover adapted the space in 1930; Franklin D. Roosevelt gutted it and built his swimming pool there in 1933; Richard M. Nixon built the Press Room there in 1970, laying a floor over the pool; today the Press Room is newly remodeled and for a few days in 2007 one could look down into FDR's pool with its handsome greenish tiles. When a builder and architect can be judged only by one building, and that structure has undergone as much alteration as the White House, then it is hard to judge the skill of the man.

However, the White House image, known to the world, is Hoban's entirely. He took up this part of George Washington's burden and designed and finished on time the first of the nation's public buildings in the new city. It is a handsome, large pile, frosted with the richest stone carvings seen in the new nation. It was a huge house for its time. In an age concerned with kingly pretensions, it was an august house, yet a house and not a palace. And when Hoban came to build it back, he was ordered to make it as it was, which he did, perpetuating the image and his own claim to a place in history.

NOTES

1. Hoban's relationship to Saint Patrick's Church is covered in William W. Warner, *At Peace with All Their Neighbors: Catholics and Catholicism in the National Capital, 1787–1860* (Washington, D.C.: Georgetown University Press, 1994), 161.

2. James Hoban to the Commissioners of the District of Columbia, Washington, December 1, 1792, Records of the Commissioners of the District of Columbia, Record Group 42, Commissioners' Letters Received, National Archives, Washington, D.C.

3. See Dublin Society, *Proceedings*, June 15 and November 4, 1780, Royal Dublin Society Library, Dublin.

4. See Edward McParland, *Thomas Ivory, Architect* (Dublin: Gatherum Series, 1973). Ivory, who was born in Cork, rose in the trades from origins as a cabinetmaker to gunstock carver to architect. He was naturally aware of the difficulties faced by poor boys getting a start in architecture and building. While he seems to have helped Hoban, one suspects that there were other forces at work in Hoban's favor.

5. I am grateful to have had several interviews with the late Mrs. Margaret Phelan and access to her extensive genealogical notes, "County Kilkenny," in my pursuit of Hoban's family. I also credit articles published in the *Irish Times* by Gertrude Higgins in January 1974. See letter Gertrude Higgins to Daisy [Margaret] Phelan, n.p., February 25, 1974, Kilkenny Historical and Archaeological Society. Pierce and Judith Hoban possibly were Hoban's parents. Both died and were buried in County Kilkenny in 1793; Pierce Hoban left an inventory of personal effects in the Records Office, County Kilkenny.

6. Dublin Society, *Proceedings*, November 23, 1780; Records of the Commissioners of the District of Columbia, Minutes, October 20, 1792, RG 42, National Archives.

7. McParland, *Thomas Ivory*, 2.

8. Dublin Society, *Proceedings*, March 5, 1780, lists the following books ordered for Ivory: James Gibbs, *Architect: A Book of Architecture* (London, 1728); Francis Price, *The British Carpenter: A Treatise on Carpentry* (Dublin, 1768); *The Builder's Guide* (Dublin, 1750); William Halfpenny, *Modern Builder's Assistant* (London, 1757); James Ferguson, *On the Art of Drawing: Perspective Made Easy* (London, 1778); Leon Gattista Alterti, *The Art of Building in Ten Books* (Florence, 1496); Andrea Pozzo, *Perspectiva Pictorum et Architectorum*, 2 vols. (Rome, 1693 and 1698). I have added the dates of the original publications. I would suppose the books ordered by the Royal Society were later editions, although the *Proceedings* do not indicate the date.

9. Robert Pool and John Cash, *Views of the Most Remarkable Public Buildings, Monuments and Other Edifices in the City of Dublin* (Dublin: J. Williams, 1780). The Dublin newspapers and the records of the Dublin Society describe an exhibition of plates from this book exhibited at the society while Hoban was a student. It is likely that Hoban owned a copy of this book, being, like the authors, a student of Ivory.

10. *Philadelphia Post*, May 25, 1785.

11. *Charleston Morning Post*, April 21, 1787.

12. *Charleston City Gazette and Daily Advertiser*, January 17, 1789, 3–4, transcription in the research files of the Museum of Early Southern Decorative Arts, Winston-Salem, N.C.

13. President George Washington to the Commissioners, Philadelphia, June 8, 1792; Jacob Read to Washington, Charleston, May 24, 1792; Aedanus Burke to Washington, Charleston, May 12, 1792, all Records of the Commissioners of the District of Columbia, Commissioners' Letters Received.

14. Commissioners to Thomas Jefferson, Washington, July 5, 1792, Records of the Commissioners of the District of Columbia, Commissioners' Letters Sent.

15. For biographical information on the Leinsters and their kin, see S. K. Tillyard, *Aristocrats: Caroline, Emily, Louisa, and Sarah Lennox, 1740–1832* (London: Vintage House, 1994); Tillyard, *Citizen Lord: Edward Fitzgerald, 1763–1798* (London: Vintage House, 1996).

16. Detailed records of the construction of the White House are housed in Washington in the records of the Commissioners of the District of Columbia, Record Group 42, National Archives. The records are near complete and splendid year-by-year accounts of change and life at the White House from its conception to the present day. No more complete and detailed record exists of any American building of two centuries of age, unless, possibly, the Capitol.

17. Benjamin Henry Latrobe to Philip Mazzei, Washington, D.C., May 29, 1806, Benjamin Henry Latrobe Papers, Library of Congress, Washington, D.C.

18. Hoban's White House drawings are: 1792 plan and section, one page, Thomas Jefferson Papers, Massachusetts Historical Society, Boston; elevation from the north, one page, drawn late 1793 or early 1794, Maryland Historical Society, Baltimore; and the sewer drawing, Prints and Photographs Division, Library of Congress. The Bulfinsh drawings for the North Portico, tracings of Hoban's originals lost in the fire, are found in Stephen V. Van Rensselaer to Commissioner Joseph Elgar, Washington, n.d. [a report for January 1829], Records of the Commissioners of the District of Columbia, Commissioners' Letters Received.

19. My descriptions of this earliest period of the White House are gleaned from hundreds of invoices, work orders, and other documents in Records of the Commissioners of the District of Columbia, Commissioners' Letters Sent and Commissioners' Letters Received.

20. The source for this description is the bills and papers of Louis Veron, a Philadelphia jobber of domestic merchandise, pertaining to the decoration of the East Room. These include not only the orders made by Andrew Jackson's agent in Philadelphia but a check list of the merchandise—chairs, tables, chandeliers—as received and installed at the White House. Records of the Commissioners of the District of Columbia, Contracts.

21. Latrobe to Mazzei, Washington, May 29, 1806, Latrobe Papers.

22. Hoban to Commissioner Joseph Elgar, Washington, D.C., February [1?], 1829, Records of the Commissioners of the District of Columbia, Commissioners' Letters Received.

23. *Times and Alexandria Advertiser*, February 3, 1798.

ATTRIBUTIONS TO JAMES HOBAN

The Charleston County Courthouse (top left), a c. 1880 photograph of the building at the corner of Meeting and Broad Streets. Washington was impressed by Hoban's abilities, which may have been illustrated to him in this structure, finished about the time he was there, 1791. Saint Patrick's Church in Washington, D.C. (top right). Hoban supplied materials for and probably largely designed James Monroe's Oak Hill (bottom left) near Leesburg, Virginia, and Col. Seabrook's house on Seabrook Island, South Carolina (bottom right).

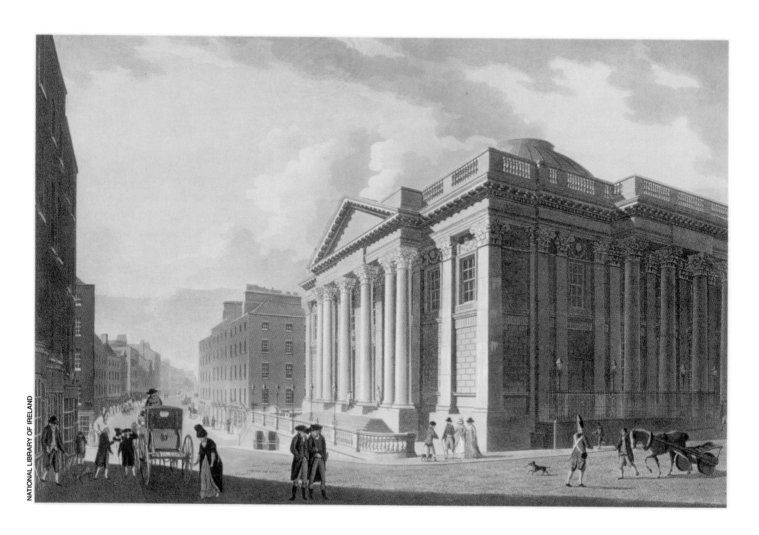

The Royal Exchange, Dublin, *by James Malton c. 1792. View of the Royal Exchange, which faces north, down Parliment Street to the Liffey River. Designed by Thomas Cooley, the Royal Exchange was one of the first important buildings in the city to follow the neoclassical style. It served as the Royal Exchange for the prosperous Dublin merchant population from 1769 to 1779. In the early 1850s, Dublin City Corporation bought the Royal Exchange and converted it for use by city government and it serves today in a perfect state of preservation as City Hall.*

"The Second City in the British Dominions":
Dublin in the Later Eighteenth Century

HOLGER HOOCK

*D*ublin in the eighteenth century was the capital city of a nominally semi-autonomous kingdom but a de facto colonial territory subject to the British throne. The city was some two and a half miles long and of nearly equal breadth; in 1763, the laying out of the North and South Circular roads gave it a sense of geographical definition, enhanced soon thereafter by the completion of the South Wall. By 1790, a trunk canal system defined the city's limits. By mid-century, it was about a quarter the size of London, comparable to Stockholm, Copenhagen, or Berlin. Dublin's population grew from an estimated 140,000 in 1760 to 154,000 in 1778 and some 182,000 in 1800, making it then the sixth largest city in Europe. This is the city the young James Hoban would have observed and occasionally moved in.

As "the second City in the British dominions," Dublin dominated Ireland in every respect.[1] It was the seat of the intermittent vice-regal court, government departments such as the Revenue, semistate bodies like the Inland Navigation Board and Turnpike Trusts, the biannual parliament, and the higher courts.[2] In this period of considerable political upheaval, the Volunteers were formed as a national defense force against a potential French invasion during the American War of Independence. The Volunteers, along with a parliamentary grouping, also supported reformist policies; by 1782, Ireland achieved temporary legislative independence from Westminster.

Dublin's political dominance was matched by its economic hegemony. It was the country's leading port and center for the distribution of goods. Laws restricted Irish trade in favor of England: all Irish goods had to pass through English ports, and Ireland could not sell directly to the colonies. It was only in 1780 that the repeal of the Trade Laws was obtained, strongly supported by the Irish or opposition party led by Henry Grattan and the Volunteers. But within the constraints of the Trade Laws, as the unrivaled economic center for the whole island of Ireland, Dublin's share of national customs receipts averaged over 50 percent throughout the century. It was the chief entry point for most primary and manufactured imports. Indeed, with accelerating national market integration and a concentration of overseas trade on four or five large ports in the whole of the island, Dublin's position was consolidated over this period. It was also a major manufacturing location, from woolen manufacture and the silk industry to iron-founding, metal-finishing trades, glass manufacture, and sugar-baking. In 1759, Guinness's Brewery was established in Saint James's Gate, to become one of the city's most successful industries. Dublin's markets offered "flesh, fowl, and fish, particularly the latter, in higher perfection than in any other capital in Europe."[3]

Moreover, Dublin was the country's center of banking and finance and for the distribution of printed materials. By 1780, the city had twenty-one master booksellers, thirty lesser dealers, and fifty printers, including newspaper publishers. Printing thrived because it did not operate under the restrictions of British copyright, and

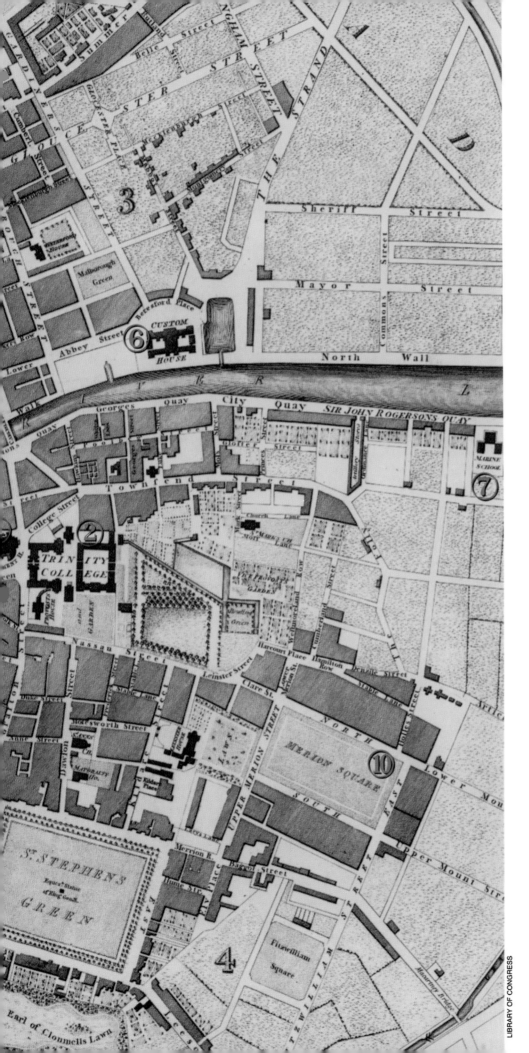

A Plan of the City of Dublin, 1797.
Places of interest are marked in blue:

1. Guinness Brewery
2. Trinity College
3. Dublin Castle
4. Parliament House
5. Royal Exchange
6. Custom House
7. Marine School
8. Sackville Street
9. Lying in Hospital
10. Merrion Square

A Prospect of the City of Dublin from the North, made by Charles Brooking, 1728.

everyone was free to reprint London works. After
Jonathan Swift and George Berkeley, there were, however, no Irish writers of comparable stature for the
remainder of the century. Dublin held a concentration
of lawyers and medical specialists as well as a monopoly on higher education in the form of Trinity College.
Trinity doubled its intake over the second half of the
century, fed by the expansion in academies and private
schools. The college taught the sons of the Irish peerage
alongside those of the professional classes and even of
butchers and builders, mostly pursuing a classical cur-
riculum. The wealthiest also continued to educate their
sons in England and on the Continent. Most future ordi-
nands of the Church of Ireland were educated at Trinity,
but no other professional education was available.
Nevertheless, the college provided an intellectual and
social focus for Dublin's intelligentsia.

Building on its political and economic dominance,
Dublin was the social hub of the landed classes who
spent the winter season from around November to
March in the city, and not just in those alternate years
between 1715 and the 1780s when parliament met
for five to eight months. A second, shorter social peak
occurred in late April and May, when the polite
indulged in an endless round of culture and consumption. Dublin was also the chief manufacturing place
for luxury and high-quality commodities for the whole
of Ireland.

Urban and Architectural Developments

"Dublin was transformed in the eighteenth century," explains the modern scholar and Dublin-based
geographer Edel Sheridan-Quantz, "from a relatively
compact single-centred walled town with incipient suburbs to what was by the standards of the time a metropolis, with a fragmented, multi-centred structure," in
political, social, and cultural as well as in economic and
retailing terms.[4] In addition to the north-south division
imposed on the city by the River Liffey, there was a
clear east-west social gradient, with the gentry's pleasant residences mostly nearer the coast and the merchants and mechanics living landward in the western
suburbs. Most investment in the urban fabric occurred
in the eastern half of the city, downriver from the
medieval core, both in terms of residential quarters and
of public buildings.

Later eighteenth-century Dublin possessed a range
of impressive public buildings, all suitably advertised
and eulogized in contemporary guidebooks. The Dublin
Castle was not unambiguously among the most magnificent and imposing. At core a thirteenth-century building, its upper court served as the residence of the Lord
Lieutenant, Ireland's viceroy. In this quadrangular
square, said R. Lewis's guide of 1787, "the state musicians appear on the birthdays of their majesties . . .
when the cavalry from the garrison are drawn up."[5] The
treasury, other public offices, and the armory were

accommodated in the lower court. The more impressive eighteenth-century structures included Parliament House (now the Bank of Ireland), begun in 1729 to the design of Sir Edward Lovett Pearse. It was far grander than the buildings that housed the Westminster Parliament at the time; indeed it was said that the whole "British Empire, [we might have added Europe herself] cannot boast of so spacious and stately a Senatorial-Hall."[6] Across the College Green from Parliament House stood Trinity College, "one of the noblest [structures] of the kind in Europe, exhibiting more the appearance of a royal mansion, than a number of collegiate cells."[7] The green itself was dominated by the equestrian statue of William III, erected in 1700–1701 by the corporation "in grateful commemoration of their deliverance from Popery and slavery." Its sides were ornamented with warlike trophies, and in the center of each side was a shield with a dedication to King William, the preserver of religion, the restorer of the laws, and the defender of liberties. The statue was the focus of an annual parade of representatives of the crown, city officials, and parliamentarians marching from the castle to College Green with orange banners and flags to celebrate the Glorious Revolution and their loyalty to the Crown. The Royal Exchange (now the City Hall), designed by Thomas Cooley and built for £40,000 raised by parliamentary grant and merchants' lotteries, was an imposing square building of Portland stone, complete with a dome and

sumptuous, highly decorated interiors. These included offices, meeting rooms, and a chamber where merchants deposited specimens of their commodities in drawers. John van Nost's cast copper statue of George III showed the king in Roman military habit, crowned with laurel and holding a truncheon.

New economic hubs developed on the city's eastern edge. Dublin merchants identified mostly with the city's medieval core and consequently opposed, unsuccessfully, the new Custom House (1781–91) in a much more easterly location and to the north, with new docks developed immediately to its east. Designed by James Gandon, this was the "clearest example of the influence of direct colonial management in the architecture of pre-union Dublin." Founded by the British government, its iconography was meant to demonstrate the harmonious union between Britain and Ireland. Lewis's guide of 1787 described the Custom House with its 125 meter wide facade as, compared to the old Custom House, a "much larger edifice, with convenient and proper offices." As a "new and magnificent" building, it promised "to be not only an honour to the city and kingdom in general, but highly useful to the interests of trade and commerce."[8]

Besides the buildings that were specific to Dublin's function as capital city, most parishes had charitable schools. There were also the Marine and Hibernian schools, which prepared for armed service the children of diseased or disabled sailors and soldiers. The city's numerous hospitals included older foundations such as the Royal Hospital, a retirement home for former soldiers, the Foundling Hospital, an orphanage, and the Bluecoat Hospital for the relief of poor children and old people. From the early eighteenth-century onward, further voluntary hospitals were founded, such as the Charitable Infirmary (1718), Steeven's Hospital (1733), Mercer's Hospital (1734), the Hospital for Incurables (1743), and Saint Patrick's hospital for "lunaticks and idiots," endowed by Dean Swift in 1745 with an £11,000 bequest; he himself later famously became a tragic resident. The Magdalen Asylum in Leeson Street received "those unfortunate females, who have deviated from the paths of virtue," and the House of Industry pursued the "benevolent purposes of receiving such of both sexes, as are by age, misfortune, or sickness, rendered incapable of earning their bread, and for relieving the public from various impostors, and those of indecent manners."[9]

Not a great deal of church building occurred in the eighteenth century itself, yet anyone walking Dublin in this period would have noticed the ubiquity of ecclesiastical structures. In 1787, a guidebook listed the two Protestant cathedrals, Saint Patrick's and Christ Church, eighteen parish churches, eight chapels of ease, four foreign churches, thirteen meeting houses of Presbyterians, Anabaptists, Quakers, and Methodists, sixteen Roman Catholic chapels, four nunneries, and a synagogue.[10] A denominational divide cut through most aspects of Dublin life. The Catholic population clearly outsized the Protestants by mid-century, but for most of the century, practicing Roman Catholics were barred from the administration, the armed forces, and the professions except medicine. Political, economic, and genetic pressure had attenuated the remaining resident Catholic peerage and even the Catholic urban gentry. In Dublin's cultural life, even Masonic societies, while theoretically open to all, probably reinforced the denominational divide, and some middle-class associations were run on explicitly anti-Catholic lines. This essay focuses on the dominant Protestant culture.

In the last third of the century, the Wide Streets Commission, one of Europe's first municipal planning authorities, widened and straightened existing streets and built new ones in the attempt to create a more coherent and "ordered" urban structure. As in previous urban developments, such as Sackville Mall, new streets were created through compulsory purchases of properties and demolition. Previous patterns of ownership were dissolved, streets widened to at least 30 meters, and new buildings constructed with facades stretching across boundaries to link discrete dwellings and properties, as in Dame or Westmoreland Streets. All this provided improved communication, suitable approaches to the castle and Parliament House, and grand vistas, such as Parliament Street. Dame Street was replanned from 1778 as Dublin's largest thoroughfare and fashionable shopping street; it was often compared to London's Bond Street. The 1780s and 1790s saw further widening and enhancing of the grandeur of the capital's central streets, with Sackville Street's width at 160 feet the most impressive. Thus emerged the new city of spectacle and "coherent façade" as a "mirror in which its dominant elite would see their entire culture reflected."[11] All new buildings had shops on the ground floor with residences above. Dublin's "chief monumental axes became more than just representative facades of officialdom," explains Sheridan-Quantz. "The integration of varied facilities into the monumental streetscape ensured that the streets would have a commercial and social life linked with their representative functions, and they thereby created new fashionable stages for conspicuous consumption."[12] To aid these developments, in 1774 an act was passed for "taking down sign-posts, pent-houses, and other projections" from the fronts of houses, as well as for the new paving of streets with flagged foot passages on each side.[13]

Genteel Haunts

Not only public, but private building activity, too, transformed the city of Dublin in this period. By mid-century, aristocratic interest in building in the city revived, and several spacious suburbs were developed with wide streets and squares, mostly north of the river, nearly all built speculatively. In architectural and artistic terms, Dublin showed no slavish dependence on English models and imports. Instead, building on long-standing Continental links and growing Continental travel, it had direct access to originals in the development of architectural classicism.

There were two large, and several smaller estates with elegant streets and squares, and large and comfortable four-story houses four or five bays wide. The most prestigious urban developments included, north of the river, the Gardiner estate, encompassing Sackville Street and Rutland and Mountjoy Squares, laid out on the

Illustrations from Views of the
Most Remarkable Public
Buildings, Monuments, and
Other Edifices in the City of
Dublin, *published in 1780 by
Robert Pool and John Cash,
included the garden front of
Dublin Castle (above); the
north front of the Royal
Exchange (right); and the east
front of the Bluecoat Hospital
(below).*

Gardiner family development (later the Viscounts Mountjoy). On Rutland Square—Dublin's earliest square, after the College Green—was a charitable venture: the Lying-In-Hospital, founded by the physician Dr. Bartholomew Mosse in the 1750s as the first hospital in the British Isles to specialize in obstetrics. In the first thirty years, almost twenty thousand poor women delivered their babies there. At the hospital, obstetrics and entertainment were integrated: it would soon include a fashionable promenade and pleasure gardens laid out to its north. These offered musical entertainment outdoors and, from 1784, indoors as well, in the specially built Rotunda to the east of the hospital. Lewis's 1787 guide described the hospital as "extremely

Kildare, then Leinster House (today the seat of the Irish Parliament), with its spacious and elegant gardens, stables, and numerous outbuildings behind its rather dour façade, was a great house of hospitality and entertainment.[16] These two eastern fashionable areas boasted about the same number of resident peers and bishops, making the geographically smaller northern estate socially the even more exclusive one. And it was Leinster House upon which James Hoban based his design for the White House.

The city's commercial topography was closely linked to social settlement patterns. In the medieval core and the Liberties were regular street markets and very small shops and hawkers for low-order goods. High-

THE CUSTOM HOUSE

The Custom House of Dublin from the City of Dublin/1728, *by Charles Brooking.*

magnificent." The total funds—through lotteries, receipts from the Rotunda concerts, gardens, benefit balls, and benefactions—totaled some £1,200.[14] We shall return to the pleasure gardens and Rotunda in a moment.

Another fashionable area, and the southern, larger counterpart to the Gardiner estate to the north, centered around the estate of Viscount Fitzwilliam of Merrion and the Earl of Kildare (later the Duke of Leinster). Merrion Square was first laid out in the 1760s, and by the 1790s a third of its lessees were titled. In 1797, a Dublin estate agent wrote to Fitzwilliam in London about this "spacious and elegant area": "Merrion Square looks so handsome it is so fashionable a walk and drive . . . you have nothing in London so handsome."[15]

order and luxury goods, serving a more prosperous clientele—perfumers, goldsmiths and silversmiths, and print and book sellers—were located at the eastern end of the medieval core and in the shopping streets serving the fashionable estates. There were three main areas of fashionable consumption: Castle Street–High Street; Parliament Street–Dame Street–College Green–Grafton Street; and Capel Street with Henry and Mary Streets. The western parishes with largely poor housing were the focus of industrial activity and the least social mixing; the center, around High, Castle, and Dame Streets and Parliament House, displayed higher-quality commercial activity; and the Gardiner estate mixed exclusive residential with some commercial and retailing streets.

In 1777, the Londoner the Reverend T. Campbell rhapsodized that "genteel company walk in the evenings, and on Sundays, after two o'clock, as with us in St. James's Park," lavishing rare metropolitan praise on one of Europe's largest, if not the largest, urban square. If the polite did not walk, they owned or hired sedan chairs, carriages, and coaches to move around the city, especially in poor weather. City guides listed, among the types of carriage available: stage and hackney coaches, chariots, chaises, and sedan chairs, all for the conveyance of persons and goods, for both pleasure and business. A coach from a given location to a set-down in an adjoining division cost £1,1s and a sedan chair sixpence during the day, but between midnight and 6 a.m. the rates were £1,4s and 1s respectively. If one hired a carriage for a twelve-hour period, a coach was 13s, and a sedan chair 4s,4d.[17] The innovative fund-raising methods for the Lying-In Hospital included a legal monopoly over licenses for private sedan chairs, with significant rates going toward the upkeep of the hospital and steep fines for noncompliance; the power of enforcement was transferred from the hospital to the police in 1787. The list for 1785 indicates that more than two-thirds were titled nobility who lived mostly in Henrietta and Sackville Streets, Rutland and Merrion Squares, and Saint Stephen's Green, the important urban square initiated by the corporation and featuring a statue of George II. By 1787, 239 names and addresses were registered for privately owned chairs in east Dublin.[18]

Polite Society's Cultural Life

The "dependent status of Ireland had practical and psychological repercussions for the standing of its capital," explains the Oxford historian T. C. Barnard. "London fashions could be slavishly and uncritically adopted, or angrily repudiated." Often dynamic, sometimes insecure, Dublin's cultural life is perhaps best compared to the urban cultures of Edinburgh or Calcutta rather than of London.[19] Whatever the exact mixture of originality and emulation, of self-confidence and a sense of inferiority, a plethora of polite entertainment was offered at Dublin's clubs, coffeehouses, assemblies, and balls, at its theaters, musical venues, and pleasure grounds.

The viceroyalty aimed at making a cultural as well as political impact, but (not so dissimilar from the Court of Saint James's) suffered from a shortage of funds, the cramped and inadequate fabric and spaces of the castle, and the lack of a suburban or country retreat from which to participate in the peerages' country house circuit. But the viceroy remained a crucial source of patronage, and the first couple's presence invariably ennobled an event or performance. At court levees on Tuesday there was a dance, and on Fridays, card-playing.[20]

Beyond the court, at various times over this period the city offered the Theatre Royal as well as playhouses in Crow Street, Smock Alley, and Chapel Street, with a seat in a box costing 5s; the pit, 3s; the gallery, 2s; and the upper gallery, 1s. Concerts could be heard in the cathedrals, churches, and the new Musick Hall in Fishamble Street, which sat seven hundred people and was the venue for the premier of George Frideric Handel's *Messiah* in 1742. During the 1750s and 1760s, the hall became the site of Lord Mornington's Musical Academy, and Italian opera was performed there from around 1777. The hall's eclectic program also featured conjuring exhibitions, ridottos, masquerade balls, lectures and political debates, and lotteries. In 1787, the Irish Musical Fund for the charitable support of "decayed musicians and their families" held its inaugural benefit concert as a Handel commemoration with apparently three hundred performers at Saint Werburgh's Church. The city's musical life was also supported by the musical bands maintained by the viceroy and the corporation and by the choirs of the two Protestant cathedrals, which performed a limited repertoire at a high standard.

Members of the university played a key part in the city's intellectual and cultural life. The Dublin Philosophical Society and the Dublin Society first meet in college rooms. The latter, founded in 1731, integrated sociability with utilitarian schemes. From the 1740s, premiums were awarded to promote improvements in agriculture, manufacture, and the arts. A lively culture of civic activism tackled a wider spectrum of social problems, too, from poverty to illness and the fate of the excluded sections of society. From the 1720s, hospitals were endowed through innovative fund-raising methods often involving concerts. Most famously, Handel's oratorio performances perfectly linked the moral concerns of the libretti and music with the benevolent causes of the sponsoring (and sponsored) hospital.[21] Some of these activities made available opportunities for women, both the titled and the richest commoners, to make a public and visible mark, for instance in the Magdalen Asylum to rescue prostitutes. Otherwise

The square at St. Stephen's Green featured a statue of King George II, as seen in this engraving by James Malton, 1799.

women were avid theater goers (but could not be proprietors). They were excluded from Masonic lodges and from much of coffeehouse and tavern conviviality.

Artistic culture flourished more selectively than musical culture. From mid-century, the Dublin Society financed the private drawing school of Robert West. Facilities included a figure drawing school with drawing from the antique and a collection of Old Master drawings. There were also departments for landscape and ornament (1756) and architectural drawing (1764); by the 1790s, life drawing had become a regular feature. It was at this school that James Hoban first studied and was awarded a prize in 1780. The training the school offered owed more to French than English principles, a connection that helps explain some of the distinctive features of Irish silver, furniture, and stucco.[22] Tuition was free, and once a week the school was open to nonstudents. Students competed for Rome scholarships, which financed studies in Italy. By 1800, some three thousand students had graduated from the school,

including a distinguished group of engravers and mezzotint scrapers—such as Charles Spooner and John Brooks who, alas, moved to London where they became known as the Irish school. The Dublin Society drawing school's landscapists enjoyed a good reputation, too. But although the city thus had one of the earliest training schools for artists in the British Isles, there were still very limited opportunities for public exhibition. To be sure, local artists intermittently exhibited at successive, short-lived societies from 1765 to 1780, but Dublin artists largely "depended on London for survival," either pursing a career there or habitually sending their works to the exhibitions at the Royal Academy of Arts. Artists in Dublin, right to the end of the century, felt themselves to be in a vacuum. Hugh Douglas, Irish portrait painter, wrote in Italian to his friend Antonio Canova, the celebrated sculptor, to describe his sense of isolation: with no one to discuss art, with no art critics or exhibitions, and with portraiture dominating what limited artistic life there was and a "total lack in this

The Parliament House *by James Malton c. 1793. View of the Parliament House, College Green, Dublin, Ireland, showing the West Front of Trinity College.*

country of an understanding or liking" for the higher forms of art, Douglas felt cultural despair.[23]

There were numerous assemblies and balls, both by subscription and privately organized. At the peak of private feting, in April 1785 rumors had it that the Duke and Duchess of Leinster had given out one thousand tickets for an aristocratic masquerade at Leinster House. Gatherings were also organized for Old Etonians, gentry originating from the same county, or the Sportsman's Club at the Rose Tavern, which arranged races and prizes at the Curragh. There was a trend toward more private, controlled settings and meetings: for instance, a gaming club started meeting at Patrick Daly's Tavern, Dame Street, but by the 1780s it had an almost exclusively parliamentary clientele and built a grand new clubhouse on Daly's site (1789–91).

The Great Assembly Halls in Brunswick Street by the mid-1760s held more than a dozen assemblies and ten balls in one season. By the 1780s, the Grand Ridotto Room and the Exhibition Room on William Street were among the most fashionable venues; balls included dancing, supper, tea, negus, and occasional card-playing. The pleasure gardens and the Rotunda at the Lying-In Hospital, which we briefly encountered before, were open for walks and concerts three days a week during the summer; at those times and on Sunday evenings, said Lewis's guide, "there is a numerous and brilliant assembly of the first people in Dublin."[24] The Rotunda at the Lying-In Hospital was built after the example of London's Ranelagh Garden, more than 20 meters in diameter but without any central support and only held by the outer walls. It ingenuously lengthened the season of entertainment by providing an indoor arena for the same activities that were carried out outdoors, most famously the promenade. As "one of the finest and noblest circular rooms in the British dominions," the Rotunda featured niches, some 4 by 3 meters large and decorated with their patrons' coats of arms, as semiprivate spaces somewhat removed from the main space.[25] The "curving wall of the sumptuous interior [was] artic-

Dublin Fireworks:

"Perspective View of the Illuminations and Fire-Works to be Exhibited at St. Stephen's Green at Dublin in Ireland on the Thanksgiving Day for the General Peace Concluded at Aix la Chapelle, 1748." An Engraving published in Universal Magazine, *1749.*

ulated with a classically inspired arrangement of a continuous pedestal supporting a series of pilasters surmounted by an entablature."[26] Six annual assemblies were held, with a concert in the Rotunda and tea, coffee, lemonade, and ices being served in the tearoom; the card room was lit for receptions, and a midnight supper was laid on for sixteen persons at each of the twenty-five tables.[27]

The origins of the new Assembly Rooms at the Lying-In Hospital were linked to the newly founded Illustrious Order of Saint Patrick. Created in 1782 as a new chivalric order specifically for Ireland, it was intended to appeal to both denominational traditions and to channel the potentially volatile passion for Irish history into more innocuous forms of entertainment. Second only to the Garter but more senior than the Bath, the Saint Patrick's Order displayed the Irish insignia of harps and shamrocks, albeit interspersed with the English rose and a combination of English, Scottish, and Irish crowns. Iconography and color schemes emphasized the interdependence and union of the three kingdoms, while recognizing Ireland's regional individuality and national emblemata. Prominent

Volunteers and opposition leaders in the House of Lords, including the Earl of Charlemont and the Duke of Leinster, were installed among the first knights. At the same time as the ballroom in Dublin Castle was renamed after Saint Patrick, in the city's Assembly Rooms the saint became a fashionable, profitable attraction.

Dublin's various pleasure gardens were arenas for conspicuous consumption and display, the "vortex of fashion, where parading the latest costumes accompanied evenings spent eating, drinking and promenading the gravel walks which snaked through its plantations and groves."[28] The latest fashionable music, usually played from a centrally located position, filled the spaces, both outdoors and indoors, where the aristocracy and gentry mingled with the upwardly mobile middling sorts. Competition among the rival venues at Saint Stephen's Green, the City Bason in James's Street, Ranelagh Garden, and Mosse's New Pleasure Garden produced ever novel musical entertainment and exotic amusements. Mosse at one stage built an illusionary waterfall; some proprietors offered free breakfast; most presented frequent fireworks. Finally, the pleasure gardens were also places of sexual intrigue. Dense planting near the outer walls, dead ends, and peripheral walkways all facilitated chance and not-so-chance encounters. An act of 1784 ordered the outer walls taken down and replaced with rails; the perimeter was lit by lamps. But despite this heightened level of surveillance, sufficient possibilities remained for those determined to seek them out, with alcohol and music helping to loosen social and sexual mores. Particular scope for play with social identities and sexual intrigue was also provided by masked balls or masquerades.[29]

In sum, Ireland's capital in the second half of the eighteenth century was a vibrant city, full of energy—economic, social, philanthropic, cultural, and political. Polite society was constantly on the move between the city's most fashionable cultural sites, indulged in conspicuous consumption, and linked morals and money with sociability and entertainment in exercising its civic duties and philanthropy. Music and the theater appeared to flourish more than literature and most branches of the visual arts, with painters, except some portraitists, finding it difficult to be supported by Dublin's modest quota of patrons. It was perhaps Dublin's urban and architectural development that most immediately, and certainly most visibly, reflected the city's consolidation of its political, economic, and cultural hegemony over the island of Ireland.

NOTES

1. Robert Pool and John Cash, *Views of the Most Remarkable Public Buildings, Monuments and Other Edifices in the City of Dublin* (Dublin: J. Williams, 1780), 6–7, quotation on 6; David Dickson, "Death of a Capital? Dublin and the Consequences of Union," in *Two Capitals: London and Dublin, 1500–1840*, ed. Peter Clark and Raymond Gillespie (Oxford and New York: Oxford University Press, for the British Academy, 2001), 111–31; Dickson, "The Place of Dublin in the Eighteenth-Century Irish Economy," in *Ireland and Scotland, 1600–1850: Parallels and Contrasts in Economic and Social Development*, ed. David Dickson and T. M. Devine (Edinburgh: John Donald, 1983), 177–92. This essay also owes much to T. C. Barnard, "'Grand Metropolis' or 'The Anus of the World'? The Cultural Life of Eighteenth-Century Dublin," in *Two Capitals*, ed. Clark and Gillespie, 185–210.

2. On municipal and national government and governance, see J. R. Hill, "The Shaping of Dublin Government in the Long Eighteenth Century," in *Two Capitals*, ed. Clark and Gillespie, 149–65.

3. R. Lewis, *The Dublin Guide; or, A Description of the City of Dublin* (Dublin, 1787), 45.

4. Edel Sheridan-Quantz, "The Multi-Centred Metropolis: The Social Topography of Eighteenth-Century Dublin," in *Two Capitals*, ed. Clark and Gillespie, 265–95, quotation on 287. Much of what follows is based on Sheridan-Quantz.

5. Lewis, *Dublin Guide*, 86.

6. Pool and Cash, *Views*, 29.

7. Lewis, *Dublin Guide*, 258.

8. Ibid., 116–17.

9. Pool and Cash, *Views*, 22–23.

10. Lewis, *Dublin Guide*, 44.

11. Gary A. Boyd, *Dublin, 1745–1922: Hospitals, Spectacle and Vice* (Dublin.: Four Courts Press, 2006), 107–12, quotation on 112.

12. Sheridan-Quantz, "Multi-Centred Metropolis," 286.

13. Pool and Cash, *Views*, 16.

14. Lewis, *Dublin Guide*, 175–76.

15. Quoted in Sheridan-Quantz, "Multi-Centred Metropolis," 274.

16. Lewis, *Dublin Guide*, 167–69.

17. Ibid., 79, 83.

18. [Lying-In Hospital], *A List of the Proprietors of Licenses on Private Sedan Chairs* (Dublin: Lying-In Hospital, 1787).

19. Barnard, "'Grand Metropolis,'" 187.

20. Ibid., 189–94.

21. Ibid., 194–203.

22. John Turpin, *A School of Art in Dublin Since the Eighteenth Century: A History of the National College of Art and Design* (Dublin: Gill & Macmillan, 1995), 1–17.

23. Quoted in Fintan Cullen, *Visual Politics: The Representation of Ireland, 1750–1930* (Cork: Cork University Press, 1997), 18, n. 13; See also Holger Hoock, *The King's Artists: The Royal Academy of Arts and the Politics of British Culture, 1760–1840* (Oxford: Oxford University Press, 2003), 98–99, with further references.

24. Lewis, *Dublin Guide*, 176.

25. Pool and Cash, *Views*, 65.

26. Boyd, *Dublin*, 80.

27. [Lying-In Hospital], *List of the Proprietors*.

28. Boyd, *Dublin*, 124.

28. Ibid., 126.

White House Irish Counterparts

DESMOND GUINNESS

*I*n February 1792, Pierre Charles L'Enfant, who had laid out the Federal City, now Washington, during the previous year, was relieved of his post. A French soldier, engineer, and architect, he would have gone on to design the public buildings, including the official residence of the president of the United States.

No time was lost in finding a substitute, because every major American city wanted the capital for the prestige and prosperity it would bring. An advertisement, amended and approved by George Washington, was published by the Commissioners of the Federal District in the newspapers of the principal cities, dated March 1792. The competition for the design of the President's House was to be judged on July 15 of that year.[1]

The winner was James Hoban, one of four to enter the competition who were born in Ireland. Hoban's architectural training was at the Dublin Society's architectural school where, in 1780, he was awarded a medal, now in the collections of the Smithsonian Institution, for drawings of "Brackets, Stairs, Roofs etc."[2] Thomas Ivory, Hoban's teacher, was born in County Cork and built both the monumental Bluecoat School and the Newcomen Bank in Dublin. Hoban's design for the

White House was modeled on Leinster House in Dublin, designed by the German architect Richard Castle in 1745 for the first Duke of Leinster; it now houses the Dáil (Irish Parliament).

George Washington decreed that the President's House should be one-fifth larger than Hoban's winning drawing,[3] but only two stories over basement instead of three, as in the winning competition drawing. As there was an applied portico supporting a pediment on the two upper stories, Hoban could not remove the top floor without radically altering the design; it was therefore the ground floor that was eliminated.

Leinster House had a ballroom taking up the entire depth of the house from front to back at the northern end of the building, now occupied by the Irish Senate. This room inspired Hoban to create the ballroom at the White House, which likewise occupies the whole building from front to back to the left of the Entrance Hall; it is much used for receptions, recitals, and the like.

James Wyatt, the neoclassical English architect who was more popular in Ireland even than Robert Adam, had an extensive Irish practice. He is thought to have inspired the oval room on axis to the Entrance Hall that is such an original feature of the White House. Wyatt definitely used it twice in Ireland, at Castlecoole, County Fermanagh (1797) and Mount Kennedy, County Wicklow (1784). He may also have designed Lucan House (1781), which also has an oval room on axis to the entrance hall. Wyatt is known to have designed the Sarsfield Monument in the grounds of Lucan House, a

The oval ballroom at Castlecoole, County Fermanagh.

handsome triangular column resting on the backs of three tortoises and surmounted by an urn; he could also have designed the house. However, Agmondisham Vesey, who owned the property, claimed to have been the architect, on the strength of which he was named professor of architecture in Samuel Johnson's Utopian University. This is a house Hoban could have known. Like the White House, it has an oval room on axis to the front hall.

Hoban emigrated to America in about 1784 and practiced architecture in the beautiful city of Charleston, South Carolina. He could not have seen Castlecoole, therefore, which is included here simply for the sake of completeness.

Castlecoole, County Fermanagh

James Wyatt's designs for Castlecoole are based on drawings (on display in the house) by Richard Johnston, the architect of the Gate Theatre in Dublin and the elder brother of the more famous Francis Johnston. Wyatt furnished designs for the ceilings and even for the curtains, which were closely followed. When the joiners had finished the doors and windows they turned their attention to the furniture. which is still in the rooms for which it was made. Unlike most Irish houses, a complete set of the building accounts has survived for Castlecoole.

Castlecoole is an uncommonly perfect house. The quality of the cut stonework, carved and dressed on the site, is as perfect on the back and sides as it is on the front. The Portland stone of which it is built was brought by sea to Ballyshannon, where a quay was constructed to receive it, and from there it was taken overland to Lough Erne. The massive blocks were then shipped to Enniskillen and brought the last 2 miles by bullock cart to the site. In February 1790 several stonecutters were at work, and by May there were eight masons. The month of June 1791 saw the work at its height; the wages bill was £159 13s 7½ d for a force of twenty-five stone cutters, twenty-six stone masons, ten stone sawyers, seventeen carpenters, and eighty-three laborers.[4]

Small wonder that when the Earl of Belmore, who built Castlecoole, died in 1802, only four years after the completion of his remarkably perfect and refined house, he left debts amounting to £70,000. Today it is the property of the National Trust.

Castlecoole, County Fermanagh (opposite), is an
uncommonly perfect house.

It was built from limestone quarried since Roman times
on the Isle of Portland in Dorset (below). At right a
structural survey is conducted by the Irish National
Trust at about the same time similar examinations
were made of the White House sandstone. The classical
expression and extreme restraint of Castlecoole, together
with the absence of a raised basement or rustic and
the opening of the principal apartments direct to the
ground, give the house a character more typically
French than Anglo-Irish. The same character is
shared by the north front of the White House.

PAM FOGG, ROPE ACCESS SPECIALISTS

RICHARD EDMONDS, JURASSIC COAST WORLD HERITAGE TEAM

COLLECTION OF THE AUTHOR

The staircase, built of limestone, with the thin treads pinned into the wall by morticing.

The state bedroom, Castlecoole, showing eighteenth- and nineteenth-century furnishings and hangings.

The oval ballroom, Castlecoole, with Regency period furnishings. The doors and niches recall the original architecture of the White House Blue Room.

Mount Kennedy, County Wicklow

Only 300 acres remain today of the estate of 64,000 acres that belonged to General Cunninghame, the builder of Mount Kennedy. He had purchased the original 10,000 acres from Elizabeth Barker, who inherited the property from the last male of the Kennedys, after whom it is named, in 1769. When Arthur Young, the agriculturalist, traveler, and commentator, visited the demesne in 1776, the house was not yet begun, but he admired the compost and the park where "every spot is tossed about in a variety of hill and dale."[5] The general lost no time in planting and improving his new acquisition, and the trees he put in are now at the height of their beauty. With the view of the sea on one side and the wild mountains on the other, the demesne of Mount Kennedy is one of the most picturesque in Ireland.

Cunninghame was the first Irish landlord to commission plans from James Wyatt for his house. Wyatt's designs are in the National Library of Ireland, Dublin. On one of them is written: "West elevation of a House designed for Major General Cunninghame intended to be built in Ireland –Jas. Wyatt 4 June 1772."[6] This was barely six months after the opening of the Pantheon in London, the design of which had made Wyatt's reputation overnight. The general waited more than ten years, however, before he commenced building, although he lost no time in embellishing the landscape that was to surround his new house.

Thomas Milton, who published in his *Select Views from the Seats of Ireland* an engraving of Mount Kennedy after a painting by William Ashford, states that the building dates from 1784 and was executed by Thomas Cooley from a design of Wyatt's.[7] That was the year of Cooley's death, and the building must have been begun a few years before. Cooley came to Dublin from London in 1769 on winning the competition for the Royal Exchange, now the City Hall, and settled in Ireland, where he developed a considerable practice. Francis Johnston was apprenticed to him and took over the practice when he died, which may be the reason that in the National Library there is a drawing in the hand of Richard Johnston of the elevation of Mount Kennedy.[8] Perhaps when Cooley died, Richard Johnston was commissioned to supervise the completion of the house. He was already 30 years old in 1784, whereas his younger brother Francis would have been a mere 24 at the time of Cooley's death.

The plan is very similar to that of Lucan House, even as to the disposition of the rooms. The large drawing room at Lucan was originally the dining room and occupies the same position as the dining room at Mount Kennedy. The two blind windows at Lucan have now been opened out, but at Mount Kennedy, although they are shown blocked on the Wyatt plan, they have always been open.

The house rises sheer out of the parkland in true Irish fashion, and the surface material is pebble-dash. The basement is constructed as thick-walled as a fort. An elaborate series of tunnels and storerooms, one of them an armory, reaches out from the area, either designed as a means of escape or for surprising an attacker from behind. In the 1798 rebellion General Cunninghame, who had by now been created Lord Rossmore, and Lord Kingsborough, at the head of their troops at Mount Kennedy, managed to beat off a body of insurgents. If the generals had lost, the rebels would have gained a commanding position over the road to Wexford, which runs between the mountains and the sea.

The chief beauty of Mount Kennedy is the elaborate plasterwork, by Michael Stapleton, which ornaments all the principal rooms on the ground floor. As at Lucan, grisaille roundels by Peter de Gree have been incorporated in the decor. A. Atkinson, in *The Irish Tourist*, described them rather naively as "Italian devices so exquisitely painted, as to render the sight dependent on the feeling for the discovery of their real character, for they swell upon the eye like groups of the finest figures done in Basso relievo, and until touched or accurately inspected, this error is scarcely discovered."[9]

Peter de Gree came to Ireland with an introduction to the viceroy from Sir Joshua Reynolds in 1785 and died in poverty in 1789. His work is often attributed to Angelica Kauffmann, who did spend a few months in Ireland in 1771 but whose name, like those of Adam and Grinling Gibbons, has been so widely used that it has come to refer to a certain style. De Gree was born in Antwerp, where he studied under M. J. Geeraerts. His grisailles for the dining room at Mount Kennedy have been supplemented there by others imported from a house nearby called Woodstock, which were originally painted for Number 52, Saint Stephen's Green, the La Touche town house. Other grisailles by him, at Lucan House, are illustrated here.

At one end of the dining room lofty Corinthian pilasters flank a rectangular recess. Two houses in County Limerick, Shannongrove and Carnelly, have a similar feature, and it has been suggested that these were used to accommodate a tabernacle for religious services of a private or family nature. It is more probable that they in fact contained a sideboard rather than an altar. The decoration in the hall incorporates General Cunninghames's arms and those of his wife, who was a Murray, above the pillars facing the main door. He died without issue in 1801, and the property was inherited by Jean Gordon, the daughter of one of his sisters. She married George Gun of Kilmorn, County Kerry, and their son added the name of Cunninghame to his own.

Mount Kennedy remained in the possession of the Gun-Cunninghames until 1930, and in 1938 it was acquired by Ernest Hull. Today it is owned by Mr. and Mrs. Cecil Quinn.

Above: The dining room at Mount Kennedy.

Left: A detail of the stucco work on the dining room ceiling.

Opposite: The front hall with its column screen and fine stucco work in the style associated with the Adam Brothers, but in this case built to designs of James Wyatt of London.

Lucan House, County Dublin

Charlotte Sarsfield, the cousin of the second Earl of Lucan, was a considerable heiress. She married Agmondisham Vesey and it was their son, also Agmondisham, who built the present house.

There may have been a house there already as well as the old castle, for in 1700 there is a claim on the "castle and great white house at Lucan" and, in 1775, Lady Louisa Conolly writes, "The house . . . is almost pulled down, and I hear won't be habitable these two years." Mrs. Vesey laments leaving "the dear old Castle with its niches and a thousand other Gothic beauties," and there are two references to the house being rebuilt after a fire.[10] Milton, in his *Select Views from the Seats of Ireland*, describes Lucan as being finished for the past two years.[11] It seems probable therefore that both the castle and the "great white house" were habitable and that the house was pulled or burned down and rebuilt as we see it today.

In keeping with many eighteenth-century amateur architects, Vesey was not above consulting professionals. He wrote to Sir William Chambers on January 3, 1773: "I have got the Landskip of Lucan and its environs and wish to shew you the Situation and aspects of a place which I am persuaded will receive great Embellishments from your hands." To this Chambers replied, "I have been out of town else your Elevation should have been done and Plans altered sooner." In a later communication, sent with his bill, Chambers mentioned that "the windows do not come perfectly regular on one side but I have contrived it so that the difference will scarcely be perceptible."[12] John Harris takes this "side" to refer to the River Liffey front, where the windows are out of balance.[13] This imbalance was probably due to the difficulty of fitting the new house into what remained of the old.

A plan of the ground floor of Lucan corresponding exactly with the existing house is in the National Library of Ireland, but it is unfortunately not signed.[14] The same collection of architectural drawings includes designs by Michael Stapleton for plasterwork on ceiling and wall at Lucan, and the ground plan can presumably be attributed to him also. As we have seen, it resembles closely the plan of Mount Kennedy, County Wicklow, and the elevation is not unlike that of Charleville, County Wicklow.

The interior is one of the finest in the Adam style to remain intact and was restored in 1960 by Baron and Baroness Winspeare Guicciardi; the architect was Brendan Ellis, and much of the delicate painting work was done by Matthew Dale. They uncovered the yellow marble painting on the columns in the entrance hall and

Lucan House (opposite), built in the 1770s, features the portico and arcade character of Irish Georgian architecture and present in the original designs of the White House. The Entrance Hall is pictured above.

improved the drawing room by opening out two windows that were formerly dummies, achieving a magnificent view up the river. James Gorry restored the painted roundels by de Gree in the Wedgwood room, which had the background painted out, depriving the figures of the sculptural quality intended by the artist. A similarly shaped room, with the corners of the ceiling pulled down to give a domed, tentlike effect, was provided by Stapleton for Powerscourt House, South William Street, Dublin. Another of the Vesey houses, Abbey Leix,

County Leix, was decorated by both Stapleton and de Gree; patronage of the same artists often went in families.

The elegant staircase leads to an upper landing, at one end of which there is an iron stove shaped like an urn, now painted white. Off this landing is a circular sitting-room, ingeniously fitted above the oval dining room, where Mrs. Vesey feared she would be "like a parrot in a cage."[15] Baroness Winspeare was even able to find some curtains for the room with parrots on them. Lucan House now serves as the Italian Embassy.

Delicate stucco or composition decorations on the plaster walls of Lucan House capture the spirit of Pompeii, the ancient Roman city being excavated at the time the house was rebuilt. The grisaille room is pictured above, the dining room opposite.

Staircase window, Lucan House.

The White House

During the presidency of Theodore Roosevelt at the start of the twentieth century, the well-known firm of New York architects, McKim, Mead & White, was chosen to restore and renovate the White House in Washington, D.C. "The first aim, therefore, was to discover the design and intention of the original builders, and to adhere strictly thereto in so far as the public or State portions of the house were concerned."[16] Fine words indeed, but that is all they were. A State Dining Room was created, as might have been found in a mid-seventeenth-century English house, with dark paneling, giant pilasters, and silver sconces. The principal staircase was sacrificed to create a good-sized room, but what was a 1680 English interior doing in a 1790s American house? The same firm, incidentally, wreaked havoc on Jefferson's amazing main or rotunda building at the University of Virginia.

The front hall of the White House had two columns to support the upstairs landing. They are shown clearly on the winning drawing that Hoban submitted, which shows the ground plan and the three-story elevation in section. The New York architects decided on two pairs of columns, although steel girders could easily by then have supported the weight of the upstairs landing.

When during the presidency of Harry Truman the whole interior of the White House was gutted, the correct arrangement of columns could have been restored. In Ireland all of the buildings of the same general period that might have inspired the architect, James Hoban, have a hall with two columns, not four. Castletown, County Kildare, Leinster House, Lucan House, Abbey Leix, Mount Kennedy, Castlecoole, and so on, all have halls with a pair of columns.

It was said by one White House curator, Clement E. Conger, that Truman did more damage to the building than had the British; many a true word is spoken in jest.

The fact that the public buildings in Washington were set fire to in direct retaliation to the torching by an American expedition of the public buildings in York (now Toronto), Ontario seems to have been forgotten, but can of course be found in the *Encyclopaedia Britannica*.

NOTES

1. This advertisement is reproduced in full in William Ryan and Desmond Guinness, *The White House: An Architectural History* (New York: McGraw Hill, 1980), 32.

2. Ibid., 70. Both sides of the medal are reproduced. One has the Dublin Society's emblem, Hibernia, with her spear and her harp, and the other bears the inscription "Presented by the Dublin Society to James Hoban for Drawings of Brackets, Stairs, Roofs, &c. Novr 23rd, 1780."

3. Ibid., 59.

4. A large collection of papers relating to the building, decoration, and furnishing of Castlecoole is preserved in the house.

5. Arthur Young, *A Tour in Ireland, With General Observations on the Present State of That Kingdom* (London, 1780).

6. Architectural Drawings Collection, National Library of Ireland, Dublin.

7. Thomas Milton, *A Collection of Select Views, From the Different Seats of the Nobility and Gentry in Ireland* (London, 1783–93).

8. Department of Prints and Drawings, National Library of Ireland.

9. A. Atkinson, *The Irish Tourist, In a Series of Picturesque Views, Travelling Incidents, and Observations, Statistical, Political and Moral, on the Character and Aspect of the Irish Nation* (Dublin, 1815).

10. John D'Alton, *The History of the County of Dublin* (Dublin, 1838). Lady Louisa Lennox married Tom "Squire" Conolly when just 15 years of age, in 1758, and became mistress of Castletown, County Kildare, the greatest house in Ireland. Mrs. Vesey was a celebrated blue-stocking, nicknamed "the Sylph." She was as much at home in London as in Dublin and a favorite of both Dr. Johnson and Horace Walpole.

11. Milton, *Select Views from the Seats of Ireland*.

12. Quoted in Desmond Guinness and William Ryan, *Irish Houses and Castles* (New York: Crescent Press, 1971), 132.

13. John Harris was for many years librarian in charge of the architectural drawings collection at the Royal Institute of British Architects, London. He also worked for Paul Mellon.

14. Plan of Lucan, unsigned, in the Architectural Drawings Collection, National Library of Ireland.

15. Quoted in Guinness and Ryan, *Irish Houses and Castles*, 134.

16. Quoted in Ryan and Guinness, *White House*, 153.

Imagining James Hoban:
Portraits of a Master Builder

WILLIAM B. BUSHONG

$\mathcal{J}$ames Hoban has been honored through the years as the Irish-born architect who built the White House. Most histories and architectural histories pass him by with a scant mention, however, his fame lies in his major achievement, a house today known around the world. Finding out about the man personally is a task, but clues do turn up from an extensive search. Seeking what he looked like is even more difficult, but in both instances, we know a few things.

In his lifetime Hoban was a leading citizen of Washington, a well-known builder who got his start with the public buildings until 1802, when President Thomas Jefferson replaced him as the government's principal architect with Benjamin Henry Latrobe. Hoban had moved to Washington toward the close of 1792 to build the White House. In his wake, in Charleston, South Carolina, the newspaper extolled him for being selected for the work:

> On this occasion we think it but justice to observe, that Mr. Hoban, as a man of abilities, is unassuming and diffident. When a mere boy, he received a

The only known life portrait of James Hoban is a small wax bas-relief in the White House collection attributed to the German-born artist John Christian Rauschner, c. 1800.

mark of distinction from the royal society of Dublin, which none else could then achieve. . . . When the President of the United States honored this city with a visit last year, Mr. Hoban was introduced to him as a man of merit and genius under the patronage of general Moultrie, Mr. Butler &c. And we may safely add that it is no small matter of universal satisfaction to the citizens of Carolina, that their fellow citizen, Hoban has succeeded in the enterprize.[1]

Hoban had not been in Washington for a year when he was instrumental in organizing Federal Lodge Number One of Freemasons, September 6, 1793, one week after President Washington laid the cornerstone for the Capitol, a ceremony in which the Masons participated. He was married, for the second time, his new wife being Susana Sewell of a prominent Maryland family. He was in Washington to stay. The Hobans probably built and lived in several houses before finally settling into a fine two-story brick house on the north side of F Street, between 14th and 16th, not far from the White House. It was a house not unlike some still seen today along Kilkenny streets that Hoban knew well.[2]

At the center of Hoban's neighborhood stood Rhodes Tavern, the first commercial building erected in downtown Washington. It was the hub of city life in the days before other buildings were built to absorb urban needs. The two-story brick tavern, which stood fairly much intact until its demolition toward the close of the twentieth century, served as an unofficial city hall where the local courts and a variety of organizations regularly assembled for business. Indeed the commission that supervised the building of the White House and Capitol met there regularly, so Hoban knew Rhodes Tavern from the first. His name frequently appears in early newspaper notices of meetings he attended or even chaired related to the militia, civic and political activities, urban improvements and services, and educational and charitable organizations.[3]

Hoban's public involvements included, in addition to the Masonic lodge, the founding of Saint Patrick's Roman Catholic Church, 1794, and convincing Father Anthony Caffry to come to America from Ireland to lead it. Hoban formed the city's first militia company, 1796, which had a profound influence upon the maintenance of law and order in the young community. Intimate to the efforts of Washington citizens to make Congress notice their local needs, and when limited municipal government was organized, Hoban was elected to the city council, on which he served for twenty years. He was also involved in establishing an early neighborhood civic association, the F Street Inhabitants and Proprietors Association, foreshadowing urban life to come. The group promoted civic improvements and even assessed themselves to pay for sidewalks and curbs, gutters and gravel for the streets. The result was a very desirable neighborhood, with big houses like his, alongside rows of lesser wooden houses, painted fences, and gardens.[4]

Hoban was active in what we would call the real estate business all his life. Rental property, land, and construction were all within the scope of his enterprises. In 1805 he advertised his own house for rent:

To be rented

For one or more years, as may be agreed upon, the house at present by the subscriber fronting F Street north near the President's square, it contains four rooms, with fire places, 2 garret rooms and a kitchen—on a lot immediately in the rear is a stable, carriage house, coalhouse and garden. Also the house adjoining the above and on the same lot, containing 4 rooms with fireplaces, kitchen and servant's room, with a good dry cellar.

The whole of the above property would accommodate a large genteel family or they will be rented separately. Possession may be had after the last day of May next. The situation is healthy and pleasant.—James Hoban.[5]

Proud of his Irish heritage, Hoban was significant in giving a voice in local politics to the great number of Irish immigrants in Washington who worked both as skilled and unskilled laborers, draymen, tavern keepers, blacksmiths, grocers, and boarding house proprietors. He founded the Society of the Sons of Erin in 1802, largely to help Irish-born workers who needed housing, food, and medical services, but also to promote naturalization. Meetings of the Sons of Erin were held at Rhodes Tavern, and the society organized parades and musical entertainments and promoted the wearing of shamrocks each year on Saint Patrick's Day.[6]

Hoban seems always to have kept a building crew available, if not in operation. In this he was served in part by slaves. He had owned slaves in Charleston, skilled carpenters. The 1800 census records four slaves and by 1820 Hoban owned three male slaves under the age of 14, two between 14 and 26, and one between 26 and 40. By 1830, shortly before his death and while he was building the North Portico to the White House, he owned only two slaves. They may have been house servants, and one African American in his household was free. Hoban himself was opposed to slavery, at least in the District of Columbia, for he signed a petition to that effect in 1828.[7]

Hoban's wife, Susana Sewell Hoban, bore him ten children, losing one in infancy and herself dying young. Their two teenage daughters Helen and Catherine died within a year of their mother in 1822 and 1823.[8] The Italian sculptor Giuseppe Valaperti, who executed the marble eagle on the frieze of Statuary Hall at the Capitol, pronounced Helen Hoban "the most beautiful female he had ever seen" and implored her to pose for him for one of the Capitol statues. She modestly declined.[9] Other children lived longer lives, two sons Edward and Francis becoming officers in the U.S. Navy. Henry became a Jesuit priest and doubtless the pride of his father. The best known was James Hoban Jr., a powerful orator and respected Washington lawyer, who climaxed his career as district attorney for the District of Columbia.[10]

What James Hoban looked like is entirely transmitted in a wax image that came down in his family. He

At the center of Hoban's F Street neighborhood was Rhodes Tavern, the oldest commercial building in downtown Washington, which served as an unofficial city hall. Most of the meetings Hoban attended relating to militia, political, civic, and charitable organizations regularly assembled for business here. Drawing by the Baroness Hyde de Neuville, 1820.

James Hoban's residence was located just to the east of Rhodes Tavern on the north side of F Street between 14th and 15th Streets. This watercolor, painted from the rear of the house on a wintry day in 1874, captured its appearance a few years before it was razed in 1880.

The Royal Dublin Society Medal presented to James Hoban in 1780 for "Drawings of Brackets, Stairs, Roofs, &c" is now in the collection of the Smithsonian Institution.

probably sat for the profile portrait. Curators attribute the miniature bas-relief to German-born John Christian Rauschner. It is in color, showing a youthful profile, thick brown hair, and a rosy complexion. The broad shoulders and chest suggest a hardy physique not alien to work with his hands, just as one might expect. Hoban just missed the age of the photograph, and thus we are without the accuracy of the camera.

Hoban died in 1831, having completed the North Portico and thus the White House. He left a large estate of more than $60,000 in value, with property both in the city and farms outside in Maryland. His children shared most of the estate. The slaves were to be sold. James Hoban, the son, and Thomas Carbery, probably a nephew of Susana's, but at the time mayor of Washington, were the executors. A special bequest was made to his brother-in-law "Mr. Stone and his two daughters Nancy and Martha," 3 acres upon which they

resided and $400 with which to build a new house.[11] Hoban was buried beside Susana in the old graveyard at Saint Patrick's Church. The graves were moved in 1863 to the new Mount Olivet Cemetery on Bladensburg Road, in Washington, where they remain.[12]

James Hoban's obituary noted that he had been architect of the White House and a superintendent of construction at the Capitol, and that he was an Irish émigré who had settled in Charleston at the close of the American Revolution about fifty years before. The notice continued: "Captain Hoban possessed, in a very high-degree the esteem and confidence of his fellow citizens. He was hospitable, generous, and charitable. In his regard for the just claims and feelings of others, he was scrupulously nice and particular. Such men are the blessings to society whilst they live, and, even after death instruct by example."[13]

According to family lore, James Hoban Jr., pictured at right, was the "spitting image" of his father. An orator and attorney, author, and 1840 mayoral candidate, he died suddenly during a yellow fever outbreak in 1846. Lithograph after a daguerreotype taken by William J. Corcoran in 1844.

The marriage of James Hoban to Susana Sewall, January 13, 1799, is recorded in the marriage registry of Holy Trinity Church, in Georgetown, Washington, D.C.

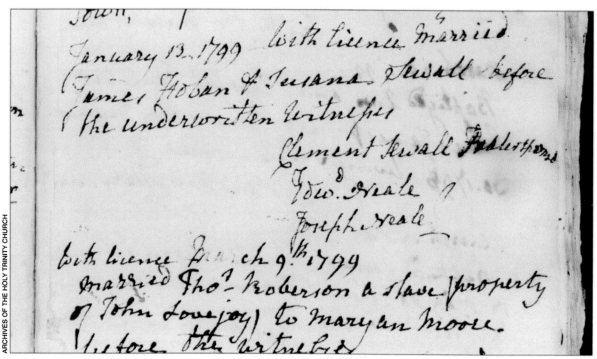

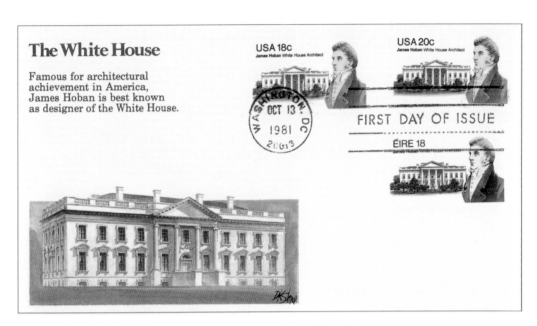

The White House

Famous for architectural achievement in America, James Hoban is best known as designer of the White House.

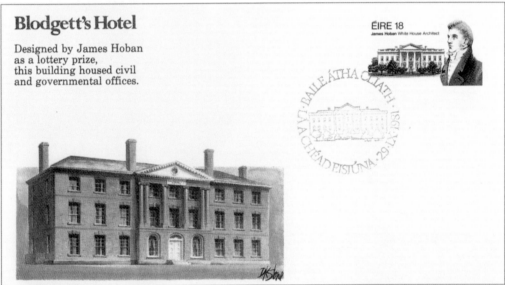

Blodgett's Hotel

Designed by James Hoban as a lottery prize, this building housed civil and governmental offices.

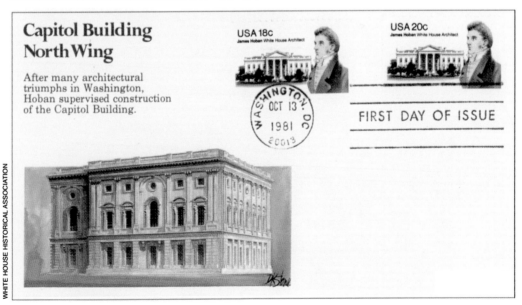

Capitol Building North Wing

After many architectural triumphs in Washington, Hoban supervised construction of the Capitol Building.

In 1981, the United States and Ireland both issued commemorative stamps to mark the 150th anniversary of Hoban's death. A collection of first day covers (opposite) feature several of Hoban's designs, including the White House (note both the Irish and U.S. stamps), Blodgett's Hotel, and the U.S. Capitol. The commemorative poster from 1981 (above) features an idealized portrait of a young James Hoban, grouped with a sketch of his meeting with President Washington during the construction of the White House and copies of his only extant White House drawings, a 1792 floor plan and a 1793 north elevation.

Died, in this city, on the 8th instant, Capt. JAMES HOBAN, aged about seventy.three years. Capt. Hoban was by profession an Architect, and emigrated to this country, from Ireland, at the close of the American Revolution. He first settled in Charleston, South Carolina, from whence he was invited to the City of Washington to superintend the erection of the Public Buildings. He designed, and obtained the premium for, the President's House, and both built and re-built it. He also superintended the architecture of the Capitol for a considerable time.

In private life, Capt. Hoban possessed, in a very high degree, the esteem and confidence of his fellow citizens. He was hospitable, generous, and charitable. In his regard for the just claims and feelings of others, he was scrupulously nice and particular. Such men are blessings to society whilst they live, and, even after death, instruct by example.

☞His funeral will take place at 10 o'clock This Morning to which his friends are respectfully invited.
Dec. 9.   A FRIEND.

WHITE HOUSE HISTORICAL ASSOCIATION

James Hoban's obituary ran in the Washington National Intelligencer *on December 9, 1831. He was reinterred in 1863 in Mount Olivet Cemetery in Washington, D.C., with his wife Susana. This monument marks their gravesite.*

WHITE HOUSE HISTORICAL ASSOCIATION

Hoban's prominence as architect of the White House grew in the twentieth century with the interest that accompanied the various renovations that took place. When researchers started trying to find about him, one of the greatest obstacles—one that still remains—is the misfortune that his business and personal papers were lost in a fire in the 1880s. The only written material that can be found is scattered through federal papers and related to public buildings. Newspapers also provide occasional notices, as he did lead, locally at least, a life of public involvement.

Engineer Frederick Owen studied Hoban's White House design in 1889 when First Lady Caroline Harrison proposed drastic additions to the house. Owen praised Hoban for seeing the house built in spite of "scarcity of labor and other obstacles almost insurmountable."[14] During the renovations and reconstruction

carried out by President Harry S. Truman from 1948 to 1952, Hoban's name again appeared. Truman's architect sought information on the man, but the furthest Lorenzo Winslow seems to have gotten was to sense his presence as the house was gutted.[15]

Hoban the builder had already become part of American history. Before the wax image was discovered among Hoban family heirlooms in 1959, the famous illustrator N. C. Wyeth had created a poster for the Pennsylvania Railroad to coincide with the George Washington Bicentennial Celebration sponsored by the Congress in 1932. Basing the subject of the painting on the personal interest President Washington took in the building of the White House, he devised an imaginary scene of Washington touring the construction site with Hoban.[16] A subsequent honor came during World War II when the *James Hoban*, a 10,500 ton ship, was launched.[17] In 1981, the United States and Ireland jointly issued a commemorative stamp.[18] In 2005 Charles De Antonio, a Charleston artist, painted an interesting portrait of Hoban for the Charleston County Courthouse, using the wax image and imaging software.

Yet with all the words, fragments of fact, and images that profile James Hoban, we still know relatively little about him. His thoughts and ideas, beyond what we can surmise from business letters and his activities, remain pieces of a puzzle largely incomplete. The most significant concept representing him and his ability is the White House.

NOTES

I would like to thank Sally Sims Stokes, Hillary Crehan, Amy Quesenbery, Gloria Beiter, and Martha Rowe for their research contributions to this article.

1. From a Correspondent, *The Mail; or, Claypoole's Daily Advertiser*, August 8, 1792, 3, digital version available by subscription online at www.newsbank.com, © Newsbank and/or the American Antiquarian Society, 2004.

2. Martin I. J. Griffin, "James Hoban: The Architect and Builder of the White House," *American Catholic Historical Researches* 3, no. 1 (1907): 35–52. Griffin interviewed James Hoban, the grandson of the White House architect, who was the source of biographical facts and the story of the destruction of Hoban's personal and professional papers by fire in the 1880s. See also William Seale, *The President's House* (Washington, D.C.: White House Historical Association, with the cooperation of the National Geographic Society, 1986), 1:40.

3. Nelson F. Rimensnyder, *James Hoban: Overlooked Civic Life of a Distinguished Washingtonian, 1792–1830*, 1992, Pamphlet Collection, Historical Society of Washington, D.C.; William W. Warner, *At Peace with All Their Neighbors: Catholics and Catholicism in the National Capitol, 1787–1860* (Washington, D.C.: Georgetown University Press, 1994), 149–51, 153, 161–62.

4. Warner, *At Peace with All Their Neighbors*, 153, 161–162. See also Morris J. McGregor, *A Parish for the Federal City: St. Patrick's in Washington, 1794–1994* (Washington, D.C.: Catholic University Press, 1994), 42–44.

5. *Washington Federalist*, March 16, 1805, 3–4.

6. McGregor, *Parish for the Federal City*, 42–44.

7. For information on Hoban's slaves, see Hoban's notice concerning a runaway slave carpenter named Peter, *City Gazette and Daily Advertiser*, January 17, 1789, 3–4, transcription in the research files of the Museum of Early Southern Decorative Arts, Winston-Salem, N.C. Hoban received the wages as owner for slave carpenters working on the White House. See Robert J. Kapsch, "The Labor History of the Construction and Reconstruction of the White House, 1793–1817" (PhD diss., University of Maryland, 1993), 392–93. See also U.S. Census, 1800, 1820 and 1830, Washington, D.C., Population Schedule, National Archives, Washington, D.C., also available online at www.ancestry.com. Finally, for the petition for the abolition of slavery in the District of Columbia, see *Norwich Courier*, April 9, 1828, 7:2, digital version available by subscription online at www.newsbank.com © Newsbank and/or the American Antiquarian Society, 2004.

8. Griffin, "James Hoban," 39–40. Death notices for Susana, Helen, and Catherine Hoban can be found in the *Washington National Intelligencer*, September 4, 1822, July 30, 1823, and December 22, 1823.

9. "Beauty and Modesty," *Providence Patriot*, December 31, 1823, digital version available by subscription online at www.newsbank.com © Newsbank and/or the American Antiquarian Society, 2004.

10. Griffin, "James Hoban," 39–40. See also John E. Norris, *Eulogy on the Life and Character of James Hoban, Esq.* (Washington, D.C.: W. Blanchard Printer, 1846), 5–16.

11. Wesley E. Pippenger, comp., *District of Columbia Probate Records, Will Books 1 through 6, 1801–1852 and Estate Files, 1801–852* (Arlington, Va., and Westminster, MD: Family Line Publications, 1996), 169.

12. Griffin, "James Hoban," 47.

13. *Washington National Intelligencer*, December 9, 1831, also quoted in Griffin, "James Hoban," 51.

14. Frederick Owen, "The First Government Architect: James Hoban of Charleston, S.C.," *Architectural Record* 11 (October 1901): 587. Study of Hoban's contributions to the public architecture of Washington had been well established by influential studies by George Alfred Townsend, *Washington Outside and Inside: A Picture and a Narrative of the Origin, Growth, Excellences, Abuses, Beauties, and Personages of Our Governing City* (Hartford, Conn., and Chicago, J. Betts and Company, 1873), 64; Glenn Brown, *History of the United States Capitol* (Washington, D.C.: Government Printing Office, 1900), 1:94–95.

15. Winslow held séances and claimed to have spoken to the dead, including former presidents. See Seale, *The President's House*, 2:1031.

16. "Artist Draws Washington at White House," *Washington Post*, May 22, 1932, M5, digital version available by subscription online at www.proquest.com, © ProQuest Historical Newspapers.

17. "Liberty Ship Named for Builder of White House," *Washington Post*, October 21, 1942, 13, digital version available by subscription online at www.proquest.com, © ProQuest Historical Newspapers.

18. "Stamps and Coins," *Washington Post*, October 25, 1981, G6, digital version available by subscription online at www.proquest.com, © ProQuest Historical Newspapers.

George Washington's Bow Window

A Lost Fragment of White House Precedence Comes to Light in Philadelphia

EDWARD LAWLER JR.

*W*hen in June 1792 architect James Hoban met with President George Washington at the red brick President's House at Sixth and Market Streets in Philadelphia, fresh in his mind was a design for the White House. A national competition for the new Executive Mansion was in progress. Hoban was the only competitor privileged to meet with the president on the subject, by virtue of influential friends in Charleston, South Carolina, where he lived. The architect was to win the competition in the next month, and what he saw in the Philadelphia house, and perhaps the conversation it inspired, may have had a major influence on his submission. Two years earlier Washington had added a large, semicircular bow or bay with three windows to the south end of the rented mansion's dining room. The bow played a key role in Washington's effort to define the presidency, as Hoban may have witnessed firsthand.

The office of president, in which the head of state and head of government were united, was brand new for its time. Washington sought to project its legitimacy, sta-

bility, and permanence in the eyes of foreign powers and American citizens as well. A useful tool for accomplishing this goal, he found, was ceremony.

But how much formality was appropriate for the elected leader of a republic? How accessible should the president be to the people? When a steady stream of well-wishers (and job seekers) knocked on the front door and interfered with his work, who then was served? Washington's response was the weekly levee or public reception. On Tuesday afternoons at three o'clock, male visitors who had applied in advance were welcomed to the house and presented to the president. In New York, the nation's first capital, Washington had stood before a fireplace. But with the transfer of the capital to Philadelphia in 1790, the opportunity arose to create a more dramatic setting. Washington loved both architecture and theater and understood the use of both in the wielding of power. By building the bow he gave himself a stage, backlit by the three windows, for receiving his callers, a formal ceremonial space in which the public would meet the president. By all accounts, it was a most impressive experience for those who attended.

Standing in his bow Washington received the Senate and the House of Representatives in the reciprocal visits that began each session of Congress. It was here that he faced down Citizen Edmond Genêt, the French minister who tried to rally the American people to oppose the president's neutrality policy. Almost without a doubt the silver peace medallion Washington

---

In March 2007, an archaeological excavation was begun at the site of the President's House, one block north of Independence Hall in Philadelphia. The house was occupied by George Washington and John Adams during their presidencies while the White House was under construction in Washington.

Below: A watercolor of the President's House in Philadelphia (c. 1795–96), by William L. Breton.

Right: The southeast corner of Sixth and Market Streets, Philadelphia, in 1949, with the outline of President's House drawn in red. The east wall of the President's House, one story of its west wall, and most of its foundations survived until the 1951 demolition of the block.

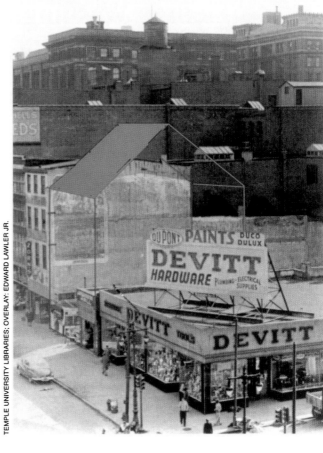

placed around the neck of the Seneca chief Red Jacket was presented in the bow. On the Fourth of July a thousand people came to call and shake the hand of the president, who stood in the bow.

In 1800 the government moved to the new capital Federal City of Washington. The Philadelphia President's House became a hotel, was gutted in 1832, and in the early 1950s its few remaining walls were demolished to make way for Independence Mall, the new setting for a preserved Independence Hall. Recent controversies surrounding the redesign of Independence Mall inspired the first archaeological investigation of the site of President Washington's residence, to determine whether anything might have escaped the bulldozers half a century ago. On May 7, 2007, archaeologists working one block north of Independence Hall unearthed the partial foundations of Washington's bow window.

Did Hoban, in seeking to please the president and win the competition, take Washington's Philadelphia bow window as the inspiration for the bow that is now the Blue Room? Ovals became a motif at the White House, climaxing more than a century after Washington and Hoban in the addition of the Oval Office in 1909. Today when we see a photograph of the president's desk positioned before the three windows of the Oval Office, we can be reminded of Washington and his callers, his rivals, his silver medals and Indian chiefs, and the whole span of the American presidency symbolized in that crumbling stone remnant of the bow window, now uncovered in Philadelphia.

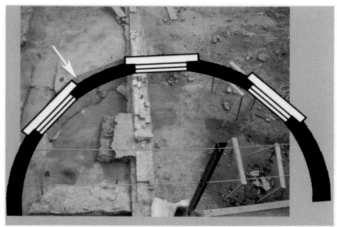

The recent archaeological dig at the site of the President's House has revealed that about a third of the foundation of the bow window survives. The photo above shows foundations of the section of the original south wall from the 1760s. Washington added the bow window in 1790.

A plan for the reconstruction of the State Dining Room in the temporary President's House in Philadelphia (right). Because of the 2007 archaeology we know that Washington's bow window was the full width of the State Dining Room instead of a smaller bow; rather like a bay-window, as has always been suspected.

STATE DINING ROOM

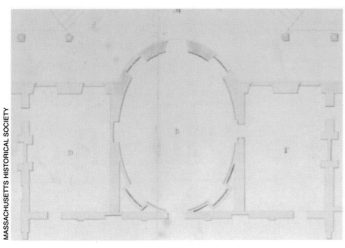

The similarly shaped oval Blue Room of the White House is seen in this detail of James Hoban's plan of the State Floor (left).

Four Places in Hoban's Dublin

A Twenty-First Century Photographer's View

PHOTOGRAPHS BY BRUCE WHITE

*T*he city where James Hoban lived when he first appeared in the written record still boasts many of the buildings he knew. It was his good luck to know some of the finest buildings of his time in Ireland: Desart Court in his Kilkenny boyhood, and major buildings in the Irish capital. Each of them could have stood on their own as excellent architecture anywhere, and all, like the White House, are in the neoclassical design vein.

The vigor and character of eighteenth-century Dublin survive in these structures. They are built of the finest materials known at the time, limestone, marble, wrought iron, slate, lead; crown glass, many kinds of wood, plaster troweled and cast. The permanency of their construction preserves the hopes of their builders for a prosperous future, inspired during a short-lived relaxation of tensions between Ireland and Great Britain.

The streets Hoban walked as a pupil of the Dublin Society are not altered entirely by later construction, although they, of course, have been shaped as well by two subsequent centuries of building and pulling down. Photographer Bruce White, covering parts of Ireland in the summer of 2007, stopped by some buildings that particularly interest us at *White House History,* three involved in the Hoban story and a fourth, which Hoban may not have known at all, very reflective of Irish support of the American Revolution.

He set his camera as best he could to avoid the rush of the modern, booming city and concentrate upon the buildings. Prosperity in Ireland today approximates that in the Dublin of the 1770s and 1780s. America's battle for independence had nearly universal support among the Irish, who saw in American victory possibilities that Ireland could escape the British thumb. Newcomen's Bank and the Royal Exchange, both worked on by Hoban in some capacity, are surrounded by traffic from early morning until late night. Leinster House, now the seat of the Irish Dáil and very much in the busy city, is banked in high-level security outside and as lively inside as any other capitol. Belcamp, the country house, quiet and alone in a tangle of modern highways and commerce, is in the hands of a sympathetic developer who has pledged its preservation and a bright future.

Looking up Parliament Street from the River Liffey to the Royal Exchange, which James Hoban knew during its construction in the 1770s.

All photographs in this article (pages 62–87) are by Bruce White for the White House Historical Association, 2007, unless otherwise noted.

NEWCOMEN BANK

James Hoban said he worked on this neoclassical structure built by Thomas Ivory, beginning in 1781. The remarkable building, tailored to a difficult lot on the steep street leading to Dublin Castle, is seen here twice its original width, the eighteenth-century half to the left in the inset view. Sir William Newcomen, who commissioned the bank, had begun life as William Gleadowe and married into the prominent Newcomen family of County Longford whose name he adopted. He was in his 80s when he engaged Ivory, having been very visible in public life, and, having pleased the British Crown along the way, first was knighted, then rose to the peerage. The bank was to be both city apartment and office, an idea stylish in cities in Europe at the time, the business rooms below and elegant residence above, all richly carried out, as befit one of Sir William's rank.

Newcomen's son, Thomas Viscount Newcomen, managed the bank well until the 1820s. Its failure obliterated his family's fortune and drove him to suicide. The title died with him. Newcomen's Bank was sold for other purposes. In 1862 the Hiberian Bank engaged the architect William Caldbeck to double the size of the building. The added section was to face the newly created Lord Edward Street and exactly mirror the old, the two parts united by a columned porch. Newcomen's Bank, today a government tax office, is one of Dublin's finest examples of late eighteenth-century neoclassicism as well as one of the earliest, perhaps, of mid nineteenth-century revivalism of that style, expressed in the addition. It is considered Ivory's finest work.

Dublin's wealth and late eighteenth-century building boom not only helped generate a strong local construction community but attracted skilled workmen from Europe, including stonemasons and stone carvers, not to mention, workers in the ornamental stucco that was very popular with the Irish.

The Portland stone walls of Newcomen's Bank are splendidly executed, rusticated externally on the public or ground level, smooth-faced above on the residential floors. Ornamental plaques, after the neo-classical fashion of Paris and London at the time, were executed by Simon Vierpyl and Vincent Waldré. The rustication suggests Hoban's treatment of the basement on the Ground Floor of the White House.

In the 1862 addition, the style was copied more successfully than the construction technique. Details pictured here include left and opposite below left examples of the 1862 replication. Opposite above left and below right, eighteenth-century walls show Ivory's elegant balance between smooth and ornamental wall treatments.

The interior of Newcomen Bank consisted of three oval rooms on the main or ground floor, so devised by Thomas Ivory to create rational spaces within the odd, trapezoid shape the building had taken to accommodate the triangular lot. One was a drawing room, where Sir William received and sometimes dined with upper-class clients, while the other two were working areas of the bank. Seeming to address more the residential quarters than the bank itself, the monumental grand stairs of stone dominating the elegant central hall sweep to the floors above, their thin limestone treads morticed into the stone walls, the fine wrought-iron railing tracing the curves two stories up to a domed skylight flamboyantly decorated with classical designs in stucco.

LEINSTER HOUSE

East Front of Leinster House, 2007

When begun in 1745, Kildare House, as it was first known, was built for the earl of Kildare in the country outside Dublin. Warned that he was building out of the way, the earl declared that society would follow him, and it did, over the years, bringing a whole townscape of fine buildings to diminish the original effect of this as a country house. Leinster House is by no means the greatest Irish country house, its architecture a little stiff, its principal facade a bit squat. Designed by Richard Cassels (Castle), a German, it was brought to completion about 1750 and altered variously through the more than half century the family remained there. The earl became the Duke of Leinster in 1766, Leinster by name for the province in which Dublin stands. It was the first duke's son William, second Duke of Leinster, a kind and popular man, who occupied Leinster House when Hoban was in school in Dublin. In 1818, the family sold Leinster House to the Royal Dublin Society for a headquarters and relocated permanently to Carton, their beloved country house.

West or Principal Front of Leinster House, 1780

Leinster House, or rather, Hoban's descriptions of the house, undoubtedly convinced George Washington that it was a worthy model for the President's House then ordered built for the new United States. Hoban probably knew the house rather well, and Washington had unquestionably heard of the duke. While Hoban was a student, the ground floor dining room was being remodeled by the prolific English architect James Wyatt, surely an event of the greatest interest to Hoban's teacher Ivory, perhaps even to the point of his taking his students there to observe the work. However that may have been, it was commonly said in the early days of the White House that Leinster House was the model. Hoban seems to have made the connection well known.

Like the exterior, the plan of the two houses is similar enough to further suggest a strong relationship. The Leinster plan was more complete, with its service wings, back halls, secondary stairs, stables, and other features, not unusual even in large American houses. Washington never considered the White House finished, but left that for the future. Today much of what was Leinster House is altered for modern legislative use and expanded around 1900 with large forward wings to the main front. Such a tall interior entrance hall as this may have been part of the first design for the White House, running from the ground floor up into the first floor (second floor, American usage). Hoban's first design suggests that if it were intended, such a hall would have been placed like that at Leinster House, entered from the ground level. As it turned out, the Entrance Hall of the White House was not dissimilar as Hoban built it and rather like the accompanying view of the hall at Leinster House, with fireplaces balanced on each side, a screen of columns at the back, which originally had arches, giving on to a transverse hall. The upper area with its cove ceiling was replaced at the White House by a flat ceiling.

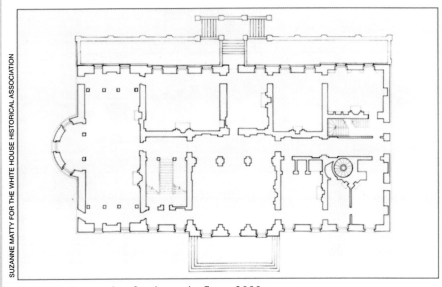

SUZANNE MATTY FOR THE WHITE HOUSE HISTORICAL ASSOCIATION

Leinster House plan for the main floor, 2000.

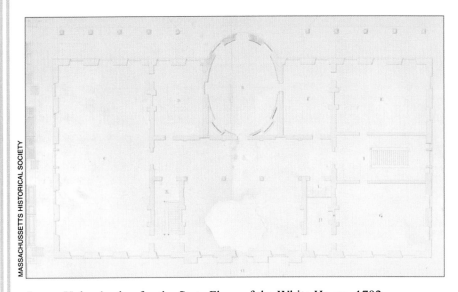

MASSACHUSSETTS HISTORICAL SOCIETY

James Hoban's plan for the State Floor of the White House, 1792.

Another major Dublin building Hoban said he had worked on is the Royal Exchange, today's City Hall, located across Castle Street from the Newcomen Bank. The construction dates of 1769 to 1779 indicate that Hoban worked on it late in the project's duration and before he entered the Dublin Society's school. Perhaps it was through this building and his stonemason cousins in Kilkenny that he got to Dublin. It is a magnificent building indeed, designed by Thomas Cooley, something of a beau ideal of architecture for a bank building of the time and certainly suggested in the design of the First Bank of the United States in Philadelphia, built while Hoban was working on the White House, its design attributed to Samuel Blodgett Jr., with whom Hoban was at the time (1795) building a Washington hotel.

The Exchange was commissioned by the Merchants' Guild of Dublin, with a design competition held in 1768. Cooley, the winner, was 28 years old, from London, where he had apprenticed in the office of the Scot Robert Mylne. It was the first monumental building reflecting archaeological neoclassicism in Ireland. Essentially a square enclosing a circle, the latter being a columned rotunda, the Exchange occupied an acutely pitched site that ran from the walls of the old Dublin Castle to the bank of the River Liffey. Parliament Street was to have framed it, although street vista and building were ultimately harmonious only thanks to the architect's skill at optical deception. Cooley's short career climaxed in this building, but he designed others, including the country house Mount Kennedy, described elsewhere in this issue.

The interior of the Royal Exchange presents a rotunda 46 feet in diameter ringed by heroic columns and crowned by a dome, all in the richest materials. Working areas of the Exchange were adjacent to this, off corridors. Obvious echoes of the Pantheon immediately establish the "antique" style then very popular in London and following more closely actual Roman ruins and remains than had been the case with such neoclassicism as Leinster House or Newcomen's Bank. Subsequent embellishment in inlaid marble and stained glass have not notably altered the original Exchange, which is handsomely maintained by the city.

Elliptical stairs, built entirely of stone, rise in the two corners of the building, executed in a very high quality of craftsmanship. Anchored in the limestone walls, the mass of the stair is reduced to the smallest dimensions possible so that the steps seem to float on the air.

The Royal Exchange was simply a place to conduct business, serving its membership and renters. A large coffee house on the second floor gave on to corridors and open halls that served offices and alcoves where brokers of all kinds dealt in wool, grain, and other products of a largely agricultural Ireland. It was a busy place when open, described as noisy. Being a prominent and quasi-public building, it was a gathering place for public meetings, many of them protests during the difficult times from its completion into the 1820s. A place where women seldom appeared, businessmen filled it in the daytime, abandoned it at night to a few guards, and kept it lively as the center of commercial transaction in Dublin well into the mid-nineteenth century.

Many highly emotional events have taken place here, from state funerals to citizen rallies. Of the latter the most notable was in 1800, when Roman Catholics assembled in the Exchange to protest the Act of Union, which, in British reaction to the 1798 revolution, had dissolved the Irish parliament. Among those who spoke was Daniel O'Connell, then 25, who would become father of Irish nationalism and who is commemorated today in the Exchange in a statue, pictured here, in the bend of the stairs, in Roman costume.

The Exchange is a very magnificent building, built entirely of Portland limestone. Massive Corinthian capitals carved by Simon Vierpyl, who executed the fine classical plaques for the Newcomen Bank, are powerful expressions of the most opulent of all classical ornaments. The Exchange fills its site, seeming almost monolithic rising among lower-standing buildings of less forceful character.

The Royal Exchange was purchased by the City Corporation of Dublin in 1852 and converted into City Hall. Various changes took place, the introduction of partitions to subdivide the open market character of the balconies, conversion of the coffee room into the council chamber, the introduction of a large staircase in the rotunda, and the usual historical and inspirational murals typical of the late nineteenth and early twentieth centuries. At the end of the last century the city restored the building generally to its appearance when completed in 1779. It is still used by the Dublin City Council and contains the city archives, but most city offices are elsewhere.

BELCAMP HOUSE

To our knowledge, James Hoban never set foot at Belcamp, but since it commemorates the early friendship between Ireland and America, White House History finds it significant, symbolically at least, in the story of the builder of the White House. Had Hoban ever visited Belcamp he would have found in the grounds the first monument ever built to George Washington, later his client and patron.

Belcamp House was commenced about 1763 by Sir Edward Newenham, who had acquired the estate when it came on the market following the death of its owner, the well-known jurist James Grattan. The estate had been in the Grattan family for more than a century, but was not passed on to Grattan's son Henry, because the father did not agree with the son's liberal politics. The younger Grattan went on to fame and glory in Irish history as an early and effective opponent of Britain's control over Ireland and a friend of America. The house Newenham found on the site was replaced by the house pictured above.

Like Henry Grattan, Sir Edward was also a great admirer
of America and the luminaries of its war for independence. He built a fine Georgian house at Belcamp, demol-
ishing the early house with apparently not a moment's
regret for losing it or its associations with Jonathan Swift
and many other famous figures. His house of brick and
stone was of a type familiar in this issue of the journal,
and has the usual Irish references to the White House in
the rustic base on the front and the protruding bow on
the rear.

As with most big houses of the time, work went on building and finishing the interior and the gardens at Belcamp for many years. An important feature was the landscape. Belcamp's extensive acreage was planted in the popular English natural mode, with groves and open meadows as well as formal arrangements. One of several garden follies is seen here, overlooking a lagoon.

Opposite: A deep areaway across the main front of Belcamp permits natural light to basement rooms, a device Hoban used in precisely this way in his plan for the White House. Indeed the areaway shown here is very reminiscent of that at the White House before the North Portico was built in 1829 and covered it.

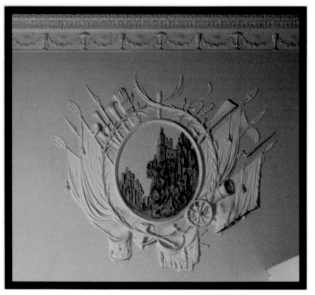

Cast plaster or composition (plaster mixed with mortar) enhanced the formal rooms of Belcamp House. Among the classical representatives is a contemplative Benjamin Franklin.

The elaborate cast plaster ornament inside Belcamp includes many neoclassical devises popular at the time, along with some surprises, as this dining room alcove, draped in cast plaster "curtains" and perhaps designed to receive a sideboard.

Sir Edward became utterly swept up in the American Revolution, beginning an almost obsessive correspondence with the American patriots. George Washington seems to have paid little attention at first, yet Sir Edward continued to write to him. In 1778 Sir Edward commissioned a little castle folly for his garden and dedicated it to George Washington. On its wall he placed a plaque proclaiming the honor it bestowed and a commentary on British governance of Ireland: "The English have long seemed to think it a right, which none could have but themselves. Their injustice has already cost them dear, and if persisted in, will be their ruin."

Washington eventually wrote a response, which Sir Edward cherished. Franklin proved a more willing correspondent. Ten or twelve letters survive in Franklin's papers to and from Belcamp. From Paris on May 27, 1779, Franklin wrote to Sir Edward: "I admire the spirit with which I see the Irish are at length determined to claim some share of that freedom of commerce, which is the right of all mankind, but which they have been so long deprived by the abominable selfishness of their fellow subjects." This comment was more commercially oriented than the abstract freedom that so attracted Sir Edward, but he idolized Franklin anyway.

WHITE HOUSE HISTORY

White House Historical Association
Washington

WHITE HOUSE FLOWERS AND GARDENS • NUMBER 23
PUBLISHED SUMMER 2008

Foreword

Flower arranging is quite an art today at the White House, as this issue shows, but fresh flowers were seldom used in early days. Old medical books warn how flowers drank up healthful air in closed rooms. The White House has been involved in gardening from the first, so flowers naturally made an early appearance inside. The first reference to flowers used for decoration in the house is in the recollections of Jessie Benton Frémont, daughter of Senator Thomas Hart Benton and wife of John C. Frémont, "The Pathfinder." She tells of "stands" of camellias in the State Rooms during Andrew Jackson's presidency. The garden-loving president, having camellia sesanqua growing in terra-cotta pots, seems to have brought the plants in full bloom to the house for special occasions, then returned them to their places in the orangery he had established in the grounds.

The affection of the White House for flower arrangements began in the late 1850s with Harriet Lane, hostess to her uncle President James Buchanan. She brought the idea home from England, where Buchanan had served as American minister. A new conservatory having replaced Jackson's orangery, flowers were close at hand, and geraniums were the rage. At the dinner table each lady was greeted with a small bouquet or nosegay wrapped in lace paper, each man a boutonniere. Fresh flowers adorned the Monroe plateau. By the 1870s bouquet makers (flower arrangers) were on the White House gardening staff. Since just before the Civil War, flowers have been a constant presence at the White House. Today flower arrangements are turned out by the hundreds, using historic vases and containers, by a surprisingly small flower shop located in the basement area.

Articles in this issue are centered in gardening, flower arranging, and table decorations. First Lady Edith Kermit Roosevelt's "colonial garden" and the fanciful French porcelain statuary with which she loved to decorate the State Dining Room table represent one who loved flowers. James Monroe's gilt bronze plateau has been used on the White House dinner table since 1818. Today's flower arranging at the White House is described by the White House florist, Nancy Clarke. Some of the most elaborate floral decorations at the White House have been for weddings, so we feature two, and have asked watercolorist Margaret Huddy to re-create for us in color some of the flowers used at the weddings of Nellie Grant and Frances Folsom Cleveland, which we can see only in black-and-white in the photography and graphics of their time.

Look for further issues on gardens and gardening in *White House History*.

William Seale
Editor, *White House History*

Terra cotta pots in Lincoln's White House, 1861, hold roses and camellia sesanquas. Photo by Mathew Brady, 1863 (detail).

First Lady Edith Kermit Carow Roosevelt's "Colonial Garden" at the White House

MAC KEITH GRISWOLD

Edith Kermit Carow Roosevelt (1861–1948), wife of the twenty-sixth president of the United States, walks toward us out of that narrow, fertile strip of the past so well tilled by Edith Wharton and Henry James: upper-class Manhattan in the post–Civil War years. She smiles graciously, and in each hand she holds a bunch of flowers: in one, green and brown orchids; in the other, white hyacinths and lilies of the valley. She carries them so it will be perfectly clear to the five to six thousand people who have come to greet her at her first large function as a public personage, the reception following the 1899 inauguration of her husband, Theodore Roosevelt, as governor of New York State (1898–1900), that she will not be shaking hands with them, a custom she considers overly familiar.[1]

Edith Roosevelt's grace, her intelligence, her self-discipline, and her quiet determination to guard her privacy and make her own life fit the template she described for it are qualities familiar to any Wharton or James reader. Unlike so many of those writers' heroines, she succeeded in realizing her goals. Her precarious childhood in New York City had been one of "keeping up appearances" and "making do."[2] She was without a permanent home of her own from the age of six until her marriage. She lived a genteel life only because of the kindness of relatives, friends, and neighbors, principally a wealthy aunt; her grandfather, Brigadier General Daniel Tyler IV, a Connecticut gentleman and successful civil engineer; and the Cornelius Roosevelts of Washington Square, whose widower son, Theodore, she would marry in 1886. Her life thereafter would be fiercely centered on her husband and six children. Her remarkable coping mechanism for dealing calmly with the unexpected, no doubt in part a legacy of that childhood, meant she was able to make a home on short notice, then pick up her tent and start again, each time shaping unpromising elements of house and garden to her design.[3] Flowers, indoors and out, were integral to her life, both as a shield and as a means of expression.

In 1902 Edith Roosevelt carried the symbolism of flowers forward as part of the first complete renovation of the White House. For her architect, Charles Follen McKim, of the renowned firm of McKim, Mead & White, to "restore" the original neoclassical White House as envisioned by George Washington was only part of a grander dream for the city as a whole. At the Corcoran Gallery of Art, just three months after Theodore Roosevelt took office following President William McKinley's assassination in September 1901, McKim and his three associates (in what later became known as the McMillan plan) mounted an exhibition of magnificent models and renderings to show how Pierre

---

First Lady Edith Roosevelt was photographed seated on a garden bench on the south side of the White House in preparation for her painted portrait by Théobald Chartran in 1902.

The huge glass conservatories prior to their demolition, 1902.

Charles L'Enfant's 1791 plan for the city, with its elegant axial and radial planning, and massing of symbolic elements such as the Mall, the Capitol building, and the White House, could be realized in the twentieth century.[4] Theodore Roosevelt visited the exhibit and was impressed. Edith Roosevelt, as a New Yorker no doubt comfortably familiar with McKim's New York firm, soon invited McKim to meet with her about much needed improvements to the White House family quarters.[5] McKim then convinced both Roosevelts that the entire house was in dire need of work. McKim pored over archival materials, studying the original plans and the first expansions to them, all brought together by the Army Corps of Engineers. More than half a million dollars was appropriated by Congress at the end of June 1902.

By November 1902, a bare five months later, the project bore evidence to McKim's *parti* for a colonial-style White House stripped to eighteenth-century simplicity (at least as McKim conceived of it) but with functional Jeffersonian-style expansions. The major additions were restoration of the vanished East Colonnade and, on the west, the new "temporary Executive Offices," which would eventually house the Oval Office.[6] After a summer at Sagamore Hill, the family's permanent home overlooking Long Island Sound in Oyster Bay, New York, Edith Roosevelt and the children moved back in.

Men at work on demolition of the conservatories, above the site of what would become Mrs. Roosevelt's garden, August 7, 1902. The columns of the West Colonnade, once enclosed by the conservatories, are again exposed.

The only major point of disagreement between the architect and his clients had been the dismantling of the huge glass conservatories, whose spread, off to the southwest of the building, by 1901, was one-and-a-half times greater than the square footage of any single floor of the White House itself.[7] Edith Roosevelt especially resisted, bolstered by letters from Henry Pfister, the White House gardener since the administration of President Rutherford B. Hayes.[8] Pfister was losing his kingdom; his drawn-out battle to save it cost him his plants. His glass palaces were demolished in September 1902, and the greenhouses being built off-site as a compromise solution were not finished in time to house his precious tropicals before a killing frost. The space, today

the Rose Garden, where Pfister's tender treasures had grown for fifty-seven years, would now be an outdoor flower garden imbued with the same spirit of colonial purity as McKim's White House. The informal style, however, is remarkably different in interpretation from McKim's stately and dignified composition.

Edith Roosevelt and Pfister took stock. The area lay in the embrasure between the bulk of the house and the new executive offices. To the north it was protected by the West Colonnade, whose handsome Tuscan columns, once buried in the conservatory, again stood in the open air. Southward, the breadth of the space opened out to a full view of the White House grounds. As seen in the old photograph on the next page, which was shot

The "colonial garden,"
c. 1902.

from above, perhaps from the roof of the executive offices, a symmetrically patterned parterre of oval and triangular beds is laid out among sanded paths. The plantings are very unlike the carefully patterned, carpet-bedded mounds that Pfister was accustomed to cutting into the turf of the White House grounds. And, even in this black-and-white image, the colors and textures appear different from Pfister's greenhouse-grown tropical cuttings, such as calceolarias, caladiums, or begonias, whose leaves are as brilliant as their flowers.

These are summer-flowering herbaceous perennials, biennials, and herbs, stretching out in patches, not patterns. Each bed is centered with taller shrubs, many of which look to be old-fashioned roses; they are growing freely and have not been clipped or tied into formal shapes. Jasmine vines clamber artlessly up simple posts. Tiny boxwoods, probably recently rooted cuttings of dwarf boxwood, *Buxus sempervirens* 'Suffruticosa,' form frilly but sober green edgings around each bed. The rectangular enclosure that stretches the length of the West Colonnade is surrounded by a low box hedge. At the end of the garden nearest the South Portico stands a sturdy white-painted wooden bench. It is a summer day: the shrub roses are in flower; some silvery white mullein spikes punctuate the masses of green; what appear to be black-eyed Susans poke their heads into the bottom of the photographic frame.

The garden's design is attributed to Edith Roosevelt herself, and to Pfister. Mrs. Roosevelt was an excellent domestic executive who preferred hands-on control. For example, when she installed her family in their new home, she dismissed the housekeeper and took on the household direction herself.[9] Her exchanges with McKim were polite, but she had very clear ideas of what she wanted and did not hesitate to state them.[10] So there is every reason to think that she did, in fact, propose the design and that Pfister planted as she directed. Where had she found her inspiration for her "colonial garden," which today would be called a "Colonial Revival garden"?

The term "Colonial Revival" is often used to describe a style in the decorative arts, architecture, and gardens. In fact the so-called colonial wallpapers, silver patterns, doorway pediments, and white-painted benches such as the one seen in the White House photograph are only the material manifestations of a profound change in American historical thinking. The Colonial Revival was

part of the nation's healing process after the Civil War ended.[11] It was more than a style; it was a national movement. In its best light the Colonial Revival represents the first time Americans, as a nation, looked back at their history and realized it really *was* a history worthy of study, one that could even hold lessons for the future. As such, the movement was a return to first principles, which included the principles of design that embodied the best of life's values—what another great Beaux Arts architect, Thomas Hastings, later hailed in "The Relations of Life to Style in Architecture."[12]

At its worst, the Colonial Revival has been justly criticized as a xenophobic reaction to the mass influx of European immigrants in the second half of the nineteenth century and as a Luddite reaction to the industrial revolution—a simplistic longing for a return to a simpler and more worthy life. It has also been character-

Photograph of Edith Roosevelt prior to her marriage.

ized, again one may say rightly, as class warfare on polite terms, waged by a New England oligarchy (which by definition included the Tylers, Kermits, Carows, and Roosevelts) that was rapidly losing power and status to an emergent cadre of post–Civil War industrial barons. As such, it was a retreat into the safety of what looked like the unchanging past. There were pitfalls in describing, reverencing, and sometimes "re-creating" this past. In 1955 the American historian C. Vann Woodward wrote, "The twilight zone that lies between living memory and written history is one of the favorite breeding places of mythology."[13] The one hundred years since the start of America's independence struggle were still within living memory.

The first national, public iteration of the Colonial Revival took place at the world's fair celebrating the nation's centennial, held in Philadelphia in 1876. Two

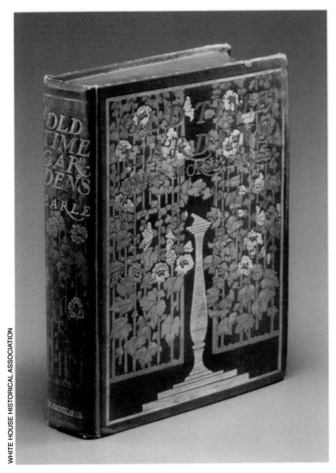

This copy of Old Time Gardens *is in the collection of Sagamore Hill today.*

log cabins—the Farmer's Home and the Modern Kitchen—with picket-fenced front dooryards, were popular exhibits.[14] The simplicity of the Farmer's Home stands at one end of the Colonial Revival spectrum, representing the American ideal of democracy's rural roots; McKim's White House represents the other—America's embodiment of a classical republic reborn.

The champion of "colonial" gardens was Alice Morse Earle (1851–1911). Born into a Massachusetts family with strong gardening and horticultural interests, Earle was a scholar and a writer specializing in the life and material culture of New England.[15] The author of dozens of articles and seventeen books with titles such as *The Sabbath in Puritan New England* (1891) and *Child Life in Colonial Days* (1899), Earle went on to publish what was probably her most influential book, *Old-Time Gardens: A Book of the Sweet o' the Year*, in 1901, the year the "old-time" or "colonial" garden at the White House was made.

Twenty-two chapters and more than two hundred black-and-white photographs of East Coast gardens old and new, and mostly in New England, lay out Earle's demands for privacy, enclosure, single rather than double flowers, simple garden furniture, formal, symmetrical design, a certain artless and discreet good taste, and the use of a green frame, preferably boxwood. She erases the Victorian garden, with its unbounded lawns and cut beds, with one phrase, calling the lawn "that dreary destroyer of a garden."[16] Her style is anecdotal; her research is deep and meticulous, though many of her conclusions as to how and when the gardens she reveres were laid out indeed lead her deep into Woodward's "twilight zone."[17]

Earle's intent is tutorial, trending always toward the inestimable value of English heritage and English stock as the basis of an upright American life, whether in gardens or out. Her passage on ancient boxwood at Sylvester Manor on Shelter Island, New York, confirms boxwood as *the* colonial garden icon, and illustrates the pull of Earle's style—and her prejudice:

Over these old garden borders hangs literally an atmosphere of the past; the bitter perfume stimulates the imagination as we walk by the side of these splendid Box bushes, and think, as everyone must, of what they have seen, of what they know; on this garden is written the history of over two centuries of beautiful domestic home life. It is well

Above left: Edith Roosevelt and son Quentin near the pet cemetery on a path ending with a wooden arbor at Sagamore Hill, c. 1901.

Above right: The garden at Sagamore Hill, c. 1918.

Left: Title page of Old-Time Gardens, *a book that Mrs. Roosevelt had in her library and a likely inspiration for her White House flower garden.*

OLD·TIME GARDENS

Newly set forth

by

ALICE MORSE EARLE

A BOOK OF
THE SWEET 'O' THE YEAR

"Life is sweet, brother! There's day and night, brother!
both sweet things: sun, moon and stars, brother! all
sweet things: There is likewise a wind on the heath"

NEW YORK
THE MACMILLAN COMPANY
LONDON MACMILLAN & CO LTD
MCMI
All rights reserved

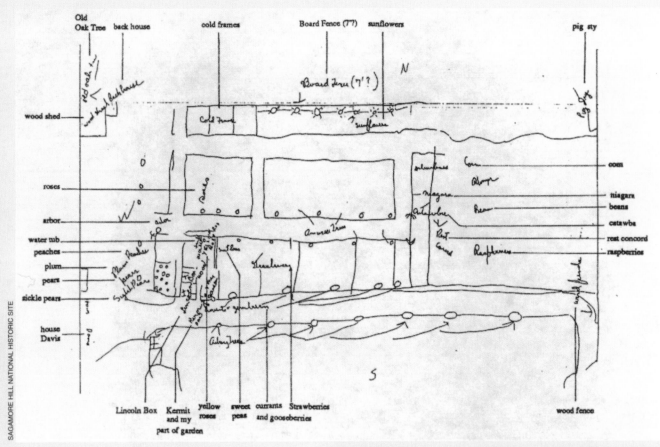

Old
Oak Tree   back house   cold frames   Board Fence (7'?)   sunflowers   pig sty

wood shed

roses

arbor

water tub
peaches
plum
pears
sickle pears

house
Davis

Lincoln Box   Kermit   yellow   sweet   currants   Strawberries   wood fence
               and my   roses   peas   and gooseberries
               part of garden

corn

niagara
beans

catawba
rest concord
raspberries

*Above: An undated sketch by Edith Roosevelt's son
Archibald Roosevelt of the flower and vegetable
garden at Sagamore Hill.*

*Right: A seventeenth-century design for a garden knot
of flowers, which was published on the dedication page
of* Old-Time Gardens.

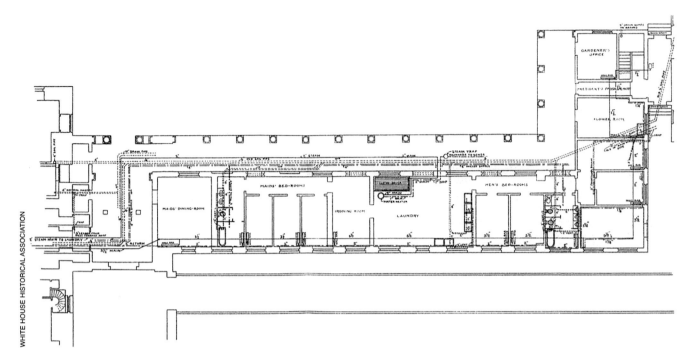

Above: West Terrace Plan for the President's House, as published in the official report, Restoration of the White House, *1902.*

Opposite: The West Terrace by Jules Guerin was included in Restoration of the White House *and may reflect architect Charles McKim's own vision for the garden, with a wide center path.*

that we still have such memorials to teach us the nobility and beauty of such a life.[18]

Whether or not Edith Roosevelt herself owned a copy of *Old-Time Gardens* (a first edition copy is on the shelves at Sagamore Hill, but it neither appears in any inventory until 1963 nor does it bear her bookplate), nonetheless, throughout her life she was surrounded by examples of such gardens. One was the garden at Oldgate in Farmington, Connecticut, the ancestral home of her sister-in-law's husband. Theodore Roosevelt's elder sister, Anna Roosevelt, had married William Sheffield Cowles in 1895, and the Roosevelts often visited there. Oldgate lay in the heart of "old-time gardens" country: northwestern Connecticut. Members of what the columnist Joseph Alsop (TR and Anna's nephew) would later wittily call the "Wasp Ascendancy" (as well as would-be Wasp Ascendants who moved to cool Connecticut as summer residents) were busy making "colonial gardens" at just this time.[19] Litchfield, Bethlehem, Sharon—all the little towns had their coteries of garden makers and historic preservationists. No

frequent visitor could have missed the fever and fervor of the Colonial Revival movement as it moved into the mainstream of domestic style in a landscape of farm and field so redolent of the Puritan past. The entire region was a talisman.[20]

At Sagamore Hill, the Roosevelts themselves maintained an "old-time garden" that Earle would have blessed. A short distance north of the house stretched an unpretentious, rectangular three-acre garden stocked with orchard trees, beds of soft fruit, roses and vegetables, cold frames, a pig sty, and, at the end of the central path, a plain wooden arbor.[21] In its amplitude and understatement, this garden is probably very like the garden that Edith Roosevelt remembered at her grandfather Tyler's.[22] When, as an elderly widow, she looked both for a refuge from her memories of her husband at Sagamore Hill and for the solace of her own family background, she bought an eighteenth-century house built by a Tyler ancestor in Brooklyn, Connecticut, only a few miles from her birthplace in Norwich.[23]

The "old-time garden" underwent an apotheosis at the White House. While the pattern and the plantings of

A recent view of the Rose Garden, c. 2000, with the watering system at work. The area once filled with flowers by Edith Roosevelt is now the grass-covered center of the Rose Garden, which is often used for special events and presidential press conferences.

a typical "old-time" or "colonial" assemblage remained the same, how the garden was most often viewed turned it into a completely different place. The flat roof of the one-story West Colonnade had been reworked into the West Terrace, an elegant promenade for White House official evening entertainment. From this important vantage point, and even in darkness, thanks to the soft brilliance of the newfangled electric globes on the terrace balustrade, the garden was transformed into a vivid American *parterre de broderie*, a palace garden attuned to the grandeur of the White House and yet homelike in its countrified plantings. For the household staff whose service rooms opened into the colonnade, for the president's staff in the new executive office—and for the president on his walks to and from that office, which he used only occasionally, preferring to work in the White House itself—it remained a sweet-smelling ramble along a maze of paths.

As usual, Edith Roosevelt seems quietly to have had the last word: the report on the restoration of the White House includes two renderings of the West Terrace and the garden below it by Jules Guerin, the fashionable Beaux Arts muralist and illustrator of the grandest estate gardens of the country place era. It seems that McKim may have envisioned something entirely different: a muscular design with a single broad central path, massive planes of turf and flower beds planted only with a single species of white flowers.[24] It is a beautiful but completely public design. Edith Roosevelt's little lace doily of a garden has a private subtext as well as a public meaning. Modest yet self-confident, it was an apron of old-time respectability in the face of the rising grandeur of the establishments of the post–Civil War era.

NOTES

1. Sylvia Jukes Morris, *Edith Kermit Roosevelt: Portrait of a First Lady* (New York: Coward, McCann & Geoghegan, New York, 1980), 199. All biographical information on Edith Roosevelt is drawn from this source.

2. Edith Kermit Carow Roosevelt's New England family history began with Job Tyler's arrival in 1638 in Massachusetts. Her mother, Gertrude Carow, traced her ancestry to the famous Puritan divine, Jonathan Edwards. Her husband, Charles Carow, was a member of an important New York City shipping family of Huguenot descent. None of this was proof against the economic currents that carried Edith Roosevelt's parents downward. Family misfortune played its part: Charles Carow was a business failure and an alcoholic; Gertrude Carow, a hypochondriac. Edith Roosevelt assiduously destroyed papers that pertained to her childhood. As a married woman, she dropped the Carow name from her habitual signature, "Edith Kermit Roosevelt." Her bookplate reads, "Edith Kermit Roosevelt." Morris, *Edith Kermit Roosevelt*, 9–10, 13, 20, 44.

3. Following Theodore Roosevelt's career, Edith spent seven years in Washington, D.C., two in New York City, two in Albany, then six months back in Washington as wife of the vice president, followed by the abrupt move to the White House.

4. Mardges Bacon, "Toward a National Style of Architecture: The Beaux-Arts Interpretation of the Colonial Revival," in *The Colonial Revival in America*, ed. Alan Axelrod (New York: W. W. Norton, 1985), 91–121, esp. 96–102.

5. For Edith Roosevelt as a New Yorker and comparison of her taste with that of Theodore Roosevelt's cousin Edith Wharton, see William Seale, *The White House: The History of an American Idea*, 2nd ed. (Washington, D.C.: White House Historical Association, 2001), 166.

6. *Restoration of the White House: Message of the President of the United States Transmitting the Report of the Architects,* Washington, D.C.: Government Printing Office, 1903, 9.

7. William Seale, *The White House Garden* (Washington, D.C.: White House Historical Association, 1996), 57.

8. For information on the greenhouse debate, see Sarah Fayen, "Inhabiting an Icon: First Ladies and the White House," *Blueprints* 18, no. 1 (Winter 2000): also at http://www.nbm.org/blueprints/00s/winter00/page2/page2.htm (accessed September 19, 2007).

9. Morris, *Edith Kermit Roosevelt*, 224.

10. Ibid., 243.

11. The Colonial Revival began before the Civil War as a literary movement: in 1827, Catharine Maria Sedgwick (1789–1867), who lived in the Berkshire Mountains of western Massachusetts, novelist, published the historical romance *Hope Leslie*, set in seventeenth-century Massachusetts. Sedgewick's historical novels turned the American imagination to the material culture of the past. Not until the Centennial Exhibition would period settings take shape on the ground.

12. Thomas Hastings, "The Relations of Life to Style in Architecture," *Harper's New Monthly* 88, no. 528 (May 1894), cited in Bacon, "Toward a National Style," 94.

13. C. Vann Woodward, *The Strange Career of Jim Crow* (New York, 1955), viii, quoted in Michael Kammen, *Mystic Chords of Memory: The Transformation of American Culture* (New York: Vintage Books 1993), 31.

14. Rodris Roth, "The New England, or 'Olde Tyme,' Kitchen Exhibit at Nineteenth-Century Fairs," in *The Colonial Revival in America*, ed. Axelrod, 159–83, esp. 174.

15. Alice Morse Earle, *Old-Time Gardens Newly Set Forth: A Book of the Sweet o' the Year* (1901), new ed. introd. Virginia Lopez Begg (Lebanon, N.H.: University Press of New England, 2005). See also the entry for Alice Morse Earle, by Wendell D. Garrett, in *Notable American Women, 1607–1950*, ed. Edward T. James, Janet Wilson James, and Paul S. Boyer (Cambridge, Mass.: Belknap Press of Harvard University Press, 1971), 1:541–42.

16. Earle, *Old-Time Gardens*, 53.

17. Earle's adjective, "old-time," was carefully chosen to cover gardens from the seventeenth century to the early twentieth century, but recent research reveals that early gardens were more rudimentary and subsistence-based than Earle believed.

18. Earle, *Old-Time Gardens*, 106.

19. Joseph W. Alsop and Adam Platt, "The Wasp Ascendancy," *New York Review of Books*, November 9, 1989, 48–56.

20. William Butler, "Another City upon a Hill: Litchfield, Connecticut, and the Colonial Revival," in *The Colonial Revival in America*, ed. Axelrod, 15–51.

21. "There are many pretty trellises and vine supports and arbors which can be made of light poles and rails." Earle, *Old-Time Gardens*, 386. See also Regina M. Bellavia and George W. Curry, preparators, *Cultural Landscape Report for Sagamore Hill National Historic Site* (repr., Boston, Mass.: Olmsted Center for Landscape Preservation, 2003), 47, 48, 51.

22. Morris, *Edith Kermit Roosevelt*, 44.

23. Ibid., 467–69.

24. "Report of Messrs. McKim, Mead & White, Architects," in *Restoration of the White House,* op.cit., 12, 16.

James Monroe's White House Plateau
"A perfect riot of festooned railings and graceful figures"

MELISSA NAULIN

*I*f, as is often stated, the Landsdowne portrait of George Washington by Gilbert Stuart is the most important piece of fine art in the White House collection, then the corollary in presidential decorative arts must be the French Empire table centerpiece and its accessories that President James Monroe purchased for the President's House in 1817. This "plateau," consisting of seven sections of mirror glass surfaces surrounded by balustrades of gilded bronze, has graced White House dining tables for almost two centuries. Its consistent use throughout such a long period of time is unusual in the history of White House furnishings, which are either worn out from use or have changed according to the tastes of the many families who have lived there. Purchased to impress the White House's most important guests with American panache, the plateau's early use at dinners for both national and international leaders quickly became tradition, thereby perpetuating its use long after the fashion for plateaus had passed. The plateau's longevity can also be attributed to its adaptability and function as a stage for decorative table props of the latest style.

When James Monroe assumed the presidency in March 1817, the White House was still being rebuilt

---

Since the early 1960s five sections of the plateau have been regularly displayed in the State Dining Room, as seen here.

after being burned during the War of 1812. Monroe made reoccupying the President's House a priority and set an initial deadline of fall 1817. He immediately engaged William Lee, who had previously served as American consul in Bordeaux, France, and remained in business in Paris, to supervise the refurbishing; but the president remained heavily involved, if only by letter. Monroe's diplomatic experience strongly influenced his furnishing decisions. His service representing the United States in France, England, and Spain in the 1790s and early 1800s exposed him firsthand to the European capitals and their leaders' residences, and provided an ample education in what was right and proper for an official house. During his foreign assignments, Monroe had avidly acquired furnishings of the highest quality both for his own homes and for those of his friends.[1] Attending to such commissions was common practice among elite Americans in the early Federal era, who relied on those living in fashion centers to relay both information and goods to those without ready access to them. Monroe was an ardent Francophile who was as enamored with French goods as he was with French politics, and thus when faced with an unfurnished executive residence, he turned to the American firm of Russell & La Farge in Le Havre, France, to supply furnishings for the two most formal spaces in the President's House, the Oval Room (now the Blue Room), and the State Dining Room. His familiarity with French domestic goods is demonstrated by the fact that his order was accompanied by specific requests regarding the finish, decoration, and costs of the desired furnishings. These wishes his agents could not always fulfill.

Although President Monroe's original order to Russell & La Farge has not survived, later correspondence between them strongly implies that Monroe specifically requested a plateau. By doing so, he indicated his desire to follow the latest European dining fashions in the President's House. Although in fashionable use since the third quarter of the eighteenth century, plateaus reached their height of popularity during the first quarter of the nineteenth century, when the very best European metalworkers produced increasingly elaborate versions made in silver, silver gilt, or gilt bronze for the tables of royalty and the rich. The use of plateaus can be traced back to medieval salt cellars, which gradually began to support additional condiments and serving pieces until separate movable table forms began to be created to both hold food and serve as decoration. Eventually, as the utilitarian characteristics of centerpieces were overshadowed by their decorative nature, strictly decorative objects began to be placed at the center of the table while food dishes were placed around the outside.[2] Mirrored plateaus like the one Monroe ordered were typically decorated with items like wax, sugar, or ceramic figurines, fresh or artificial flowers, or metal baskets or urns. Scattered over the mirror and in the glowing of yellow candlelight, the decorations could be very beautiful.

James Monroe was not the first American president to believe a plateau was a necessary dinner ornament for the executive residence. When a plateau was not among the goods provided by Congress for the first president's house in 1789, George Washington decided to use his own money to acquire one. Washington's secretary, Tobias Lear, tried to purchase a plateau in Philadelphia but could not find any that were large enough for Washington's needs. Washington therefore wrote to Gouverneur Morris, then residing in France, to ask him to secure a plateau. Morris dutifully sent a nine-piece silver plateau along with biscuit porcelain figurines, which Washington immediately put into use, as recorded by the accounts of guests to the President's House.[3]

It is not known whether John Adams used a plateau during his presidency, although Thomas Jefferson provided him with a French example in 1785 when Adams was serving in diplomatic service as American minister to England. Thomas Jefferson owned a number of plateaus during his years in France and continued to use the form back in America both at Monticello and at the White House.[4] In the inventory of White House furnishings taken just before Jefferson left office, "1 plateau in five parts with a set of ornaments," probably statuettes, is listed in "Store Room No. 2."[5] This may have been the same "tarnished" plateau that an 1813 visitor to the Madison White House noted seeing.[6] This plateau was probably destroyed when the White House was burned in 1814.

Thus while the use of a plateau at the President's House was well established by Monroe's administration, the gilded bronze plateau that Russell & La Farge provided was far more elaborate and expensive than those used by his predecessors. Mercury-gilded bronze, also called *ormolu*, was a Parisian specialty and was at the height of its popularity during the Empire period.[7] In a letter to Monroe written on September 15, 1817, Russell & La Farge commented on the quality and price of the plateau, or *surtout de table*,[8] that his firm had commissioned for the refurbished President's House: "The surtout is very handsome; it has been made by the best manufacturer in Paris, who lost by it near 2000 francs."[9] As the total cost of the plateau and its accompanying accessories was 6,000 francs, Russell & La Farge was emphasizing that the United States government was getting a good deal for the set, although the plateau was still the most expensive furnishing provided for the White House. Fortunately, the plateau is marked on the face of one of its plinths by its maker, Denière et Matelin, revealing whom Russell & La Farge considered "the best manufacturer in Paris." Without this mark, the plateau would probably be attributed to Pierre-Philippe Thomire, largely regarded as the best bronze craftsman of the Empire period.[10] Jean-François Denière and François Thomas Matelin were chief competitors to Thomire during this period and owned one of the largest bronze workshops in Paris at the time.[11]

Russell & La Farge's itemized listing of goods supplied for the White House is wonderfully detailed, listing the plateau as "1 chased bronze Surtout de table, mat gilt with garlands of fruit and vines with figure of Bacchus and Bacchantes and pedestals on which are 16 figures presenting wreaths for receiving lights [candles] and 16 cups for changing at will, composed of 7 pieces altogether 13 feet 6 inches long [actually 14 feet 6 inches

The plateau is marked on the face of one of its plinths by its maker, Denière et Matelin.

long] , over 2 feet wide, set with mirrors."[12] The plateau consists of two D-shaped ends with five interchangeable rectangular sections to fit in between, allowing its length to be accommodated to the size table being used. All seven pieces are set with mirrors on their horizontal surface and surrounded by a gilded bronze balustrade featuring Bacchus, the Roman god of horticulture and wine, and his followers supporting swags of grapevines, ivy, and fruit.

Bacchus sits on an overturned ewer in the center of each balustrade, holding a drinking vessel in one hand and a thyrsus (staff with a pine-cone end) in the other. Bacchantes (Bacchus's female devotees) recline on either end of the balustrades, also holding thyrsi. A laurel leaf border runs below the balustrades. Each of the plateau's sections feature two plinths with a wreath mount on its face, with the exception of one of the end sections, which has four plinths. Each plinth supports a

An overall view of the plateau, with all seven pieces, the Three Graces baskets, and the tripod stands.

removable classically dressed woman balancing on a sphere with both outstretched arms holding a wreath. Alternatively, the plinths can be set with sixteen shallow, oval-shaped bronze dishes decorated with grapevines and acanthus leaves that were also provided by Denière et Matelin.

Russell & La Farge also sent seven gilded-bronze containers to be used with the plateau to form a complete ensemble. A set of three baskets, each supported by three female classical figures assumed to represent the Three Graces, stand on circular plinths. Both the one large and the two smaller versions of these baskets came with removable candelabra inserts of six arms each, but none of these inserts have survived. A pair of stands "copied from the ancient style" and featuring three winged sphinxes sitting on top of animal legs also accompanied the plateau.[13] The model for these stands was recovered from the excavation of the Temple of Isis at Pompeii and was copied widely in the classical decorative arts of the early nineteenth century.[14] A pair of

Detail of female figure holding two of the thirty-two small bowls supplied for the plateau in 1853 by Bailey & Co.

vases in the "Etruscan" form with wreath mounts encircling classical masques completed the plateau decorations. All seven of these containers remain in the White House collection, although the vases are not regularly displayed.

The powerful impression the plateau made on guests to the White House in the early nineteenth century cannot be overstated. Almost every known written account of dining at the President's House during this period comments upon the centerpiece. The frequency of comment and the level of detail that visitors recorded speaks to the rarity of plateaus in America.[15] New York Congressman Thomas Hill Hubbard's complimentary and detailed account of experiencing the President's House plateau in February 1818 is not uncommon:

> We had a good dinner and the table was more richly furnished than any that I have yet seen. There were about thirty sat down to dinner. . . . The plateau was the most elegant thing that I ever saw. It is as much as twelve feet long and two feet wide, oval at the ends. The bottom, which is raised on little gold balls or feet, is a mirror edged around with a gold border about two inches high, beautifully wrought, and at equal distances, about eighteen inches apart, on the outer edge, stands a female figure about eight inches high, of gold with her arms extended over her head, holding a gold branch or candlestick in each hand, so that there were about forty candles burning around this superb article. There were also three large flowerpots [probably the Three Graces baskets], whether gilt or plated I cannot tell, filled with a variety of artificial flowers. The whole had a most pleasing and brilliant effect and as you looked across the table you saw in the mirror the ladies and gentleman who were sitting opposite you with their faces inverted. All the furniture of these rooms is rich beyond anything I ever saw.[16]

Descriptions like Hubbard's help us visualize the dazzling effect of seeing the candlelit plateau in the age before electricity. Although Americans in this period typically ate their main meal of the day in the late afternoon when natural light would have still been available, genteel diners preferred to eat with the shutters or curtains drawn and rely on artificial light. Due to the expense of fine-quality candles and the fashion for candleholders made of precious metals, a well-lit room demonstrated both wealth and hospitality.[17] The brilliance of the State Dining Room must have been a sharp contrast to the dark, empty streets upon which visitors travelled home.

When all the sections were in use, the classical female figures standing on the sixteen plinths of the President's House plateau held thirty-two candles, whose light was in turn reflected and magnified by the sheets of mirror glass below. The gilding of the plateau and its accoutrements would have further amplified the light. Thus the plateau would have quite literally glowed at the center of the dining table. Seeing the plateau in candlelight would have also emphasized its superb craftsmanship such as the subtle finish differences between the plateau's matte and burnished components.

What some visitors to the President's House saw as elegance, others saw as unjustified extravagance for the head of a republican government. The expensive French furnishings that Monroe had selected inspired extensive criticism, both in his own day and for years to come.[18] Newspapers frequently published letters like the one from "a journeyman cabinet maker" who wrote to the *Washington Gazette* in 1818 to complain that the French furnishings at the President's House were all about "pomp, and parade, extravagance, and profligacy." In the same issue, an "unostentatious Republican" wrote that "the real friends of the President lament that he has committed the direction of these [furnishing] matters to the hands of those who seem to have gratified an itch for introducing the mock-grandeur of a late emperor."[19]

The question, in George Washington's words, of "the style proper for the Chief Magistrate to live in" had been debated since Congress selected and furnished the first executive residence in New York City in 1789.[20] The dual needs for the President's House to represent the values of the United States' republican government while simultaneously commanding respect from foreign officials who were accustomed to their leaders living in great opulence inevitably evoked criticism from both those who believed the furnishings were too grand and those who believed they were insufficient. American painter and inventor Samuel F. B. Morse articulated this conflict when he observed in 1819 that some of the President's House is "decorated in the most splendid manner, some think too much so, but I do not. Something of splendor is certainly proper about the Chief Magistrate for the credit of the nation."[21] Writing

One of a pair of "Etruscan" vases attributed to Denière et Matelin, 1817, and intended to be used with the plateau.

Above: March 12, 1870, wood newspaper engraving of a State Dinner.

Left: A wood newspaper engraving of an 1871 dinner honoring the Joint High Commission with Britain, assembled to settle American Civil War maritime claims against the Crown. Note First Lady Julia Grant's floral arches for the plateau, which were made using copper chicken wire and lamp parts.

in 1823, Virginia Senator John Taylor similarly observed that the highest quality furnishings in the President's House were "designed to impress upon foreign ministers a respect for the [United States] government, which may have a valuable influence upon our foreign relations."[22] Thus while European visitors to the President's House tended to find it modest, they at least did not accuse the Americans of being ignorant of fashion. When Englishman William Faux, who visited the President's House on July 6, 1820, found it "neither so elegant, superb, nor costly as the seats of our nobility," he still declared it "a good, substantial, pleasant abode."[23]

As beautiful and elaborate as the White House plateau is in its own right, its real role was to display additional decorations. Throughout Europe and America, wealthy hosts competed to adorn their plateaus with increasingly imaginative and costly displays of flowers, sugar sculptures, vases, figurines, baskets, and candleholders. Although not mentioned in Russell & La Farge's itemized listing of furnishings, their packing list notes that package 21 contained "The Flowers for the surtout."[24] Thus artificial flowers, often of wax, were part of the original plateau ensemble, and many early visitors report seeing them in the gilded bronze stands, vases, and baskets that accompanied the plateau.[25] During this period, artificial flowers were considered more appropriate than fresh flowers for this purpose.[26] By the 1850s, however, that was beginning to change. A guest who reported seeing artificial flowers on the plateau in 1850 during the Millard Fillmore administration went on to comment that "we saw very few natural flowers, and there was no conservatory at the White House."[27] The White House gained its first greenhouses in 1853, and thereafter, fresh flowers predominated on the plateau.[28]

The capability the plateau gave one to adapt to changing fashions allowed its continued use past the time when plateaus fell out of fashion in the mid-nineteenth century. President Franklin Pierce deserves much of the credit for perpetuating the plateau's use by deciding to invest almost $600 from his congressional appropriation to the White House fund to overhaul the table ornament. It appears that the entire plateau and its accessories were sent to Philadelphia in 1853, where the silver and fine jewelry firm of Bailey & Co. oversaw their regilding and repair, including the resilvering of the plateau's mirrors.[29] Bailey & Co. also supplied new accessories for the plateau in the form of thirty-two

small cut-glass bowls fitted with pegs that could be inserted into the wreaths held by the female figures on the plateau. Two larger compote bowls with identical cutting in a Moorish arch pattern, also with plugs on their bottoms, were acquired at the same time. "Artificial Flowers & Fruits" completed the new plateau decorations.[30] A few years later, a guest at one of President James Buchanan's dinners noted that the "small crystal dishes" on the plateau were used to hold "bonbons and cakes."[31] In order to accommodate the fashion for extravagant fresh flower displays on the table, First Lady Julia Grant had wire and mesh arches built for the plateau that could be decorated with greenery and support additional flower baskets.[32]

During the third quarter of the nineteenth century, the significance of the President's House plateau shifted from fashionable ornament to historic relic. With the exception of the Stuart portrait of George Washington, the furnishings purchased by Monroe in 1817 for the White House were the longest serving, and thus the most historic. The practice during the nineteenth century of auctioning off undesired or damaged furnishings from the President's House had led to the removal of many of Monroe's purchases. The expensive but sturdy suite of French furniture that Monroe had been sent for the primary drawing room (now the Blue Room) was finally replaced in 1859, and sold soon after, leaving the more durable metal objects, such as clocks and the plateau, to represent Monroe's French purchases. The French furnishings had received so much press through the years that visitors to the President's House often spoke of seeking these items out to judge their reported extravagance for themselves. Thus, after attending dinner at the President's House in 1841, William Greene reported inaccurately to his daughter that "the gold Plateau and spoons which you have heard so much about made their appearance and are simply *silver*, gold washed."[33] Visitors expecting to see the plateau at important dinners at the President's House probably helped perpetuate its use at such events, which in turn contributed to its historic significance for being used at such a large number of these dinners.

The earliest known images of the plateau in use date from President Ulysses Grant's administration. The March 12, 1870, issue of *Harper's Weekly* included a wood engraved print after Theodore Russell Davis depicting a State Dinner at the White House. Although

Stereoview of the State Dining Room during Benjamin Harrison's administration showing the plateau on display. The Hiawatha Boat centerpiece purchased for the White House by First Lady Julia Grant is at the center of the plateau.

barely visible, all seven sections of the plateau appear to be in use in this image, as it is shown supporting seven bouquets of fresh or artificial flowers down its center. The large glass compote bowls purchased in the Pierce administration are clearly visible atop a pair of gilded French candlesticks believed to have been acquired at the same time as the plateau.[34] The bowls are filled with large fruit and floral displays. Julia Grant's floral arch addition is seen in a wood engraving of the March 9, 1871, State Dinner for the Joint High Commissioners, which appeared in *Frank Leslie's Illustrated Newspaper* on April 1. The plateau's original female figures stand on the plinths with each arm supporting either one of the small glass bowls from 1853 or a section of one of the three decorated arches that soar above the plateau, topped with an additional floral display. A tall candelabrum, also adorned with flowers, stands at the center of the plateau. One of the Three Graces baskets appears

at the very far end of the table near the mantel. The pair of gilded French candelabra supplied by Russell & La Farge for the Sitting Room (Red Room) in 1817 can be identified on either end of the table just outside the plateau.[35] Although the width and probably the length of the plateau are greatly exaggerated in the drawing, the image conveys how the plateau dominated the dinner table when in use.

The plateau's growing history along with the demand for inventive table decorations inspired a number of presidential families to make their own contributions to the plateau ensemble. The glass bowls for the plateau purchased by President Pierce proved to be very popular and were used often. First Lady Julia Grant selected a silver centerpiece representing Hiawatha's boat that was displayed at the 1876 Centennial Exposition in Philadelphia.[36] Although the high-masted canoe was already mounted on a silver plateau with a

A State Dinner during the administration of President Herbert Hoover for Pierre Lavalle, prime minister of France, 1931. The plateau is seen at the far right of the table with its center filled with floral arrangements.

mirrored surface representing the water on which the canoe floated, later this centerpiece was frequently placed on top of the Monroe plateau. This arrangement can be seen in late nineteenth-century photographs of the State Dining Room when the room was not in use. First Lady Lucy Hayes purchased two pairs of gilded brass candelabra from Tiffany and Company in 1880 for the State Dining Room.[37] With their classical motifs, the candelabra were immediately put into use with the 1817 plateau and accessories. These candelabra became so quickly associated with the Monroe pieces that throughout much of the twentieth century, White House staff did not recognize that the candelabra were a later addition.

The plateau accommodated the growing taste for elaborate displays of fresh flowers in the late nineteenth century by serving as a base and support structure for the flowers. Flowers were used so abundantly as table decorations during this era that it can be difficult to

determine from images of events at the President's House whether the plateau is beneath all the floral displays. Visitor accounts confirm that it usually was there. A guest at President Chester A. Arthur's cabinet dinner in January 1884 noted:

> The table decorations were more unique than is usual on State occasions, a large centre-piece, called the "Swinging Garden of Babylon" being entirely new. This was about four feet long and one and half feet high, and was composed of red and white carnations, honeysuckles, Marechal Niel and other roses, massed in separate colors. The piece was more suggestive of a temple than a garden and on the top were clusters of rare and curious blossoms of the nun-plant. It rested on a long mirror, and at the ends were stands of Marechal Niel and Jacqueminot roses. Beyond these were circular

pieces of mixed flowers and baskets of lilies of the valley and roses.[38]

President Arthur took a special interest in White House entertaining and reportedly personally oversaw the decoration of the plateau at State Dinners. Like President Pierce, he invested in having the plateau repaired and regilded early in his administration so it would look its best at his dinners.[39]

In 1902, President Theodore Roosevelt oversaw a complete renovation of the White House, which included expanding the State Dining Room. All of the room's former decor was replaced, with the exception of the Monroe plateau and its accessories.[40] Although the annual inventories of White House furnishings list the plateau as being located in the State Dining Room during the administrations of Theodore Roosevelt and William Taft, photographs of the room during this time do not show it. It therefore does not appear that it was kept on display when it was not in use, as had been the tradition in the late nineteenth century. The new English baronial State Dining Room furnishings may have contributed to the arrangement. Although a long rectangular table was initially provided for the room, the Roosevelts desired a smaller table for daily use and thereafter used a small round table or one of two small square tables that had been created from the original long table. The gilded plateau set may have also seemed incompatible for daily display with the new silver-plated chandelier and sconces supplied for the room by Edward F. Caldwell & Co.

The tradition of using the plateau on the State Dining Room table for important meals, however, remained uninterrupted. In her memoirs, First Lady Helen Taft recalled using the "massive silver-gilt ornaments which President Monroe imported from France" when entertaining large groups. She went on to describe the plateau:

> Based on oblong plate glass mirrors, each about three feet in length, they stretch down the middle of the table, end to end, a perfect riot of festooned railings and graceful figures upholding crystal vases. Then there are large gilded candelabra [probably the Tiffany candelabra added by Mrs. Hayes], centre vases and fruit dishes to match. In their way they are exceedingly handsome, and they certainly are appropriate to the ceremony with

which a state dinner at the White House is usually conducted.[41]

A photograph of the State Dining Room set for one of the diplomatic receptions during the Taft administration shows the plateau at the center of a large crescent-shaped table. The plateau was decorated with large floral displays, and the Monroe stands and the Three Graces baskets were filled with fruit and placed at even intervals around the table. The four candelabra purchased by Mrs. Hayes were also distributed around the large table.

After the Taft administration, the plateau was kept in storage except when it was being used for formal entertaining, but the tradition of using the plateau remained strong for the next several decades. First ladies and their staff expressed their creativity through floral arrangements and sometimes in table configurations at formal events, but the use of the Monroe pieces remained a constant. Henrietta Nesbitt, housekeeper during the twelve years of the Franklin Roosevelt administration, expressed the sense of inevitability that the plateau had achieved by the time of her tenure when she recalled, "The centerpiece for the family was always a bowl of flowers. A big silver ship [the Hiawatha boat] in full sail was for teas. But for the formal affairs we used the Monroe gold service."[42]

Because the plateau was used so consistently for formal events, it often inspired first ladies' decisions on other formal tableware. First Lady Florence Harding commissioned a service of gold flatware to complement the plateau by gold plating some existing sterling silver cutlery and supplementing with newly purchased pieces. Head housekeeper Elizabeth Jaffray recalled using the new gold flatware service with the plateau assemblage (which she incorrectly refers to as the "Dolly [sic] Madison service"):

> During the social season of 1922–1923, which was the last one during the Hardings' time, I hit upon the idea of using this Dolly [sic] Madison service with the Wilson china and the gold knives, forks and spoons of the Hardings. I would have the bowls filled with fruit, with ripe Malaga grapes hanging over the sides. The candles in the gold candlesticks would be lighted, and with the gold knives and forks, and the exquisite cream and gold Wilson china, it really made as beautiful a table as

State Dining Room with three sections of the plateau on head table and small banquet tables, during the John F. Kennedy administration. Selections from the White House vermeil collection, acquired in 1958, ornament the plateau.

anyone could wish to see. I know that foreign diplomats, attending the great diplomatic dinners at the White House, were overwhelmed by the beauty of this great dining-room table.[43]

Mrs. Harding's gilded flatware in turn inspired Mamie Eisenhower to choose a heavily gilded pattern for the formal service plates that she ordered in 1955.[44] Mrs. Eisenhower also accepted a large bequest of gilded silver (vermeil) for the White House collection and promptly incorporated many of the pieces into the formal table setting with the Monroe service. Vermeil tureens or wine coolers were frequently used thereafter to hold flowers on the plateau. Jacqueline Kennedy was so enamored with the gilded Monroe tableware that she was working on designing a new state porcelain service to complement them when her husband's administration ended prematurely. When Lady Bird Johnson solicited Mrs. Kennedy's advice in 1966 on White House furnishings, the latter advocated completing her plan to acquire a new state porcelain service, suggesting "an Empire design that would go with all the magnificent Monroe gilt centerpieces."[45]

Jacqueline Kennedy's interest in the historic furnishings of the White House and subsequent campaign to furnish all of the White House interiors in the style of the early occupancy resulted in a new appreciation for the plateau ensemble. Mrs. Kennedy highlighted the plateau's importance by deciding to display it prominently on the State Dining Room table for public tour visitors to admire. Her decision to redecorate the State Dining Room in a gold and white color scheme appears to have literally revolved around the gilded centerpiece. She had the existing 1902 silver-plated chandelier and sconces in the room gilded to match the plateau. Mrs. Kennedy introduced many changes to formal dining practices at the White House, but she continued to use the plateau and its accessories. She experimented with table arrangements, creating one large rectangular table with an opening on one side to allow access and with the plateau on the longest side opposite the opening. Mrs. Kennedy finally settled on using a number of small, round banquet tables in conjunction with one long head table for the president, first lady, and other prominent guests for formal dinners. To suit the shorter length of this head table, fewer sections of the plateau were used. Since more guests could be accommodated in the State Dining Room at the small round tables than at any of the large table formations, presidents following Kennedy began to use this arrangement with greater frequency, eventually eliminating even the head table to make more room. The plateau is rarely used for formal

Three sections of the plateau in use at a lunch for Baudouin, King of the Belgians, held in the East Room April 22, 1980.

dining anymore, but sections continue to be displayed on the State Dining Room table when the room is not in use, allowing millions of White House visitors to admire it in the last forty years.

Almost two hundred years ago, President Monroe's purchasing agent, William Lee, justified to Congress the expense of the plateau and the other French purchases by arguing "that the articles are of the very first quality, and so substantial that some of them will last and be handsome for 20 years or more." He went on to express his philosophy that "in furnishing a government house, care should be taken to purchase substantial heavy furniture, which should always remain in its place and form as it were a part of the house, such as could be handed down through a succession of Presidents, suited to the dignity and character of the nation."[46]

Lee and Monroe have certainly been vindicated by history, as the once-controversial French furnishings are now among the most highly treasured objects in the White House collection. If they had not sought out such exceptional craftsmanship, the furnishings they selected would have never survived the strenuous schedule of White House entertaining to attain their status today.

The mirror glass in the plateau has been replaced often, and regilding has been necessary in certain sections, but on the whole, the plateau has survived in remarkable condition.[47] Five sections of the plateau and the Three Graces baskets filled with fresh floral displays still impress visitors today on the State Dining Room table, serving as a tangible link to the United States' earliest presidents and their efforts to secure the respect that allowed the young country to flourish.

NOTES

1. For examples of furnishings purchased abroad by the Monroes, see Lee Langston-Harrison, *A Presidential Legacy: The Monroe Collection* (Fredericksburg, Va.: James Monroe Museum, 1997).

2. Amelia Fearn, "From the Salt to the Centrepiece, 1580–1780" and "Serving Sweetmeats," and Hilary Young, "Sculpture for the Dessert, 1680–1910," in *Elegant Eating: Four Hundred Years of Dining in Style*, ed. Philippa Glanville and Hilary Young (London: V&A Publications, 2002), 64–67, 82–85, 92–95.

3. Six sections of Washington's plateau survive: five are in the collection of Mount Vernon, and one is in the collection of the National Museum of American History. For more on Washington's plateau, see Carol Borchert Cadou, *The George Washington Collection: Fine and Decorative Arts at Mount Vernon* (Manchester, Vt.: Hudson Hills Press, 2006), 129 and cat. 38; Susan Gray Detweiler, *George Washington's Chinaware* (New York: Harry N. Abrams, 1982), 107–18; Kathryn C. Buhler, *Mount Vernon Silver* (Mount Vernon, Va.: Mount Vernon Ladies' Association of the Union, 1957), 49–56.

4. Susan R. Stein, *The Worlds of Thomas Jefferson at Monticello* (New York: Harry N. Abrams, 1993), 26, 86.

5. Inventory of the President's House, February 19, 1809, Thomas Jefferson Papers, Library of Congress, Washington, D.C.

6. Quoted in Conover Hunt-Jones, *Dolley and the "great little Madison"* (Washington, D.C.: American Institute of Architects Foundation, 1977), 40. Hunt-Jones argues that the plateau must have belonged personally to the Madisons since there is no record that a plateau was purchased during their administration and because no plateau is listed in the inventories of White House furnishings taken during the Adams or the Jefferson administrations. Since the last assertion is incorrect, the noted plateau may have been public rather than private property.

7. Mecury gilding, also known as fire gilding, involved coating an object with an amalgam of gold and mercury and then heating it until the mercury evaporated. Mercury gilding is no longer practiced in the West because of the harmful effects to craftsmen.

8. A wide variety of terms have been used historically to describe this form of table centerpiece, including plateau, *surtout de table, plat de ménage, table-centre, epergne,* and dessert. In the period, Americans tended to use the term "plateau," and thus this is the term I use.

9. Russell & LaFarge c. September 15, 1817, to James Monroe, National Archives, House of Representatives, Record Group 233, House Report 79, 262.

10. The White House plateau is very similar to a marked Thomire plateau that belonged to Napoleon's brother, Prince Lucien. See Madeline Deschamps, *Empire* (New York: Abbeville Press, 1994), 169.

11. Ibid., 96.

12. Russell & LaFarge, Bill for 41 Assorted Packages," September 15, 1817, National Archives, Miscellaneous Treasury Accounts of the General Accounting Office, 1790–1894, Record Group 217, Account 37131, voucher 3. Original in French, English translation by the State Department.

13. Ibid.

14. Catalog entry for lot 121, Christie's sale 9656, May 24, 2001. The original stand is now in the Museo Archeologico in Naples, Italy. English designer Thomas Hope appears to have used the same stand as inspiration for the supports on both a large stand and a table included in his 1807 book, *Household Furniture and Interior Decoration* (repr., New York: Dover, 1971), pl. XI, no. 5., and pl. XXV, no. 2.

15. The rarity of plateaus in America is also demonstrated by the fact that there are only three known examples made by American silversmiths: two by New York silversmith John W. Forbes (one in the White House collection, 1962.267.1, and a similar but smaller example at the Metropolitan Museum of Art, 1993.167) and a one-piece example by New York silversmith Benjamin Halsted. Louise Conway Belden, *The Festive Tradition: Table Decoration and Desserts in America, 1650–1900* (New York: W. W. Norton & Company, 1983), 63.

16. Thomas Hill Hubbard to Phebe Hubbard, February 21, 1818, copy, Office of the Curator, The White House.

17. I am indebted to English scholar Lisa White's lectures on historic lighting for understanding the important difference in the way objects are seen today and how they were seen in their period. See also Elisabeth Donaghy Garrett, *At Home: The American Family, 1750–1870* (New York: Harry N. Abrams, 1990), 93–94, 140–62.

18. Pennsylvania Congressman Charles Ogle's famous "Gold Spoon Oration," delivered in 1840 to denounce the extravagant lifestyle led by President Martin Van Buren, criticized the plateau's cost and extravagance. See *White House History*, no. 10 (Winter 2002), dedicated to Ogle's speech.

19. "To Corn-Planter" and "For the Gazette," *Washington Gazette*, May 28, 1818, 3.

20. George Washington to James Madison, March 30, 1789, *The Papers of George Washington, Presidential Series.* (Charlottesville: University of Virginia Press, 1987) 1:464.

21. Samuel F. B. Morse, journal entry for December 17, 1819. *Samuel F. B. Morse: His Letters and Journals*, ed. Edward Lind Morse (New York: Kennedy Galleries, 1973), 1:227.

22. John Taylor to John H. Bernard, January 5, 1823, Robb-Bernard Papers, Special Collections Research Center, Earl Gregg Swem Library, College of William and Mary, Williamsburg, Va.

23. William Faux, *Memorable Days in America: Being a Journal of a Tour to the United States* (London: printed for W. Simpkin and R. Marshall, 1823), 443.

24. Russell & La Farge, Contents of the 41 Packages, c. September 15, 1817.

25. Rosalie Stier Calvert to Henri Joseph Stier, March 13, 1819, *Mistress of Riversdale: The Plantation Letters of Rosalie Stier Calvert, 1795–1821*, ed. Margaret Law Callcott (Baltimore: Johns Hopkins University Press, 1991), 343–44; Samuel Breck, December 30, 1823, in "Broken Journal of a Session Δ20of Congress," 18th Cong., Historical Society of Pennsylvania, Philadelphia; William Preston to Susan Marshall Preston, December 28, 1839, Preston Family Papers, Davie Collection, Filson Club, Louisville, Ky.

26. Belden, *Festive Tradition*, 79; Jim Cheshire, "Flowers and Garlands," in *Elegant Eating*, ed. Glanville and Young, 58.

27. Unidentified visitor, 1850, quoted in Dare Stark McMullin with Lou Henry Hoover, untitled study of White House furnishings, 1932, 68, Lou Henry Hoover Papers, Herbert Hoover Presidential Library, West Branch, Iowa.

28. William Seale, *The President's House: A History* (Washington, D.C.: White House Historical Association, with the Cooperation of the National Geographic Society, 1986), 1:310–13.

29. Bailey & Co. began in 1832 as Bailey & Kitchen, and changed its name to Bailey & Co. in 1846. In 1878, the company became Bailey, Banks, & Biddle Co., and as such remains in business today. Dorothy T. Rainwater, *Encyclopedia of American Silver Manufacturers* (New York: Crown Publishers, 1975), 16–17.

30. All thirty-two of the small cut-glass bowls and the two larger bowls remain in the White House collection. National Archives, Miscellaneous Treasury Accounts, Record Group 217, account 113810, voucher 3.

31. Sara Agnes Rice Pryor, *Reminiscences of Peace and War* (New York, Macmillan, 1904), 51, quoted in Jane Shadel Spillman, *White House Glassware: Two Centuries of Presidential Entertaining* (Washington, D.C., White House Historical Association, 1989), 62.

32. Seale, *The President's House,* 1:466.

33. William Greene to Catherine Ray Greene (Roelker), March 9, 1841, Greene-Roelker Papers, Cincinnati Historical Society Library, Cincinnati Museum Center, quoted in Belden, *Festive Tradition*, 64.

34. See Betty C. Monkman, *The White House: Its Historic Furnishings and First Families* (Washington, D.C.: White House Historical Association, 2000), 58, 283.

35. Ibid., 64, 284.

36. Ibid., 151–53, 293.

37. Ibid. 156, 294.

38. Quoted in McMullin and Hoover, untitled study, 39.

39. William Friederich of Washington, D.C., was paid $75 in November 1881 "for repairing, soldering and gilding parts of frames of seven mirrors being part of centerpiece of State Dining Table" and $20 "for furnishing 2 plate glass mirrors for centerpieces of State Dining Room." National Archives, Office of Public Buildings and Grounds, Record Group 42, Accounts, voucher 31, 4th quarter, 1881.

40. John Pearce, "The 1817 Catalogue Drawing of the White House Plateau," *Connoisseur*, August 1971, 285.

41. Mrs. William Howard [Helen] Taft, *Recollections of Full Years* (New York: Dodd, Mead & Company, 1914), 357, 358.

42. Henrietta Nesbitt, *White House Diary* (Garden City, N.Y.: Doubleday, 1948), 114.

43. Elizabeth Jaffray, *Secrets of the White House* (New York: Cosmopolitan Book Corporation, 1927), 111–12. The plateau was commonly believed during this time period to have been bought by Dolley Madison, so Jaffray was not alone in this belief.

44. See Margaret Brown Klapthor, *Official White House China: 1789 to the Present*, 2nd ed. (New York: Harry N. Abrams, 1999), 169–71.

45. Quoted in ibid., 171.

46. "Statement of William Lee, Esquire, Agent for procuring furniture for President's House," March 9, 1818, *House Report* 143 (Washington, D.C.: E. De Krafft, 1818), 4, 5.

47. Examination of the plateau by a conservator in 1990 revealed that the plateau's female figures retain large portions of original or early mercury gilding, but the base and galleries were electroplated with 24K gold at some point. This treatment may have happened during the Franklin Roosevelt administration, as housekeeper Henrietta Nesbitt records having had the plateau "redipped." Nesbitt, *White House Diary*, 115.

Flowers on the President's Table
State Dining Room Splendor

NANCY CLARKE

Stepping into the State Dining Room of the White House minutes before the guests enter on the evening of a State Dinner is a magical experience. Thirteen tables are set with glistening crystal, presidential china, and beautiful centerpieces on elegant tablecloths. On either side of the portrait of President Abraham Lincoln, abundant fresh flowers spill from the slender vermeil vases on the mantel. A large floral arrangement in a historic gold container is reflected in the gilded mirror above the eagle pier table. The television light towers and cameras are in position, ready to illuminate the entire room. The air is charged with a sense of excitement as the butlers fill the stemware with wine and chilled water. There are low whispers among the staff reviewing the order of events. The ambience in the room softens when the candlelight rises and the lights are dimmed. The evening is about to unfold as everyone moves into place. The chief usher, dressed in his crisp black tuxedo, slides open the double pocket doors of the State Dining Room, and the honored guests enter the room to share a magnificent dinner with the president and first lady.

Floral arrangements placed in the State Dining Room on the mantel and tables prior to a dinner in April 1992 include peach peonies, peach tulips, and pink delphiniums.

All photographs in this article are White House photos courtesy of the author, unless otherwise noted.

The State Dining Room is host to events every day, ranging from formal State Dinners, breakfasts, luncheons, private dinners, and receptions to coffees and afternoon teas. Depending on the occasion, each event has its own feel or theme that is designed into every aspect, from the type of food served to the flower arrangements. The many factors that influence the selection of flowers include the season of the year, the type of event, and the decorative elements of the State Dining Room, such as the subtle stone gray-colored walls and ceiling and the rich, warm tones in the carpet and draperies. Even the gilded chandelier and sconces with their red undertones influence the color ranges that work well in the room.

A mahogany table is centered in the room for the majority of breakfasts, receptions, coffees, teas, or any other event for which the guests are not seated at individual tables. Even this beautiful table with the rich auburn-colored wood influences the flower selections. The historic Monroe plateau with its lovely gilded bronze figures and mirrored base is usually the focal point on the White House table, as it has been for nearly two centuries. Centered on the mirrors of the plateau, three tall gilded bronze fruit baskets supported by female figures are the ideal containers for every style of floral display from very formal, precise arrangements of roses and orchids to loose-flowing casual styles of summer daisies and lilies with trails of ivy that cascade over the edges and flow gracefully down the sides.

The first lady's preferences, the guests who will

attend, the type of event, the seasons of the year, and the time of the day determine the style and colors of flower arrangements. In selecting flowers for a breakfast buffet for a children's organization, bright colorful shades of reds, oranges, and yellows arranged in a casual style are more appropriate than very formal arrangements of pastel shades and subtle textures. Casual style and bright colors are easily integrated into the color ranges used in the decorative appointments of the room. If the event is an evening black tie reception instead of a breakfast, more formal arrangements of flowers are preferred. Seasonal flowers such as roses, tulips, hydrangea, and often orchids of softer colors arranged in a reserved style are more appropriate.

The White House staff manages the president and first lady's calendar and schedules. Advanced planning varies: larger more formal events are often scheduled months in advance to give all parties ample time to plan; others may be set weeks or only days ahead of time. When an event appears on the schedule, the first lady's social secretary is notified. She then works closely with the usher's office, which is the operational center for the White House residence and the source of information for all the residence staff, to plan and coordinate the event.

An initial meeting is set up with the social secretary and the chief floral designer to determine specific requirements and to specify flowers for various locations. Several factors are taken into consideration during these preliminary discussions, always keeping in mind what the first lady may want.

Frequently, the first lady deals directly with the flower shop to discuss her preferences. She might explain the general "look" she would like for a function and sometimes indicates the specific flowers she prefers. These discussions with the first lady take place when planning any large events such as ladies' luncheons, special dinners, and, of course, formal events such as black-tie dinners or State Dinners.

A State Dinner is an official function given by the president and first lady for a head of state or government from another country. By tradition, each country may be honored with only one official State Dinner during an administration, so each aspect will be carefully orchestrated. The White House typically hosts several State Dinners a year. Costs for these are covered by the Department of State.

Once a State Dinner appears on the schedule, the State Department Office of Protocol provides information to the White House staff that is helpful in entertaining foreign guests, often in great detail. Food and flower restrictions might be specified, as in some countries certain flowers and colors are considered offensive in a centerpiece. For example, in Muslim and many Pacific Rim countries, the color white is reserved for funerals. In many of the Central and South American countries, the same is true of the color yellow. Sometimes it is the type of flower that must be avoided; in some countries and regions, lilies, mums, or carnations are used only for funerals. The State Department also provides information on the personal preferences or allergies of guests. All of this information is sent to the East Wing social office and then to the usher's office, which in turn gives it to all Residence staff department supervisors. A State Dinner requires extensive planning by everyone from the housekeepers to the chefs, and of course the floral designers.

Conversations about the "look" of the floral designs with the first lady and her staff begin in the earliest stages of planning a State Dinner. Occasionally, the first lady has a particular gown she would like to wear and the "look" for the evening will be designed to coordinate with her dress. Additional dialogue includes questions like: What did we use the last time the country visited? What containers are available based on the number of tables we plan to have? Do we have enough of the gilded silver candelabra or containers? Other considerations, such as the season or preferences of the visiting head of state, help determine the general mood and feel of the event. Should it be a light, summery look, with garden flowers, or a rich autumn feeling of fruits and rust-colored roses? Light-colored tablecloths or dark colored tablecloths? Many options for centerpieces, tablecloths, china, crystal, and candlesticks must be considered.

Once the overall look for a State Dinner has been thoroughly discussed and agreed upon, the local wholesale floral suppliers are contacted to be sure the desired flowers will be available for that particular date. A few weeks before the dinner, a sample order of the flowers arrives. It is checked for quality and color and then conditioned or prepared to be used and last as long as necessary in a vase. The flower shop designers make up several sample centerpiece options for the first lady and

Right: Nancy Clarke at work in the flower shop arranging ambrosia roses, 2000.

Sample arrangements are often prepared during the planning for an event. Below left: A sample arrangement made prior to a State Dinner for Singapore in October 1985 includes white orchids, cream fuchsia, and lemons. Below right: A sample made in 1990 includes white freesia, pink gerber daisies, lavender asters, and pink roses.

Unique arrangements are made for each State Dinner and for other special events held in the State Dining Room. Clockwise from top left: An arrangement of branches of ivy, red tulips, and pink carnations; a centerpiece of white lilies and pink nerines; and arrangements of white amaryllis with white french tulips.

Opposite, clockwise from top left: arrangements of white gerber daisies and white lilies; cream, white, and peach roses; and assorted tulips.

Above: The State Dining Room prior to an event in July 1994. Opposite: Arrangements of orange floribunda roses, movie star roses, orange unique roses, and apache roses were created for a dinner for France in November 2007.

the social secretary to review. Once the samples are approved, time is scheduled to view sample setups with the first lady. For these sessions, three or four different tables are set in the State Dining Room, complete with china, tablecloths, glassware, and candles. These sample choices can range from glass vases filled with vibrantly colored anemones, to historical candelabra filled with cascading roses, to vermeil containers from the White House collection overflowing with fresh seasonal fruits and amaryllis blooms. These trial viewings create a preview of the event in the actual room where it will take place.

The first lady sometimes rearranges flowers within the centerpiece, removing flowers or asking to add specific colors to give it her personal touch. She may move the centerpiece from one brightly colored tablecloth to a softer, pastel one or change the china or stemware, or rearrange the candlesticks. When she is satisfied that we have achieved what she wishes to portray, the final selection is made of the flowers and plant material that

will be used throughout the rest of the White House.

The sample is refrigerated and kept as a reference for the dinner and also as a guide for ordering the actual flowers for the dinner. Local floral wholesalers are asked to place the final flower orders immediately so the best growers for those particular flowers can be found. Caterers are asked to provide the tablecloths if the White House does not already own the style that the first lady wants. Because of the scale and preparations required for a State Dinner, part-time service staff are also scheduled at this time.

The week before the State Dinner, the activity level increases throughout all departments of the White House as well as in the flower shop. The part-time workers begin reporting to help with the early preparations. Flower orders begin to arrive on different days, allowing each flower to be processed individually so it will reach its peak on the day of the dinner. Stems are cut and placed in fresh water; some flowers are refrigerated, while others may be left out to quickly open. The

Special arrangements are placed in rooms other than the State Dining Room that are open to guests during dinners and special events. Opposite, clockwise from top left: a seasonal arrangement of yellow snapdragons, gerber daisies, roses, and lilies on the East Room mantel in October 1987; an arrangement of pink lilies and pink larkspur in the Red Room in September 1991; and white peonies, calla lilies, and snapdragons in the Blue Room in 1988.

Floral arrangements often incorporate objects related to the event. Above: Needlepoint animals were used in arrangements made for a luncheon for governors' spouses in spring of 1992. They included white lilies, pink September asters, and pink nerines. Right: A ceramic figure was used in November 1989 with an arrangement of Queen Anne's lace, pink nerines, and pink floribunda roses.

White House butlers prepare tables set with the Reagan china service prior to an event held in April 1985. Dogwood adorns the Monroe plateau.

A U-shaped table set for a NATO Summit dinner in April 1999 in the East Room is decorated with white hydrangea, white dendrobiums, gardenias, green grapes, white roses, smilax, and maiden hair ferns.

containers are polished and liners are filled with floral foam, which is then covered with a thin layer of natural moss. Candles are prepared, and the tablecloths arrive. The members of the flower shop staff finalize the appropriate timing for the placement of the various flower arrangements and assign individual responsibilities on the day of the dinner.

The day before the State Dinner, floral designers arrange the conditioned flowers and then place the coordinating arrangements in each room of the White House. The National Park Service brings in elegant plants carefully maintained in its greenhouses to place in predetermined locations. All the rooms on the State Floor except the State Dining Room, which remains closed until the dinner, are filled with lush bouquets and plant material. By the following morning, the state rooms of the White House are ready. The formal reception of the guest of state takes place outside at about 10:00 a.m., after which the first lady serves tea in one of the state parlors.

For the State Dinner all of the carefully laid plans come to life. The entire staff of the White House as well as the flower shop designers busily prepare for the event. Exact replicas of the sample centerpiece are created for each table. The coordinating flowers for the mantel and pier table in the State Dining Room are fashioned and put in place. Television crews position lights in preparation for the broadcast of the president's and foreign head of state's toasts during the dinner. Silver and china are brought out from storage. The butlers polish the flatware and candlesticks, wipe down each plate, and clean each piece of glassware. The tablecloths are put in place for the housekeeping staff to carefully press. The butlers place the china and stemware on the tables. Then the flower shop staff positions the centerpieces and arranges the candlesticks or votive candles on each table. Once the butlers have completely set the tables, an inspection of each centerpiece follows and the stage is judged set and ready for the performance to come.

Meanwhile, the first lady's staff and often the first lady herself walk through to make last-minute adjustments before the afternoon press preview. The press preview is an opportunity for members of the media to photograph the State Dining Room and to interview members of the White House staff about what the evening's decor will be like. Following the press preview, the centerpieces are photographed for future reference.

Approximately an hour before the guests are scheduled to arrive, every detail has been attended to and every effort has made by the staff to guarantee that the foreign dignitaries and other guests have a memorable evening. An ending has come to the months of planning and coordination involving so many people. The butlers now slip away to put on their tuxedo jackets and straighten their ties, while the housekeeping staff do a last check to make certain every piece of furniture is dusted and gleaming. The stemware and gold-banded china on the tables in the State Dining Room sparkles. Flower arrangements are checked again for the final time. The red carpet is in place, and the North Portico doors stand open as the bright spotlights shining against the White House cast reflections across the polished marble floors. The White House is truly never more magnificent than at this moment.

Smilax

Tuberose

Fern

Orange Blossoms

Tea Rosebud

Spiraea

Rose

Lilies of the Valley

Miniature Oranges

Margaret Huddy AWS, NWS

White House Brides and Envisioned Flowers:
Two Nineteenth-Century White House Weddings

ILLUSTRATIONS BY MARGARET HUDDY

*T*he first really grand White House wedding was Nellie Grant's. For this President and Mrs. Ulysses S. Grant had the East Room redecorated entirely, adding to James Hoban's original architectural detailing matching columns and extending the cornice into beams, all gleaming white, with accents in gold leaf. Andrew Jackson's three chandeliers were replaced by much grander "French" models, boasting thousands of glass pieces showered over a nickel-plated framework, with gas flames shaded by cut and frosted glass shades.

Like all great events, this one had its problems and tensions. The president and his wife were hesitant about the upcoming marriage, Nellie being only nineteen, headstrong and spoiled, and the prospective groom, Algernon Sartoris, perhaps less than an ideal son-in-law. Being English, he would take Nellie far away; he was a bit idle and for all his good breeding, somewhat inclined, they feared, toward the stage. The White House had been in mourning in the spring for Millard Fillmore. The death of a president called for thirty days of official mourning. Where at most locations, flags at half staff was sufficient, at the White House chandeliers and mirrors had to be draped in black crape, with crape on the

front door and around the windows. This was torn away as soon as possible so that the various decorating establishments could return and complete their work for Nellie.

By May 21, 1874, the house was put in final preparation. In the upstairs rooms the presents were displayed

This recent watercolor by artist Margaret Huddy captures the variety of flowers used in the decorations and bouquets for first daughter Nellie Grant's White House wedding in 1874. Right: The menu from the wedding reception.

Nellie Grant, c. 1874, at the time of her White House wedding at age nineteen to Englishman Algernon Sartoris.

Frances Folsom on the day of her marriage to President Grover Cleveland in 1886.

(according to the stores where they were bought), the state parlors were set up for light breakfast, and the State Dining Room fixed for a seated breakfast, the table massed with pink and white roses and azaleas. In the East Room a platform was built before the broad east window, over which the curtains were shut. A bell made of pink roses was suspended above, and along the walls palms and arrangements of roses stood in lines. In recalling the decorations, one of the doormen, Tommy Pendel, was not specific about flowers but captured the scene: "There was a beautiful marriage bell suspended over her [the bride's] head. The four large columns supporting the girders were all entwined with the beautiful national colors. Palms and other plants were artistically placed around the room, the windows were closed and the room brilliantly lighted. The effect was beautiful in the extreme."

White orchids and orange blossoms from the conservatory formed a crown to hold Nellie's rose-point lace veil. The wedding dress itself was white satin, falling into a six-foot train. The bride carried a bouquet of roses fixed to a pearl fan, a gift from her parents. The groom gave her a bouquet of rare flowers, of what sort unrecorded, but a point was made that they came from Manhattan's finest florist. Army and navy officers in dress uniforms stood at attention in a double row down the Cross Hall to the East Room altar. Nellie and her eight bridesmaids all in white, descended the Grand Staircase. Two hundred and fifty guests witnessed the spectacle, which for many years would be remembered as the most elaborate occasion at the White House.

Yet a mere twelve years later floral art reached another high point in the decorations for the marriage of President Grover Cleveland to Frances Folsom on June 2, 1886. The bride was not yet 22, and the groom 49. For a year the romance of the president and his former ward, the daughter of his late business partner, had captivated the American public. Frances Folsom, known popularly as "Frankie," had become the first celebrity first lady overnight. To the president's great disapproval, she was a staple feature on the front pages of every major paper in the United States.

When the fifty wedding invitations went out, two weeks before the event, they bore the full names of both the president and his bride. The floral decorations did not suggest so small an event. It might be assumed that Frances Cleveland's mother Mrs. Oscar Folsom and the

A modern watercolor depiction of the colorful flowers used to decorate the White House for President Grover Cleveland's wedding to Frances Folsom in 1886.

president's sister Rose Cleveland ordered the decorations, but Cleveland himself kept a heavy thumb on all wedding plans and this president dearly loved the conservatories and their floral stock. The head gardener at the White House was Henry Pfister of Cincinnati, whom President Rutherford B. Hayes had appointed nearly a decade before and who had transformed the greenhouses from what one might find in a private house to a series of botanical conservatories filled with remarkable specimen plants and flowers. Cleveland had given him full support.

For the wedding the conservatories were literally extended into the State Rooms. The East Room was banked in palms, set in porcelain jardinières. It being summer, the fireplaces were closed and their hearths and mantels massed with flowers. In the Cross Hall the columns were entwined with garlands of greenery and smilax and adorned by large Union shields made of red, white, and blue roses, carnations, and immortelles. The Red and Green Rooms were similarly decorated, leaving just about enough room for guests, but the Blue Room, where the ceremony took place, had the most splendid flowers. The hearth blazed with red begonias symbolizing fire, with a border of centaureas to symbolize ashes; over the mantel a confection of pansies formed the initials "C" and "F." The gas chandelier was decorated with roses and smilax. Palms surrounded the walls.

The wedding supper was held seated, in the State Dining Room. On the white damask cover of the long table an ocean of flowers swelled up from the Monroe plateau and upon it, sheets to the wind, a floral ship, the *Hymen*, sailed toward Victorian bliss.

While the photographers and newspaper artists gave us fairly good records of this splendor, together with the documentary materials Henry Pfister preserved in the National Archives, one longs for color.

With this in mind, *White House History* brought a sheaf of the photographs and papers to me in my studio at the Torpedo Factory across the river in Alexandria and asked me to select flowers to paint from the pictures and records. The accompanying watercolors are the result.

WHITE HOUSE BRIDES

Left: This double portrait by artist Ralph Earl depicts two White House brides. Mary Eastin, left, was married to Lucius Polk in the White House in April 1832, and Mary Anne Lewis, right, married Alphonse Pageot in November of the same year.

Opposite: President Theodore Roosevelt's daughter Alice Roosevelt, on her wedding day in 1906.

John Adams, or at least his wife Abigail Adams, just may have been host to the first White House wedding. It is hinted in a letter from Mrs. Adams to her sister Mary from the White House, January 15, 1801, that her lady's maid, who was Betsy Howard, and Betsy's "lover," were married Sunday evening the week before, presumably at the White House.[2] Betsy Howard had been one of three who worked for Mrs. Adams at the President's House in Philadelphia. She was ill at one point, but did join the first lady in Washington. Abigail Adams spoke affectionately of Betsy in her letters.

James Monroe's daughter Maria Hester Monroe married her first cousin (nephew of her mother) Samuel L. Gouverneur on March 9, 1820, at the White House. There were forty-two guests, and Washington people not invited were vocal in their annoyance. The Monroes considered the marriage a private family affair. Sam Gouverneur was from New York and served as postmaster there, appointed through the intervention of President Monroe.

John Quincy Adams's second son John Adams II was married in the Blue Room on February 25, 1828, to Mary Catherine Hellen, one of three sisters who lived with the Adams family in the White House. The wedding took place only about ten days before the end of the Adams administration. Young Adams was not much like his scholarly, bookish relatives. He was expelled from Harvard for inciting a student riot and was skilled at fist fighting.

Andrew Jackson, on April 10, 1832, held a wedding for his niece Mary A. Estin, who married Lucius J. Polk in the East Room. Mary Ann Lewis, daughter of Jackson's aide Major William Lewis, married the French diplomat Alphonse Pageot, November 29, 1832, in the only Roman Catholic marriage ceremony ever held in the White House. The cabinet was in attendance.

John Tyler's daughter Elizabeth married at the White House on January 31, 1842, to William N. Waller, an old family friend from Williamsburg, Virginia. Tyler himself was married while president, following the

Two of President Woodrow Wilson's daughters married in the White House. In 1913 Jessie Wilson (above) married Francis B. Sayre, and in 1914 Eleanor (right) was married to William G. McAdoo, secretary of the treasury in Wilson's cabinet.

death of his wife, but his June 1844 wedding to Julia Gardiner took place in New York. The bride was 24 and the groom 54. Many in the public raised eyebrows not only for the age difference but also for the all-too-short mourning period that preceded the wedding, both for Tyler's first wife and for his new bride's father. David Gardiner, a former New York state senator, had been killed aboard the the US Navy's first screw-propelled steamer, USS *Princeton*, when a cannon breach burst while the gun was being demonstrated for President Tyler and his guests during a cruise on the Potomac.

Abraham Lincoln was credited with seeing to the marriage in the White House of a couple he did not know. The following story appears in a clipping from a newspaper published in 1906: One Mrs. James Chandler, Elizabeth, from Virginia, was 16 and her parents would not allow her to marry James. They got a Virginia license and fled to Washington, having been told that they might be married in a public building. They found their way to the White House, where Lincoln answered the door. They explained their wishes, and he took them to the East Room, which was decorated with flags, and summoned a Baptist preacher. There before President and Mrs. Lincoln and "some ladies," they were married. Then they were taken to the State Dining Room—"the longest table I ever saw"—and dined with a crowd. There were punch toasts; the Lincolns asked them to stay over, which they did, and

The wedding of Franklin D. Roosevelt's aide Harry Hopkins to Louise Macy was held upstairs at the White House, in 1942.

they went home to forgiving parents the next day with the news that they had been "married in the White House."

Ulysses S. Grant's only daughter Ellen ("Nellie") Grant married Algernon C. F. Sartoris, a wealthy Englishman. He was a singer and also a nephew of the controversial British actress Fanny Kemble. The Grants were not happy with the match but staged a lavish wedding on May 21, 1874. The couple moved to England and within a decade were separated but never divorced. She returned to the United States. He died in 1890 an alcoholic.

Rutherford B. Hayes held at the White House the marriage of his niece Emily Platt, age 28, to General Russell Hastings, a widower, aged 42, who had served under Hayes in the Civil War. She was the child of his late sister Fanny and had lived in the Hayes household most of her life, and the president considered her as a daughter. Hastings, an intimate of the president's, was also much like a family member. The marriage took place June 19, 1878, in the East Room beneath a giant bell made up by the gardener from 15,000 rosebuds.

Theodore Roosevelt's daughter Alice Lee married Nicholas Longworth of Cincinnati on February 17, 1906, in the White House. She was 22. The wedding was almost a national event, with crowds of thousands packed outside in the streets and Lafayette Park. The couple honeymooned in Europe, greeted as royalty.

Former White House bride Alice Roosevelt Longworth greets President Johnson's daughter Lynda and her new husband Charles Robb at their White House wedding in 1967.

Longworth became Speaker of the House. Alice lived well beyond his time into old age, one of the great characters of Washington.

Woodrow Wilson had two daughters marry in the White House—Jessie to Francis B. Sayre on November 25, 1913, and Eleanor ("Nell") on May 7, 1914, to William G. McAdoo, secretary of the treasury in Wilson's cabinet and a widower, much older. Eventually they divorced. The president himself, after his wife's death in 1914, married the widowed Edith Bolling Galt, but the wedding took place at Mrs. Galt's house, not at the White House.

Franklin D. Roosevelt's top aide Harry Hopkins married upstairs at the White House, July 30, 1942, to Louise Macy, former Paris editor of *Harper's Bazaar.* Hopkins, a widower, and Macy, who was divorced, moved to a house in Georgetown.

President Richard Nixon's daughter Tricia married in the Rose Garden of the White House in a televised ceremony on June 14, 1971.

Lyndon B. Johnson's eldest daughter Lynda Bird was married to Charles S. Robb at the White House on December 9, 1967, in the East Room. Robb was to become governor of Virginia and United States senator from Virginia.

Richard M. Nixon's daughter Patricia ("Tricia") married Edward F. Cox in a well-attended ceremony in the Rose Garden outside the Oval Office on June 12, 1971. Decorations were elaborate, recalling White House weddings of the nineteenth century.

"The Most Beautiful Things"
Gifts from France in the Roosevelt White House

AMY VERONE

Theodore Roosevelt's home at Sagamore Hill sits on top of a hill overlooking the Long Island Sound, nestled between properties once owned by his aunts, uncles, and cousins. Built in 1885, it was Roosevelt's home for thirty-four years, and his wife Edith's home for another twenty-nine years after his death in January 1919. The house is filled with an eclectic assortment of family furniture, gifts from heads of states, tag sales finds, books, hunting trophies, sculptures and paintings, souvenirs from their travels, and mementos of their family life. Many of these objects are well documented, and their history and significance to the Roosevelts are clear; but for other objects, their "backstories" have been lost or obscured by the passage of time. One of those mysteries concerns a group of ceramic figures of women dancing.

The six bisque figurines stand about 24 inches high and were designed by French sculptor Agathon Léonard. Léonard based his designs on the dances of Loie Fuller, an American-born proponent of modern dance. Fuller's dances emphasized natural and abstract movements and

A detail of one of the six Sèvres dancers now in the collection of Sagamore Hill, which were given to Edith Roosevelt by a French delegation attending the unveiling of the Rochambeau statue in Lafayette Park in 1902. President Theodore Roosevelt was photographed (above right) in the reviewing stand erected for the ceremony.

used colored lights, fabric, and other props to create unique effects and illusions. These characteristics are shown in the figures' flowing gowns and swaying postures, and in the torches, tambourines, and scarves they are holding.

The dancers were produced by the National Porcelain Factory of Sèvres and were available individually or as part of a set of fifteen figures intended for use as a table centerpiece. The "Scarf Dance" set was featured in the Sèvres exhibit at the Paris Exposition in 1900 and was both a critical and a commercial success. The French government presented the full set to Tsar Nicholas II during his visit to France in 1901. It is now part of the collections at the Hermitage in St. Petersburg.

Six bisque figurines designed by French sculptor Agathon Léonard produced by the Sèvres Porcelain Factory now in the collection of Sagamore Hill Historic Site, were used in the White House during the Theodore Roosevelt administration. Léonard based his designs on the modern dances of Loie Fuller. Born in Illinois in 1862, Fuller grew up performing in travelling shows, vaudeville, and the theatre before becoming interested in dance in the early 1890s. Inspired in part by sunlight shimmering on silk, Fuller realized that dance could be a free-flowing combination of light with movement. She developed a series of "serpentine" dances that copied the movements of flowers, butterflies, flowing water or flickering flames and used colored lights and the manipulation of scarves and props to enhance the emotional quality of the performance.

Lois Fuller depicted dancing in her signature full-length costume, c. 1898. Her dances are preserved in a film for which she performed.

The six figures at Sagamore Hill were apparently given to Edith Roosevelt by a French delegation that came to the United States for the dedication of the statue of the Count de Rochambeau in Lafayette Park in May 24, 1902. At the time, relations between France and the United States were strained due to the United States' recent war with Spain, a longtime ally of France. French envoy Jules Boeufve thought that the statue of the Count de Rochambeau, whose troops had supported George Washington's victory at Yorktown, would remind both countries of their historical friendship. The dedication ceremony included two thousand official guests and thousands of spectators, speeches by President Roosevelt and French Ambassador Jules Cambon, the presentation of a wreath from the Colonial Dames, and a parade after the official ceremony.[1]

Edith Roosevelt did not attend the dedication or the State Dinner that had been held on the evening of May 23, 1902. She was still recovering from an illness, possibly a miscarriage, which had kept her bedridden for almost two weeks. Newspaper accounts of the dinner noted her absence and that sixteen-year-old Alice stood in for her stepmother. At the dinner, Alice accepted a set of forty sketches and engravings of Paris as a gift for her mother from the French delegation.[2] Curiously, the news article makes no mention of the Sèvres figurines, and, to date, no references to the presentation of the figurines have been found in Edith Roosevelt's diaries or letters.

Although it is unclear when the figurines arrived at the White House, there is no question that they were used there. Captain Archie Butt referred to "the Sevres figures which the Rochambeau Commission brought from France and which are always used on the table at state dinners" in a letter to his sister-in-law in 1908.[3] In 1922, Edith Roosevelt described the statues to her daughter Ethel as part of a project to document the history of their household furnishings, confirming that they were a gift from the Rochambeau delegation and had been used as centerpieces in the White House.[4]

More curious is the question of why are there only six figurines. If the French government had given an entire set to the Russian tsar, wouldn't diplomatic protocol dictate that it give a full set to the American president? If a full set were presented, what happened to the other nine figurines?[5] There are no indications that Edith Roosevelt left any of the statues behind at the White House. Given her affection for them, it is doubtful that she would have given any of the statues away as gifts, although doing so was common practice for both her and her husband.

Regardless of when she received them, what is clear is that Edith Roosevelt was very fond of the figurines. In 1909, when an opposition newspaper implied that the Roosevelts were trying to take government property to Sagamore Hill, Edith angrily refused to take a small sofa that she had purchased for use in one of the sitting areas. (President William Howard Taft later paid to have a copy of the sofa made and sent her the original.)[6] But even in the midst of that outcry, she never considered leaving the figurines behind. She told Archie Butt that they had been given to her personally and that she had "the documents to prove it."[7] At Sagamore Hill, she displayed them prominently in the new North Room, where they still reside today.[8]

NOTES

The author thanks Barbara Nicolls, Charles Markis, Catherine Forslund, and William Seale for their assistance with this article.

1. "The unveiling of Rochambeau's Statue," *New York Times*, May 25, 1902.

2. "President Receives French Visitors," *New York Times*, May 23, 1902; Edith K. Roosevelt diary, Theodore Roosevelt Collection, Houghton Library, Harvard University, Cambridge, Mass.

3. Archie Butt to his sister-in-law Clara Butt, December 11, 1908, *The Letters of Archie Butt: Personal Aide to President Roosevelt*, ed. Lawrence Abbot (Garden City, N.Y.: Doubleday, Page & Company, 1924), p. 239.

4. David H. Wallace, *Sagamore Hill: Historic Furnishings Report*, vol. 1, *Historical Data* (Harpers Ferry, W. Va.: Harpers Ferry Center, National Park Service, U.S. Department of the Interior, 1989), 406.

5. A photograph taken in the White House about 1908 dimly shows the figures, perhaps in greater number, but this is not absolute. It is the only reason to think that Mrs. Roosevelt may have been presented with more than the present number. Future research will doubtless clarify this.

6. Sylvia Jukes Morris, *Edith Kermit Roosevelt: Portrait of a First Lady*, Coward, McCann & Geoghegan, Inc., New York, 1980, p. 337–38.

7. Quoted in ibid., 337.

8. Wallace, *Sagamore Hill*, 406.

WHITE HOUSE
HISTORY

White House Historical Association
Washington

LIFE IN THE LINCOLN WHITE HOUSE: PART ONE • NUMBER 24
PUBLISHED FALL 2008

Foreword

The year 2009 marks the bicentennial Abraham Lincoln's birth, which took place in Hardin County, Kentucky, on February 12, 1809, about a month before Thomas Jefferson surrendered the keys to the White House to James Madison. Fifty-two years later Abraham Lincoln would move to the same house—rebuilt after the War of 1812—as sixteenth president of the United States. The nation Jefferson and Madison had helped create was falling apart.

Although all the presidents except for George Washington had occupied the house prior to Lincoln and all would live there after him, it was Lincoln's tenancy of four years and a few days less than six weeks that fixed the White House immovably in the American imagination. In the President's House Lincoln administered and inspired the nation during the Civil War; but the White House has been the scene of many great events. More important for its own preservation through time, the White House was the stage of Lincoln's personal life, an unfolding melodrama that paralleled the experiences of loss and anguish suffered by Americans North and South. Thereafter an emotional knot bound the house to Americans' sensitivities. Otherwise, it is questionable whether the White House would have survived the years since.

This is the first of two issues of White House History commemorating Lincoln. We feature life in Lincoln's White House, meeting his son's tutor, exploring the music he loved, meeting some of his intimates, from the boyish, ill-starred Colonel Ellsworth, to the beautiful Kate Chase, to Laura Keene, the actress who held the dying president. We are lucky as historians that the camera was there and at work during Lincoln's time. An amazing portfolio of views of the White House while Lincoln lived there takes us beyond word descriptions to gain a more precise idea of the place as it actually was.

The White House, 1861, as it was when Lincoln moved in (detail of photo, page 31).

William Seale
Editor, *White House History*

nesses." Upon this, the miller began a discourse, which discovered such a vast penetration of judgment, such extensive knowledge

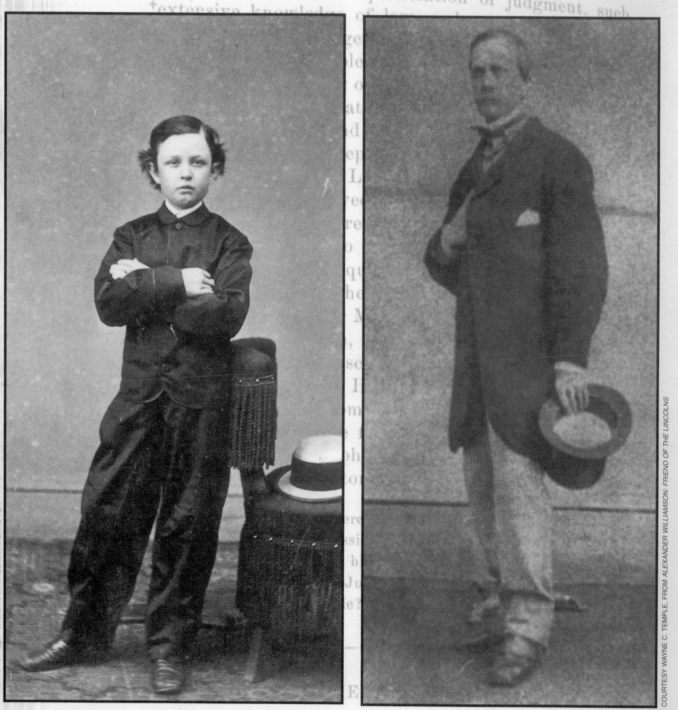

in the following words, sound the last consonant distinctly.

(After such exercises as this, it will be necessary to guard against a drawling style of reading).

Or-*b*, ai-*d*, fa-*g*, Geor-*ge*, a-*ll*, ai-*m*, ow-*n*, li-*p*, wa-*r*, hi-*ss*, ha-*t*, gi-*ve*, a-*dd*, so-*ng*, brea-*th*, tru-*th*, pu-*sh*, bir-*ch*.

Mo-*b*, la-*d*, ru-*f*, ha-*g*, ca-*ge*, ta-*ck*, fi-*ll*, ri-*m*, si-*n*, ho-*p*, fa-*r*, pa-*ce*, hi-*t*, ha-*ve*, ha-*s*, pa-*ng*, ba-*nk*, soo-*the*, pi-*th*, wi-*sh*, ri-*ch*.

Tad Lincoln and His Tutor Alexander Williamson

ELIZABETH SMITH BROWNSTEIN

Tad Lincoln, the president's youngest son, was an irrepressible, warm-hearted boy who would have loved the internet, had he been born a century later. But he would have had a slight problem using its riches to satisfy his boundless curiosity. By the time the Lincoln family moved from Springfield into the White House on March 4, 1861, Tad, nearly eight years old, still could not read or write.

Whatever formal education might have been imposed on an unwilling Tad back home was clearly ineffective. Even his conscientious oldest brother, Robert Todd, managed to flunk fifteen of the sixteen exams required for acceptance by Harvard University, despite his four years at the new Illinois State University in Springfield (an ambitious but abortive attempt by distinguished local citizens to establish a school of hopefully higher learning in that small town on the edge of the prairie). So Robert was sent off to a first-rate New England private school to prepare himself—successfully—to enter Harvard as a freshman in 1860. "I never knew what the word 'study' meant until I came here," said one of Robert's Springfield classmates, at Yale.[1]

Tad Lincoln and his tutor, Alexander Williamson. The date of the photograph of Williamson is unknown, but he is probably in his mid-40s, about the time he was employed by the Lincolns.

But prep school anywhere as a remedy for Tad's illiteracy was not an option. Tad had "a very bad opinion of books, and no opinion of discipline,"[2] observed John Hay, Lincoln's literate secretary. In "Deportment in School and General Conduct" alone, which were among the twenty-eight "Studies" offered at the capital's exclusive Emerson Institute, Tad Lincoln would not have lasted long. The city's public schools were hardly suitable for a president's son either. In his Annual Report of 1861, Mayor Richard Wallach described the system as "very defective, regrettable, and mortifying."[3] Despite its flaws, neither the subjects taught, nor the behavior expected of the few hundred white boys and girls enrolled, would have suited the fiercely independent Tad.

Abraham Lincoln would have applied the mayor's criticisms to his own formal education. In an 1858 forty-seven-word sketch of his life for the *Dictionary of Congress*, Lincoln admitted bluntly, "Education defective."[4] But unlike Tad, he was what a fellow congressman had once called him—a bookworm. Old friends recalled how he grabbed the chance to read anywhere, anytime: sitting with his back against a tree, behind the plow, between customers at his New Salem store, day or night—in a dogged but remarkable effort to educate himself, as it turned out, far beyond the grammar school level of most of his countrymen. Mary Todd Lincoln's education was much different. Nine years of excellent schooling in Lexington, Kentucky, more than most young women were given then, prepared her well in many ways to meet the challenges she faced as first lady.

One of the many convictions and interests the Lincolns did share was their philosophy of child rearing. Both agreed that their own childhoods had been desolate. So "it is my pleasure," said Lincoln, "that my children are free, happy and unrestrained by parental tyranny. Love is the chain whereby to bind a child to its parents."[5] What was to be done with Tad? "I suppose you want to grow up as a great dunce,"[6] Mary scolded, even after they had left the White House in 1865, as she and her dressmaker Elizabeth Keckley were trying to convince Tad that the word "ape" did not spell monkey. He was just guessing by the illustration accompanying the text, and the quick-witted boy held his ground. After all, he did know his monkeys. Hadn't he seen plenty of them with the organ-grinders passing by the White House? Yet Mary had often said during the White House years she wanted the children to have a good time, and Lincoln agreed. "Let [Tad] run—he has time left to learn his letters and get pokey. Bob was just such a little rascal, and now he is a very decent boy."[7] When Robert told his father he wanted to continue on to law school, Lincoln reminisced, "If you do, you should learn more than I ever did, but you'll never have as good a time."[8]

Perhaps Lincoln empathized with Tad's wide range of interests, hints of the diversity he had experienced as a young man on the frontier, before he turned to the law: surveyor, postmaster, army officer, riverboatman, merchant, clerk. He respected those brought up in the school of hard knocks, which he called "the school of events . . . I mean one in which, before entering real life, students might pass through the mimic vicissitudes and situations that are necessary to bring out their power and mark the caliber to which they are assigned."[9]

In his own imaginative way, Tad took daily advantage of every "vicissitude and situation" the hectic, often traumatic Civil War White House had to offer. He delighted in shaking down the steady stream of office-seekers for five cents for the Sanitary Fairs or for refreshments he had bought from street vendors. He took on weeping petitioners whose cases he would try urgently to bring to his father's attention. Noah Brooks, the Maine journalist and friend of the president, concluded that Tad "comprehended many practical realities that are far beyond the grasp of most boys. Even when he could scarcely read, he knew much about the cost of things, the details of trade, the principles of mechanics, and the habits of animals, all of which showed

the activity of his mind, and the odd turn of his thoughts."[10]

But then there was brother Willie. His obvious intellectual abilities had to be attended to. Since he and Tad were close in age, and in White House mischief-making, perhaps Tad would settle down and learn something by copying his brother. As Mary would rationalize later, "Few children learn well, without someone, sharing their lessons. If his darling brother Willie had lived, he Tad, would have been much further advanced."[11]

The only practical answer to educating the Lincoln boys was a private tutor, and soon they found an ideal candidate in Alexander Williamson, a Scotsman in his mid-40s. Williamson had been recommended as an experienced teacher by Major Thomas Alexander, acting governor of the Soldiers' Home, 3 miles northeast of the White House, where the Lincolns for three summers sought desperate relief from the "city of stink" that was the nation's wartime capital.[12] Lincoln liked Williamson immediately. A few minutes together in the White House library and Lincoln concluded, "I like this way of doing business—quick and to the point and satisfactory to both parties."[13] Mary was not so sure. Paying his salary was the problem, since she was already convinced that she would not have enough money to refurbish the dilapidated White House, let alone dress and entertain in the style she thought appropriate as first lady. Finally, Mary came up with a solution.[14] Williamson would work in the morning at the post office for pay and come later to the White House for free (his "unofficial hours," as Robert Todd Lincoln put it years later). This arrangement was neither unique nor new; John Hay and several other staff worked under somewhat similar terms, paid from distant government coffers. The naturalist and fellow Scot John Muir, writer Herman Melville, and poet Walt Whitman were among the needy "notables" who at one time or another found government employment in the Department of the Treasury, as Williamson would in 1863, thanks to Lincoln.

On September 5, 1861, the pedagogical experiment began at the far end of the State Dining Room, where Mary set up a blackboard and a desk for Mr. Williamson. The two Lincoln boys were probably put at the dining table, together with their close friends invited to share instruction, Horatio Nelson ("Bud") Taft Jr. and Halsey Cook ("Holly") Taft. Williamson was delighted by Willie's "aptitude in mastering the studies he was

The Lincoln Family *painted by Francis Bicknell Carpenter in 1865, is a portrayal of the president's family set in 1861, the year that Alexander Williamson began his work as the younger boys' tutor. Left to right are Mary Todd Lincoln, Willie (who died in 1862), Robert, Tad, and the president.*

pursuing . . . his memory was so wonderfully attentive that he had only to con over once or twice a page of his speller and definer, and the impression became so fixed that he went through without hesitation or blundering, and his other studies in proportion."[15] Willie was also a regular at Sunday school. Tad, on the other hand, was once seen emerging from church draped over his father's strong arm like a saddlebag, for misbehaving during the service. Occasionally Lincoln did put his foot down, or resorted to small bribes to make Tad behave. The new tool kit had to be taken away, the door to the attic locked. But Tad's antics usually entertained his father enormously.

It is not difficult to guess how Tad reacted to the new classroom. One day, Williamson later remembered,

"I was in the library reading when Mr. Lincoln came in with a candle in his hand—the afternoon being dark and hazy—and began looking over the shelves, as if in search of some book. By and by he said, 'Tad is a terrible fellow. He puts everything in confusion.'" Lincoln had come looking for a particular biblical concordance, and Williamson knew exactly where to find it. "That is a book that in Scotland you would find in almost every library," he told Lincoln, who replied, "You Scotch folks know your Bibles better than we do. The more pity for us."[16] But Lincoln did know his Bible. For him it was an indispensable daily source of comfort.

What might Williamson have used to teach the Lincoln and Taft boys? It's likely he had in his school-bag the wildly popular McGuffey Readers, their lessons

Tad in a Zouave uniform like that of his hero, Elmer Ellsworth.

Above: *Tad was given a courtesy commission by Secretary of War Edwin M. Stanton and is seen here wearing a lieutenant's uniform in 1864.*

Left: *Tad in mourning for his father in 1866. A black mourning band is seen circling his hat.*

Tad was photographed with his father, President Abraham Lincoln, by Anthony Berger of the Mathew Brady Studio in 1864 (above) and by Alexander Gardner in 1865 (right).

Tad on his pony at the White House, November 16, 1863.

Tad Lincoln, toward the end of his life, while a student at Dr. Hohagen's Institute in Frankfort, Germany, 1868–70.

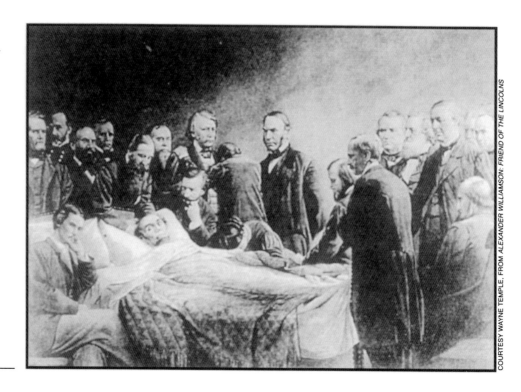

Alexander Williamson (eighth from right) was present at Abraham Lincoln's deathbed in the Peterson House. This depiction of the scene, entitled The Last Moments of Lincoln was published by Philip & Solomons in 1866.

about morality, manners, and taste compatible with his own Calvinist upbringing. Like him, William Holmes McGuffey was of Scottish ancestry. Millions of his Readers had been sold by 1861. Historian Henry Steele Commager a century later maintained that "they helped shape that elusive thing we call the American character. The Readers were more than a textbook. They were a portable school for the new priests of the republic."[17] Henry Ford once opined that McGuffey was a national giant who ranked with George Washington and Abraham Lincoln.[18]

There was another phenomenon that must have shaped Williamson's approach to teaching, the Scottish Enlightenment, that "hotbed of genius"[19] boiling up in late eighteenth-century Scotland. The philosopher David Hume, James Watt, inventor of the steam engine, economist Adam Smith, and architect Robert Adam were among the array of scientists and thinkers whose achievements and attitudes of curiosity, optimism, and tolerance would have a permanent global impact.

Willie Lincoln would have reveled in the McGuffey Readers' compilations of essays, orations, and poems by worthies of ancient and modern times, perhaps prompting him to write a respectable (and published) poem mourning the death of one of the war's earliest casualties, Edward Dickinson Baker, for whom the Lincoln's second son, dead in 1850, had been

named. But Tad was too busy with his pet goats and Jack the turkey, his elaborate miniature theater, his rooftop fort, the pony he rode fearlessly, his visits to Grover's Theater (with occasional surprise appearances on stage), and his daily visits in his "lieutenant's" uniform to the camps of Company K, 150th Pennsylvania Volunteers, Lincoln's guard for three years, to have been attracted to mere lessons in books.

Opinions differed about Tad's behavior. The soldiers of Company K showed their appreciation of Tad's generosity by presenting him an expensive album of photographs of each of them, in return for the huge flag and other gifts he brought back from trips with his mother. To his father and mother, Tad, Mary's "little troublesome sunshine,"[20] could do little wrong after Willie's death on February 20, 1862, just a few months after classes had begun. Any thought of continuing this educational experiment came to an abrupt end. The Taft boys no longer came to the White House. The sight of them was more than Mary Todd Lincoln or Tad could bear. Without Willie, Tad turned to his father, becoming the best companion Lincoln ever had, according to White House doorman William Crook. Tad would "laugh enormously whenever he saw his father's eyes twinkle, though not seeing clearly why."[21] He would rush to his father in his office, even at cabinet meetings, give his father a huge hug, and rush right out. He loved to accompany his father to military parades, once racing ahead on his pony shouting, "Make way, men. Make way, men. Father's a-coming."[22] He would fall asleep on the floor by his father's desk as Lincoln worked into the night, then be carried gently by his father to bed, often his own.

Others saw Tad as "the Madam's wildcat,"[23] the "little tyrant of the White House,"[24] "a lawless little prankster"[25]—in other words, a spoiled brat. But most who knew him well were fond of him. "He gave the White House the only comic relief it knew. His gayety and affection were the only illumination of the dark hours of the best and greatest American who ever lived," wrote Noah Brooks.[26]

Williamson had his own tragedies to cope with. His son James, Willie's age, had died a month before Willie. Three of his seven children were buried even before the family left Scotland in 1855. Only two daughters and the eldest son, William, were left.

Given Williamson's disapproval of "the fearful condition of the city" during the war, it would not have been surprising had he moved away. It was, he reported,

swarming not only with troops but with vagabonds, vampires, and harpies of every description . . . poisonous whiskey sold to the soldiers at four or five dollars a bottle, and citizens clothes kept for soldiers to desert . . . whole streets occupied by prostitutes, who never numbered less than twenty thousand . . . churchgoing almost given up . . . churches indeed were converted into hospitals and filled with wounded and dying men. . . . Then such a roar as there was continually in the city day and night. Droves of mules, horses by the thousand, herds of cattle. . . . Then there were the dying and the dead . . . columns of rebel prisoners, regiments innumerable crowding through the city on their way to the front.[27]

But Williamson stayed, now more of a companion to Tad than a tutor. A year after Willie died, a harried Lincoln responded quickly to Williamson's request for a letter of recommendation to the treasury secretary for a position as clerk. This position became Williamson's security for many years. And it was clear that Williamson by then had gained a privileged place in the Lincoln White House. In July 1864, Lincoln wrote to Williamson's mother in Edinburgh to thank her for a gift of hand-woven plaid given him by her "kind and worthy son."[28] Lincoln immediately took to wearing it when riding.

There were many foundations to the friendship that grew between Lincoln and Williamson. Both shared a love of Robert Burns's poems. Williamson was a staunch Republican, joining the new party at a time, he maintained, "when it was as much as a man's life was worth to espouse its principles."[29] Lincoln told Williamson he was grateful to the Scots Presbyterian Church for its stand, "one of the most complete arguments against slavery I ever read."[30] The tutor was a fervent supporter of the Union. He sheltered many members of a regiment of Highlanders in his home and joined the Treasury Department's volunteer militia. He and his wife, like the two Lincolns, were constant visitors to the wounded in the city's hospitals. The four parents shared the same anguish as their oldest sons faced the prospect of going into battle. The saddest evidence of Williamson's close link to the Lincolns was his presence among the group of intimates who gathered in the small room across from Ford's Theatre to watch Lincoln die.

Mary Todd Lincoln clearly shared her husband's respect and affection for Williamson. After Lincoln's murder, she gave Williamson the plaid shawl, as well as his slippers and dressing gown. Tad saw to it that Williamson got the inkwell Lincoln had supposedly used to sign the Emancipation Proclamation. Just two weeks after the assassination, Mrs. Lincoln was composed enough to write to Lincoln's successor, Andrew Johnson, recommending Williamson for a position she knew Lincoln had promised him in March 1865, in the new Freedmen's Bureau. "Mr. Williamson has all along been a devoted friend of our family and an unconditional friend of the Union," she wrote.[31] A few weeks after Mary and her two sons had quietly left the White House for Chicago, she wrote to Williamson, "Taddie . . . bids me write & thank you truly, for all your kindnesses to him. . . . He is at length seized with the desire to be able to *read & write,* which with his *natural* brightness will be half the battle with him. I hope he will be able to write by fall, so that he may be able to write you a letter inviting you *out here,* to see him. For all your great kindness, to my darling boys, may Heaven forever bless you!"[32] In the fall of 1866, when Williamson was worried by the prospect of losing his Treasury job to the vagaries of the patronage system, Mary wrote a letter on his behalf to her husband's longtime, well-placed friend,

Alexander Williamson, pictured here at about age 67, died at age 89 in 1903. His obituary (below) was published in the Washington Post.

Former White House Tutor Dead.

New York, June 4.—Alexander Williamson, who was the tutor of Abraham Lincoln's younger children, died to-day at his home in Brooklyn. He was eighty-nine years old. Mr. Williamson was born in Edinburgh. Coming to this country nearly sixty years ago, he was for a time a teacher in the South. During the civil war, after being employed by Mr. Lincoln, as a tutor for his children, Mr. Williamson received an appointment in one of the government departments at Washington, a post which he held until Mr. Cleveland's first administration. He will be buried in Washington.

Orville Hickman Browning, describing Williamson as "an honest upright man . . . a devoted friend, of my beloved husband."[33]

By then, a bitter Mary was using Williamson as her unlikely liaison to dunning merchants, ungrateful politicians, and other prominent men, in a frantic effort to raise money to pay her many debts and live in a style she felt appropriate to her position as widow of the martyred president who had not only saved the Union but given many of them their opportunities for success. In the hands of anyone of lesser integrity, Mary's financial and personal disasters would not have remained private for long. For several years, Williamson quietly did what he could, but failed. Like Elizabeth Keckley, Williamson never saw a penny of Mary's promised commission on whatever money he might have raised. Pitifully, both Keckley and Williamson themselves turned to Mary for loans. Pleading poverty herself, she gave nothing.[34]

Robert Todd Lincoln continued all his life, in his dignified way, to support Williamson, once recommending him for a consular post in Britain. "I take great pleasure in vouching for his learning, ability, and faithfulness, as well as for his loyalty."[35] Years later, Robert

was still trying to help. Williamson had finally lost his job at the Treasury Department and moved to Brooklyn. Repeated pleas by both men for his reinstatement ended in 1901 with a cruel dismissal by a department official, who wrote to Williamson: "It would not be in the interest of the service to reinstate any man so old as you as the record shows you to be, viz. eighty-six years."[36] Two years later, Williamson was dead, the heading of his obituary attesting to his memorable role in White House history, "Former White House Tutor Dead."[37]

As for Tad, that "complete embodiment of animal spirits and one of the historic boys of America,"[38] he faithfully and compassionately accompanied his mother on her years' long wanderings in Europe, "putting the waters between me and unkindness," she explained.[39] Tad's father had once said, in an eerie presentiment, "If he grows to be a man, Tad will be what the women all dote on—a good provider."[40] But Tad died in Chicago in 1871, having diligently learned to read and write and conquer his childhood speech impediment with tutors and at schools in Germany and England. His health had been impaired by the parlous and stressful conditions in the White House, and he could not shake off the fatal illness that began as a bad cold on his voyage home to America with Mary, eager to see his new niece, Robert's first child, Mary.

Of the four Lincoln sons, now only Robert lived. In a heartbroken epitaph, he wrote to Noah Brooks that Tad "was only eighteen when he died, but he was so manly and self-reliant that I had the greatest hope for his future."[41]

NOTES

I am particularly grateful to Dr. Wayne C. Temple for his wonderful study *Alexander Williamson: Friend of the Lincolns* (1997), which provided firm ground on which to base my essay.

1. Quoted in Ruth Painter Randall, *Lincoln's Sons* (Boston: Little, Brown, 1955), 97.

2. John Hay, *At Lincoln's Side: John Hay's Civil War Correspondence and Selected Writings*, ed. Michael Burlingame (Carbondale: Southern Illinois University Press, 2000), 111.

3. *Seventeenth Annual Report of the Trustees of Public Schools of the City of Washington, September 1, 1861*, 8. Charles Sumner School Archives, Washington, D.C.

4. Abraham Lincoln, statement for the *Dictionary of Congress*, 1858, In *The Collected Works of Abraham Lincoln*, ed. Roy P. Basler et al. (New Brunswick, N.J.: Rutgers University Press) 2:459.

5. Quoted in David Herbert Donald, *Lincoln* (New York: Simon & Schuster, 1995), 109.

6. Quoted in Elizabeth Keckley [Keckly] *Behind the Scenes; or, Thirty Years a Slave and Four Years in the White House*, 1868 (Reprint, London and New York: Oxford University Press, 1988), 215–19.

7. Quoted in Hay, *At Lincoln's Side*, 12.

8. Quoted in John S. Goff, *Robert Todd Lincoln: A Man in His Own Right* (Norman: University of Oklahoma Press, 1969), 60.

9. Quoted in Francis B. Carpenter, *The Inner Life of Abraham Lincoln: Six Months at the White House* (New York: Hurd and Houghton, 1867), 15.

10. Noah Brooks, "A Boy in the White House," *St. Nicholas Magazine for Young Folks* 10 (November 1882–May 1883): 61.

11. Mary Todd Lincoln to Alexander Williamson, September 9, 1865. *Mary Todd Lincoln: Her Life and Letters*, ed. Justin G. Turner and Linda Levitt Turner (New York: Fromm International Publishing, 1987), 272–73.

12. Ruth Painter Randall, *Mary Lincoln: Biography of a Marriage* (Boston: Little, Brown, 1953), 292.

13. Quoted in Wayne C. Temple, *Alexander Williamson: Friend of the Lincolns*, Special Publication 1 (Racine, Wisc.: Lincoln Fellowship of Wisconsin, 1997), 15.

14. Ibid.

15. Quoted in ibid., 16.

16. Quoted in David Macrae, *The Americans at Home* (New York: E. P. Dutton, 1952), 103–4.

17. Quoted in John H. Westenfelt, *McGuffey and His Readers: Piety, Education, and Morality in the Nineteenth Century* (Nashville: Parthenon Press, 1978), 16.

18. "That Guy McGuffey," *Saturday Evening Post*, November 26, 1927, 16.

19. See David Daiches, *A Hotbed of Genius: The Scottish Enlightenment, 1730–1790* (Edinburgh: Edinburgh Free Press, 1986).

20. Quoted in Randall, *Lincoln's Sons*, 97.

21. Quoted in John Hay, *Inside Lincoln's White House: The Complete Civil War Diary of John Hay*, ed. Michael Burlingame and John R. Turner Ettlinger (Carbondale: Southern Illinois University Press, 1997), 188.

22. Quoted in Harry M. Kieffer, *Recollections of a Drummer Boy* (Mifflinburg, Pa.: Bucktail Books, 2000), 61.

23. Julia Taft Bayne, *Tad Lincoln's Father* (Lincoln: University of Nebraska Press, 2001), 48.

24. Brooks, "Boy in the White House," 58.

25. Randall, *Lincoln's Sons*, 155.

26. Brooks, "Boy in the White House," 65.

27. Quoted in Macrae, *Americans at Home*, 109.

28. Quoted in Temple, *Alexander Williamson*, 23.

29. Alexander Williamson file, Treasury Department General Records, Record Group 56, National Archives II, College Park, Md.

30. Quoted in Macrae, *Americans at Home*, 104.

31. Mary Todd Lincoln to Andrew Johnson, April 29, 1865, *Mary Todd Lincoln*, ed. Turner and Turner, 226.

32. Mary Todd Lincoln to Alexander Williamson, June 15, 1865, ibid., 250.

33. Mary Todd Lincoln to Orville Hickman Browning, September 24, 1866, ibid., 391.

34. Mary Todd Lincoln, letters to Williamson, in *Mary Todd Lincoln*, ed. Turner and Turner, passim; see esp. 472.

35. Robert Todd Lincoln, letter of February 16, 1869, Williamson file, National Archives.

36. Treasury Department official to Williamson, March 28, 1901, ibid.

37. *Washington Post*, June 5, 1903.

38. Noah Brooks, *Washington in Lincoln's Time*, ed. Herbert Mitgang (Athens: University of Georgia Press, 1979), 246.

39. Quoted in Elizabeth Smith Brownstein, *Lincoln's Other White House: The Untold Story of the Man and His Presidency* (New York: Simon & Schuster, 2005), 224.

40. Quoted in Brooks, *Washington in Lincoln's Time*, 250.

41. Quoted in Randall, *Lincoln's Sons*, 212.

Music in Lincoln's White House

ELISE K. KIRK

*A*braham Lincoln was one of America's most unmusical presidents. He could neither play an instrument nor carry a tune, yet he had a passionate love of music. Many times he left the White House during his tenure to attend the opera at Washington theaters, and when duties held him to the mansion, he invited performers to entertain him and his family "at home." For Lincoln, however, music was more than mere entertainment. It was a form of therapy, a panacea, a way to touch the soul of beauty. Friends noted that his reaction to the mysterious powers of music was often intense and highly personal. Certain songs would "mist his eyes and throw him into a fit of deep melancholy."[1]

Lincoln had been responsive to music from his earliest boyhood days, when his mother, Nancy Hanks, sang lyrical ballads to him. For the young man in America's frontier wilderness, songs such as "Kathleen Mavourneen," "Old Rosin the Beau," and "Annie Laurie" had their own special poignancy and charm. Lincoln's musical friend from the Shenandoah Valley, Ward Lamon, once recalled: "Many a time, in the old

---

This ornately carved grand piano was ordered from Schomacker and Co. of Philadelphia, by Mary Todd Lincoln in 1861. It was placed in the Red Room and used by the Lincoln children for their music lessons and by performers who entertained in the White House.

days on the Illinois circuit, and often at the White House when he and I were alone, have I seen him in tears while I was rendering in my poor way that homely melody ['Twenty Years Ago']."[2] But Lamon had a way of cheering Lincoln, too. His interpretation of the spirited banjo tune "The Blue Tail Fly" was a special favorite with the president. With its comic lyrics and syncopated beat, this type of song formed the core of the popular new minstrel shows of the time.

If Lincoln's tastes in music were eclectic, they were perhaps no more so than those of most Americans. But music in those days was not as clearly delineated into "popular" and "classical" as it is today. There were no CD bins in music stores, no videos, iPods, or TVs, and no radios or movies to provide entertainment and respite from everyday cares. Theaters with live performers, therefore, were kept very busy. And while Ford's Theatre and Grover's Theater showcased plays, tableaux, and revues, they also presented fully staged operas. Most of these were produced on East Coast tours by New York's elegant new Academy of Music. Thus, Washingtonians, young and old, enjoyed the greatest operas of Gioacchino Rossini, François-Adrien Boieldieu, Wolfgang Amadeus Mozart, Richard Wagner, Giuseppe Verdi, Vincenzo Bellini, Gaetano Donizetti, Carl Maria von Weber, Giacomo Meyerbeer, and Ludwig van Beethoven, and President Lincoln saw most all of them.[3]

Lincoln attended the opera more than thirty times during the four years he was in the White House. He

Two weeks before his inauguration, Lincoln attended the American premiere of Giuseppe Verdi's A Masked Ball—*which ominously told the story of the assassination of another head of state, King Gustav III of Sweden. The opera is still performed today. This still shows the "Death of the King" during a performance by the San Diego Opera in 1999.*

In Washington, President Lincoln often attended the opera at Grover's Theatre on Pennsylvania Avenue. Today's National Theatre is the sixth theatre to stand on the site. The fourth (pictured opposite) was constructed in 1873.

had never heard an opera before his election to the presidency. Sometimes he went with Mrs. Lincoln or with friends, but often alone. He especially liked Charles-François Gounod's *Faust* with its rousing "Soldiers' Chorus," which he saw at least four times. When criticized for attending the opera so much while real life dramas raged at Bull Run and Harpers Ferry, he retorted: "The truth is I must have a change of some sort or die."[4] His passion for opera, in fact, was so pronounced that at one point the *New York Herald* suggested that President Lincoln visit Manhattan, "where Mrs. Lincoln can shop, and the president can have his fill of opera."[5] But opera in New York also had a darker tone for him. When Lincoln attended his first opera on February 20, 1861, two weeks before his inauguration, it was the American premiere at the Academy of Music of Giuseppe Verdi's *Masked Ball*—the story of a monarch's brutal assassination. For Lincoln it was a chilling prophecy.[6]

While her artistic interests were not as fervid as the president's, Mary Todd Lincoln found her own special joy in music. Shortly after moving into the White House, she ordered a fine new grand piano made by the Schomacker Company of Philadelphia (c. 1860).[7] With its one-piece cast-iron frame and graceful foliate carving, the piano occupied a prime spot in the lush, Victorian-style Red Room, Mrs. Lincoln's favorite sitting room. Here the two unruly Lincoln boys, Willie and Tad, took music lessons from their Polish instructor, Alexander Wolowski. The scholarly professor had recently set up a studio in Washington and styled himself "court musician" to the Lincolns. But the Schomacker piano had other important duties. It became the focal point for many musical programs that the Lincolns held in the White House—entertainment as varied as the president's own preferences and as kaleidoscopic as American taste itself.

When the Lincolns invited the young American opera singer Meda Blanchard to perform for them in the White House, they were unaware that they had inaugurated an important American cultural tradition. Since that time, literally hundreds of fine singers have entertained at important White House functions for every American president to modern times.[8] Forgotten today, Meda Blanchard had studied abroad, and as the *Sunday Morning Chronicle* of June 30, 1861, proudly reported,

"She returns to America laden with the highest encomiums."[9]

At her program for the Lincolns and their guests in July 1861, the young diva sang "in a manner that charmed everyone present." Seated at the piano, she "laid off the shawl from shoulders that no 'South' would have ever seceded from [with its eyes open]," wrote the press.[10] Among her selections was the famous "Casta Diva" from Bellini's *Norma* and two of Lincoln's favorite ballads. At the president's request, she finished up with the "Marseillaise." Four days later the Lincolns attended Blanchard's concert at Willard's. The *Evening Star* noted that "our Republican President seemed to have been oblivious to the cares of office and wholly absorbed by the syren [*sic*] voice of the fair cantatrice."[11] As for the young singer, did it matter that she would never soar to stellar heights? She had sung for the president. He had even sent her a bouquet of flowers.[12]

If the president craved diversion from the increasing gloom of the war, he found it in four disparate entertainers, whom he welcomed on different occasions at the Executive Mansion: a Native American soprano, a P. T. Barnum entertainer, a nine-year-old piano prodigy, and a

vocal ensemble that, beginning with John Tyler, would sing for a total of seven presidents. Several months before Meda Blanchard sang, another young woman presented a program for the president and his guests at a White House reception. She was called simply "Larooqua," and the papers noted her "woodnotes wild" and "mellifluous voice."[13] Probably politics as much as artistry brought the young Native American to the White House. She was in Washington at the time assisting John Beeson, who was giving a series of lectures on the plight of the Indians in Oregon. But there would not be another like her until Chief Yowlache of the Yakima tribe of Washington sang for President Herbert Hoover in 1933.

When Commodore Nutt entertained President and Mrs. Lincoln on October 17, 1862, the distressed president had just witnessed his darkest hour through the disastrous carnage at Fredericksburg. To brighten his spirits—if even for a moment—the great American showman, Phineas T. Barnum, brought one of his stars to the White House. The gentleman, 29-inches-high, barely reached the president's knee. Advertised in the *National Republican* of October 17, 1862, as the

"smallest man in the world," George Washington Morrison Nutt was also considered a very fine entertainer. He delighted the president and his cabinet with his interpretation of David T. Shaw's "Columbia, the Gem of the Ocean," a song made popular recently at concerts in Boston, New York, and Philadelphia.[14]

Another small White House entertainer went on to become one of the century's finest concert pianists. The amazing Venezuelan prodigy, Teresa Carreño, was only nine when she came to the White House with her father in the fall of 1863. But she exhibited the temperament that was to become her hallmark. Recalling the event in her later years, she wrote:

> The President and his family received us so informally, they were all so very nice to me that I almost forgot to be cranky under the spell of their friendly welcome. My self-consciousness all returned, however, when Mrs. Lincoln asked me if I would like to try the White House grand piano. . . . Without another word, I struck out into Gottschalk's funeral *Marche de Nuit*, and after I had finished, modulated into *The Last Hope*, and ended with *The Dying Poet*. . . . Then what do you think I did? I

During his presidency, Lincoln attended many opera productions in Washington, including Carl Maria von Weber's Der Freischütz *on April 4, 1864, which featured Theodore Habelmann (above left c. 1870), as Max. In May 1862 he saw the 19-year old American, Clara Louise Kellogg (opposite, top right) in Gaetano Donizetti's* Daughter of the Regiment.

Among the many Lincoln performers who entertained in Lincoln's White House were the Hutchinson Family (above c. 1880) a nineteenth-century American family singing group who for generations sang about social issues and political causes. In various combinations, the group sang for seven presidents. Commodore George Washington Nutt (opposite left) a 29-inch tall singer, was brought to the White House in 1862 to cheer up Lincoln, who was distressed following the Battle of Fredericksburg. Teresa Carreño (opposite bottom right) was a child prodigy pianist who performed for the Lincolns at age nine.

Artists of the period sometimes exaggerated the size of the East Room of the White House, as in this hand-colored wood engraving entitled Grand Presidential Party at the White House, Washington—Wednesday Evening February 5th, *which was published in* Frank Leslie's Illustrated Newspaper *on February 22, 1862.*

Five hundred guests were invited to this grand gala, which featured an elaborate buffet and music by the Marine Band, performing in the Entrance Hall (seen in the distance through the open doors on the left). Although the Marine Band usually provided the music at social and ceremonial events, it was often crushed by the festive crowds.

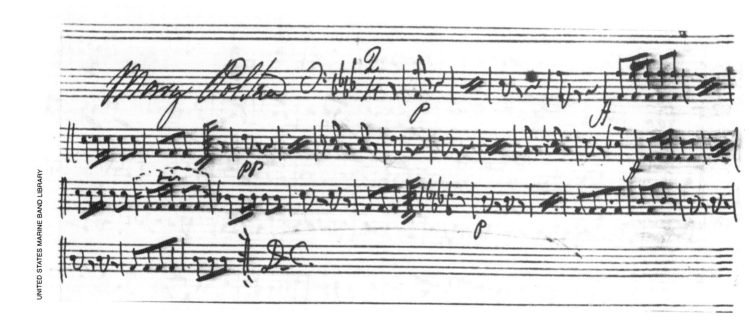

The Marine Band in Lincoln's time had a large repertory that included popular songs and dances. Their famous "Mary Lincoln Polka" was first played at the White House in 1862. The handwritten bassoon part (above) illustrates the characteristic 2/4 time and rhythmic patterns of the polka.

jumped off the piano stool and declared that I would play no more—that the piano was too badly out of tune to be used.[15]

Though the vertiginous pieces by Louis Moreau Gottschalk were meaty fare for a nine-year-old, Carreño's complaints about the piano were not alone. When the Hutchinson Family Singers sang for the Lincolns' reception on January 7, 1862, John Hutchinson remarked: "We suffered a slight inconvenience in singing . . . no music stool could be found, and altogether it was evident that Mr. Lincoln and his family were thinking of something else than music in those days." Hutchinson felt that it would be "little less than treason" to attempt "Yankee Doodle" on the out-of-tune piano, so he sent for his melodeon instead. At the president's request he played Henry Russell's dramatic "Ship on Fire," a descriptive American classic that had all the earmarks of a D. W. Griffith silent film score. "I can seem to see our martyred President now as he stood only a few feet from me, holding his sweet boy, Tad, by the hand," wrote Hutchinson. "We were warmly applauded as our program concluded. The room was as full as it could be."[16]

While guest artists were still relatively infrequent at the White House, one musical ensemble had been an integral part of the mansion's cultural life from its earliest days—the United States Marine Band. Appearing first at the White House for John Adams's New Year's Day reception in 1801, the band became known as "The President's Own" from the time of Thomas Jefferson. On July 25, 1861, President Lincoln established the first act to recognize the Marine Band by law, and the ensemble, now greatly enlarged, played for nearly every White House ceremonial and social event. Public band concerts, begun by John Tyler, were also held weekly on the White House grounds. The only exception was a period of almost two years when Mrs. Lincoln ordered them to cease after the death of her son Willie.

The repertory of the Marine Band in those days was unusually large and varied. In addition to polkas, waltzes, and quicksteps, there were numerous selections from opera, for lyrical opera tunes were "popular music" to many Americans—rather like Broadway show tunes are to us today. The tradition of Italian opera was also born into the distinguished Marine Band leader, Francis Scala, who had come to America in 1842 from his

The first known photograph of the United States Marine Band was taken in 1864 at the Marine Barracks in Washington, D.C.

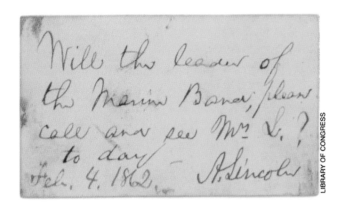

A note requesting that the Marine Band leader Francis Scala call on "Mrs L" was signed "A. Lincoln" on February 4, 1862. Scala, pictured at right, c. 1865, served as director under five presidents.

President Lincoln was especially fond of patriotic tunes popular during the war including George F. Root's immortal "Battle Cry of Freedom" (1862).

native city of Naples. When he left the band in 1871, Scala had served under nine presidents and had greatly improved the balance, technique, and repertory of the ensemble.

Although Lincoln attended the Marine Band concerts whenever he could, an account written at the time only underlines what little peace he had to pursue his own pleasures. One Saturday afternoon, when the lawn was crowded with people enjoying the concert, the president appeared on the portico. "Instantly there was a clapping of hands and clamor for a speech. Bowing his thanks, and excusing himself he stepped back into the retirement of the circular parlor, remarking with a disappointed air, as he reclined upon the sofa, 'I wish they would just let me sit out there quietly, and enjoy the music.'"[17]

But the music closest to Lincoln were those tones bound most intimately with Americans during their turbulent war years—melodies that revealed the spirit of a people who knew the powers of both tragedy and joy, defeat and victory. "We are coming, Father Abraham, three hundred thousand more!" sang thousands of volunteer soldiers before the White House, responding to the president's call. Strong men cheered, cried, and bellowed out George F. Root's immortal "Battle Cry of Freedom"—"Yes we'll rally round the flag, boys, we'll rally once again!" On July 4, 1864, thousands of black people gathered on the White House lawn to sing spirituals commemorating both Independence Day and the Emancipation Proclamation. And on January 27, 1865, five hundred members of the Christian Commission called on the president, singing various hymns and the "Soldiers' Chorus" from Gounod's *Faust.*

After the fall of Richmond, crowds gathered at the White House far into the night. They waved flags and serenaded victory with Julia Ward Howe's "Battle Hymn of the Republic" and vaudeville star Dan Emmett's "Dixie." "Let's have it again!" cried the president, who first heard "Dixie" at a minstrel show in Chicago. "It's our tune now!" he said, implying that both North and South would find unity and fellowship

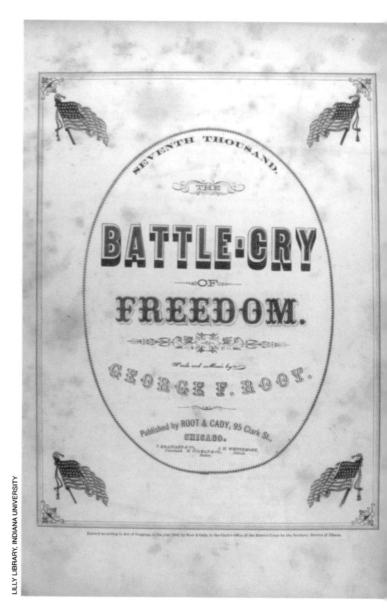

in this common musical expression.[18] How deeply the president was moved by musical demonstrations has been recorded by those close to him. He was known to have called for certain pieces again and again.

A philosopher once said that music reaches beyond language and expresses our highest and deepest longings. But for Abraham Lincoln music was much more. "Listening to melody," he once said,

every man becomes his own poet, and measures the depths of his own nature, though he is apt to lose the line as the sound dies away. As a student in a rugged school, I have through life been obliged to

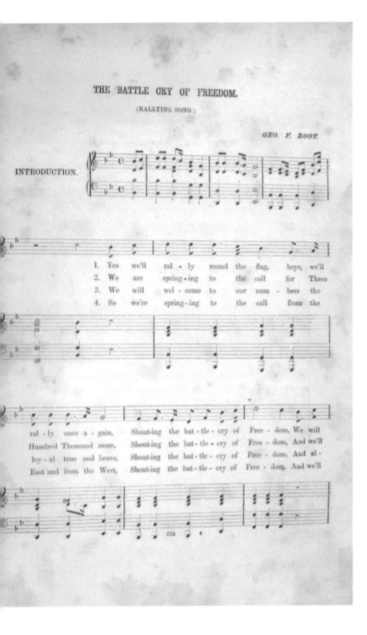

strip ideas of their ornaments, and make them facts before I conquered them. . . . Still a few, soft heart-searching notes will often remind me of a want, convincing me that, like other hard workers, I may have gained in precision and concentration at the cost, maybe, of the silent pleasure an eye educated to beauty can always drink in at a glance.[19]

Perhaps we find a little bit of ourselves in these words. But more important, we gain fresh insight into this dedicated leader, his lively curiosity, his sensitivity, and his soul.

NOTES

1. John Lair, *Songs Lincoln Loved* (New York: Duell, Sloan and Pearce, 1954), ix.

2. Quoted in Carl Sandburg, *Abraham Lincoln: The War Years* (New York: Harcourt Brace, 1939), 596–97.

3. The *National Intelligencer* usually reported the times President Lincoln took his special box at the opera. Many of the productions he saw featured the greatest singers of the time, such as Marie Frederici and Joseph Hermanns in *Faust* (April 2, 1864). Hermanns's interpretation of Mephistopheles so captivated the president that he invited Hermanns to the White House for a visit. Lincoln also saw Bertha Johannsen in her celebrated role as Leonora in Ludwig van Beethoven's *Fidelio* (June 8, 1864), Theodore Habelmann as Max in Carl Maria von Weber's *Der Freischütz* (April 4, 1864), and the 19-year-old American, Clara Louise Kellogg, in Gaetano Donizetti's *Daughter of the Regiment* (May 28, 1862), among many other productions.

4. Quoted in *New York Herald*, April 23, 1863.

5. Ibid.

6. The play, *Our American Cousin*, which Lincoln attended at Ford's Theatre on April 14, 1865, contained music. But the special feature of the evening, "Patriotic Song and Chorus, Honor to Our Soldiers," Lincoln never heard. He was assassinated by John Wilkes Booth while seated in his box overlooking the stage.

7. The piano had a compass of seven octaves plus a minor third. It was delivered to the White House sometime after June 21, 1861, by the firm of William H. Carryl & Bros, Philadelphia. Stanley McClure to Paul Angle, October 1, 1948, Chicago Historical Society. Today the piano is in the collection of the Chicago Historical Society. Carryl Brothers had provided the now famous Lincoln Bed.

8. For a history of the musical programs and performers at the White House, see Elise K. Kirk, *Musical Highlights from the White House* (Malabar, Fla.: Krieger, 1992) and *Music at the White House: A History of the American Spirit* (University of Illinois Press, 1986).

9. *Washington Sunday Morning Chronicle*, June 30, 1861.

10. Quoted in Kenneth A. Bernard, *Lincoln and the Music of the Civil War* (Caldwell, Idaho: Caxton Printers, 1966), 36.

11. *Washington Evening Star*, July 7, 1861.

12. Meda Blanchard's handwritten reply to the president is in the John Nicolay Papers, Library of Congress, Washington, D.C. She was a native of Washington, D.C.

13. Quoted in Bernard, *Lincoln and the Music of the Civil War*, 16–17.

14. *National Republican*, October 17, 1862.

15. Quoted in "Living Stage Folk Who Knew and Cheered Lincolns," *Montgomery Advertiser*, February 12, 1911. Carreño was described at the height of her career as "the Valkyrie of the piano." She also became a fine singer, conductor, and composer. Lincoln often attended Gottschalk's concerts when this pianist performed in Washington.

16. John Wallace Hutchinson, *The Story of the Hutchinsons* (Boston: Lee and Shepherd, 1896), 2:380.

17. Quoted in Francis B. Carpenter, *The Inner Life of Abraham Lincoln: Six Months at the White House* (New York: Hurd and Houghton, 1867), 143. Ironically, Lincoln's funeral ceremony held at the White House contained no music, but the thirty-five piece Marine Band played as the solemn cortege left the mansion for the Capitol.

18. Quoted in Bernard, *Lincoln and the Music of the Civil War*, 298–99.

19. Quoted in *San Francisco Bulletin*, May 12, 1865, in David Rankin Barbee, "The Musical Mr. Lincoln," *Abraham Lincoln Quarterly* 5, no. 8 (1949): 446–47.

Photographs of the Lincoln White House

LYDIA TEDERICK

*A*braham Lincoln assumed the office of president of the United States on March 4, 1861, an innovative period for photography. He was the first president to be photographed extensively and is thought to have sat for as many as thirty-six photographers on sixty-six occasions.[1] His White House also became the subject matter for a growing number of photographers. Their work enables us to see the Executive Mansion at an important time in our nation's history.

By the 1860s, photography had undergone several important developments. The most significant change was the ability to produce paper prints from glass negatives. Photographic images no longer had to be unique but could be reproduced for a larger audience. Average people could now afford to have their portraits made at a studio and to buy images of celebrities and scenic sites for their own collections.

Early photographic formats, such as daguerreotypes, ambrotypes, and tintypes, were unique, or one-of-a-kind, images exposed on nonpaper supports. A daguerreotype, for example, was a positive image made directly on a sheet of copper, plated with a highly polished coating of

Tad Lincoln stands on the North Drive of the White House in this carte de visite by Henry Warren, a detail of the photograph reproduced in its entirety on page 34, taken in March 1865.

silver. It could appear as either a positive or a negative depending on the angle it was tilted. The only way it could be copied was by rephotographing the original. Subject to corrosion and abrasion, the fragile daguerreotypes were displayed behind glass in small hinged cases.[2]

Prints on paper, on the other hand were easier to produce and display. Made from glass plate negatives, they could be copied endlessly and were subsequently more affordable. Glass negatives were prepared using the wet collodion process, a technique that was popular from 1855 until it was replaced in the 1880s by the gelatin dry-plate negative process. In a dark room, a glass plate was covered with collodion, a syrupy liquid, and a silver nitrate solution and then placed into a special holder for protection. If the photographer was outside the studio, this step was undertaken in a specially constructed tent or covered wagon. Timing was important because the exposure had to be made while the plate was still damp. The subject was posed and placed into focus before the plate holder was inserted into the camera. A protective shield and the lens cap were then removed to expose the plate. The exposure could take approximately fifteen to thirty seconds. To avoid blurriness, studios often used props or headrests to help the sitter remain still. The exposed plate then had to be developed in a darkroom and washed. When the negative was dry, it was placed on a sheet of light-sensitive paper and exposed to the sun to create a positive print. The paper most commonly used from the mid-1850s until the early twentieth century was coated with albumen, an emulsion of egg white, and brushed with light-sensitive silver salts.[3]

Multilens cameras were developed that could expose several images simultaneously on a glass plate. With a four lens camera, where two pairs of images were created, each pair was stereoscopically related. When printed, the images could be mounted as two stereographs or separated as four smaller cartes de visite. A large number of photographs could be produced quickly from original negatives.[4]

Cartes de visite and stereographs were perhaps the most popular photographic forms available during the 1860s. A carte de visite was a photograph mounted onto a card that was similar in size to a calling card, approximately 2¼ by 4 inches. A stereograph had two nearly identical images mounted side-by-side. When seen through a special viewer, a three-dimensional effect was achieved. Any antique shop today is likely to have for sale "stereo slides." Perhaps millions were made, many by amateurs, and among the amateurs were many women.

Cartes de visite were acquired to such an extent that special albums were sold to house the collections. Prints of family members were displayed along with Civil War heroes, political leaders, and scenic views. The Lincoln family was no exception and had an album while living in the White House. Their album contained views of Washington, D.C., including the White House, Lafayette Square, the War Department, the Treasury Building, the Capitol, the Post Office Department, and the Smithsonian Institution.[5]

Determining the photographer of a particular image can be very difficult. Many were simply not identified. At that time, it was not uncommon for publishers or major studios to buy the negatives from other photographers and print and publish them as their own. E. & H. T. Anthony & Company, for example, was a New York publisher and photographic supply firm that employed many photographers and purchased negatives from outside sources. Images published under the Anthony logo rarely name the actual camera operator. Mathew Brady's studio, while it was managed by Alexander Gardner, did make a special agreement with Anthony. The publisher was furnished with negatives to be mass-produced and distributed, for which Brady was paid a fee and given a credit line. Operators working for Brady, however, were not recognized.

Photographs made by his employees were credited to Brady himself.[6]

Photographs of the White House from this period predominately feature the exterior of the building. Lighting interior spaces presented many challenges for photographers, and there are only a few images that show the interior of the house prior to the later 1860s.[7] The photographs selected for this article are from the White House collection unless otherwise noted. The dates of some examples are not known, but they were selected because they reflect the appearance of the Executive Mansion while Lincoln was president.

Mathew B. Brady

With a gallery already established in New York, Mathew Brady opened a studio in Washington, D.C., in 1849 in hopes of making daguerreotype portraits of important Americans. The National Photographic Art Gallery, located on Pennsylvania Avenue between Fourth and Sixth Streets, NW, was not profitable, however, and closed after a few months. Brady returned to Washington in 1858 and tried again with Brady's National Photographic Art Gallery on Pennsylvania Avenue near Seventh Street in the top three floors of Gilman's Drugstore. This venture, initially managed by photographer Alexander Gardner, met with great success. It was established at a time when the innovative wet collodion process was being used and photographs were more affordable. Bad business deals and financial problems would eventually cause Brady to close his New York studio and declare bankruptcy in 1872. His Washington business did not close until 1881.[8]

Among his many accomplishments, Brady is also remembered for his efforts to document the Civil War. Under his name, teams of camera operators in specially equipped wagons were sent on location to photograph military life, battlefields, and the war's aftermath. Brady himself appeared in several of the images.[9]

Portrait of Abraham Lincoln, Carte de Visite by Mathew Brady, 1864

Mathew Brady was well known to the Lincoln family, all of whom were photographed in his Washington studio. Lincoln was first photographed by Brady on February 27, 1860, prior to the presidential candidate's delivery of his seminal speech at the Cooper Union in New York. That portrait was widely distributed, appearing on campaign buttons and cartes de visite. It was also copied by engravers for newspapers, books, and campaign posters. Lincoln would later say the Brady portrait and the Cooper Union speech put him in the White House.[10] From a January 8, 1864, sitting at Brady's gallery, five poses were taken of the president, including this carte de visite image.[11] The reverse is marked with Brady's logo.

North Facade, Carte de Visite by Alexander Gardner, 1862

On various occasions during the Civil War, crowds were permitted to assemble around the North Portico for presidential addresses. From the center window over the main doorway, visible between the columns, the president would appear and speak to the gathering. It was from this location on April 11, 1865, two days after the Confederates surrendered at Appomattox Court House, that Lincoln spoke publicly for the last time.

Photographed from the central lawn, the north façade appears beyond an iron anthemion-patterned fence. The iron fence was placed along the north edge of the driveway in 1833 and, until its removal in 1872, enclosed a small garden where a bronze statue of Thomas Jefferson was displayed. A similar railing was also installed between the North Portico columns and as a parapet on either side of the portico; both were removed in 1902. The ornamental fences were inspired by an anthemion-band cornice placed in the East Room by architect James Hoban.

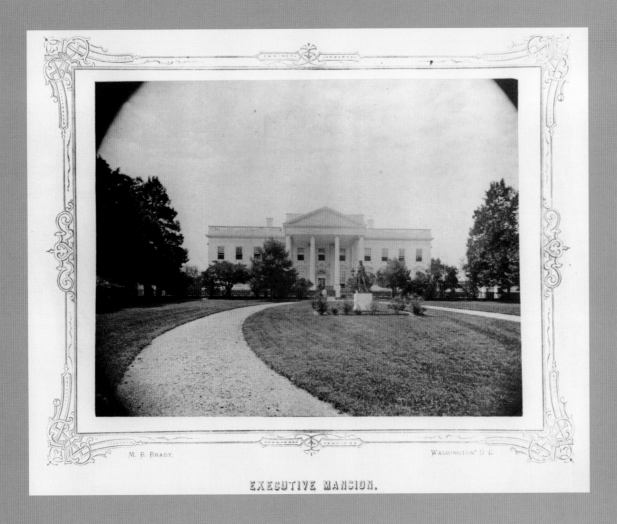

EXECUTIVE MANSION.

M. B. BRADY.   WASHINGTON, D. C.

The White House, by Mathew Brady, c. 1860s

This photograph is affixed to a decorative Brady mount and shows the bronze statue of Thomas Jefferson that was a prominent fixture in front of the Executive Mansion during the mid-nineteenth century. Made in 1833 by French sculptor Pierre-Jean David (1788–1856), it was a gift to the United States Capitol by Uriah Phillips Levy (1792–1862), a naval officer and Jefferson admirer who purchased the late president's home, Monticello, in 1834.[12] At the request of President James K. Polk, the statue was moved to the North Lawn of the White House in 1847. It was returned to the Capitol in 1874 when President Ulysses S. Grant had it replaced by a fountain.

North Drive, 1860s

Opposite: Seen here as a carte de visite, this northeast view was also published as a 3-D stereograph (No. 1304 by E. & H.T. Anthony & Co.) and as such doubtless adorned many a souvenir album and parlor table. It shows Lincoln's White House from the northeast, looking up the broad stone sidewalk beside the graveled drive. This was the public entrance to the president's office and residence. The two lanterns in front of the corner of the building were added to the stone piers of an interior gate in 1852. The gates were removed in 1872 along with the northernmost lanterns and piers; the remaining lanterns were taken down in 1902. The southern gate piers remain to the present day.

Above: The camera has been moved a bit to the west in this similar view of the north side of the White House dated 1864. General Montgomery C. Meigs (1816–1892), the owner of this print, was an engineer and architect who served as the quartermaster for the Union Army during the Civil War. A camera buff, he occasionally supplied images to Mathew Brady.[13]

Tad Lincoln, Carte de Visite by Henry Warren, March 1865

The boy standing on the roadway in front of the north facade is Lincoln's youngest son, Thomas "Tad" Lincoln (1853–1871). Soldiers appear in the background and may well be members of Company K, the 150th Pennsylvania Volunteers, also known as "Bucktails." The Bucktails, so nicknamed because of deer tails worn on their hats, provided protection for the president and his family during the war. Tad was popular with the soldiers, and as a memento, the Bucktails presented him with an album containing their autographed photographs.[14]

Late in the war, photographer Henry F. Warren from Waltham, Massachusetts, hoped to photograph the president but had no means of gaining access to him. A chance meeting with Tad, however, enabled Warren to establish a contact using the boy as an intermediary. On March 6, 1865, the busy president agreed to pose on the South Portico, and three images were taken.[15] These are believed to be the last photographs taken of him.

The White House Draped in Mourning, Stereograph, 1865

This haunting stereographic slide is a rare view of the White House draped in black crape for the slain Lincoln. It must date from between April 15 and May 22, 1865, thirty days being the official period of mourning for a president. The photographer is not known. The house has been decorated by the longtime White House decorator and upholsterer, John Alexander, who supervised the other funeral arrangements, including building the catafalque, which still survives, upon which Lincoln's coffin rested in the East Room and in the Capitol. Note the platform or drawbridge built to the East Room window, to allow exit to viewing mourners and the six hundred people invited to attend the funeral.[16]

The moment captured by the picture gives pause: It might be surmised that the black crape is either being put up or taken down. If the latter, then perhaps the carriage—a White House carriage—is that which transported a grieving Mrs. Lincoln, Tad, and her seamstress, Elizabeth Keckley, to the railroad depot. While pure speculation, the sad, quiet departure might certainly have inspired a photographer as well as explain the odd angle of the picture.[17]

COLLECTION OF BOB ZELLER

Encampment on the South Grounds, Stereograph, c. 1861

A stereograph view, No. 1311 published by E. & H. T. Anthony, shows troops encamped on the South Grounds.[18] *The President's House and the East Terrace are visible through the trees in the background. During the initial months of the Civil War, troops were quartered in public buildings throughout Washington, including the East Room of the White House. Army barracks were also placed nearby on the "White Lot"—one day to become the Ellipse, an open space located south of the White House.*

Children on the South Grounds, Carte de Visite, c. 1861–66

Children in Lincoln's time pose around a fountain that was built on the south grounds in 1858. It was a striking fountain consisting of two tiers and a shaft of entwined sea serpents rising over a large round pool, but the water jet rarely worked. By 1869, the fountain itself was removed.

But there is more. The west and east colonnaded terraces, seen to the left and right of the residence respectively, built at the suggestion of Thomas Jefferson to house service areas, were topped on the west in 1857 by a simple wood and glass greenhouse, seen at left. It burned in 1867 and was replaced with a larger structure. The East Wing was demolished in 1866 and not replaced for thirty-six years.

Who the children might be is not known—possibly Tad and Willie and their friends, as the grounds were made public only at special times so the boys could play there.

Soldiers on the South Wall, Carte de Visite by Mathew Brady, 1862

In this carte de visite, which is actually dated, soldiers pose on the 12-foot stone wall built by Jefferson fifty-four years before to terminate the south grounds. The wall was demolished 1871–72. In the background, in front of the South Portico, the fickle fountain gives one of its rare performances, while the flagpole awaits its weekly surround of a tented platform from which the Marine Band played for a public afternoon. Performances were held on these otherwise restricted grounds throughout the Civil War, with the exception of the coldest winter weeks and the mourning period for Lincoln's son Willie. The president liked to lie on a sofa in the Blue Room, which opened at the top of the portico steps, and with shutters closed listen in privacy to the music.[19]

Workers Rolling the Grounds, Carte de Visite by Mathew Brady, 1862

Grounds workers "roll" smooth the president's graveled walks with heavily weighted, water-filled "rollers." At one time the grass had also been rolled regularly, but since the invention of the lawn mower in the 1830s the more or less level cutting reduced the desirability; yet the lawn was still occasionally rolled in the Lincoln period, to create the perfect carpet. This rare image of a commonplace activity at Lincoln's White House is probably the earliest photograph of White House staff members at their daily work.

ALEXANDER GARDNER

Lincoln's Last Sitting, Carte de Visite by Alexander Gardner, 1865

Alexander Gardner (1821–1882) emigrated from Scotland in 1856 and began working for Mathew Brady in New York. In 1858, he moved to Washington to manage Brady's newly opened gallery. In addition to being a savvy business manager, he was a talented photographer who was an expert in the wet collodion process. He left Brady in 1862 to work for the Army of the Potomac, under General George B. McClellan, photographing soldiers, campsites, and battlefields, especially the carnage left behind. Gardner photographed Lincoln on numerous occasions in the studio and at outside locations. When Gardner's own establishment opened, the president agreed to be his first subject and posed on August 9, 1863.[20] Gardner was on hand to document several momentous occasions during Lincoln's presidency, including both the 1861 and 1865 inaugurations, the president's meeting with General George McClellan after the battle at Antietam, October 3, 1862, and the dedication of the cemetery at Gettysburg, Pennsylvania, where the president delivered his famous address, November 19, 1863. He also photographed the Lincoln assassination conspirators and their executions on July 7, 1865.

Along with Mathew Brady, Gardner was an early advocate for photographic documentation of the Civil War. In 1866, his war photos were published in a two-volume set entitled, Gardner's Photographic Sketch Book of the War. *One hundred hand-mounted photographs were featured and captioned by Gardner. For each, he added a credit line that acknowledged the work of the photographers under his employ and the individuals who made the prints.[21]*

The image above is a retouched print of a likeness from Lincoln's last sitting with Gardner on February 5, 1865. The addition of the ribbon suggests that it was printed after Lincoln's death.[22]

NOTES

1. Lloyd Ostendorf, *Lincoln's Photographs: A Complete Album* (Dayton, Ohio: Rockywood Press, 1998), ix.

2. James M. Reilly, *Care and Identification of 19th-Century Photograph Prints* (Rochester: Eastman Kodak Company, 1986), 50.

3. Ibid., 4–5. Mary Panzer, *Mathew Brady and the Image of History* (Washington, D.C.: Smithsonian Institution Press for the National Portrait Gallery, 1997) 11, 13. See also www.npg.si.edu/exh/brady, a special website presentation that was created in conjunction with *Mathew Brady's Portraits* an exhibition held at the National Portrait Gallery, September 26, 1997–January 4, 1998. The site includes a glossary and an animated demonstration of the wet collodion process.

4. Ostendorf, *Lincoln's Photographs,* 81, 83, 131.

5. Mark E. Neely Jr. and Harold Holzer, *The Lincoln Family Album: Photographs from the Personal Collection of a Historic American Family* (New York: Doubleday, 1990) ix–x, 74. Photographs were removed from the family albums long ago. The albums and family-owned photographs, many of which could have been in the albums, are now in the collection of Abraham Lincoln Presidential Library in Springfield, Illinois. The Lincoln Museum in Fort Wayne, Indiana also has family-owned photographs that may have been in the albums. E-mail correspondence of the author with James M. Cornelius, Curator, Lincoln Collection, July 8, 2008, Abraham Lincoln Presidential Library.

6. D. Mark Katz, *Witness to an Era: The Life and Photographs of Alexander Gardner* (Nashville: Rutledge Hill Press, 1991), 19, 31.

7. Photographs of Lincoln-era rooms include those taken by Anthony Berger, of Brady's gallery, of the president in his office on April 26, 1864, one of which will be illustrated in William Allman's article in *White House History* no. 25, and a northeast view of the East Room published previously by the White House Historical Association. See William Seale, *The White House: The History of an American Idea*, 2d, ed. (Washington, D.C.: White House Historical Association, 2001), 104.

8. Kathleen Collins, *Washingtoniana Photographs* (Washington, D.C.: Library of Congress, 1989), 24–25. See also Panzer, 18–20.

9. Dorothy Meserve Kunhardt and Philip B. Kunhardt Jr., and the Editors of Time-Life Books, *Mathew Brady and His World* (Alexandria, Va.: Time-Life Books, 1977), 200–11.

10. Ostendorf, *Lincoln's Photographs,* 34–37. See also Panzer, *Mathew Brady,* 15, 17.

11. Ostendorf, *Lincoln's Photographs,* 168–69.

12. The sculptor was David d'Angers. Susan R. Stein, *The Worlds of Thomas Jefferson at Monticello* (New York: Harry N. Abrams, 1993) 120.

13. Katz, *Witness to an Era,* 20. Collins, *Washingtoniana Photographs,* 142.

14. I would like to thank Dr. Wayne C. Temple for his observations and for the suggestion as to the identity of the soldiers. See also Margaret Leech, *Reveille in Washington* (New York: Harper & Brothers, 1941), 303. Tad's album with its contents is in the Abraham Lincoln Presidential Library. See also Neely and Holzer, *The Lincoln Family Album,* ix.

15. I would like to thank Keya Morgan, Keya Gallery, New York, for his assistance with documenting this carte de visite. This image, as well as several others that appear in this article, were acquired from Mr. Morgan. See also Ostendorf, *Lincoln's Photographs,* 213–15, 365–66, and Clifford Krainik, "Face the Lens, Mr. President: A Gallery of Photographic Portraits of 19th-Century U.S. Presidents," *White House History,* 16:28–30.

16. Leech, 422. William Seale, *The President's House: A History* (Washington, D.C.: White House Historical Association, 2008), 408.

17. Seale, *President's House,* 411

18. Garry E. Adelman and John J. Richter, *99 Historic Images of Civil War Washington* (Oldsmar, Fla.: Center for Civil War Photography, 2006), 3.

19. This custom began during the presidency of John Tyler and ended during the Herbert Hoover administration. Elise K. Kirk, *Music at the White House: A History of the American Spirit* (Urbana: University of Illinois Press, 1986), 56. See also Seale, *President's House,* 390.

20. Katz, *Witness to an Era,* 50–51. See also Collins, *Washingtoniana Photographs,* 212 and Ostendorf, *Lincoln's Photographs,* 122–23, 130.

21. Alexander Gardner, *Gardner's Photographic Sketch Book of the Civil War* 1866 (Reprint: New York: Dover Publications, 1959), introduction.

22. Ostendorf, *Lincoln's Photographs,* 230–31.

A Gallery of Individuals,
Major and Minor, from Lincoln's Time
in the White House

*T*he house the American people provided for their sixteenth president was the stage for most of the Lincoln melodrama, the last hours of which passed at Ford's Theatre April 15, 1865. These two buildings—White House and Ford's—dominate our memory of President Lincoln, confining the action of his history in a way shared by no other presidency. The event at Ford's was a moment; his life at the White House covered four years and a little over a month. In and out of Lincoln's White House moved numerous figures important to his presidency and his private life, family, friends, military and political associates, as well as the orbit surrounding what was known as the "Republican court."

In the first of two Lincoln issues, *White House History* has taken a sampling of the people who figured in the Lincoln story. There were many more. These are representative. John Hay was in the White House nearly the whole time; Ellsworth's brief time is indelible in the history of the house; John Ford may have attended a Fourth of July or New Year's reception, or may never have crossed the threshold, but he figures in the climax of Lincoln's story. To some of these figures Lincoln was close, indeed intimate, while others he kept at arm's length. Yet they all were there. As it was with Lincoln, for most of them this four year interlude in the long White House past was the high point of their lives. Lincoln did not live to serve his entire second term, nor to move to Chicago and practice law after that, as he planned. Most in this gallery enjoyed longer lives.

Col. Elmer Ephraim Ellsworth, 1861

Posing in his oilcloth raincoat, Col. Elmer Ephraim Ellsworth (1837–1861) became the toast of the town when he moved to the capital with President-elect Lincoln, who called him "The greatest little man I know." A colonel in the National Guard Cadets in Chicago, the native of New York State became close to Lincoln during the 1860 campaign, vowing to defend the candidate against harm. He was 23 when he moved with the Lincolns to the White House, sharing a room with the eldest son Robert Todd Lincoln. Flamboyant and energetic, Ellsworth brought a regiment of New York firefighters to Washington, trained in gymnastics. They performed amazing feats weekly on the White House lawn, and once, in a human pyramid, rescued a damsel in distress from the upper floor of a burning hotel.

This member of the Lincoln household was to be the first Union casualty of note in the Civil War. When Virginia seceded April 17, 1861, Ellsworth and his regiment were part of the capture of Alexandria, across the Potomac River the following morning. Eager for Lincoln to have as a souvenir the Confederate flag visible from his office window, which he had seen waving proudly over a King Street hotel, Ellsworth was shot dead in the attempt. The Lincolns wept over his body when the steamer brought it to the dock at the Navy Yard. The president ordered the remains brought to the White House, where he lay in state in the East Room, beneath a wreath of flowers woven by Mary Lincoln.

Willie and Tad Lincoln, 1861

Robert Todd Lincoln, 1862

The president's sons Willie (1850–1862) and Tad (1853–1871) pose with their first cousin, Lockwood Todd, at Brady's studio in 1861. Todd, who was in town seeking a presidential appointment that would allow him to locate in California, never got to claim his prize. He died of malaria in the next year. Willie, center, also died in that year probably of typhoid, in the bed known as the Lincoln Bed. He was a thoughtful, studious boy and his mother's favorite. Tad Lincoln, for his father's position and his own many publicized antics, was the most famous child in the war-torn nation. Of a creative bent, he had a theater on the Second Floor of the White House and commanded all White House employees to attend. In April 1865 Tad walked through the ruins of the Confederate capital, Richmond, with his father, while Union soldiers and freed slaves cheered. The pillar of his mother during her difficult widowhood, Tad Lincoln died while still in his teens.

Robert Todd Lincoln (1843–1926) turned twenty during his father's presidency (one month after Gettysburg and the fall of Vicksburg). He was a somewhat distant youth, who was away at school most of Lincoln's term. Over his mother's tearful objections, he joined the Union Army in 1865 and was present with Ulysses S. Grant at the surrender at Appomattox. In later life he served as secretary of war under Garfield and Arthur and was American minister to St. James's, 1889–93. His achievements in business and government were always overshadowed by his being Lincoln's son, and he sometimes reacted angrily when his father's name was brought up to him. Bob Lincoln was the longest-lived of Lincoln's private White House circle. When he died he was chairman of the board of the Pullman Palace Car Company.

Mary Todd Lincoln, 1861–65

LIBRARY OF CONGRESS

Mrs. Abraham Lincoln (1818–1882), often the subject of derision even in her time, was the first presidential wife subjected to negative press. She suffered not always in silence; hers was not yet the time when a first lady might be hardened to unkind reporting, and the situation was unique. Mary Lincoln's was a transitional time. An intellectual by nature, she loved literature and was probably far better read than Lincoln. Nervous and high-strung, she was an insecure woman whose appearance was so in contrast to Lincoln's homely ways that she never settled well as first lady. Although easy with the refinements of social and diplomatic Washington, she dealt entirely in personalities; she interpreted those who objected to her as being against her and too often coddled even the most brazen sycophants. Privately she was an affectionate wife and mother, and Lincoln, if not a particularly attentive husband, seems to have been devoted to her. After the war and his death, what appears to have been a mildly manic condition sharpened until in one brief period she was declared insane. As a widow she lost her son Tad, who lived with her, and after that was left only with the chilly Robert Todd Lincoln, to whom she was not close.

George Nicolay, 1863　　　　　　　　*John Hay, 1863*

Nicolay (1832–1901), a journalist and newspaper editor, came to America from Germany as a boy, and by 1860 was secretary to Lincoln during the presidential campaign. He moved with Lincoln to the White House, to live in the office section on the east end of the Second Floor with his assistant John Hay and work in the southeast corner room known today as the Lincoln Sitting Room. Efficient and wise, he was not only Lincoln's right-hand man but a close friend. His life was on hold during his White House years, his marriage postponed; he was at Lincoln's continual service, valuable for his writing skills and discretion on special missions, one of which took him as far away as Colorado. Nicolay resigned at the close of the war, married his fiancée, and took a job at the American legation in Paris. For many years he was marshal of the Supreme Court in Washington and wrote books and articles on Lincoln, notably with John Hay, a biography and writings serialized 1888–90 in Century Magazine, *that became the twelve-volume classic* Abraham Lincoln: A History, *published 1890–94.*

Hay (1838–1905) was the assistant secretary, who dealt with letter-writing and, toward the end of the war, some secret missions. No two people outside the Lincoln family had closer interactions with the president. Living in the White House, Nicolay and Hay were accessible to the president at all hours; when he could not sleep, he often woke them in early hours to talk. Hay resigned at the war's end and was preparing to enter the diplomatic service when Lincoln was assassinated. In Spain he began to write and gained some popularity for his Indiana tales. Like Nicolay, he returned to Washington eventually and with his large family occupied a double house, built with his friend Henry Adams, on Lafayette Square where the Hay-Adams Hotel now stands. He began what might be considered a new life when McKinley appointed him American ambassador to Britain in 1897, and in 1898 he became secretary of state, a position he held with distinction until his death.

Ward Hill Lamon, c. 1855–65

Benjamin Brown French, c. 1861–65

Ward Hill Lamon (1828–1893) was a fixture in the Lincolns' lives at the White House. A lawyer, he had met Lincoln on the circuit in the 1850s, but his marriage in 1860 to Sally Logon, daughter of one of Lincoln's early law partners and an old friend, gave him full access. Lamon was many things, not least a sort of court jester. Lincoln delighted in his banjo playing and renditions of popular minstrel songs; he could be found with Lincoln most any time, at the White House or on the road, banjo in hand. Ward Lamon became Lincoln's self-appointed bodyguard after the election of 1860. Often at odds with Allan Pinkerton, the detective hired for the purpose, Lamon remained determined to satisfy himself that Lincoln was safe and the president seems to have endorsed what Pinkerton for four years called intrusions. Lamon's absence from town when Lincoln was assassinated was a source of great pain to him, and rained down popular criticism he was to try to thwart for the rest of his life.

Benjamin Brown French (1800–1870), commissioner of public buildings under Lincoln, was in charge of maintenance and many functions at the White House. A lawyer and office-seeker, French had been an appointee to the same office under President Franklin Pierce, but became a Republican and went after an appointment from Lincoln in 1861. As commissioner he was put in direct touch with the Lincolns, now and then as a mediator between them. He courted favor with Mrs. Lincoln, doing most of what she wished, including buying the famous Lincoln Bed, in the White House today, at which Lincoln flew into a rage at him over spending money on "this damned old house" when the soldiers needed blankets. While an able commissioner in most respects, his delicate dealings with the erratic first lady seem to have made him steer clear of the domestic staffing of the White House, thus leaving the door open to spies and other undesirables who infiltrated the enclave.

Rosa Greenhow with her daughter, 1862

The famous Confederate spy, Rose O'Neal Greenhow (1817–1864), a well-known Washington hostess before the Civil War, fell under the influence of John C. Calhoun while a young girl and when the war broke out became outspoken in her southern sympathies. Allan Pinkerton learned of her connection as a secret agent to General P.G.T. Beauregard and had her arrested in January 1862. She is shown here in prison, posed hugging her daughter "Little Rose," with crafted pathos. Her network of secret correspondence extended beyond prison walls. Toward the end of 1862, weakened by the pressures the clever woman was able to muster from outside, federal officers sent her to Richmond. From the Confederate capital, where she was celebrated, she sailed to Europe, where she was presented at court in France and Britain and even became engaged to a peer. Returning home via Bermuda on a blockade runner with $2,000 in gold to present to the Confederacy, she saw a Union Coast Guard cutter on the horizon, and boarded a lifeboat, which capsized in the surf near Wilmington, North Carolina. Very heavy with the gold she had sewn into her dress, Rose Greenhow sank to the bottom. She was buried in Wilmington with full Confederate military honors.

Elizabeth Keckley

LIBRARY OF CONGRESS

The skills of Elizabeth Keckley (1818–1907) a well-known Washington "mantua maker," or shawl and dressmaker were called to the White House for Mrs. Lincoln early in the war. Born a slave in Hillsborough, North Carolina, Mrs. Keckley took in sewing to buy her freedom, which was made possible for herself and her son George ultimately by a grateful customer. She was not a member of the White House staff but was often there, and Mrs. Lincoln relaxed in her company. Soon the work at the White House became all consuming, threatening the Keckley shop in town; still Lizzie Keckley was the only woman who seems to have been able to calm Mrs. Lincoln in her difficulties. The government employed her to hurry Mrs. Lincoln's departure after Lincoln's assassination and accompany her to Chicago, for which all the bills survive. Mrs. Keckley in 1868 published Behind the Scenes: Formerly a Slave, but More Recently Modiste, and a Friend to Mrs. Lincoln, or Thirty Years a Slave, and Four Years in the White House. *Viewed at the time as a betrayal of confidence, and denounced by Mrs. Lincoln, it prevails as one of the best-detailed recollections of life in the White House. While it may appear otherwise, Mrs. Keckley's book, written during a storm of criticism of Mrs. Lincoln, at least seems on one level an honest and kind effort to set the record straight.*

General Winfield Scott, c. 1861

General George B. McClellan, 1862

NATIONAL PORTRAIT GALLERY, SMITHSONIAN INSTITUTION

LIBRARY OF CONGRESS

General in chief of the army, Winfield Scott (1786–1866) had a long and visible military career both in strong leadership and sure strategy. His actual rank since 1856 had been brevet lieutenant general, the only man to hold that title since George Washington. By the time Lincoln took office he was in his 70s, weighed in excess of three hundred pounds and suffered agonizing gout. Strict and practiced in the exercise of authority, Scott made people stand back and give him his way; in this at first Lincoln was no exception. He resigned as chief of the army on November 1, 1861, but lived on to honor requested ceremonial appearances at the White House. Sometimes the effort was so tiring he was taken upstairs and put to bed before the evening ended.

General George Brinton McClellan (1826–1885) frequently made the trip up the carpeted stairs to Lincoln's office, often to explain himself. He followed Scott as general in chief in 1861 and founded the Army of the Potomac. While a very popular public figure during the earlier war years, his failures and only near successes, together with his arrogant attitude, shrank Lincoln's opinion of him. In 1862 he was removed as general in chief and left in command of the Army of the Potomac. A year later he was removed entirely from command. He ran unsuccessfully as a Democrat against the Republican Lincoln for the presidency in 1864 and lived on after the war to become governor of New Jersey.

General Daniel Sickles, 1860–70

Walt Whitman, c. 1867

General Daniel Sickles (1819–1914) entered the military in 1861. This followed a career in Congress during which he earned a notorious reputation for killing, in front of the White House, Philip Barton Key, the husband of his mistress and son of Francis Scott Key. Saved from the gallows by a clever lawyer, and quite notorious as a result of the trial, he went on to redeem himself at the Battle of Gettysburg, where his brilliance in battle was commemorated in the loss of a leg. He was a constant visitor to the Lincoln White House, where he assumed great familiarity, often lounging on the sofa in the office, smoking cigarettes, and talking, while Lincoln and his secretaries worked. After the war Dan Sickles enjoyed a long, lively career in diplomacy and added heroic chapters to his love life.

Novelist, essayist, and poet Walt Whitman (1819–1892) moved to Civil War Washington in pursuit of his brother, a soldier believed wounded. In the midst of war excitement, Whitman decided to remain, to play some role. He had difficulty getting work because of the sexual subject matter, considered pornographic, in his book of poems, Leaves of Grass, *first privately and anonymously published in 1855, then released under his name in 1860. He at last found part time work in the army paymaster's office, giving him spare time to work in the army hospitals, where he took on the most menial tasks and comforted wounded soldiers. When Lincoln died, Whitman wrote the memorable poem, "When Lilacs Last in the Dooryard Bloom'd," expressing in personal terms the tragedy of Lincoln's death and the national mourning that accompanied the long funeral journey back to Springfield.*

Kate Chase c. 1864

Kate Chase (1840–1899) was the daughter of Governor Salmon P. Chase of Ohio, who had longtime presidential ambitions. Reigning beauty of Civil War Washington, the proud, elegant Miss Chase was the center of society— and political to her toes. John Hay knew "Katie" well enough to express no surprise at her schemes to win over the great and powerful. Her marriage to Senator William Sprague, one of the richest men in New England, was the event of its time. For all the brilliant diamonds and costly parties that surrounded the marriage, it was not a love match, but her union to a fortune that might oil the tracks for her husband or her father to the presidency. Plans went awry; the marriage was unhappy. Kate Chase left Washington and eventually returned, forgotten. Finally, in her 50s, desperately sunk in poverty at a crumbling estate near town, she raised a meager income send- ing milk from her cow to Eastern Market. News of her death broke over the news pages of a nation newly inter- ested in the Civil War period, one of the dramatic, tragic characters of the Lincoln circle.

John T. Ford, c. 1865

Laura Keene c. 1855–65

NATIONAL PARK SERVICE, FORD'S THEATRE NATIONAL HISTORIC SITE

LIBRARY OF CONGRESS

Whether John T. Ford (1829–1894) ever formally met President Lincoln is unknown but probable; Ford served the president various times in his theaters. A native of theater-loving Baltimore, John Ford was a theater owner and manager for twenty years before the appeal of a thickly populated wartime Washington lured him to seek profits there. When his first Washington theater, of three, burned, he rebuilt it as Ford's Theatre, where he fashioned a gaslit presidential box, with rocking chairs and an engraving of George Washington and encouraged patronage from the president. Ford booked the best performers and plays. It was at Ford's Theatre that Lincoln was assassinated by Ford's friend, the matinee idol John Wilkes Booth, on April 14, 1865. Ford was arrested with his brothers as suspects and held for a month, until released. His theater was bought by the government for $100,000 and stands restored today, while Ford continued in the theater business in Baltimore.

Actress and theater entrepreneur Laura Keene (1826–1873) was the star of Our American Cousin, *performed at Ford's Theatre the night Lincoln was shot. She was the first woman theater manager in the United States. British born, and reared in the theater, she was a clever businesswoman, not at all liked by most actors who had to work for her. She demanded star status in every play. When Lincoln lay mortally wounded, she grasped the moment and, coming down from the stage, cradled his bleeding head in her lap.*

COFFEE URN PRESENTED TO JEFF. DAVIS, BY HIS FRIENDS IN FRANCE.

TENDER TO THE COFFEE URN PRESENTED TO JEFF. DAVIS.

The Locomotive Tea Set:
A Gift from France

JOHN H. WHITE JR.

*T*he Statue of Liberty that stands in New York Harbor is surely the largest gift from France to this country. A smaller French gift arrived in Richmond during the early years of the Civil War, when the Confederate Capitol felt on top of the world—that the Confederacy might win the war. A decorative tea maker in the shape of a locomotive was presented to Jefferson Davis. Was it an official gift of the Second Empire and Napoleon III? No evidence has been found to support this notion, and it was more likely sent by someone hoping to establish business relations with the Confederate government, or perhaps it was only a wealthy admirer of President Davis. It was surely a unique and costly ornament that would brighten any room with its glossy china body and gilt hardware. It was displayed in the Confederate White House.

A rather sizable piece of tableware, it measures 23 inches long by 15 inches high by 7 inches wide. Technically it is not an accurate likeness of a real locomotive and appears to have been perhaps a manufactured pull-toy for children. Yet it has cylinders, a single pair of driving wheels, and a substantial smokestack. Most people would recognize it as a locomotive, which

These drawings of the decorative locomotive-shaped teapot given to Jefferson Davis by France during the early years of the Civil War were printed in Frank Leslie's Illustrated Weekly Newspaper *in July 1866.*

is likely about all the engine maker intended. The lack of a cowcatcher, headlight, and other American features suggest that the prototype was European. The buffers on the engine and tender confirm this supposition. From a decorative perspective it was splendidly customized, with elegant scrolls, lettering, banners, and flags. A panel on the side of the boiler is inscribed "President Jefferson Davis." On the front of the boiler or smokebox, the top banner reads "Confederate States of America." The Confederate flag and its battle flag are entwined with the French national insignia. Just below the flags is another banner lettered in Latin with the familiar motto: "God helps those who help themselves."

Mechanically, the tea maker was a simple device. The smoke stack was the hopper for the tea leaves; a loose-fitting cap could be lifted up to make an opening. A glass tube served as a siphon to direct the hot water from the boiler to the tea hopper. Just behind the tube is a funnel-shaped opening with a china plug. This is where water is introduced into the boiler. Behind the water plug is a brass turn-cock that, when left open, will indicate when the water is at a boil. The little platform behind the boiler once supported the china figure of an engineer or fireman ringing a huge dinner bell. Below the boiler on a sheet metal platform is a small spirit or alcohol lamp that keeps the water hot. A spigot at the very front of the locomotive delivers brewed tea to a cup or glass.

The tender is the small four-wheel car just behind the locomotive. When new it had several small cut-glass

The locomotive on display at Tusculum College in the 1990s.

---

tumblers inside the railing now occupied by two large china cups. A cognac decanter fit just behind the tumblers. At the rear a china tea decanter may also have served as a sugar bowl. Below this rectangular container is a music box that could play eight popular tunes of the day. This mechanism no longer plays, but it is likely "Dixie" was one of those airs. Six hoops on each side of the tender were arranged to hold cigars.

We assume Davis and his family were pleased with this delightful and decorative breakfast room novelty. Surely it became a plaything for the grandchildren. By the spring of 1865 there was little feeling for play or

merriment in Richmond as the Union Army put an end to the Confederacy. Davis packed hurriedly to escape from the doomed capital. Much was left behind and consigned to Bell, Ellett & Company's auction house on Pearl Street. A Richmond newspaper for April 17, 1865, reported on the sale of the locomotive tea set to an Italian named A. Barratti.[1] Within a few days he resold it to Colonel Friedman of Philadelphia, who intended to give it to President Abraham Lincoln as a souvenir of war. Lincoln did not live to receive the intended gift. Friedman presented it to Andrew Johnson instead. Ironically, the china tea server went from the

Confederate executive mansion to the U.S. White House.

Johnson was inaugurated as the seventeenth president upon Lincoln's death and should have by rights occupied the White House on becoming the commander in chief. But he took pity on Mrs. Lincoln's state of near-total collapse and advised her to remain in the Executive Mansion so long as it suited her needs. Meanwhile, Johnson was invited to share the apartment of Treasury Secretary Hugh McCulloch in the Treasury Department Building, which stood next to the White House.

Johnson was a southerner and McCulloch born a New England Yankee, but the men got along famously. Each day during Johnson's long exile they shared tea together, made in the locomotive tea maker. When Sir Frederick Bruce presented President Johnson his credentials as the British envoy, tea was served from the Davis tea urn. After Johnson took up residency in the White House, the tea server was placed in the library on the second floor as a display piece but was no longer used.

Few presidents had a more miserable time in office than Johnson. When his term was over in the spring of 1869, he was surely ready to return to his home in Greeneville, Tennessee. The china and gilt tea maker was among the objects returned to his eastern Tennessee home. It was passed down through succeeding generations and became the property of his great-great granddaughter, Mrs. Margaret P. Bartlett. She was a graduate of the local school, Tusculum College, in 1924, and was devoted to preserving papers and artifacts associated with her illustrious ancestor. Tusculum eventually became the repository for the Johnson papers. Mrs. Bartlett also attempted in other ways to keep his memory alive. In the fall of 1959 she visited First Lady Mamie Eisenhower in the White House and brought the tea locomotive with her.

The tea maker was loaned to the Treasury

Shaped Like Locomotive

Teapot Given Jeff Davis by France, Used by President Johnson, Found

By Francis de Sales Ryan
Washington Area Historian

A locomotive-shaped teapot that France gave to Confederate President Jefferson Davis has been found and is on temporary exhibit in the Treasury Building.

Souvenir hunters had searched for it more than half a century. Records in the Federal Archives show, that the teapot was sold at auction after the evacuation of Richmond and the purchaser, Anthony Barratti, sent it as a gift to the new President, Andrew Johnson.

Johnson was using Room 3434 in the Treasury Building as a temporary White House because illness kept Mrs. Lincoln from moving from the Executive Mansion. Secretary of the Treasury Hugh McCulloch described how the President's tea was made every day:

"The boiler received the tea and made it, and then dis charged it through a spigot a miniature steam-whistle and a little tinkling bell indicating when the beverage was ready. The tender carried sugar and glasses and a container for

Picture on Page A4

cognac. Its sides carried racks for cigars; and a tiny secret music box, when set, played eight popular airs.

"On the side of the locomotive 'President Jefferson Davis' was emblazoned in gold. In front, the Confederate banner and battle flag, entwined with the ensign of France, was fashioned into a charming design." Below this design is a Latin inscription reading, in

English, "God helps those who help themselves."

On April 20, 1865, when Sir Frederick A. Bruce presented to the new President his credentials as envoy from Britain, tea was served from the Davis pot by the President's daughter, Mary Stover, an ancestor of President Eisenhower's mother.

Isabella S. Diamond, librarian of the Treasury Department, succeeded in tracing the teapot, made of silver, bronze and enamel, to the home of a great-great-granddaughter of Johnson, Margaret Patterson Bartlett of Greenville, Tenn.

Bringing the teapot with her on a recent visit to Mrs. Eisenhower, Mrs. Bartlett lent it to Miss Diamond for temporary exhibit. It will be forwarded this week to the Andrew Johnson National Monument at Greenville.

Department for display after the visit. A short article in the *Washington Post* alerted curators at the Smithsonian Institution that this national treasure was on exhibit just blocks away.[2] W. E. Washburn, then chief of the Political History Division, made contact with Mrs. Bartlett. After a year of negotiations, the tea maker was lent to the Smithsonian. I remember it being on exhibit in the original First Ladies Hall in the Arts and Industries Building, which was one of the first modern galleries in this branch of the Smithsonian. In about 1964 the First Ladies Hall and all associated specimens were moved to the Museum of History and Technology, now renamed the National Museum of American History. In 1982, Mrs. Bartlett recalled the loan, and the Davis tea maker returned to Greeneville. Perhaps she wanted the relic near at hand in her advanced years. Mrs. Bartlett considered lending it to the World's Fair in nearby Knoxville, but it is uncertain if that loan was ever honored. Sometime in the 1990s the tea maker joined the other Andrew Johnson memorabilia in the Tusculum College archives, where it remains to the present time.

NOTES

1. *Richmond Whig,* April 17, 1864.

2. "Teapot Given Jeff Davis by France, Used by President Johnson, Found," *Washington Post*, October 19, 1959. p. A1.

WHITE HOUSE
HISTORY

White House Historical Association
Washington

LIFE IN THE LINCOLN WHITE HOUSE: PART TWO • NUMBER 25
PUBLISHED SPRING 2009

Foreword

Across Lafayette Park from this journal's office, Saint John's Episcopal Church is known for good reason as "the Church of Presidents." Designed originally by Benjamin Henry Latrobe for a rich parishioner, John Tayloe, the church was uninhibited by committee votes and stood in secular glory for nearly thirty years, until the addition of columns and a steeple brought it into conformity. Only on the interior does one still meet the liberality of the original builder.

Most of the nation's presidents have worshipped at Saint John's from time to time, thanks to its convenience to the White House and a history of compelling preachers. President Abraham Lincoln, who regularly attended New York Avenue Presbyterian Church in Washington, liked to cross Pennsylvania Avenue alone, enter Saint John's Church unnoticed through the outside door pictured here and ease into pew 89 for Evensong. "Before the service was ended," remembered the rector Rev. George Williamson Smith, "he would slip out as quietly and unostentatiously as he had come."

Pew 89 at historic Saint John's is a Lincoln site in Washington as is, of course, the White House. Indeed the capital is filled with Lincoln places, as our authors show in this second number of the White House Historical Association's commemoration of Lincoln's administration. Harold Holzer takes us inside Lincoln's White House, while Anthony Pitch describes the chaos of the assassination and its aftermath. Michele and Clifford Krainik have drawn together and analyzed here for the first time photographs taken of visiting native Americans after their 1863 meeting with President Lincoln in the East Room. I have gone to the Confederate capital, Richmond, to find out how the president of the Confederacy lived in his official house. White House curator William G. Allman introduces our readers to the revised Lincoln Bedroom, redecorated with an eye to evoking Lincoln's White House.

President Lincoln preferred to slip in and out unnoticed from services at Saint John's Church. He sat in pew 89, the last pew in the back corner beside the door.

In planning our two Lincoln issues we were reminded constantly of the monumental place the Civil War or Lincoln years hold in the history of the White House. The question was for a long time where to begin. This we believe you will find makes an interesting companion to the previous number, also on Lincoln.

William Seale
Editor, *White House History*

Abraham Lincoln's White House

HAROLD HOLZER

O n a hot summer day in August 1864, Abraham Lincoln strolled from his Second-Floor office to the lawn outside the Executive Mansion to greet a regiment of Ohio soldiers en route home after surviving some of the bloodiest fighting of the Civil War. Thanking the men profusely for their bravery and sacrifice, Lincoln implored the veterans to remember that the nation remained "an inestimable jewel" well "worth fighting for," not just for their own generation, but to guarantee "equal privileges" for "our children's children" as well. As he put it: "I happen temporarily to occupy this big White House. I am a living witness that any one of your children may look to come here as my father's child has."[1] By the time he spoke these heartfelt words, it might be fair to say, Lincoln had endured nearly as much suffering and heartache in that "big White House" as the soldiers had on the battlefield.

However much the Lincolns—particularly Mary Lincoln—may have hoped for a glorious four years of social triumph and renewed intimacy at the nation's

---

Detail of Peter Rothermel's The Republican Court in the Days of Lincoln *(see p. 460), oil on canvas, painted in c. 1867 to recall the ebullient spirit of Union in the recent Civil War.*

most famous residence, rebellion, civil war, and family tragedy conspired to puncture their dream. Although Mary dutifully hosted her share of public and diplomatic receptions, her husband grew increasingly occupied with running the government and the war, and before long the couple found themselves spending fewer hours together than at any time since his circuit-riding days as an attorney.

Mary's fond hopes for a palatial new existence in Washington were in a way dashed almost as soon as she took up residence in March 1861. As Lincoln's clerk William O. Stoddard conceded, many once glittering areas of the house were run down; even the East Room had "a faded, worn, untidy look."[2] Mary's visiting cousin Lizzie Grimsley thought the "deplorably shabby furnishings" looked like they had "survived many Presidents," although the house had been extensively refurbished twice in the previous decade. Concluding that it would be "a degradation" to subject her family— and her guests—to such surroundings, the new first lady launched a monumental redecorating project, purchasing new carpets, draperies, wallpaper, furnishings, china, and books, and modernizing plumbing, heating, and lighting.[3]

No doubt much of this renovation initiative was sorely needed, but when Mary overran a generous congressional appropriation allocated for the effort— by nearly 30 percent—Lincoln "*swore*" to the commissioner of public buildings in December 1861 that "he would never approve the bills for *flub dubs for that*

damned old house!" As Lincoln viewed matters, it was "furnished well enough when they came—better than any house *they* had ever lived in—& rather than put his name on such a bill he would pay it out of his own pocket." As the weary commander in chief declared: "It would stink in the land to have it said that an appropriation for $20,000 for furnishing the house had been overrun by the President when the poor freezing soldiers could not have blankets."[4]

Eventually, the overrun was hushed up and made good—Lincoln was not required to make up the difference "out of his own pocket" after all, and Congress quietly supplemented the appropriation the following year—but the episode revealed the strains that White House life had already exacted on the president's marriage after only nine months in the mansion. Mary would not even tell her husband directly that she had overspent on its decor; she compelled the hapless commissioner of public buildings to bring him the bad news, and bear the brunt of his outrage.

One aspect of White House life that made family life particularly difficult for the Lincolns was the mansion's open-door policy to the public, war notwithstanding. Virtually from Lincoln's first day in office, a crush of visitors besieged the White House stairways and

Left: North Front of the White House at the time of Lincoln's inauguration. Iron fences and railings control public access to the grounds. The graveled walk, set in a flat-rolled lawn, encircles the Pierre Jean David d'Angers statue of Thomas Jefferson, placed there by President James K. Polk in 1847 and since 1874 in Statuary Hall in the Capitol. To the right of the house barely can be seen the Conservatory, which was built atop the west terrace in the later 1850s and was filled with tubbed camellias and fruit trees.

Opposite bottom: Anthony Berger of Mathew Brady's Gallery photographed Lincoln in his White House office and Cabinet Room on April 26, 1864. The picture was set up by the painter Francis Bicknell Carpenter. The damage to Lincoln's face may have been caused when Tad locked the photographer out of the temporary darkroom in the house.

Below: The Lincoln Family, *oil on canvas, 1865, by Francis Bicknell Carpenter, was widely published as an engraving and hung in many an American parlor through the balance of the nineteenth century. If it was posed, the sittings probably took place in the Soldiers' Home. From left to right, Mrs. Lincoln, Willie (whom Carpenter added, for Willie died in 1862), Bob, Tad, and the president.*

Frank Leslie's Illustrated Newspaper *of April 6, 1861, included this illustration along with a scathing article about the "office-seekers" who gathered outside Lincoln's meeting rooms and aggressively sought employment. Favor-seekers were a fact of life in the nineteenth century White House, and in Lincoln's time those approved for appointments crowded into the East Hall outside his office to await their turn. Some wanted salaried government positions, others wanted their special requests granted. They paced and huddled on the oilcloth floor, used the numerous spittoons, and were a general nuisance, although their right to be there was staunchly defended by the president.*

OFFICE-SEEKERS IN WASHINGTON.

Scene Outside the Room in the White House where the President Holds his Cabinet Meetings.

OFFICE-SEEKING has become, of late years, quite a science in this great Republic, and, as an illustration of the manners of the present time, our artist in Washington has given a graphic sketch of the "mob of gentlemen" which generally gathers around the door of the room in the Executive Mansion where Mr. Lincoln holds his Cabinet meetings. When one of the Secretaries comes out from the "Sacred Presence" he is eagerly seized upon by some one who has the good fortune to know him, and is compelled to undergo the purgatory of a series of introductions almost fabulous in extent. The unhappy Minister escapes from his tormentors with the vague idea that he has been captured by a crowd of Smiths, Browns, Joneses and Robinsons. Indeed, he sometimes feels more like the fag-end of a mob himself. The enormous amount of intellect, labor, time and patriotism wasted by office-seekers always puts us in mind of poor Nym's adventure of the fiddle-case, as narrated by that veracious historian, Shakespeare, who deposes that the aforesaid Nym stole a fiddle-case, carried it half a score of leagues, and then, to save himself from being hanged as a thief, sold it for a penny! If our office-seekers would bestow on some reputable calling the energy and toil they waste in securing a spoonful of Government pap, they would die happier and wealthier men.

OFFICE-SEEKERS IN WASHINGTON SCENE OUTSIDE THE ROOM IN THE

E HOUSE WHERE THE PRESIDENT HOLDS HIS CABINET MEETINGS.—From a Sketch by our Special Artist in Washington.—See Page 310.

corridors, climbed through windows at levees, and camped outside Lincoln's office door "on all conceivable errands, for all imaginable purposes."[5] Neither custom nor security precautions shielded the president from his voraciously demanding public. Office-seekers were the biggest drain on the president's time and energy—among them, his wife's own relatives—crowding the hallways all the way down the front stairs in an endless effort to importune him for lucrative government appointments. As the first Republican president, Lincoln was expected by his party to cleanse the bureaucracy of Democratic holdovers, and when he failed to do so by the time of his inauguration, job aspirants made their way to Washington in quest of the loaves and fishes they believed theirs by right.

too burdensome, the public hours were cut back to "only" three hours per session. Under the revised system, Lincoln joked, every applicant had to take his turn "as if waiting to be shaved at a barber's shop." But even with a truncated schedule, each open house, Lincoln continued to maintain, served "to renew in me a clearer and more vivid image of that great popular assemblage out of which I sprung. I tell you," he lectured one visitor, "that I call these receptions my '*public opinion baths*,'" and their effect was for him "renovating and invigorating."[7] At least that is what he said publicly. To his assistant secretary Edward Duffield Neill, who was often required to referee the onslaught of callers, Lincoln "playfully" admitted that the crush reminded him more of a "Beggar's Opera."[8]

WESTERN RESERVE HISTORICAL SOCIETY

President Lincoln's office and cabinet room on the second floor of the White House became the Lincoln Bedroom in the twentieth century. C. K. Stellwagen made a pen-and-ink sketch of it in October 1864. At the long cabinet table the Emancipation Proclamation had been signed on January 1, 1863.

At first, Lincoln rejected his staff's efforts to spare him by limiting public access. "For myself," he insisted, "I feel—though the tax on my time is heavy—that no hours of my day are better employed than those which thus bring me again within the direct contact and atmosphere of the average of our whole people."[6] Eventually, however, the crush proved too much even for the generous Lincoln to bear, and his staff secured some concessions and organized a formal schedule.

The original, daylong "promiscuous receptions," as Lincoln had taken to calling them, were thenceforth limited to twice weekly, for five hours each session, from 10 a.m. until 3 p.m. When even this arrangement proved

The White House architecture did little at first to protect Lincoln. In fact, only when he found himself unable to navigate between his office and the family parlor unmolested did White House maintenance men erect a partition that finally divided public and private spheres and allowed him at least to retreat for meals without running the gauntlet of assembled strangers. Those who were prevented from seeing him left stacks of letters, petitions, and pleas—and in some cases, inventions for his inspection. Clerk William O. Stoddard testified that so many newfangled weapons were deposited in the White House office that it came to resemble "a gunshop."[9]

Historical illustrator Tom Freeman painted for the White House Historical Association in 1999 this representation of President Lincoln and companions departing the North Portico as night is falling and the gaslight rises from the great lamps mounted to the columns.

For a year, at least, the White House rang with the laughter of the Lincoln's two energetic young sons (the eldest was off at college). Eleven-year-old Willie and eight-year-old Tad explored the vast mansion and merrily conducted such mischief as playing havoc with its intricate bell system for summoning servants, galloping a pet goat down the central corridor, and cutting up tablecloths to shreds with pocket knives.[10] To all of this, Lincoln turned a blind eye. A White House clerk observed Willie and Tad repeatedly burst into his office and interrupted meetings with "grave statesmen and pompous generals" but maintained that their company was "of more value to their father and to his work than anybody knew."[11]

The White House was always more to the Lincolns than a family home, of course. It simultaneously served as a seven-days-per-week presidential office, a military hub, a magnet for tourists and favor-seekers, and at times, even a funeral chapel. When the Lincoln's young family friend, Colonel Ephraim Elmer Ellsworth, became the first officer killed in the Civil War in May 1861, a teary-eyed president ordered his body brought back to the White House for a state funeral, at which Mary placed the slain hero's photograph and a wreath on his casket.[12] A few months later, Lincoln ordered the mansion draped in black once again to mourn the death of his old political rival, and Mary's onetime admirer, Stephen A. Douglas.[13]

In many ways, just as the president had declared,

the White House was far better than any place the Lincolns ever lived in. Its family quarters boasted indoor plumbing (a luxury their Springfield, Illinois, home lacked), gas-fed lighting, separate bedrooms for the children, and a handsome suite and dressing chamber for Mr. and Mrs. Lincoln. The family no longer needed a kitchen, as meals were cooked and served from the White House galley below. Though the Lincolns' Springfield residence had two small parlors and a tiny dining room and the private quarters upstairs at the White House provided only one common room—a combination library, dining area, and parlor—the Oval Room, as it was known, proved nearly as large as all three of the Lincoln home's rooms combined. Besides, the Lincolns were free to entertain small or large groups downstairs in the intimate Green, Blue, or Red Rooms, or hold levees in the vast East Room, the scene of many public receptions during their four years in residence.

For a time, the first lady appreciated the perquisites she now enjoyed. The living situation was "very different *from home*," Mary breathlessly observed soon after her arrival. "We only have to give our orders for the dinner, and *dress* in the proper season."[14] The Lincolns now had several servants at their disposal, including doorkeeper Edward Moran, seamstress Rosetta Wells, cook Cornelia Mitchell, butler-waiter Peter Brown, and valet William Johnson, who traveled with the president to Gettysburg.[15] Helping the president with his day-to-day routine was a valet, and Mary was frequently

attended by her seamstress, Elizabeth Keckly. The president's two private secretaries, John George Nicolay and John M. Hay, lived in a room next to their outer office, constantly at Lincoln's beck and call. It is little wonder that Mary wrote just a few weeks after moving in, "I am beginning to feel so perfectly at home, and enjoy every thing so much." "Every evening," she marveled, "our *blue room*, is filled with the elite of the land." The "pleasure grounds" were "exquisite," she recalled, and the adjacent Conservatory "delightful," yielding "so many choice bouquets." A bit boastfully, she wrote that her visiting sister would probably never again be able to "settle down at home, since she has been here." Of her family, she added, "We *may perhaps*, at the close of *four*, years, be glad to relinquish our claims."[16] But her joy proved brief, and not just because of the imbroglio over redecoration.

Their grand new situation did not automatically bring the Lincolns closer together, as Mary hoped; ultimately, it conspired in a sense to drive them farther apart. Although before his presidency Lincoln had never made his office in his home, his new proximity to his family did not guarantee them more shared time. Mary's

Above: Peter Rothermel's East Room painting uses some enlargement of the interior's true scale to allow portraits of the numerous guests. The picture is believed to be symbolic, not representational. Yet General Ulysses S. Grant's presence at center suggests his triumphant appearance at the White House following the victory at Vicksburg in 1863. But the picture also evidences a reception at the time of Lincoln's second inaugural in 1865. A detail that perhaps favors the Grant interpretation is the presence of the orator Edward Everett, seated on the left, who had died prior to the second inauguration; still, it would be odd at the earlier representation to have included Andrew Johnson so prominently, before he was vice president, in Lincoln's second term. Nearly all the celebrities of Lincoln's era in the White House are represented, including the old military hero General Winfield Scott, seated because he was suffering from gout and his feet failed him.

Opposite top: A hand-colored wood engraving from Frank Leslie's Illustrated Newspaper *captures President Lincoln welcoming guests to a New Year's reception at the White House on January 1, 1862.*

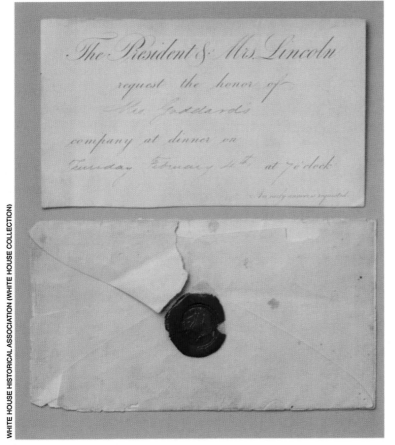

This invitation to dine at the White House with the President and Mrs. Lincoln on February 4, 1863 (left) is a traditional presidential engraved invitation blank filled out in ink. The wax seal that secured the envelope is impressed with the presidential seal (above) and was not only an ornament but assured on delivery, if intact, that the invitation had not been opened en route from the White House.

Opposite: Francis Bicknell Carpenter's The First Reading of the Emancipation Proclamation Before the Cabinet *was painted in oil at the White House in 1864. The artist used the State Dining Room for his studio studying firsthand every detail of the president's office and the individuals represented, to make his work accurate to history.*

Right: The unfinished Washington Monument, seen to the right in a Civil War period photograph, was not the capital landmark that it is today. Simplified from the original 1836 design by Robert Mills, the Washington Monument was not to be totally completed inside and out for twenty-five more years, in 1888. In Lincoln's presidency it remained the stub seen here, construction halted. Even had it been finished, it likely would have been eclipsed by the colossal new dome on the Capitol, completed during the war, that won Americans' hearts as the symbol of Union.

cousin Lizzie, who remained in the White House for six full months after the inauguration, rationalized her delayed departure by explaining that the first lady "hates to be alone"—a strong indication that the busy president was growing increasingly unable to provide his wife the companionship she needed. The Lincolns' eldest son, Robert, who spent his college vacations at the White House, later complained that once his father moved there, "any great intimacy between us became impossible. I scarcely even had ten minutes quiet talk with him during his Presidency, on account of his constant devotion to business."[17] To Robert, who decades later rejected appeals that he run for the presidency himself, living in the White House was like being confined to a "gilded prison."[18]

The cruelest blow to afflict the Lincolns during their time in the White House was undoubtedly the death of their beloved middle son, Willie, following an agonizing struggle with what is believed to have been typhoid fever. To make matters more difficult to bear, his decline followed on the heels of Mary's greatest social triumph, an invitation-only ball that one Washington newspaper declared "a brilliant spectacle."[19]

Two weeks later, on February 20, 1862, Willie succumbed, and his body was removed to the Green Room. Mary not only refused to attend the services for the boy; she never set foot in his White House bedroom again. "Our home is very beautiful," she acknowledged a few months later, still deep in mourning, in a desperately sad letter to a Springfield friend, "the grounds around us are enchanting, the world still smiles & pays homage, yet the charm is dispelled—everything appears a mockery."[20]

Mary never recovered from the loss of her son. She found solace not at the White House, where she felt beset by critics and memories, but at the Soldiers' Home, the summer presidential retreat north of town, and on occasional trips to New York or the White Mountains in Vermont. Social life at the mansion dwindled to such an extent that at one point Lincoln was compelled to ask that weekly Marine Band concerts be suspended because Mary could not bear the sound of music in the midst of her affliction.

Two weeks after Lincoln's reelection in November 1864, even as Mary boasted with renewed energy that "the White House, has been quite a Mecca, of late,"

she confided her lonely White House isolation to her Springfield friend, Mercy Conkling: "I consider myself fortunate, if at eleven o'clock, I once more find myself, in my pleasant room & very especially, if my tired & weary Husband, is *there*, resting in the lounge to receive me—to chat over the occurrences of the day."[21]

The crush of visitors was not the only "occurrence of the day" to require Lincoln's constant time and attention. His daily work routine at the White House was crowded with military conferences, political meetings, speechwriting, and cabinet sessions, all of which took place in his bustling Second Floor corner office, its view of the ugly, unfinished Washington Monument a constant reminder of the fickle nature of public gratitude. Here Lincoln also attended to his vast and growing correspondence with the help of his clerks. Oddly, and inexplicably, the White House was never equipped with a telegraph system during Lincoln's occupancy. For the latest news from the front—which he required often— the president had to walk across the West Yard to the War Department, where he spent many long and anguished nights waiting for news from the battlefield.

Not that his office lacked for historic events. Here,

at his cabinet table, in what is now the Lincoln Bedroom, immediately following a long and exhausting New Year's Day reception on January 1, 1863, Lincoln signed the Emancipation Proclamation, surely the most history-altering document ever promulgated in this house. And here, Lincoln inaugurated what years later became a routine White House occurrence—the photo opportunity. On April 26, 1864, at the request of painter Francis B. Carpenter, Lincoln posed in his office for Mathew Brady cameraman Anthony Berger.[22] It was one of the first times a president was ever photographed inside the White House, Polk having been the first in 1846. Lincoln also posed for a photographer on the mansion's portico on March 6, 1865.

Lincoln sat here for painters and sculptors, too. Philadelphia artist Edward Dalton Marchant spent three months at the White House in 1863 creating a canvas of Lincoln signing the Emancipation Proclamation. Secretary of the Navy Gideon Welles hired Connecticut portrait painter Matthew Henry Wilson to depict Lincoln from life in February 1865. At around the same time, the precocious teen-age sculptor Vinnie Ream enjoyed several sittings with Lincoln on the way to producing

Lincoln also posed for artist Edward Dalton Marchant who spent nearly four months at the White House in 1863. The president is depicted seated beside a draped table, his arm resting on a document representing the Emancipation Proclamation.

the bust portrait she later adapted into the full-length statue now gracing the Capitol Rotunda.

Perhaps the most famous artistic project at Lincoln's White House was the effort by New Yorker Carpenter, who arrived in February 1864 and spent the next six months working freely in the building to create his history painting of *The First Reading of the Emancipation Proclamation Before the Cabinet*—an event that had taken place in Lincoln's office (or, some have maintained, the upstairs family parlor) in July 1862. Carpenter produced countless sketches during his sessions in the mansion, painted a model head of Lincoln, and then set up a 8 by 14 foot canvas inside the State Dining Room and there commenced painting the eight figures gathered around the cabinet table. Appropriately, Lincoln offered the East Room for the first public viewing of the finished work, where the president declared the work "perfectly satisfactory," to

the artist's delight. But when Mary Lincoln took her first look at the group portrait of her husband with the ministers with whom he had grown so close over the years—at her expense, she believed—she slyly dubbed it "The happy family."[23] Her comment spoke volumes.

The Lincolns' "last best hope"[24] of making a new start in the White House ended almost as soon as it began. Only a month after Lincoln's second inauguration, Robert E. Lee's surrender at Appomattox at last brought the Civil War to an end. But less than a week later, on April 14, just hours after sharing a carriage ride during which they pledged to each other to be "more cheerful in the future,"[25] the Lincolns drove off to see the play *Our American Cousin* at Ford's Theatre. Mary returned to the White House the following morning a widow. She clung to the mansion for five weeks more, unable to summon the strength to leave and cede it to Andrew Johnson and his family until May 22, 1865,[26]

The teenage sculptor Vinnie Ream was one of the several artists for whom Lincoln posed. She produced a bust that she later adapted into the full-length statue now in the Rotunda of the U.S. Capitol.

and finally departing in "painful" silence, Elizabeth Keckly remembered, "with scarcely a friend to tell her good-by."[27]

"Bidding Adieu, to *that house*," she bitterly remembered, "would *never* have troubled me, if in my departure, I had carried with me, the loved ones, who entered the house, with me." Her memory of the White House was only that "all the sorrows of my life, occurred there."[28]

NOTES

1. Abraham Lincoln, speech to the 166th Ohio Regiment, August 22, 1864, in *The Collected Works of Abraham Lincoln*, ed. Roy P. Basler et al. (New Brunswick, N.J.: Rutgers University Press, 1953–55), 7:512.

2. William O. Stoddard, *Inside the White House in War Times* (New York: Charles L. Webster and Co., 1890), 13.

3. Elizabeth Todd Grimsley, "Six Months at the White House," *Journal of the Illinois State Historical Society* 19 (October 1926–January 1927): 47, 59.

4. Quoted in Benjamin Brown French, *Witness to a Young Republic: A Yankee's Journal, 1828–1870, by Benjamin Brown French*, ed. Donald B. Cole and John J. McDonough (Hanover, N.H.: University Press of New England, 1989), 382.

5. W. H. Crook, *Memories of the White House: The Home Life of Our Presidents from Lincoln to Roosevelt, Being Personal Recollections of Colonel W. H. Crook*, ed. Henry Rood (Boston: Little, Brown, 1911), 27.

6. Quoted in Francis B. Carpenter, *Six Months at the White House: The Story of a Picture* (New York: Hurd and Houghton, 1866), 281.

7. Quoted in ibid.

8. Quoted in Rufus Rockwell Wilson, ed., *Intimate Memories of Lincoln* (Elmira, N.Y.: Primavera Press, 1945), 604.

9. William O. Stoddard Jr., "Face to Face with Lincoln," *Atlantic Monthly* 135 (March 1925): 334–35.

10. Stoddard, *Inside the White House in War Times*, 50.

11. William O. Stoddard, *Abraham Lincoln: The Story of a Great Life*, rev. ed. (New York: Fords, Howard & Hulbert, 1884), 343–34.

12. Earl Schenck Miers, ed., *Lincoln Day by Day: A Chronology, 1809–1865* (Washington, D.C.: Lincoln Sesquicentennial Commission, 1960), 3:44.

13. Ibid., 3:46.

14. Quoted in Mark E. Neely and Harold Holzer, *The Lincoln Family Album: Photographs from the Personal Collection of a Historic American Family*, rev. ed. (Carbondale: Southern Illinois University Press, 2006), 13.

15. John E. Washington, *They Knew Lincoln* (New York: E. P. Dutton, 1941), 105–26.

16. Mary Lincoln to Hannah Shearer, March 28, 1861, in *Mary Todd Lincoln: Her Life and Letters*, ed. Justin G. Turner and Linda Levitt Turner (New York: Alfred A. Knopf, 1972), 82.

17. Robert T. Lincoln to J. G. Holland, June 6, 1865, in *Intimate Memories of Lincoln*, ed. Wilson, 49.

18. "Highest Office was 'Prison' to Robert Lincoln," n.d., unidentified clipping in the Lincoln Museum, Fort Wayne, Indiana.

19. *Washington Evening Star*, February 6, 1862.

20. Mary Lincoln to Julia Ann Sprigg, May 29, 1862, in *Mary Todd Lincoln*, ed. Turner and Turner, 128.

21. Mary Lincoln to Mercy Levering Conkling, November 19, 1864, in ibid., 187.

22. Charles Hamilton and Lloyd Ostendorf, *Lincoln in Photographs: An Album of Every Known Pose*, rev. ed. (Dayton, Ohio: Morningside, 1985), 190–95.

23. Quoted in Francis B. Carpenter, "Anecdotes and Reminiscences," in Henry Raymond, *Life and Public Services of Abraham Lincoln* (New York: Derby & Miller, 1865), 763.

24. Lincoln actually used this famous phrase to characterize the struggle to save the Union, in his Annual Message to Congress, December 1, 1862, in *Collected Works of Lincoln*, ed. Basler et al., 5:537.

25. Mary Todd Lincoln to Francis B. Carpenter, November 15, 1865, in *Mary Todd Lincoln*, ed. Turner and Turner, 285.

26. Jason Emerson, *The Madness of Mary Lincoln* (Carbondale: Southern Illinois University Press, 2007), 20.

27. Elizabeth Keckley [Keckly], *Behind the Scenes; or, Thirty Years a Slave and Four Years in the White House* (New York: G. W. Carleton, 1868), 191.

28. Mary Lincoln to Elizabeth Blair Lee, August 25, 1865, and to Alexander Williamson, September 9, 1865, in *Mary Todd Lincoln*, ed. Turner and Turner, 268, 273.

The Other White House

WILLIAM SEALE

For a four-year period in American history, two official houses carried the name White House. Standing 90 miles apart, across the Virginia landscape, one overlooked the Potomac River and the other the James. They were the same age and architecturally were cousins. Designed by James Hoban, the White House had been rebuilt by him and completed late in 1817, after its destruction in the British invasion three years before. The house in Richmond, built by one John Brockenbrough to designs by Robert Mills, once a draftsman for Hoban, was completed in 1818. This was a glorious year in the period buoyantly called the Era of Good Feelings.

By the time the Lincolns moved there, the White House in Washington had been improved with the addition of porches north and south, making it the house we recognize today. The building in Richmond, which was built with a tall, columned porch on the rear or south side, had gained a third floor not so long before it was

The Confederate White House, Richmond, Virginia, photograph of the garden front in the 1890s. The core of the house was built in 1818, remodeled in Greek Revival style about 1840, and the third floor added 1857, four years before it was occupied by the president of the Confederate States of America. It became a museum in 1893, under the Confederate Memorial Literary Society. Today it is part of the Museum of the Confederacy.

purchased by the city and furnished for Jefferson Davis as the presidential residence of the Confederate States of America. The Lincolns moved to the White House for a four-year term on March 4, 1861, immediately following the inauguration. The Davises moved into the Richmond house on August 1 for a six-year term. They had lived in a two-story frame house in Alabama during the three months the Confederate capital was at Montgomery, where Davis had been inaugurated in February. Both men went to their capitals on the train, and both took their families. Before each was a future that can only have seemed puzzling and, at its worst moments, rightly imagined as an impending nightmare. To his friends in Springfield, Lincoln spoke from the back of the departing train: "No one, not in my situation, can appreciate my feeling of sadness at this parting. . . . I now leave, not knowing when, or whether ever, I will return, with a task before me greater than that which rested upon Washington. Without the assistance of that Divine Being, who ever attended him, I cannot succeed. With that assistance I cannot fail. . . . Let us confidently hope that all will yet be well."[1]

Two days after his inauguration in Montgomery, Davis wrote to his wife: "I was inaugurated on Saturday night. The audience was large and brilliant upon my heavy breast was showered smiles plaudits and flowers, but beyond them I saw troubles and storms insurmountable. We are without machinery without means and threatened by powerful opposition but I do not despond and will not shrink from the task imposed upon me."[2]

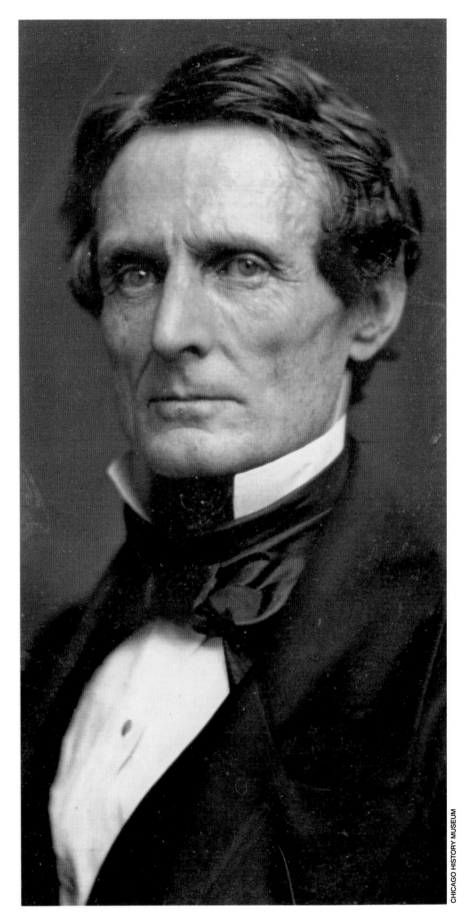

Long before the storm, the two Civil War presidents as younger men, Abraham Lincoln, left, taken about 1846, probably as a member of the U.S. House of Representatives from Illinois, and Jefferson Davis, about 1850, when he was serving as a U.S. senator from Mississippi.

CHICAGO HISTORY MUSEUM

Sarah Knox Taylor, whom Jefferson Davis married in 1835, was the daughter of Colonel Zachary Taylor (later President Taylor), then commander of Fort Crawford in Wisconsin. "Knox," as she was called, died three months later and is buried near St. Francisville, Louisiana. The heavily retouched miniature at left belonged to her family. Varina Howell Davis, second wife of Jefferson Davis, was from Natchez, Mississippi, where she and Davis were married at her family's home The Briers, on February 26, 1845. This is a detail of a daguerreotype taken of them in that year.

Each man hoped politics might solve the problem, and each soon realized that a peaceful solution was not possible. Both children of the generation that followed the American Revolution, Lincoln and Davis were born about 100 miles apart, not quite a year apart. It must have seemed incredible to them that the nation was falling apart. Just eighty-five years separated their inaugurations from the signing of the Declaration of Independence.

Roads to Two First Houses

The Lincolns, Abraham, age 52, and his wife Mary Todd Lincoln, age 42, moved to Washington under the most perilous circumstances. A plot to kidnap or murder him was bypassed through the skillful management of Allan Pinkerton, a detective on the Chicago police force who also ran a private detective agency. Traveling with Mrs. Lincoln by another route were the three sons. Four boys had been born to the Lincolns in their hometown of Springfield, Illinois. Eddie had died in 1850. Robert, the eldest, turned 18 in 1861; Willie 11; and Tad 8.

The Lincolns were hardly the nobodies one is sometimes led to think. Certainly by any measure the father was among the most prominent corporation lawyers in the Midwest. Had Lincoln not remained close to politics and his life become less entwined in the new Republican Party with its key issue the prevention of slavery into the territories, he eventually might well have taken his family from Springfield to booming Chicago. It was only a matter of time. His humble origins are well known, and the idea was even promoted by him. When asked about his family history, he called

Mary Todd Lincoln, a native of Kentucky, married Abraham Lincoln on November 4, 1842, the groom 33 and the bride 23. The wedding took place in the Springfield, Illinois, home of her sister Elizabeth Todd Edwards, who objected to the match. Mary Lincoln was bookish and shared Lincoln's interest in intellectual matters. He had the wedding ring engraved "Love is Eternal." This early daguerreotype of her was taken probably about the time they moved for the first time to Washington, 1847, when he served in Congress.

up a line from Thomas Gray's "Elegy Written in a Country Churchyard": "The short and simple annals of the poor." "That's my life," he said, "and that's all you or any one else can make of it."[3]

It was what Lincoln wanted known but not entirely accurate. He was seventh-generation American, from stable, if not always prosperous stock, with some history of public service. He had self-educated himself to become a lawyer and while serving in the Illinois legislature was admitted to the bar. The interest in politics had taken him as a Whig to the Congress in 1847, where he opposed the Mexican War. An effort to gain a public appointment and remain in Washington failed, and back home he did not run for reelection, but while not setting politics entirely aside, he devoted his interests to business for some years, in various law partnerships in the Illinois capital at Springfield. That he had married "up" when he married Mary Todd of Kentucky in 1842 was no secret, and in Springfield they occupied the only house they ever owned, a cottage to which she, with inherited money, added a second floor.

The Kansas-Nebraska Bill, which negated the Missouri Compromise, brought Lincoln back on the platform in 1854 in passionate opposition. Strong in his feeling for preserving the Union, he believed that the compromise, whatever faults it may have had, provided a basis for that preservation. The Democratic Party's radical branch disagreed. His 1858 Senate campaign debates (using more or less the same speech) with the sponsor of the bill, Senator Stephen A. Douglas, attracted news as a flea attacking a giant; his success was notable if not profound and Douglas defeated him in the election. But Lincoln kept talking, remaining a platform speaker for the next two years, when at last in 1860 his speech at the Cooper Union in New York made him a national figure. In that year he won the presidency over a divided Democratic Party.

Jefferson Davis, age 53 and his wife Varina, who was 35, moved to the White House of the Confederacy with a daughter, Maggie, age 6, and the two surviving of their three sons, Jeff, 4, and Joe, 2. They shared with the Lincolns the tragic loss of a son, Sam, who had died in 1854. Mrs. Davis was pregnant when they moved to the Confederate White House and gave birth to Billy four months later, in December 1861. Their last child, a girl named Varina but called Winnie (her mother was nicknamed Winnie by Davis), would be born in that house in 1864.

Davis had been a well-known public figure since his late 30s, first as a military man and then as a politician. A West Pointer, he first married Knox Taylor, daughter of his disapproving commander, Zachary Taylor; and he left the army to do so. Knox died very soon of a fever, while with Davis headed for Baton Rouge for a reconciliation with her parents. Davis was remarried to Varina Howell at Natchez in 1845, the year he was first elected to Congress. Ambitious and excited by the prospect of the Mexican War, he resigned in 1846 and served with distinction as colonel in command of the First Mississippi Volunteers.

Reunited in Mexico with General Taylor, the two became almost inseparable. It was Davis's military skill that devised the famous V formation strategy that won the battle of Buena Vista, for which he became known in military circles the world over. The victory, in part, took Zachary Taylor to the White House in 1849. Sent to the Senate from Mississippi, Davis and Varina took every advantage of their White House connection to become social stars in the capital. After President Taylor's death in 1850, Davis returned home to run for governor and lost, but his political influence was so strong nationally that he soon returned to Washington, appointed secretary of war by Franklin Pierce in 1853. His reforms in the military were highly influential in shaping the Union Army he was to fight later on. He was elected to the Senate in 1857 and, as a radical Democrat, was present as the fires of the oncoming Civil War burned away in the capital. A much-sought-after orator, Davis was cheered on platforms North and South. He never wanted to destroy the Union, but he believed that the Constitution, which he admired above all documents of government, allowed a state to secede if it wanted to. He held on to the last, and then supported secession ardently.

The Roles of the Two Official Houses

The two presidents had some things in common, and much that they did not share. One thing certain: they did share commitment to their points of view. Both firmly believed that the paths they had taken would have been approved by the Founding Fathers. The events of the Civil War and the two men's involvements are well known. Their offices were not dissimilar, each with walls covered by large maps, dotted with pins and flags. Americans, whether Union or Confederate, still looked over a vast, virtually empty continent. Davis believed the Confederate empire would extend west, indeed perhaps even into Mexico. Lincoln saw expansion only as the new territories would become allies and hurried to make them states, lest they side with the Confederacy.

Each house, Washington and Richmond, served three roles: office, ceremonial place for entertainment, and home for the head of state. As such they were often crowded, the stairs trod muddy by people seeking favors. In each, secretaries and aides learned that they had to protect their presidents for their health and that the stream of callers would never end unless arbitrarily stopped. Lincoln was served by two, then three secretaries; Davis had two secretaries and four aides. Being able to see the president in person was a feature of the democratic ideal by then natural to the presidency and adapted by the Confederacy. The area in front of both presidential houses was as crowded as a county fair most days. Filtering this onslaught took tact and sometimes even muscle.

Neither house was heavily guarded by our standards today. At the start of the war Jim Lane's Frontier Guard from Kansas camped in the East Room of the White House. Cassius Clay of Kentucky, sporting two pistols and an Arkansas Toothpick, bivouacked his Clay Guards outside at the foot of the stairs to the South Portico. Both soon went off to try their skills elsewhere on the battlefield. All during the war a patrol walked back and forth down the long Second Floor corridor of the White House. Two guards were at the north door. In Richmond a guard was stationed at the front door and one at the basement door; outside a dozen or more soldiers sat around a campfire. No one else guarded Jefferson Davis except his secretaries, who slept in the house with firearms close at hand.

The wartime White House of Abraham Lincoln was open to the public most mornings. People walked into the East Room and sometimes into the Green, Blue, and Red Rooms and then back out again, to satisfy their curiosity. Now and then for a souvenir an East Room tassel was cut off or a book was taken from a Red Room table. Opening the house to tourists had been started by Thomas Jefferson in 1801, recalling how he had been able to see great houses in Europe because they were available to the public. During the Civil War, newspapers abounded in letters to the editor and columns describing the White House, its big rooms, the crowds waiting to see Lincoln. Written descriptions of the Richmond White House are rare, suggesting that, being a smaller house, it was not usually open to the public. Jefferson Davis's appointments secretary sat at a table at the foot of the main stair, which curved up to the second floor office, which had the master bedroom

Both presidential mansions were guarded outside and within. The main entrance to the Confederate White House is pictured above during the Civil War. Davis's callers passed guards at the front steps and in the hall, where they waited approval to ascend the circular stairs to the office. Lincoln's White House, surrounded by heavy iron fencing, was guarded closer-in at secondary gates, one of which is shown in the Civil War photograph at left, and also in the Entrance Hall inside, from which, if authorized, business callers likewise climbed to the second floor office.

THE DAVIS FAMILY

Varina Howell Davis (1826–1906) photographed by Mathew Brady in 1860, at the peak of her social prominence in antebellum Washington.

William (Billy) Howell Davis (1861–1872) was born shortly after the Davises arrived in Richmond. He played with neighborhood children rather freely throughout the war and fled with his parents in the spring of 1865. Billy died of diphtheria just before his 11th birthday, while the family was in residence in Memphis, Tennessee, where Jefferson Davis was employed by an insurance company.

Jefferson Davis Jr. (1857–1878), second son born to Jefferson and Varina Davis, the first having died in Washington earlier, just before his second birthday. "Jeff," as he was known, accompanied his parents through the Confederate episode of their lives and is shown here in the uniform of an army major.

Joseph Evan Davis (1859–1864), was killed while "tightrope" walking the railing of the presidential mansion's columned gallery, pictured at the beginning of this article. His tombstone, above, at Richmond's Hollywood Cemetery, is near that of his parents.

Family group: Jefferson and Varina Davis's eldest child, Margaret Howell Davis (1855–1909) is seated with her brothers and sister, Jeff, left; Billy and Winnie (1864–1898), right, in a photograph from the mid-1860s.

Jim Limber, a free African American orphaned in Richmond, was a character in the drama of the Confederate White House. Taken from a cruel guardian in the winter of 1864 by Varina Howell Davis, he lived in the presidential family. Jefferson Davis registered his "free papers" with the city, to assure his status and thus independence from the guardian. While Mrs. Davis noted on this picture that his name was John Henry Brooks, he usually went by the name Jim Limber, apparently a nickname he preferred. He lived with the Davises for the balance of the war, best friend to their son Billy, and was along with the family when it fled Richmond just before the city's fall. After the capture of Jefferson Davis in Georgia, Union troops took Jim Limber with Mrs. Davis and the other children to Savannah, where they were confined to a hotel. Unsure of their future and thwarted in an attempt to escape to Europe, Mrs. Davis sent her own children to Canada with her mother and Jim Limber to live with the Davises' old friends General and Mrs. Rufus Saxton. At some point thereafter, he vanished from the written record.

John Henry Brooks, "Jim Limber," c. 1864.

Varina "Winnie" Davis, named for her mother and carrying her mother's nickname, was born at the Confederate White House in June 1864. Mrs. Charles Barnes, a free African American nurse in Richmond, was employed to attend the baby. She became close to the family, joining in its flight on March 29, 1865, and remaining at Mrs. Davis's side, even after her own widowhood, until Jefferson Davis was released from prison in May 1866. While in Baltimore with Mrs. Davis in 1866 she met and married Frederick Maginnis and remained in that city for the rest of her life. Winnie Davis became a novelist, but more, a famous symbol of the Lost Cause. When she died at the age of 34, the New York Times lamented the passing of one who was "the darling of half a nation at arms."

The infant Winnie Davis held by Ellen Barnes, 1865.

Refugees in Canada: Robert Brown, former slave of Jefferson Davis, went with members of the Davis family to Montreal when the war ended. Brown is standing; Jeff is on the left, Margaret, right; Jefferson Davis's brother and mentor, Joseph P. Davis, a wealthy Mississippi planter, holds Billy. The year is 1865 and the former Confederate president was in prison, threatened by charges of treason.

Business callers at the Richmond White House registered with presidential aide Burton Davis (above), whose desk was inside the window beneath the stair (top right), and were likely to wait quite a while before admission to the president's office (right). The rooms in the Confederate White House are restored to their appearance during the Civil War.

Jefferson Davis and his cabinet, lithograph by Thomas Kelly, 1866. The room is identified as the "council chamber," which was in the former customhouse on Main Street, several blocks from the executive mansion, but some of the details of the room seem to come from Francis B. Carpenter's painting of Lincoln's cabinet and the first reading of the Emancipation Proclamation, which was a depiction of Lincoln's office at the White House.

on one side and the children's nursery on the other. The arrangement was eased by creation of another office for Davis in the customhouse, where he met the greater number of his guests. Lincoln, however, kept his office in the White House, perhaps seeing it as more peaceful than one of the departments, which were all overrun with callers looking for wartime jobs.

In the hall of the White House in Washington guests registered with two "ushers," only recently given that title instead of "doormen." At both houses, visitors wrote their names on a blank card or presented their printed card, which was sent upstairs by a household messenger to the secretary to determine admission or refusal. Some people called every day until they were admitted. Some never got to see the president at all.

Public receptions were held from time to time in both houses. The Confederates still celebrated the Fourth of July and also New Year's, as had long been the case at the White House. In Washington, when Andrew Jackson took over in 1829, January 8, the anniversary of the battle of New Orleans, became a regular reception day, but it was dropped during the 1850s, as the Democratic party began moving away from Jacksonian ideals and sought other heroes.

Life in the Washington White House

Inside both presidential houses, the dynamics behind the scenes were directed toward a smooth public presentation. Backstage all was by no means calm at the White House in Washington. Well before he went to the White House, Lincoln was concerned that all ceremonial activities be conducted properly. He sent his secretary George Nicolay to Jeremiah Black, outgoing secretary of state, for instruction on how dinners, receptions, and

Lincoln's East Room, the earliest known view, taken by an unknown photographer probably about 1865, shows the decor as it was for all the events of Lincoln's presidency. The three great chandeliers, installed by Andrew Jackson more than thirty years before, had been converted to gas by President James K. Polk in 1848. The colors of the East Room were bright. Carpeting selected by Mrs. Lincoln was acclaimed for suggesting ocean waves casting up masses of red roses. Huge mirrors reflected endless perspectives across the room's span.

other events were traditionally handled. Nicolay was supplied with seating charts he might use as models and made notes on other details. Once Lincoln was in the White House, his secretary managed social affairs. Mrs. Lincoln, cut out of the basics, was allowed to advise only on menus and the like. She resented this as a violation of her rights and, given the anxieties from which she suffered, felt people in Washington were laughing about it behind her back. Her predecessor, Harriet Lane, had found Mrs. Lincoln too "western" for polite society, and the opinion was not exclusive to her.

For his power over matters Mrs. Lincoln wished for herself, she loathed the Belgian George Nicolay. He seems to have returned the favor with chilly silence, but not a word to her face. While Nicolay resigned at the end of the first term, in part because of her, to go elsewhere, he stuck it out for four years, greatly imposed upon. Lincoln, however, stood by his staff. So Mrs.

Lincoln turned her rage on the servants—there were fourteen—as her enemies and began to drive them away on various pretenses. She created little crises; she harassed and threatened them—notably James Buchanan's English domestics. They slowly departed, taking jobs in the government departments, joining the army, and leaving a dubious, rather low-brow crew as survivors; the replacements that came in were some of the most devious characters that could be imagined. The worst of them knew how to flatter the president's wife to serve their own ends. Mrs. Lincoln, with little to occupy her and personal tragedy to wear away at her emotionally, was constantly in trouble, whether spending too much to buy and drape the bed we know as the Lincoln Bed or welcoming fortune-tellers and mediums to the Red Room to communicate with "the other side." She was the first president's wife criticized openly in the press.[4]

Henry Wikoff was a popular social dandy in wartime Washington. The clever "Chevalier," as he was known, amused Mrs. Lincoln and her friends with gossip about European courts, but when one of Lincoln's speeches appeared in the New York Herald *before Lincoln had given it, and Wikoff's name turned up in the investigation, the president sent him to jail. Under questioning, Wikoff admitted that he had taken it down verbatim from the gardener, John Watt, who memorized the text from copy he saw on the president's office table. Released from jail, the Chevalier called at the White House for tea, and an angered Lincoln interrupted the tea party to personally order him out.*

The White House was a much larger house than the one in Richmond. Lincoln had his office in the east end of the Second Floor. There his secretaries had a bedroom in addition to several workrooms and a reception room. At the opposite end of the hall were the seven rooms of the family quarters. The large formal rooms downstairs were usually only for social occasions. The Lincolns did sit in the Red Room to read newspapers. In the evenings Mary awaited her husband there when he spent late hours in the telegraph office next door. The Lincolns were the last family to use any of the State Rooms for everyday pursuits.

Life in Lincoln's White House was thus fraught with tension, not only because of the war being conducted outside its doors but because of the little wars going on inside. Lincoln and his secretaries formed almost a unit. He enjoyed the company of these two young men, John Hay and George Nicolay. Often with them and his sons Tad and Willie he went about town or visited battlefields after the smoke had cleared. Sometimes they were joined by William Slade, a quiet, gentlemanly man who served as Lincoln's valet, an African American who took no part in the machinations of the other staff. Work hours were long. Late at night Lincoln was likely to waken the secretaries and talk to them for hours as they dozed against the bedposts. Years later the secretaries tried to remember every word he said.

Among the members of the staff who gained access to Mary Lincoln was John Watt, a gardener with about a decade's White House service. He made himself a presence in the Conservatory at the right times and thus put himself close to Mrs. Lincoln when she went there for sun and to enjoy the flowers. She was too naive to keep her distance. A talkative Scot, he was soon advising her on important matters and personalities, and he gained access to the entire house. His tenure climaxed when in collusion with another man he took a copy of one of Lincoln's speeches from the office and sold it to the press.

Similar difficulties arose with Henry Wikoff, a flashy Frenchman who styled himself a chevalier of France and claimed fond intimacy with Louis Napoleon III and the Empress Eugenie. He called on Mrs. Lincoln frequently, a giddy, entertaining man amply supplied with gossip from the European courts. She unburdened herself to him. He betrayed her also by stealing and selling papers. Lincoln, who found him repulsive anyway, personally appeared in the Red Room at a tea and ordered the Chevalier out of the house on threat of arrest. Notwithstanding the dramatic denunciation by her husband, Mrs. Lincoln kept her fondness for the Chevalier and counted him as her friend.

The formality of White House life necessarily proceeded. Dinners were held for forty once or twice a week from about November to April. The fare was French, by long White House tradition; six wines were poured. Toasts had been déclassé for a while, so there was no fanfare except a march from the Blue Room to the State Dining Room with the Marine Band, stationed in the hall, playing a waltz. Thanks to gaslight, White House dinners were no longer at 4:00 in the afternoon, but were at 8:00 p.m. Guests were expected to arrive within fifteen minutes of the time designated on the invitation. At the close of fifteen minutes, the president appeared with Mrs. Lincoln. A receiving line formed, after which, two by two, the guests followed the president to the State Dining Room, where seating was carefully arranged by rank, the president and his wife sitting across from each other on the long side of the table.

After dinner, when the president rose from his chair, all the men stood; then the women departed to the Second Floor Library to freshen up for half an hour. Chamber pots were brought out in the dining room and a screen set up around them. Men and women joined after that in one of the parlors for coffee. When the band struck "Yankee Doodle," the president and Mrs. Lincoln went upstairs and the party was over. Most of the time these dinners were all business, at least around the edges of the social interaction. A preoccupied Lincoln was likely to pull men guests aside for a talk. More than once he assembled the whole cabinet in a room for discussion and pulled the doors closed.

The White House was elegant, make no mistake. In the winter of 1862 the servants were newly attired in mulberry livery (it had always been blue) to match the new state china Mrs. Lincoln had purchased. Invitational receptions required a ticket of admission, as did all dinners and afternoon parties. For a reception for five hundred in February 1862, the guests were directed to the East Room, where the president awaited in a finely tailored new suit and Mrs. Lincoln was in a black and white ball gown with a tall headdress of flowers. A feast was served at midnight, ordered from the Manhattan confectioner Henry Maillard. In the center of the table were large models in sugar of Fort Sumter, Fort Pickens, and the Ship of State. The Marine Band played "The Mary Lincoln Polka."[5]

Great receptions sometimes greeted six thousand people. The line always had to be cut off, and some went home never having entered the White House. Again, the Lincolns had little to do but be there. Mrs. Lincoln always dressed in grand style, with a court train (4 yards from the shoulder to the tip). Diplomatic rules were maintained, assuring deference to rank. At that time the highest rank foreign powers sent to the United States were ministers plenipotentiary; there were no ambassadors for another thirty years. Always the diplomats were admitted an hour early, received by the president, and given time to station themselves through the State Rooms. The court uniforms were varied and exotic, from the British velvet trimmed in gold lace, with tricorn hat and medals on a cross-ribbon, to the Turks with their turbans, magnificent jewels, and shocks of ostrich plumes. No food was served. Ice water stations were provided on the Fourth of July. For those receptions anticipated to be very large, steps were put up to the windows of the East Room to encourage early exit.

It was during the 1863 New Year's reception that Lincoln signed the Emancipation Proclamation. His hands were black and blue from shaking hands downstairs. He rubbed them to be sure his writing was firm, commenting that, by the steadiness of his hand history would judge whether he hesitated or did not.

Life in the Confederate White House

In Richmond, social responsibility was an easier matter for Varina Howell Davis. President Davis took no part in planning anything, so capable was his wife. An aggressive woman by nature, she had gone to Washington in 1845 and again in the 1850s and demanded and won a place at the head of political society. Her access to the White House during the administrations of Zachary Taylor and Franklin Pierce gave her a certain cachet, but her husband's position in the Democratic Party and generally in all the events in Washington was very center stage. They were what would be described today as a power couple, and she relished capital life far over that of Davis's Mississippi River plantation Brierfield.

It was Davis who provided Stephen A. Douglas with access to President Pierce when Douglas sought to gain Pierce's support for the Kansas-Nebraska Bill in 1854. Promoting the bill into law behind the scenes with all the influence he had, Davis emerged before the public as never before. Within three years he had returned to the Senate, where he would remain until he resigned and headed south in January 1861. The morning he departed Washington he wrote to former President Pierce: "I leave immediately for Mississippi. Civil War has only horror for me, but whatever circumstances demand shall be met as a duty and I trust be so discharged that you will not be ashamed of our former connection."[6]

Emerging from the national political drama and onto another stage as wife of the president of the Confederacy, Varina Howell Davis had every credential for her role in such a challenge. She knew social Washington by heart, and under her direction social life in the Confederate capital became a clear reflection of Washington as it had been in the 1850s. (Witness the name "White House" for the president's residence.) Engraved invitation cards, engraved menus, orchestras, flowers, French cooking, and lots of wine and spirits were all a part of official entertaining at the Richmond White House. Receptions, dinners, balls, and garden parties characterized the social seasons, as they had in Washington.

Where Lincoln functions were stiff, the Davises had a way of seeming almost casual in the midst of the strictest formality, a charming manner entirely Washingtonian in character. As dinner ended and the guests rose from the table, the Davis children were likely to appear with their nurse, descending the staircase for a brief introduction. The two little boys had Confederate uniforms. Unlike Lincoln's, the Davis children were well behaved, receiving daily attention and schooling from their mother in spite of her busy schedule. Varina Davis once wrote of bedlam breaking out in the nursery as the strong-willed children objected to some order. Mother "scolded, laughed, cried." But they did her bidding.[7]

Two of the mansion's servants were slaves from Brierfield, the Davis's Mississippi plantation (named for Mrs. Davis's family home in Natchez, The Briers—the word spelled as in Sir Walter Scott's romances). The rest were hired and never stayed long. In addition to an excellent cook (who had been chef on one of the transatlantic Cunard steamers), there were dining room

attendants, a coachman, grooms, butler, valet, lady's maid, never large in number. By White House tradition, Lincoln's servants were paid as laborers by the various departments of the government, while officially the Confederate president was supposed to pay them from his own pocket; Mrs. Davis made unsuccessful application to the Confederate treasury for pay for her servants. The turnover of employees was very trying upon Mrs. Davis, who was demanding enough in what she expected of them to personally attend to their training. Even the steward Jim Pemberton, a slave and son of a man also enslaved, who had been at Jefferson Davis's side most of their lives, disappeared one night, as the Confederacy's fortunes sank.

Whether she had adequate assistance or not, the routine of entertaining had to go on, and Mrs. Davis, rarely complaining, pressed the schedule forward through her four years even after the blockade made delicacies so dear that only the minimum of refreshments could be served to the sweet-toothed Rebel court. The president needed to meet with particular people, and, as with Lincoln, social occasions were perfect for this. The Confederate White House was aglow with parties. Furnished from auction house and estate furniture, the house was not beautiful, nor did Mrs. Davis have the funds to expend as did Mrs. Lincoln. The furniture she ordered from Europe fell to the Union blockade. So she did her best. She enlivened her reception room by adorning it with whittled curios made by the soldiers and given to her on her visits to the hospitals. That room had a carpet with a cream-colored field that always gave General Robert E. Lee pause, fearing his boots would muddy it. She planted the garden behind the house, overlooked by the long-columned porch, in peonies and roses, and its fragrance was more often noted than other details of the house. Summer slipcovers covered worn damask in the parlors. Crisp lace curtains at the windows, starched and stretched in the sun on wooden frames, kept the rooms looking fresh.

Davis's recent biographer, William Cooper Jr., wrote that the bill of fare at the Confederate White House varied from the "sumptuous" to the "simple." He continued: "One meal included gumbo, ducks, liver, chicken in jelly, oysters, claret soup, champagne, salad, and chocolate jelly cake. Another time brains *en papillote* adorned the table."[8] The Davises' close friend, cabinet member Judah P. Benjamin, was especially delighted

Saint Paul's Episcopal Church, situated across the street from Capitol Square, was a walk of some six blocks from the Confederate White House and a walk taken often by Jefferson Davis. He was attending a service here when informed that Richmond was falling to the Union assault, and within hours had led his cabinet in flight from the doomed Confederate capital.

when Mrs. Davis served him anchovy paste on bread baked locally with Crenshaw's flour (a noted miller in Virginia) and scattered over with crushed walnuts (which came from the garden) and a glass of McHenry sherry. Davis himself, like Lincoln, was indifferent to food and rarely cared whether he ate or not. A plate of turnip greens and cornbread were a repast for him, and

he might taste a little pork and beef. He also was pleased when fish was put before him.[9]

Being a bit happy with itself already, Richmond tried to look down upon the occupants of the Confederate White House. If Davis did not care, Mrs. Davis did and was astute in dealing with female enemies, a skill honed by her experiences in Washington.

She somewhat kindly noted Richmond's "offish" provinciality in not trusting new people and speculated that their attitudes against the new government's officials probably were in reaction to the changes they saw all around them. Small town folk never welcomed change. Others found Varina Davis, as they said, "too much"; nor were Richmond Confederates the first and only ones to say so. She did unmistakably have her pushy side. Grumpy diarist Mary Boykin Chesnut perceived beneath the polish a sarcastic tongue that Mrs. Davis usually—but not always—masked with a pretty smile.[10]

Not far away, old Richmond society flourished in the Virginia Governor's Mansion, a house of similar vintage to the Confederate White House. Governor Henry A. Wise greeted party goers there, but seldom the Davises. He was a teetotaler who boasted that he had never felt "obliged to raise the familiar cup" and had reservations about those, like the Davises, who did. When Stonewall Jackson was killed, his body was brought to Richmond. Davis offered the Confederate White House where it might lie in state. Local politics intervened. Stonewall lay instead in the Governor's Mansion.

Now and then papers in the Union reported on life in the Davis White House. There was a controversial report in 1863 that a ball held at the mansion featured a United States flag drawn and colored in chalk over the floor; the dancers danced it away. While this event was denied, it is hard to doubt. One of the popular things to do in 1850s Washington was to call in a decorative painter to use colored chalks and decorate in scenes and designs the "crash" or linen cloth that was stretched over the carpets and waxed to make a floor compatible to those athletic dances treasured at the time, like the gallop and the quadrille, where twirling, hurried steps, and other fast movement caused the slippers of the dancers to "dance the chalk away." Why not at a Confederate ball, and why not the enemy flag?

Family Tragedies and Last Days

Both the Lincolns and the Davises lost sons in the White House. Willie Lincoln died at the White House, in the Lincoln bed, on February 20, 1862, probably of typhoid. He was a sickly child. The illness dragged out. At a state reception the Lincolns took turns climbing the stairs to sit beside him. When he died they were discon-

solate. The body was embalmed and laid out in the Green Room, the funeral adjacent in the East Room. Willie was put temporarily in a borrowed tomb, awaiting the end of the presidency when the body was to be returned by the family to Springfield.

In the spring of 1864, Joseph Davis II, age five, out of sight of his nurse and siblings, climbed upon the railing of the rear porch and attempted to walk across it, like a trapeze artist he had admired at the circus. He fell on the brick terrace below and crushed his skull. There was no saving him, but he lingered for hours. The parents, away in the city, were brought to the scene and Davis, stone-faced, and Mrs. Davis barely in control of her anguish, watched as Joe died. Friends and the public called to view the child's coffin at the White House. The funeral was held at Hollywood Cemetery in Richmond, where Joe Davis was buried. Two months later, Winnie, the last of the Davis children was born in the Confederate White House.

The Davises absorbed the tragedy and lived with it, moving on. Lincoln was eventually able to do the same, but Mary Lincoln did not and after Willie's death was never really herself again. At one point she seems to have been coming out of her melancholy, right at the close of the war; then Lincoln was assassinated.

In Richmond, President Jefferson Davis, with the advice of Lee, held on as long as he could. By March 1865, when he knew it was only a matter of time to the end, he and Mrs. Davis decided that she would leave with the children. She seems to have made little secret of her departure. A sale was made of some of the furniture in the house, personal items were stored, and many things left behind in the big rooms as she prepared herself and the children to leave. Davis gave her a pistol and instructed her in its use, firing off the rear gallery to targets on the garden's brick walls. He advised her to keep running, not to get caught if at all possible. She was to make her way to Florida, there to take a boat out of the country. He gave her all the gold in his possession, retaining $5 for himself, and on March 29 she departed Richmond by train with her four children, two maids, and the president's secretary Burton Harrison.

On the morning of April 2, 1865, General Ulysses S. Grant's army broke through Confederate lines and marched on Richmond. Jefferson Davis was attending the church service at Saint Paul's Episcopal Church, across from Capitol Square. Seated in his pew, he was

President Lincoln, with his son Tad and his valet William Slade, traveled to Richmond soon after the Confederate capital fell. On April 4, 1865, he entered the city in triumph, laboring to make his appearance as little warlike as possible. Former slaves and unionists flocked to see him and cheer his tour of the landmarks, as shown in this illustration from Frank Leslie's Illustrated Newspaper published eighteen days later, after Lincoln's death.

The Confederate White House as a prisoner of war: Union officers gather on the back steps of the house, the Confederate occupants of which had so recently left. Parlor chairs have been pulled out on the porch, while Varina Davis's lace curtains blow in the spring breeze. The house would be held by the government until 1870, those of its contents that the Davises had not sold just before the fall of Richmond apparently kept intact.

given a message from General Lee saying that Richmond must be evacuated. He rose and walked out, every eye in the congregation on him.

Davis had no intention whatsoever of yielding to defeat. That afternoon he finalized a plan some time in the making of meeting Lee in Danville, Virginia, near the North Carolina line, and proceeding through the "lower Confederacy" to Texas, where he felt the men and loyalty were strong enough to sustain victory. Appomattox ended that plan, and the government fled. United on the road with Mrs. Davis, Jefferson Davis was apprehended in Georgia. Mrs. Davis, following his direction, headed with the children for Florida but stopped at Savannah and booked passage on a boat to England. Union troops stopped the boat and put her under house arrest in a Savannah hotel, from which the spunky former first lady began firing off letters on behalf of her husband to Union celebrities she had known, entertained, and even helped in Washington before the war.[11]

After the Civil War

The two houses lived on in history. The White House in Washington probably would not be standing today had Lincoln not lived there. His triumph in saving the Union, and also the melodrama of his life there, fairly much sanctified the house in the minds of the American people. Already in the summer of 1865 a new house was ordered, to be built in the Washington suburbs on a large tract of land. By the 1870s it became clear that Congress would never dare fund such a new mansion, so adamant was the public that the president remain in the White House.

The White House of the Confederacy had a historical moment after Davis left. After the fall of Richmond, Lincoln and his son Tad went by train to view the captured city, a landscape of ruins, except for the Capitol, Governor's Mansion, and the White House, which were among those that survived the fires caused by the invasion. Lincoln went to the White House, climbed the curving stairs, and sat at Jefferson Davis's desk. An aide signaled through the window, and huzzas rose from the thousands assembled outside. Davis at that time was in flight overland through North Carolina, headed south. Lincoln would be dead within a week.

The Confederate White House was locked. An inventory taken in 1870 listed a good bit of furniture collected in the rooms downstairs, rather haphazardly, seemingly piled, rug upon sofa upon bed, upon box. Before the century's close the house would be acquired and renovated to serve as an archive for Confederate records and a museum. Each state of the old Confederacy sponsored a room. They were odd assemblages. The Texas room was outfitted with longhorn furniture. Mrs. Davis, who lived until 1906, surviving her husband by seventeen years, took tremendous interest in the museum, visiting it often and donating generously of artifacts she had. The museum today still uses some labels written in her hand.

Mary Lincoln and Tad left the White House in May 1865, more than a month after Lincoln's death. They were driven in a carriage to the train station. All along Pennsylvania Avenue and in front of the White House bleachers were being built for the Grand Review of the Armies of the Union, a two-day event that would be the largest and longest parade ever held in American history up until that time. Her departure was barely noticed. Very few came to say good-bye. While she was to refer to the White House now and then in the hundreds of letters she was to write, her feeling was always the same: "It broke my heart." She never returned.

NOTES

1.   Quoted in David Herbert Donald, *Lincoln* (London: Jonathan Cape, 1995), 273.

2.   Jefferson Davis to Varina Howell Davis, Montgomery, Alabama, February 20, 1861, Jefferson Davis Papers, Museum of the Confederacy, Richmond. See also Varina Howell Davis, *Jefferson Davis, Ex-President of the Confederate States of America: A Memoir by His Wife* (New York: Belford Company, 2 vols. 1890).

3.   Quoted in Donald, *Lincoln*, 20.

4.   Mrs. Lincoln's various domestic trials as well as her attitudes are vividly shown in her letters. See Justin G. Turner and Linda Levitt Turner, eds. *Mary Todd Lincoln: Her Life and Letters* (New York: Alfred A. Knopf, 1972).

5.   *New York Herald*, February 6, 1862; see also Jean H. Baker, *Mary Todd Lincoln: A Biography* (New York: W.W. Norton, 1987), 206; William Seale, *The President's House: A History*, 2nd ed. (Washington, D.C.: White House Historical Association, 2008), vol. 1.

6.   Jefferson Davis to Franklin Pierce, Washington, D.C., January 20, 1861, *Jefferson Davis: Private Letters 1823–1889*, ed. Hudson Strode. (New York: Harcourt Brace and World, 1966), 122.

7.   Varina Howell Davis to Jefferson Davis, Mill View, Georgia, September 22, 1865, Eleanor Brockenbrough Library, Museum of the Confederacy.

8.   William J. Cooper Jr., *Jefferson Davis, American* (New York: Vintage Books, 2000), 463.

9.   Robert Douthat Meade, *Judah P. Benjamin: Confederate Statesman* (New York: Oxford University Press, 1943), 285.

10. Mary Chestnut, diary, *Mary Chesnut's Civil War*, C. Vann Woodward, ed., (New Haven: Yale University Press, 1981), 85, 609, 746, 747, 785.

11. Varina Howell Davis to General Montgomery Meigs, n.p., n.d.; to Mrs. John Tyler, Savannah, July 24, 1865; to Frances P. Blair, Savannah, June 6, 1865, all Davis Papers.

The Davis family plot in Hollywood Cemetery in Richmond where the graves of Varina and Jefferson Davis are surrounded by those of their children. Modern buildings block what was once a clear view from the cemetery to the Confederate White House across the James River.

Above and right: The corner of Twelfth and Clay Streets in Richmond, Virginia, 2009. The Confederate White House now stands in the threatening shadows of the Virginia Commonwealth University Hospital and Medical School buildings.

Ford's Theatre, the presidential box seat photographed in a long gas-lit exposure by Mathew Brady a few days after Lincoln's assassination. Nothing in the scene had been changed since the tragic night, April 14, 1865. The American flag decoration, which still bears the tear from Booth's spur, would soon be taken and draped over the door of the new president's temporary office at the Treasury. Brady's picture was taken on the sly, in violation of an order not to do so.

The White House and Lincoln's Assassination

ANTHONY S. PITCH

*A*braham Lincoln had never been more cheerful and carefree in the White House than on his last day alive. Richmond, the Confederate capital, had recently fallen, and it was only five days since Washingtonians had celebrated the deliriously exciting news of Robert E. Lee's surrender to the Union victor, Ulysses S. Grant. The grinding war was all but over, barring a few weeks of inconsequential skirmishes, and the president could look with confidence beyond the ghastly battlefields. The burden had been visibly telling on his prematurely aging face. With more than 600,000 Americans dead in the North and the South, Lincoln had forecast the year before, "This war is eating my life out. I have a strong impression that I shall not live to see the end."[1] Yet he had survived and was now on the threshold of leading the nation into a period of reconciliation and reconstruction. The 56-year-old father had good reason to feel buoyant when he breakfasted on Good Friday, April 14, 1865, with his oldest son, Robert, on leave from Grant's staff, telling him they would soon live in peace "with the brave men of the South."[2] It was vintage Lincoln, displaying reason and magnanimity with an impulse to conciliate and heal.

The president was even jubilant by the time he greeted Senator John Cresswell of Maryland, who sought a pardon for an imprisoned Confederate friend. "Hello, Cresswell. The war is over!" Lincoln exulted. "It has been an awful war. But it's over!"[3] His genial mood carried over into a White House meeting of the cabinet, where he predicted invigorating news of General William Tecumseh Sherman's thrust through the Carolinas. He had even resorted to comic relief during a serious discussion on how to treat leaders of the failed rebellion, suggesting it might be a good idea to turn a blind eye to any escaping across the country's borders. "The situation reminds me of an old Irishman in Illinois," he said, "who, having been a hard drinker, finally signed the pledge, and was living up to it until one day he went into a drug store and asked for a glass of water. The clerk, knowing his propensities, said 'Pat, shall I put a stick in it?' The Irishman replied, 'Well, if you please. I've signed the pledge, but if you do it *unbeknownst to me*, it will be alright.'"[4]

During an afternoon carriage ride, Mary Todd Lincoln was taken aback by Lincoln's "playful" nature. "Dear husband," she observed, "you almost startle me by your great cheerfulness." Joyfully, he responded, "And well I might feel so, Mary. I consider this day, the war has come to a close." Recalling the death of their son, Willie, three years earlier, he reflected, "We must both be more cheerful in the future. Between the war and the loss of our darling Willie, we have both been very miserable."[5]

Lincoln arrived late at Ford's Theatre for the comedy, *Our American Cousin*, but the actors joined the audience of more than 1,600 people in rousing applause for the president as the band struck up "Hail to the Chief." The beloved chief executive, who had secured victory and preserved the Union, acknowledged the ovation and took his seat in the private box to the right, overlooking

The barouche in which President Lincoln rode to Ford's Theatre was built by Wood Brothers of New York, from whom it was purchased by a group of Lincoln supporters and presented to him on the occasion of his first inaugural. Elegantly lacquered outside and upholstered within, the carriage was mounted on six springs and drawn by a pair of horses.

President Lincoln wore his "silk finish" felt top hat (opposite), to Ford's Theatre the night he died.

the stage 12 feet below. His wife sat beside him with their guests, Major Henry Rathbone and his fiancée, Clara Harris.

In the second scene of the third act John Wilkes Booth passed unobtrusively into the closed alcove between the dress circle audience and the door to the president's box. He leveled the single shot Derringer pistol and fired at point blank range behind Lincoln's left ear. The assassin warded off, then stabbed and wounded Rathbone, leaped onto the stage, screamed out the Latin motto of Virginia, "So always to tyrants," escaped out the back door onto his waiting horse, and galloped off into the night.

Shortly afterward a frenzied man rushed into Grover's Theatre, where the president's youngest son, Tad, 12, was watching a performance of *Aladdin; or,*

The Wonderful Lamp with a White House staffer. "President Lincoln has been shot at Ford's Theatre!" he shrieked.[6] When Tad got back to the White House he ran up to the assistant doorkeeper, Thomas Pendel, crying out, "Oh, Tom Pen! Tom Pen! They have killed papa dead!" They've killed papa dead!" Pendel, a former marine, sat by the boy's bedside beyond midnight before sleep finally overcame the shattered child.[7]

Doctor Charles Leale, the first surgeon to reach the wounded president, turned down suggestions to transport Lincoln back to the White House, intimating the bumpy road and upright position in which he would have to be positioned might quicken his death. Volunteers carried the unconscious president across the road to a boarding house, where the 6 feet 4 inch supine leader labored throughout the night, exhaling for the last

THE ASSASSINATION OF PRESIDENT LINCOLN.

Top and right: The assassination of President Lincoln as illustrated in publications of the day. The Assassination of President Lincoln, *a popular print sold in the 1860s for framing, probably hung in many a residence and was found in even more scrapbooks, while the print showing Booth's leap from the box was less familiar, but also printed for a public hungry for illustration of the event.*

time at 7:22 a.m. the following day. "Now he belongs to the ages," said Secretary of War Edwin Stanton.[8]

Lincoln's body was still limp and warm when taken out of the temporary coffin and placed on a cooling board in the Prince of Wales Room, the guest suite in the White House. Named for Queen Victoria's son and heir who had slept in it five years earlier, the west front corner room overlooked crowds of mostly black men, women, and children, weeping in the rain in a stoic vigil extending over days. Less than a week had passed since thousands of joyful freed slaves had massed to sing "The Year of Jubilee" after learning of Lee's surrender.[9] One of their emancipated race would later lament the loss of their "Moses."[10]

The lights had dimmed forever in the life of Mary Todd Lincoln. She kept to her darkened bedroom overlooking grounds at the back of the White House, crying and wailing so pitifully that even young Tad had pleaded, "Don't cry so Mama. Don't cry or you will make me cry, too. You will break my heart." Only then did she stifle her tears and squeeze tight the youngest of her two surviving sons.[11]

Mary Jane Welles, wife of the secretary of the navy, was one of a select few allowed into Mrs. Lincoln's room in futile efforts to offer companionship and gentle comfort. Gideon Welles conferred briefly with his wife in the White House Library, then, as he walked downstairs on his way out with Attorney General James Speed, a tearful Tad turned from a window on the landing and asked, "Oh, Mr. Welles, who killed my father?" Both Welles and Speed, eminent and skilled in persuasive talk and opinion, now faltered, unable to give the boy an answer as each fought hard to blink back tears.[12]

A series of mix-ups and mishaps had delayed the arrival of Mary Todd Lincoln's closest confidante and companion, her seamstress Elizabeth Keckly, who could have provided immediate support and succor. The widow had sent messengers to summon the African American Keckly to the White House on the night of the assassination, but they had botched the instructions and got lost. Keckly had learned of the murder within an hour of the gunshot and instinctively raced to her friend at the White House, but armed guards made no exception in denying her and others entry in the night of unprecedented turmoil. When she finally entered the darkened room in the morning, Mrs. Lincoln could only murmur,

"Why did you not come to me last night, Elizabeth? I sent for you." Keckly felt profound sympathy as she rested her hand on the feverish brow of her friend, who would in time be committed to a sanitarium.[13]

The autopsy began less than five hours after death, with Lincoln's unclothed body covered only by sheets and towels as it lay stretched out on boards brought into the Prince of Wales Room by the embalmer. As Dr.

NATIONAL MUSEUM OF HEALTH AND MEDICINE

Edward Curtis prepared to start the postmortem with Dr. Janvier Woodward, he marveled at Lincoln's muscular form, unexpected in an elongated man who stooped.[14]

While the surgeons fingered the spongy brain, tracing the path of the lead ball along a line of torn tissue and congealed blood, a messenger came in from Mrs. Lincoln requesting a lock of her husband's hair. Dr. Robert Stone, the Lincolns' family physician, snipped some strands off the broken skull, then gave the same treasured keepsakes to each of the attending doctors.[15]

When Curtis got home later that day his wife cut off the bloodstained shirt cuffs for instant preservation as historic relics. With equal reverence, her husband delicately removed for personal safekeeping a splinter of Lincoln's skull stuck to one of his surgical instruments.[16]

German-born medical illustrator Hermann Faber of Philadelphia accompanied the army Surgeon General Joseph Barnes to Lincoln's bedside. Immediately after the body was removed to the White House, Faber made two pencil sketches of the room and the men present as the president lay dying. General Barnes and Dr. Joseph Janvier Woodward pronounced it accurate. The portrait figures developed subsequently, following Dr. Woodward's recollection, are 1) Gideon Welles, secretary of the navy; 2) Salmon P. Chase, secretary of the treasury; 3) Robert King Stone, Lincoln's personal physician; 4) Charles Sumner, U.S. Senator; 5) Charles Crane, assistant surgeon general; 6) Joseph Barnes, surgeon general 7) Major General Henry Halleck; and 8) Edwin M. Stanton, secretary of war.

PHOTOGRAPH BY BRUCE WHITE FOR THE WHITE HOUSE HISTORICAL ASSOCIATION

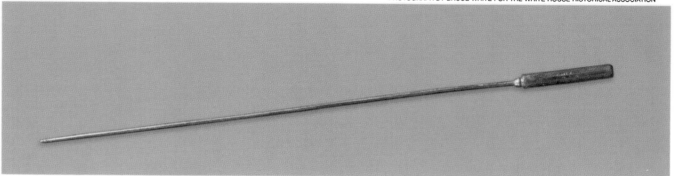

Top: Lincoln's body was moved to the White House, where an autopsy was performed in the Prince of Wales Room by doctors attached to the Office of the Surgeon General, pictured above. Those performing the autopsy included Joseph Barnes and Edward Curtis (fifth and sixth from the left) and Joseph Javier Woodward (far right). The bullet probe used by the doctors in their examination is now in the collection of the National Museum of Health and Medicine in Washington, D.C.

The bullet that killed President Lincoln was marked with the initials A. L. by Dr. Stone who described it as a "leaden-hand made ball flattened somewhat in its passage through the skull." It measures 43.75 mm and is composed of a mixture of antimony, tin, copper, and soft lead.

A lock of President Lincoln's hair preserved by Mrs. Lincoln is now in the collection of the Chicago History Museum.

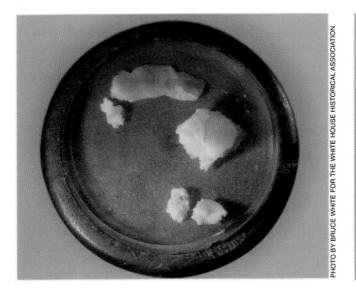

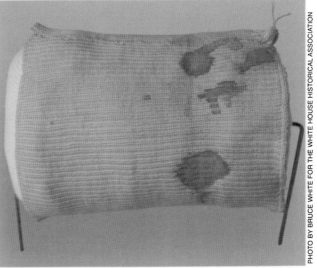

Following the autopsy Dr. Edward Curtis preserved a splinter of the president's skull, which he had delicately removed from one of his surgical instruments. A cuff from Dr. Curtis's bloodstained shirt was removed by Mrs. Curtis for safekeeping.

Crowds line the sidewalks on Pennsylvania Avenue to view the mile long funeral procession from the White House to the Capitol. Details also show spectators sitting on rooftops, and leaning from windows.

The black crape customary at presidential funerals was used abundantly for Lincoln, wrapping columns as seen above and opposite on the Capitol and Treasury Department Building, draped from windows and doorways, and visible also in black armbands worn by men and black scarves and ribbons for women. Below is the funeral train that would carry Lincoln's body in doleful parade to most of the Union's statehouses, to be viewed by millions. Less than two weeks before, Lincoln had declined to use the brand-new presidential car, built in Alexandria, Virginia, for his triumphal trip to fallen Richmond, believing it too opulent and thus the wrong tone for the occasion. The painted decorations of the car, itself lost in a fire, survive in the Union Pacific Railroad Historical Museum, Council Bluffs, Iowa.

Black mourning material quickly appeared all over the capital, hanging as sheets or stretched in folds across the face of the White House and many homes, offices, hotels, shops, and places of business. The traditional outward sign of grief wound around columns and pillars of government buildings and dropped limply from roofs and windows. Black mourning cloth bordered oversize mirrors in the East Room of the White House in readiness for the arrival of invitees bearing black-bordered admission cards to the funeral service. Lincoln's principal private secretary, George Nicolay, arrived back from a visit to Charleston two days after the president's death to find the White House "dark and still as almost the grave itself."[17]

The following day a front gate admitted thousands of Washingtonians and others who had lined up for hours to pay their last respects before the mahogany coffin. The embalmer, Henry Cattell, had shaved off Lincoln's beard, leaving only a tuft of hair on the chin. The tallest president lay solid as marble in a 6 feet 6 inch coffin bearing the simple wording etched into a silver plate:

Abraham Lincoln
16th President of the United States
Born February 12th 1809
Died April 15th 1865[18]

One woman who had waited steadfastly in line while it rained, wrote, "We were not permitted to wait a moment near the corpse, so it was impossible to obtain a satisfactory view."[19] But she had at least come close to the object of her devotion, an honor denied "tens of thousands" of others turned away when guards closed the gate for the day.[20]

As dignitaries crammed into the spacious East Room for the funeral service four days after Lincoln's death, Mrs. Lincoln remained reclusive upstairs, unresponsive to the solicitude of others and weakened by lack of sleep and loss of appetite, yet left alone to writhe in the harrowing isolation of her trauma and sorrow.

President Andrew Johnson stood near the long coffin resting above a raised catafalque under an ornately domed canopy. The grandeur was fitting for the passing of a president but out of character for the simple preferences of Lincoln. His ravaged remains had been cosmet-

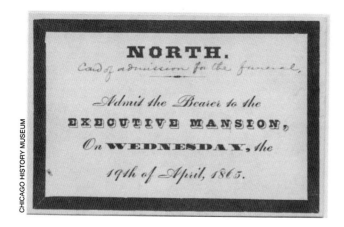

NORTH.

Card of admission for the funeral,

Admit the Bearer to the

EXECUTIVE MANSION,

On WEDNESDAY, the

19th of April, 1865.

This black-bordered card admitted one person on a very restricted list to Lincoln's funeral in the East Room. White House stationery and that of the upper officials of the government were reprinted with the black border and used for thirty days following Lincoln's death.

ically disguised for the public. The untested seventeenth president was one of the few who had seen Lincoln's brain lifted out of the gaping skull during the cranial autopsy. Others were unaware that the jugular had been cut to drain blood out of the body and that the top of his skull had been sawn off to get at the brain. But all were aware of a historic passing, and a profound sadness filled every onlooker. Even Lieutenant General Ulysses S. Grant, inured to carnage on a scale unimaginable to those who had never walked among battlefield dead, wept openly near the coffin. His own grief was deep and immediate and in time he would write fondly of Lincoln's "goodness of heart and his desire to have everybody happy."[21]

The Reverend Doctor Phineas Gurley extolled Lincoln's virtues in nostalgic remembrance of a friend. "We admired his childlike simplicity, his freedom from guile and deceit," said the Presbyterian family pastor, given the honor of leading the service in the presence of dozens of clergymen from different denominations. But he could not hide his own bafflement by the terrible turn of events. "We will wait for His interpretation," he declared, as if fumbling for a meaningful answer and settling for unconditional faith.[22]

So many delegations and individuals took part in the mile-long funeral procession to the Capitol that those in the lead reached the end before the last had even left the White House. A U.S. Army regiment of black infantrymen, included at the insistence of Secretary of War Stanton, proudly led the extended cortege.[23]

Forty thousand mourners filed by the casket while it lay in the Rotunda of the Capitol during fourteen hours of viewing the next day. Again the dignitaries

were on hand at the train depot for a final farewell as the remains were taken across country for the funeral in Springfield, Illinois.

But the widow did not budge from seclusion. Five weeks would pass before she finally took leave of the White House, though encased in mournful misery until her own death seventeen years later. Only another who had suffered a similar loss, she wrote to the widow Queen Victoria, "can appreciate the intense grief I now endure."[24]

NOTES

1. Quoted in Francis B. Carpenter, *Six Months at the White House with Abraham Lincoln: The Story of a Picture* (New York: Hurd and Houghton, 1867), 17. See also the White House Historical Association edition edited by Harold Holzer, 2008.

2. Quoted in Elizabeth Keckley [Keckly], *Behind the Scenes; or, Thirty Years a Slave and Four Years in the White House* (New York: G. W. Carleton, 1868; repr. New York: Arno Press and New York Times, 1968), 137–38.

3. Quoted in A. S. Draper, "Lincoln's Parable," *Harper's Weekly*, October 26, 1907, 1567.

4. Quoted in James Speed to Merrill Watson, summer 1885, David Homer Bates Papers, container 2, reel 1, Library of Congress, Washington, D.C.

5. Mary Todd Lincoln to Francis B. Carpenter, November 15, 1865, *Mary Todd Lincoln: Her Life and Letters*, ed. Justin G. Turner and Linda Levitt Turner (New York: Fromm International Publishing, 1987), 284–85.

6. Tanner to Frear, May 7, 1926, 69th Cong., 1st sess., *Congressional Record* (June 1, 1926): 10419.

7. Quoted in Thomas F. Pendel, *Thirty Six Years in the White House* (Washington, D.C.: Neale Publishing, 1902), 10, 44.

8. Tanner to Frear, May 7, 1926, 10420; John George Nicolay and John Hay, *Abraham Lincoln: A History* (New York: Century Company, 1917), 10:302; Charles F. Taft, "Abraham Lincoln's Last Hours," *Century Magazine* 45, no. 4 (February 1893): 635.

9. Noah Brooks, *Washington in Lincoln's Time*, ed. Herbert Mitgang (New York: Rinehart, 1958), 225.

10. Keckley [Keckly], *Behind the Scenes*, 190.

11. Ibid., 192.

12. Gideon Welles, diary, April 15, 1865, Gideon Welles Papers, reel 3, Library of Congress.

13. Keckley [Keckly], *Behind the Scenes*, 184–88.

Upon receiving a note of sympathy from Queen Victoria, Mary Lincoln wrote the following response: "I have received the letter which Your Majesty has had the kindness to write and am deeply grateful for its expressions of tender sympathy, coming as they do from a heart which from its own Sorrow, can appreciate the intense grief I now endure. Accept, Madam, the assurances of my heartfelt thanks and believe me in the deepest sorrow, Your Majesty's Sincere and grateful friend." The queen's letter to the widowed Lincoln had been intended, of course, for publication and was not in fact a personal letter. Mrs. Lincoln, who seems to have missed this point, responded intimately, referring to the death of Victoria's consort, Prince Albert, who had died four years before and for whom the queen's tireless mourning was well known.

14. Edward Curtis, "Was at Lincoln Autopsy," *New York Sun*, April 22, 1903.

15. Taft, "Lincoln's Last Hours," 636.

16. Augusta Curtis affidavit, May 11, 1926, accession file 29719, Armed Forces Institute of Pathology, National Museum of Health and Medicine, Washington, D.C.

17. John George Nicolay to Therena Bates, April 18, 1865, John George Nicolay Papers, box 3, Library of Congress.

18. *Washington Daily National Intelligencer*, April 16, 1865.

19. Helen McCalla, diary, April 18, 1865, Helen McCalla Papers, Library of Congress.

20. George Coffin, diary, April 18, 1865, Special Collections, Gelman Library, George Washington University, Washington, D.C.

21. Ulysses S. Grant, *Personal Memoirs* (New York: Charles Webster, 1886), 2:508–9.

22. Quoted in Frank E. Edgington, *A History of the New York Avenue Presbyterian Church* (Washington, D.C.: New York Avenue Presbyterian Church, 1961), 249–50.

23. Official Records of the Union and Confederate Armies, ser. 1, 46:816, pt. 3 National Archives; Brooks, *Washington in Lincoln's Time*, 235.

24. Mary Todd Lincoln to Queen Victoria, May 21, 1865, *Mary Todd Lincoln*, ed. Turner and Turner, 230–31.

The Lincoln Bedroom: Refurbishing a Famous White House Room

WILLIAM G. ALLMAN

*P*resident Abraham Lincoln's office and Cabinet Room—the large southeast room on the Second Floor of the White House—has been called the Lincoln Bedroom since 1945, when President Harry S. Truman directed that Lincoln-era furnishings be assembled there. In the Truman renovation of the White House (1949–52), only the muted Brussels-style carpet gave a reasonably appropriate design context for the celebrated suite of bedroom furniture acquired by the president's wife Mary Todd Lincoln in 1861.

The addition of a mid-nineteenth-century gaslight chandelier and Victorian-style draperies in the 1970s weighted the decor more toward the Lincoln era. Still, much of what President Truman had provided in 1952 was intact after fifty years when, in January 2002, First Lady Laura Bush expressed an interest in refurbishing the Lincoln Bedroom along historical lines.

As part of the private quarters, the Lincoln Bedroom is not technically a "State" or official room. Therefore funding its decoration and furnishing is out-

---

side the purview of the Committee for the Preservation of the White House, which was created in 1964 to advise on the maintenance of the museum character of the State Rooms; nor is it eligible for the funds provided for the public rooms by the White House Endowment Trust, which is managed by the White House Historical Association. Yet over time the Lincoln Bedroom has achieved the status of a State Room, being as famous as any on the State Floor or the Ground Floor, and as the Lincoln bicentennial was approaching, the White House Historical Association agreed in 2002 to finance a historical refurbishing project, the character of which was to be determined by Mrs. Bush, the preservation committee, and an expert subcommittee that helped with the planning.

Two separate channels of historical evidence were available for the refurbishing project. A few annotated drawings and photographs of the room in use as Lincoln's office helped document the carpeting and wall covering, both in green and yellow. A description of what was then known as the Prince of Wales Room, down the hall, where the furniture had originally been installed by Mrs. Lincoln, indicated the use of purple bed hangings and yellow draperies. The refurbishing project was based on these sources.

Fortunately, the May 12, 1862, issue of a San Francisco newspaper called the *Daily Alta California* described both Lincoln's office and the Prince of Wales Room. Of the office it said: "very neatly papered, but should be better furnished. All the furniture is exceed-

The Lincoln Bedroom, 2005. The suite of bedroom furniture was among of Mrs. Lincoln's costly acquisitions. The massive bed—rosewood and rosewood-paint-grained walnut—was accompanied by a handsome marble-topped center table made by the New York shop of John Henry Belter.

ingly old, and is too ricketty to venerate."[1] A familiar image of the office is an 1866 engraving entitled *The First Reading of the Emancipation Proclamation Before the Cabinet* by Alexander Ritchie, after the painting by artist Francis B. Carpenter now in the U.S. Capitol. Carpenter created the painting while he worked and lived in the White House for six months in 1864, so he knew the room firsthand. Even more important for the refurbishing project were Carpenter's study sketches and the photographs taken in the Cabinet Room at his direction by Anthony Berger of Mathew Brady's studio on April 26, 1864. Of similar specific relevance is an

October 1864 drawing of the Lincoln's office by C. K. Stellwagen.[2]

Stellwagen's drawing housed in the collections of the Western Reserve Historical Society and Carpenter's painting rather schematically suggest that the carpet in the room had a large diamond pattern. Greater detail appears in one of Berger's photographs. Stellwagen noted on this drawing that the carpet was "dark green with buff figure in diamonds," and on one of his sketches Carpenter had noted that the patterned stripes were "dark green," creating a grid centering medallions described as "yellow." This carpet was presumably the

The French "portico" mantel clock was purchased under President Andrew Jackson and used in President Lincoln's office. The mantel was reproduced from late nineteenth-century photos showing the 1853 mantel Lincoln would have known in the room.

119½ yards of "G&O Wilton" provided for the president's office in 1861 by the New York City department store, Alexander T. Stewart & Co.[3]

For the refurbishing project, White House curators returned to files on the carpet from 1995, when then curator Betty C. Monkman had consulted with rug specialist John Burrows about the possibility of deriving a carpet design from the 1864 documentation. Burrows had extrapolated a bold design from one of Berger's photographs, but a carpet was not commissioned at the time. Now Burrows was able to provide computer-generated images. It was surmised that the "G&O" in the

accounts stood for the period colors "green and oak," so brown was among the colors selected for the new carpet and gold yarns were chosen for the yellow or buff elements. To enliven the design and complement the proposed bed hangings, purple was introduced as well. Small woven hand trials were used to help make the final design decisions.

Inasmuch as the original Wilton carpet probably would have been made in England, it was decided that that the new carpet should be made by the venerable English firm of Woodward & Grosvenor, specialist in reproduction rugs and possessor of a vast archives of

Above: The Lincoln Bedroom evolves. Left to right: This 1889 view of the northwest corner of the room shows the Lincoln period mantel in detail. The second image, southwest view, shows the room as President Truman completed it in 1952. The third image shows the room in the 1990s as it was before the Bush restoration.

Right: The Lincoln bed in the 1870s sported hangings that may be the purple ones selected by Mrs. Lincoln in 1861. Far Right: View of the Lincoln Bedroom furniture as Theodore Roosevelt used it in the master bedroom, honoring the bed's tradition with gilded cornice and hangings.

historic rug designs and actual point papers to help assure accuracy. The carpeting was produced in its original Wilton or cut-pile form, woven in traditional 27-inch-wide strips, hand-sewn together, and fitted wall-to-wall.

The documentation indicates that the walls of Lincoln's office were covered in wallpaper colored green and gold. Decorative arts scholar, Richard Nylander, a member of the subcommittee and chief curator of Historic New England, identified in his institution's large collection of wallpapers a fragment of a very similar period paper—dark green with a gilt grid and medallions trimmed in purple and red. This fragment provided a model very similar in design to the documentation; to better suit a functioning bedroom, the green field color was changed to yellow in a block printed paper.

The suite of bedroom furniture now used in the Lincoln Bedroom was one of Mrs. Lincoln's many and often costly acquisitions of household furnishings for the White House. The massive bed—rosewood and rosewood-paint-grained walnut—was accompanied by a handsome marble-topped center table made by the famous New York shop of John Henry Belter, known for using strong, bendable laminated rosewood, and by a chest of drawers and a set of chairs also attributed to Belter.

Of this room the *Daily Alta California* said:

> The principal feature of the room is the bed. It is eight feet wide and nine feet long, of solid rosewood. The sides are cushioned and covered with purple figured satin. The headboard is a piece of rich carved work, rising eight feet above the bed, and having an oval top. Twenty feet above the floor, overspreading the whole, is a magnificent canopy, from the upper carved work of which the drapery hangs in elegant folds, being in the form of a crown, the front ornament upon which is the American shield with the Stars and Stripes carved thereon. The drapery is a rich purple satin fringe, and otherwise ornamented with finest gold lace. The carved work is adorned with gold gilt. The curtains to the room are made of the finest gold damask, and trimmed to correspond with the canopy. The centre table is of solid carved rosewood, is quite costly, and exceedingly beautiful.

With the bed as the focal point of the Lincoln Bedroom, one fascinating prospect was to re-create the demilune gilded bed cornice or corona from which the purple hangings and lace curtains had been suspended. Used with the Lincoln bed in the bedroom of President and Mrs. Theodore Roosevelt, it was later used also by Edith Wilson (1915–21) over a bed she owned personally and again with the Lincoln bed by Grace Coolidge (1923–26). When the Coolidge bed hangings were destroyed in 1928, it seems likely that the bed cornice was destroyed as well.

Bedrooms at the west end of the Second Floor have higher ceilings than those at the east end, so the proportions of the hangings had to be adjusted. The shield on the bed cornice is repeated across the room on a similar shield in the cresting of the newly installed rococo revival mirror purchased for the Green Room by President Franklin Pierce in 1853. Old photographs taken in the White House revealed large gilded window cornices that were clearly related to the bed cornice, so they were reproduced accordingly. A rich yellow silk brocatelle of a mid-nineteenth-century pattern and color was selected to hang from them, consisting of panels trimmed with purple and gold bullion fringe and open-scroll braid. These were topped by valence-like swags of cords and tassels, in yellow and purple, matching those on the purple silk bed hangings, designed to closely follow the documents—the Carpenter sketches, the Stellwagen drawing, and an 1858 fashion plate advertising merchandise for W. H. Carryl, the firm that provided the Lincoln White House with the bedroom suite of furniture and some draperies.[5]

Nearly all the furniture used in the room prior to the current refurbishing was returned. A rosewood dressing chest—of undetermined acquisition but long used with the Lincoln suite—was kept in the room and placed against the north wall. A large walnut wardrobe was conserved to hold one modern device— a television. Used with the Lincoln suite since 1930, a slant-front desk—transferred from the Soldiers' Home in Washington, D.C., the Lincoln summer White House—has a history of having been used there by President Lincoln when drafting the Emancipation Proclamation. An oak armchair from a set made for the U.S. House of Representatives in 1857—and of a type often used in Mathew Brady's photographs—remains as the desk chair. The marble-topped center tables flanking the bed were made by Anthony Quervelle of Philadelphia and purchased by Andrew Jackson for the East Room in 1829.

Highlights of the room are objects documented as having been used by President Lincoln. Four Gothic Revival walnut side chairs, of a type clearly identifiable in the Carpenter painting, are the only ones remaining from the set used around President Lincoln's cabinet table; three of these were installed in the bedroom, one in the Lincoln Sitting Room. Acquired in 1846 in the Polk administration, they were made by J.& J. W. Meeks of New York. On the new white marble mantel, carved from photographs of the 1853 mantel Lincoln knew in the room (removed in 1902, location unknown), stands a French "portico" mantel clock purchased for the nearby waiting room in 1833 under President Andrew Jackson but used on the mantel in President Lincoln's office.

In Lincoln's time, a portrait of President Andrew Jackson had hung above that clock, attributed to Miner Kilbourne Kellogg (1814–1889), c. 1840. It now hangs above one doorway. Among the other artwork retained in the room is the 1866 engraving, *The First Reading of the Emancipation Proclamation Before the Cabinet*, after the painting by Francis B. Carpenter and a miniature of Lincoln and his youngest son Tad by Carpenter that was inspired by a photograph taken in the artist's presence by Anthony Berger in February 1864. Other portraits of Lincoln displayed in the room include *Lincoln, The Ever-Sympathetic* by Stephen Arnold Douglas Volk, 1931; a bronze statue by Jeno Juszko, 1925, that portrays President Lincoln in a relaxed, seated pose echoed in the depiction of him in the *First Reading* engraving; and an 1866 print by William Edgar Marshall, one of the most widely distributed and best known post–Civil War works, this example having once been owned by Frederick Douglass.

On the room's north wall hangs *Watch Meeting— Dec. 31st 1862—Waiting for the Hour* by William Tolman Carlton, an oil on canvas that depicts slaves and friends waiting for midnight on December 31, 1862, when the Emancipation Proclamation went into effect. It is a study for a painting sent to Abraham Lincoln by abolitionist leader William Lloyd Garrison. *The Republican Court in the Days of Lincoln,* by Peter Frederick Rothermel, c. 1867, is an imaginary scene of a reception in the East Room—showing President and Mrs. Lincoln, Vice President Andrew Johnson, members of the cabinet, and prominent Union officers, including

Generals Winfield Scott, Ulysses S. Grant, and William Tecumseh Sherman—was probably intended to be a model for an engraving. At no time did all of these leaders ever assemble in the White House.

The refurbishing of the Lincoln Bedroom and the adjoining sitting room—a strong period decor derived and adapted from the historical evidence of the Lincoln era—was completed in November 2005.

NOTES

1. "Lincolns Redecorate," *San Francisco Daily Alta California,* May 12, 1862.

2. The Berger photographs are found in the Keya Morgan collection and with the Carpenter family [see Charles Hamilton and Lloyd Ostendorf, *Lincoln in Photographs: An Album of Every Known Pose* (Dayton: Morningside, 1985, 190–95).] Carpenter's sketchbook remains in family hands [see Stefan Lorant, *Lincoln: A Picture History of His Life* (New York: Bonanza, 1979, 165).] The drawing by C. K. Stellwagen is now in the collection of the Western Reserve Historical Society, Cleveland, Ohio.

3. Miscellaneous Treasury Accounts 141262, May 24, 1861, National Archives, Washington, D.C.

4. "Lincolns Redecorate."

5. "Fashion Plate./From the Establishment of W.H. Carryl and Brother," *Godey's Lady's Book,* Vol. LVII, August 1858, 77.

Photographs of Indian Delegates in the President's "Summer House"

CLIFFORD KRAINIK
AND MICHELE KRAINIK

*I*n the early spring of 1863 a delegation of Southern Plains Indians, members of the Apache, Arapaho, Caddo, Cheyenne, Comanche, and Kiowa tribes, were invited to Washington to meet with President Abraham Lincoln at the height of the Civil War. The purpose of the visit was to secure peaceful relations with the Indians and to dissuade them from joining forces with the Confederacy. Recruitment of Native Americans to fight for the South had met with some success, notably among the Cherokee Nation in the Trans-Mississippi West, and overtures were being made to other tribes in the Indian Territory, now Oklahoma. The Indian delegation accompanied by their agent, Samuel G. Colley, and their interpreter, John Simpson Smith, were escorted into the East Room of the White House, where they were immediately confronted by a large assembly of gentlemen and ladies including foreign ministers and their families, secretaries of the interior, state and treasury, the commissioner of Indian affairs, and a host of distinguished guests. According to newspaper accounts, "The savages were dressed in full feather—buffalo robes, Indian tanned, and bead worked leggings, with a profusion of paints upon their faces and hair, etc. . . . They squatted themselves down upon the floor in a semicircle—fourteen chiefs and two squaws—and were instantly surrounded by the curious crowd."[1] One of the delegates, a Kiowa chief named Yellow Wolf, drew special attention for the large silver peace medal he wore, given to the Kiowas by President Thomas Jefferson. The medal had been

handed down for generations and was held in the highest esteem by the tribe.[2]

After a brief wait President Lincoln entered the room and listened attentively to introductory remarks by Superintendent of Indian Affairs William P. Dole. Then the interpreter, John Smith, introduced each of the chiefs to the president, who solemnly shook their hands. The president, speaking to the Indians through their interpreter, told the chiefs that he was eager to hear anything they wished to say. Two Cheyenne chiefs, Lean Bear and Spotted Wolf, each addressed the president with expressions of amazement for all the wonderful things

they had witnessed; they pledged their tribal friendship but expressed dire concern about the encroachment of white settlers on their lands. President Lincoln responded by telling the Indians that "It is the object of this Government to be on terms of peace with you and all our red brethren. We constantly endeavor to be so. We make treaties with you, and will try to observe them" Lincoln continued, "The palefaced people are numerous and prosperous because they cultivate the earth, produce bread, and depend upon the products of the earth rather than wild game for a subsistence. This is the chief reason of the difference; but there is another. Although we are now engaged in a great war between one another, we are not, as a

Chiefs of the Southern Plains Peace Delegation to the White House (left to right) have been identified as Standing in Water, War Bonnet, and Lean Bear, Cheyenne; and Yellow Wolf, Kiowa. This is a detail of one of three photographs taken of the delegation in the White House Conservatory, March 27, 1863, by an unnamed photographer working for Brady's National Photographic Portrait Galleries, in Washington, D.C. The three photographs are published here together for the first time.

The subjects seated in the front row, left to right, have been identified as Standing in Water, War Bonnet, and Lean Bear, Cheyenne; and Yellow Wolf, Kiowa. In the middle row at left is the Kiowa woman, Coy, beside her husband, White Bull. An unidentified white child stands among the Indians. To the viewing right of the child is Lone Wolf, a Kiowa, and Etta, wife of Little Heart. The gentlemen standing at left in the back row are John Simpson Smith, interpreter and Samuel G. Colley, Indian agent. Standing next to Colley are Miss Geralt and Miss Lisbon. The tall figure at center is Lincoln's personal secretary, 31-year-old, John George Nicolay. To the viewing right of Nicolay are Miss Kennedy and another Miss Geralt. The four women and the white child were probably family members of visiting diplomats. The bonneted woman at far right has occasionally been identified as Mary Todd Lincoln, but positive identification remains unresolved. Less than two years after this photograph was taken all four of the Indian peace delegates seated in the front row were dead. Yellow Wolf succumbed to pneumonia days later and was buried with his Jefferson Peace Medal in Congressional Cemetery. The noncombatant Cheyennes, War Bonnet and Standing in Water, were slaughtered by Colorado Territory Militia in the Sand Creek Massacre on November 29, 1864. On May 16, 1864, mistaken for a hostile, Lean Bear protested that he had "visited the home of the White father" but fell under a volley from the same militia. Brady negative number 2735, published as a stereoview by E. & H. T. Anthony, New York.

Interpreter John Smith and the six Indian men and two women who posed in the group portrait with Nicolay appear again with a new set of visitors to the White House Conservatory. Standing in the back row at left are two unidentified gentlemen. The young woman to their right is Kate Chase, the charming daughter of Secretary of the Treasury Salmon P. Chase. The three other women remain unidentified, though they are no doubt family members of visiting diplomats. The large silver peace medal given by President Thomas Jefferson to the Kiowas is visible around the neck of Yellow Wolf, seated in the first row at far right.

The third group portrait taken in the White House conservatory depicts only members of the Southern Plains Peace Delegation with their interpreter, John Smith. Seven other unidentified Indian men have joined the group portrait. In the back row, obscured behind the figure of John Smith, two top hats reveal the presence of other visitors. At left, partially hidden by a potted plant, is a young boy wearing a hat seen in profile regarding the Indian visitors. Brady negative number 2734, published as a stereoview by E. & H. T. Anthony, New York.

race, so much disposed to fight and kill one another as our red brethren."[3] The bitter irony of telling the chiefs of the Southern Plains that the white race was not as warlike as the Indians were inclined was not lost on the crowd of guests who were painfully aware of the enormous carnage of the ongoing Civil War. Lincoln then concluded the meetings by telling the chiefs that the commissioner of Indian affairs would see that the delegation would soon be returned home. The president rose and once again shook hands with each of the chiefs. Later that afternoon the delegation was ushered to the west end of the White House and crossed the path to the Conservatory, where one of Mathew Brady's cameramen was busily preparing to take group portraits.

The Lincoln White House Conservatory, also known as the greenhouse or "President's Summer House," was actually the second building used for the purpose of botanical retreat. The first stood on the east side of the mansion near the old stable. Both decrepit structures were torn down to make way for the Treasury Building extension. The inception of a new White House Conservatory began with President Franklin Pierce, but actual construction of the building did not start until President James Buchanan assumed office. Located just 12 feet west of the White House and connected by a narrow glazed passage, the large wooden structure was completed in 1857 at a cost of $16,000. "The glass roof and sides made it seem light, despite its mass . . . Inside, the conservatory had one grand central room, very high and with a steeply slanted ceiling; it housed rows of heavy, green-painted tables. On them plants en mass created a thick growth of greenery and bloom."[4] President Lincoln's personal secretary, George Nicolay, attended the meeting with the Southern Plains Peace Delegation at the White House and after the adjournment accompanied the visitors to the Conservatory. A few weeks later Nicolay wrote to his future wife, Therena Bates, a firsthand account of the event:

Executive Mansion, Washington, April 9, 1863.

Dear Therena

I am still enjoying the quiet in the house produced by the President's absence. He has not yet returned from Fredericksburg, or rather Falmouth, and consequently the crowd that usually haunts the interchamber and my office keep at a distance. He

will probably be back again by tomorrow, when they will once more swarm in upon us like Egyptian locusts.

I enclose you a little picture of a group taken about two weeks ago, in our conservatory here. A delegation of Indians from the plains were here to see the President, and afterwards they were taken out into the greenhouse and photographed as you see them, original copperheads[5] against a background of palefaces. The young ladies are, counting from the left, Miss Geralt, Miss Lisbon,[6] Miss Kennedy, and another Miss Geralt, all but Miss Kennedy belonging to the Diplomatic Corps. I have a stereoscopic view of it which shows to better advantage.

Your

George.[7]

The "little picture" which Nicolay included in his letter is preserved in the Manuscript Division of the Library of Congress, an unmounted albumen carte de visite—size photograph—approximately 2 by 3½ inches. The carte de visite or visiting card photograph was a favorite format for paper photographs taken during the Civil War. Nicolay further stated that he had a stereoscopic view of the group portrait, referring to the popular mid-nineteenth-century double-image card that, when seen through a stereoscopic viewing device, produced a three-dimensional picture.[8]

Mathew Brady, the noted Civil War photographer, produced three distinct views of the Indian delegation taken in the White House conservatory. In each of the three photographs the most influential members of the Southern Plains Delegation were prominently posed in the front row. Three Cheyenne chiefs—Standing in Water, War Bonnet, and Lean Bear were seated next to the Kiowa leader, Yellow Wolf. In two of the photographs Yellow Wolf's Jefferson Peace Medal is plainly visible. The two front rows of Indians and their interpreter remained for all three photographs, creating a setting for the other visitors to be included in the historic record.

Two of the three Brady negatives for the Indian photographs were numbered and published as stereoviews by E. & H. T. Anthony, New York City. One image (not published as a stereoview) includes Kate

Chase, the vivacious daughter of Secretary of the Treasury Salmon P. Chase, standing next to three gentlemen—the interpreter John Smith and two unidentified guests. To the right of Miss Chase are three women whose identities remain unknown but may have been family members of visiting dignitaries. Another group portrait portrays only Native Americans with their interpreter, John Smith. In the third conservatory portrait George Nicolay is positioned at center in the back row, flanked by four identified family members of the diplomatic corps. At the far left of the image in the back row stand John Smith and Indian agent, Samuel G. Colley. The enigmatic bonneted woman in the back row, far right, has sometimes been referred to as First Lady Mary Todd Lincoln. No contemporary identification, however, supports the claim, and even George Nicolay who named all the other non-Indian guests in the picture, failed to provide her identity.[9]

Just eight days after Yellow Wolf visited the White House, he died of pneumonia at his Washington hotel. His personal effects—bow and arrows, buffalo robes and blankets, and the large silver peace medal, a present from President Jefferson to Yellow Wolf's ancestors, were buried with the Kiowa chief in a government-furnished coffin. Yellow Wolf was laid to rest far from his native Plains in Congressional Cemetery.[10] The fates of the three Cheyenne chiefs photographed next to Yellow Wolf are equally sad. Less than two years after their peace mission to Washington, all three chiefs were killed. War Bonnet and Standing in Water were slaughtered in the Sand Creek Massacre. Lean Bear was mistaken for a hostile and killed in May 1864 by Colorado troops intent on following orders to shoot Indians wherever they were found on the Plains.

The peace medal given to Lean Bear during his visit to the White House was found on his bullet-riddled body and in his hand was clutched a piece of paper verifying that he was a peaceful friend of the whites—signed, A. Lincoln.[11]

NOTES

1. *Washington Daily National Intelligencer*, March 28, 1863, quoted in Stan Hoig, *The Peace Chiefs of the Cheyennes* (Norman: University of Oklahoma Press, 1980), 70.

2. The Jefferson medals of the first grade were the largest peace medals struck at the United States Mint. Like all the Jefferson medals, they were hollow shells held together by a silver rim. . . . The Jefferson medals set the pattern for presidential peace medals in three sizes [105 mm, 76 mm, and 55 mm], with a bust of the President on one side, and a message of peace and friendship on the other." Francis Paul Prucha, *Indian Peace Medals in American History* (Bluffton, S.C.: Rivilo Books, 1994), 92–93.

3. *Washington National Republican*, March 27, 1863, quoted in Hoig, *Peace Chiefs of the Cheyennes*, 72–73.

4. William Seale, *The President's House: A History* (Washington, D.C.: White House Historical Association, with the cooperation of the National Geographic Society, 1986), 1:343–45.

5. Nicolay plays on words. The name "copperhead" referred to the vocal group of northern Democrats who opposed the Civil War and demanded an immediate peace with the Confederacy.

6. Some sources cite this name as Lisboa.

7. Illinois newspaper publisher John George Nicolay (1832–1901) met Lincoln in Illinois during the presidential campaign of 1860. Through Lincoln's first official act in office Nicolay became the president's personal secretary. He served in that capacity until Lincoln's death in 1865. Nicolay was U.S. at Paris, marshal of the U.S. Supreme Court, and with John Hay wrote a biography of Abraham Lincoln in 1890.

   Therena Bates Nicolay was born May 31, 1836, at Pittsfield, Berkshire County, Massachusetts. She was the daughter of Dorus and Emma Norton Bates. She married John George Nicolay, Lincoln's private secretary, on June 15, 1865, in Cook County, Illinois, and had two children, Helen and George. She died on November 25, 1885, and is buried in Oak Hill Cemetery, Washington, D.C.

8. The stereoview was published from Brady's negative 2735 by the firm of E. & H. T. Anthony & Co., New York. It appeared in the series *Washington City Views. President's Summer House, Washington*. The dual albumen photographic prints, each 3 by 3 inches, were placed on a flat, yellow cardboard mount, 3½ by 7 inches, with printed white paper label affixed to the verso. The identification of the delegates was provided by Nicolay, while the determination of the Native Americans was the result of research by Paula Fleming, retired photographic archivist, National Anthropological Archives, and Herman Viola, former director of the National Anthropological Archives and author of *Diplomats in Buckskins: A History of Indian Delegations in Washington City* (Washington, D.C.: Smithsonian Institution Press, 1981).

9. See Charles Hamilton and Lloyd Ostendorf, *Lincoln in Photographs: An Album of Every Known Pose* (Dayton, Ohio: Morningside, 1985), 300–301; and Lloyd Ostendorf, *The Photographs of Mary Todd Lincoln* (Springfield: Illinois State Historical Society, 1969), 50–51. Ostendorf was in error as to the date of the photograph and misidentified all of the Native Americans. He claimed, "Mrs. Lincoln appears older than she does in some other pictures taken that year, possibly because of the harsh side lighting on her face."

10. "Death of an Indian Chief," *Washington Evening Star*, April 6, 1863.

11. Hoig, *Peace Chiefs of the Cheyennes*, 67.

About the Authors

WILLIAM G. ALLMAN is the curator in the Office of the Curator, the White House.

SISTER WENDY BECKETT is an art historian and a contemplative nun who has appeared in several television series, and has written many books on the subject of art.

ELIZABETH SMITH BROWNSTEIN is an author and was the director of research for the PBS series *Smithsonian World*.

WILLIAM B. BUSHONG is the historian and webmaster of the White House Historical Association.

NANCY CLARKE began working as a volunteer in the White House flower shop during President Jimmy Carter's administration and retired in 2009 as the chief floral designer.

CRISTETA COMERFORD has been executive chef at the White House since 2005.

CLAIRE A. FAULKNER is a member of the Usher's Office in the Executive Residence at the White House.

MAC KEITH GRISWOLD, a journalist, garden historian, and author, is currently the director of archival research at the Sylvester Manor Project in Shelter Island, New York.

DESMOND GUINNESS founded the Irish Georgian Society to help preserve Irish architecture of all periods.

BARBARA HABER is an award-winning food historian and author.

HAROLD HOLZER serves as co-chair of the U.S. Lincoln Bicentennial Commission and has authored numerous books, including *Lincoln at Cooper Union*, which won the 2005 Lincoln Prize.

HOLGER HOOCK is associate professor in British history and director of the Eighteenth-Century Worlds Centre at the University of Liverpool.

MARGARET HUDDY is a Washington, D.C.–based painter specializing in watercolor landscapes.

ELISE K. KIRK is an award-winning author, lecturer, and musicologist.

CLIFFORD KRAINIK is an independent historian, dealer, and appraiser of nineteenth-century photography.

MICHELE KRAINIK is an independent historian, dealer, and collector of nineteenth-century photography and historic Americana.

MARTHA JOYNT KUMAR is a professor at Towson University whose scholarly research focuses on White House press relations and communications.

EDWARD LAWLER JR. is the historian of Independence Hall Association, a nonprofit dedicated to promoting the teaching of American history through its congress of websites at www.ushistory.org.

EDITH MAYO is curator emeritus in Politics and Reform at the National Museum of American History, Smithsonian Institution.

DENNIS H. J. MEDINA is curator of the Dwight D. Eisenhower Library and Museum in Abilene, Kansas.

ROLAND MESNIER was head pastry chef at the White House from 1979 to 2004.

MARSHA MULLIN is director of museum services and chief curator at The Hermitage, Home of President Andrew Jackson.

MELISSA NAULIN is assistant curator in the Office of the Curator, the White House, where she focuses on the decorative arts.

ANTHONY S. PITCH is an award-winning book author and gives anecdotal history tours of Washington, D.C.

ALICE ROSS is a food historian with particular interest in evolving American home cookery and foodways.

WILLIAM SEALE is the editor of *White House History*. An architectural historian, he is the author of *The President's House: A History* and other books on American architecture and cultural history.

DANIEL SHANKS oversees food and beverage operations at the White House, where he has served as assistant usher in the Usher's Office in the Executive Residence since 1995.

CANDACE S. SHIREMAN is curator of Blair House, the President's Guest House.

LYDIA BARKER TEDERICK is assistant curator in the Office of the Curator, the White House.

AMY VERONE is the chief of cultural resources at Sagamore Hill National Historic Site in Oyster Bay, New York.

GWENDOLYN K. WHITE is currently a fellow at George Washington's Mount Vernon, and was formerly a research assistant at the White House Historical Association.

JOHN H. WHITE JR. is a professor at Miami University in Oxford, Ohio, where he teaches the history of travel and technology.

CONTRIBUTING PHOTOGRAPHERS

GAVIN ASHWORTH is a photographer specializing in fine and decorative arts photography for museums and private collections.

MAGGIE KNAUS is a professional photographer and artist who has used many non-traditional photographic processes in her work.

The late ROBERT C. LAUTMAN was an architectural photographer and honorary member of the American Institute of Architects.

BRUCE WHITE photographs works of art and historic architecture for the books and exhibitions of leading cultural institutions in the United States and abroad.

INDEX

Page numbers in *italic* refer to illustrations

Logon, Sally, *437*
Long, Ava, 141
Longworth, Alice Roosevelt, *380*
Longworth, Nicholas, 379–380
Lovell, William, 11
Lucan House, 267–268, 273, 276–277, *278–280*

Macaroni, 57, *61*
Macy, Louise, *379*, 380
Madison, Dolley, menus, 137
Madison, James, 137, 248, 390
Maginnis, Frederick, *476*
Maher, James, 14
Maillard, Henry, 482
Malton, James, *252*, *262*, *263*
Manning, Helen Herron Taft, 216
Marchant, Edward Dalton, 463, *464*
Marcus, Lawrence, 175
Marcus, Stanley, 175
Marcy, William, *232*, 233
Marine Band
    Cleveland, 140–141
    Lincoln, *409*, 410, *410*, *411*, 462, 482
Marling, Karal Ann, 174–175, 178
Marshall, William Edgar, 511
Masked Ball, 404, *404*
Mason, John Young, *230*, *232*, 233
Matelin, François Thomas, 342
Mayer, Louis, 227
Mayo, Edith, 170–181, 530
McAdoo, William G., *378*, 380
McCaffree, Mary Jane, 178, 208
McClellan, George Brinton, 29, *430*, *440*
McClure, Stanley, 208

McCulloch, Hugh, 447
McGuffey, William Holmes, 398
McGuffey Readers, 395, 398
McKim, Charles Follen, 246, 327, 328, 333
    gardens, *336*
McKim, Mead & White, 281
McKinley, William
    assassination, 327
    funeral, 45
    horses and carriages, 20
McParland, Edward, 241
Medina, Dennis, 192–201, 530
Meeks, J. & J. W., 511
Meigs, Montgomery C., *421*
Melville, Herman, 394
menus, 104, *131*, 137, 139, 140, 143, 179–180, *180*
    Grant wedding reception, *371*
    Prince of Wales dinner, 112–125, *114–116*, *125*, *131*
Merrion Square, 260
Merry, Mrs. Anthony, 137
Mesnier, George, 109
Mesnier, Roland, *91*, 92–111, *93–95*, *97*, *100–103*, *110*, *111*, 125, 530
    retirement, 109, 111
Mexican War, 471, 472
Miller, Gladys, 222
Miller, Nyle, 201
Mills, Robert, *462*, 467
Milton, Thomas, 273, 276
Mion, Lance, *122*
Missouri Compromise, 471, 483
Mitchell, Arthur, *131*
Mitchell, Cornelia, 459
Moaney, John, 184
The Modern Cook: A Practical Guide to the Culinary Arts, 112, 113
Moeller, John, *122*
Monkman, Betty C., 218, 507

Monroe, Elizabeth, 249
Monroe, James, 138, *232*, 249, *251*, 341–342, 376
    furnishings, 208, *209*
    kitchen equipment, 70
    stables, 11
Monroe, Maria Hester, 376
Monroe plateau, 340–355, *341*, *343*, *344*, *346*, *348*, *350*, *351*, *353*, *354*, *367*, 374
    Adams, John, 342
    Carter, *354*
    cost, 342
    Grant, 349–350, *350*
    Harding, 352–353
    Hayes, 352
    Hoover, *351*
    Jefferson, 342
    Kennedy, 353, *353*
    Pierce, 349, 350
    Roosevelt, Theodore, 352
    Taft, 352
    Washington, 342
Monroe Room, 209, *209*
Montgomery, Robert, *163*, 166, *166*
Moran, Edward, 459
Morris, Gouverneur, 171, 342
Morrison, Suzie, 110, 119, *122*, 125
Morse, Samuel F. B., 347
Mosbacher, Emil Jr., 223
Mosbacher, Patricia, 223, 226
Mosse, Bartholomew, 260
Mount Kennedy, 267, 272–273, *274*, 276, *307*
Mount Vernon, fireplace, *246*
Muir, John, 394
Mullett, Alfred B., 14
Mullin, Marsha, 46–55, 530
Museum of the Confederacy, *467*
music, Lincoln and, 402–413
Mylne, Robert, *307*

National Defense Highway Act, 201
National Park Service, flowers, 369
National Race Course, 21, 24, 57
National Society of Interior Designers (NSID), 216, *217*, 218
Naulin, Melissa, 202–219, 340–355, 530
Neill, Edward Duffield, 458
Neiman-Marcus, *171*, 175
Nesbitt, Henrietta, 135, 141, 143, *143*, 352
    kitchens, 77–78
Newcomen, Thomas, *298*
Newcomen, William, *298*, *302*
Newcomen Bank, 242, 297, *298–303*
Newenham, Edward, *314*, *315*, *320*
Newenham, Henry, *314*, *315*
Nicholas II, 383, 387
Nicolay, George / John / John George, 14, *436*, 460, 479–480, 481, 501, *514*, 516, 517
Nixon, Patricia "Tricia," 44, 140, *176*
    wedding, 381, *381*
Nixon, Richard M., 31, 36, 381, *381*
    Blair House, 223
    funeral, 44
    kitchens, 78, *89*, *90*
    West Wing, 249
North Front (1792), *241*, *245*
North Portico, 148, *149*, *150*, 248
    inspiration, *316*
    Lincoln, *418*, *459*
Nutt, George Washington Morrison, 405–406, *406*
Nylander, Richard, 510

WHITE HOUSE HISTORY

Please visit www.whitehousehistory.org for more information about
subscribing, purchasing back issues, and other books.